*The publisher gratefully acknowledges
the generous contribution to this book
provided by The General Endowment
Fund of the Associates of the University
of California Press.*

A Golden State

California History Sesquicentennial Series
Edited by Richard J. Orsi

1. *Contested Eden: California before the Gold Rush,* edited by Ramón A. Gutiérrez and Richard J. Orsi
2. *A Golden State: Mining and Economic Development in Gold Rush California,* edited by James J. Rawls and Richard J. Orsi
3. *Rooted in Barbarous Soil: People, Culture, and Community in Gold Rush California,* edited by Kevin Starr and Richard J. Orsi
4. *Taming the Elephant: Politics, Government, and Law in Pioneer California,* edited by John F. Burns and Richard J. Orsi

A Golden State

MINING AND ECONOMIC
DEVELOPMENT IN GOLD
RUSH CALIFORNIA

Editors

JAMES J. RAWLS and RICHARD J. ORSI

Illustrations Editor
ANTHONY KIRK

Associate Editor
MARLENE SMITH-BARANZINI

Published in association with the California Historical Society

UNIVERSITY OF CALIFORNIA PRESS
Berkeley · Los Angeles · London

University of California Press
Berkeley and Los Angeles, California

University of California Press, Ltd.
London, England

© 1999 by the Regents of the University of California

Library of Congress Cataloging-in-Publication Data

A golden state: mining and economic development in gold rush
California / editors James J. Rawls and Richard J. Orsi; associate editor
Marlene Smith-Baranzini.
    p.   cm.   (California history sesquicentennial series; 2)
  "Published in association with the California Historical Society."
  Includes bibliographic references and index.
  ISBN 0-520-21770-5 (cloth : alk. paper).—ISBN 0-520-21771-3 (pbk. : alk.
paper)
  1. California—Economic conditions—19th century.   2. Gold mines
and mining—California—History—19th century.   I. Rawls, James J. II.
Orsi, Richard J. III. Smith-Baranzini, Marlene. IV. Series.
HC107.C2G59   1999
  330.9794'04—dc21   98-26238
                                                          CIP

Printed in the United States of America

08 07 06 05 04 03 02 01 00   99 10 9 8 7 6 5 4 3 2 1

The paper used in this publication meets the minimum requirements
of ANSI/NISO Z39.48-1992 (R 1997) (*Permanence of Paper*). ♾

Contents

PREFACE · Michael McCone and Richard J. Orsi · ix

1. *A Golden State: An Introduction* · James J. Rawls · 1

2. *Making Old Tools Work Better: Pragmatic Adaptation and Innovation in Gold-Rush Technology* · Ronald H. Limbaugh · 24

3. *Capitalism Comes to the Diggings: From Gold-Rush Adventure to Corporate Enterprise* · Maureen A. Jung · 52

4. *"We all live more like brutes than humans": Labor and Capital in the Gold Rush* · Daniel Cornford · 78

5. *Environmental Changes before and after the Gold Rush* · Raymond F. Dasmann · 105

6. *"I am resolved not to interfere, but permit all to work freely": The Gold Rush and American Resource Law* · Donald J. Pisani · 123

7. *Mother Lode for the West: California Mining Men and Methods* · Duane A. Smith · 149

8. *Seeing the Elephant* · Anthony Kirk · 174

9. *The Gold Rush and the Beginnings of California Industry* · David J. St. Clair · 185

10. *From Hard Money to Branch Banking: California Banking in the Gold-Rush Economy* · Larry Schweikart and Lynne Pierson Doti · 209

11. *"Property of Every Kind": Ranching and Farming during the Gold-Rush Era* · Lawrence James Jelinek · 233

12. *The Golden Skein: California's Gold-Rush Transportation Network* · A. C. W. Bethel · 250

13. *A Veritable Revolution: The Global Economic Significance of the California Gold Rush* · Gerald D. Nash · 276

LIST OF CONTRIBUTORS · 293

INDEX · 297

Preface

In January 1848, in California, one of the most remote and primitive of all North American frontiers, James Marshall noticed a glimmer in the bottom of a millrace, and changed the history of the world. In the weeks, months, and years following Marshall's fateful gold discovery, "the world rushed in" on California. The early 1848 population of 10,000 persons, excluding Indians, swelled by hundreds of thousands within only a few years and by 1880 reached nearly one million people from across the globe. In the early years, most headed directly for the gold fields of interior foothills and mountains, where they started small placer mining operations as individuals and in small partnerships. Visions of golden fortunes had lured thousands of modern-day Argonauts to California, forsaking the company and comfort of loved ones and gambling what money they had in the high cost of passage and outfit. Dreams of riches were fulfilled for some in the early days of virgin diggings, but most miners discovered only short supplies, high prices, overcrowded river bottoms, body-breaking labor, elusive gold, and loneliness and longing for home. "Nearly every person . . . ," Dame Shirley reported with her knack for seeing to the core of her world, "received the same step-mother's treatment from Dame Nature, in this her mountain workshop."

Most Argonauts returned home or voyaged on to new diggings out of state, but after the early 1850s, as the ore was rapidly depleted, those few who chose to stay founded mining companies, which grew ever larger and more complex, searching for gold with huge machines and forces of industrial laborers, new immigrants to the mines from Great Britain, Ireland, Mexico, China, and other far-off lands. Some former miners—successful and disappointed alike—remained in California and joined other newcomers in starting ranches, farms, stores, banks, factories, water companies, and steamboat and stagecoach lines. Within a decade or two of the Forty-niners' arrival, California boasted not only large quartz and hydraulic mines, but a host of other enterprises even more productive, and the state had outgrown its gold-rush childhood. Although California remained in its adolescence, pioneers had transformed it into something other than just a mining state.

The Gold Rush that followed James Marshall's gold discovery is undoubtedly the most well known event in California history, particularly to people living elsewhere; indeed, it is one of the most famous events in the history of the United States and the world. It is also, of course, the impetus and the central organizing event for the state's Sesquicentennial from 1998 through 2000. But in all of the hoopla of popular and scholarly gold-rush history, and of the Sesquicentennial itself, generally ignored are the event's larger economic dimensions: how a mining-dominated society organized its people, productive systems, technologies, and laws to encourage unprecedented development; how individual and collective decisions in the pioneer period profoundly affected the future economic development of the state, even to the present; and how California's gold, people, machines, capital, and companies crossed the state's borders back into the West, the nation, and beyond. Indeed, after the world had "rushed in" on it, California "rushed out" to the rest of the world. Those are the subjects the authors of *A Golden State* explore—the development of corporate mining in the state; technological change of a most rapid and eclectic sort; the transformation of miners from entrepreneurs into industrial laborers; the emergence of ancillary businesses in transportation, finance, agriculture, and manufacturing; the exportation of the mining economy to Colorado and the Comstock Lode, and even to far-away Idaho, Montana, New Mexico, Dakota, British Columbia, and Australia; and the impact of California mining on the national and world economies.

This book is the second in the California History Sesquicentennial Series, presented by the California Historical Society—the state's officially designated historical society—and the University of California Press, with the support of California State University, Hayward, and many other partners. Four topical, but interrelated, volumes, one published in each year from 1997 through 2000, will reexamine the meaning, particularly from today's perspective, of the founding of modern California in the pre-1848 and gold-rush era experiences. Each of the volumes will collect essays by a dozen authors, drawn from the ranks of leading humanists, social scientists, and scientists, reviewing the best, most up-to-date thinking on major topics associated with the state's pioneer period through the 1870s. The authors have been asked to consider, within their area of expertise, the general themes that run through all four volumes: the interplay of traditional cultures and frontier innovation in the creation of a distinctive California society; the dynamic interaction of people and nature and the beginnings of massive environmental change; the impact of the California experience on the nation and the wider world; the shaping influence of pioneer patterns on modern California; and the importance and legacy of ethnic and cultural diversity as a major dimension of the state's history.

The four California History Sesquicentennial volumes will be published simultaneously as expanded issues of *California History,* the quarterly of the California Historical Society, and as books for general distribution. Each volume will be coedited by a consulting editor who is a leading scholar in the specific field and by Richard J. Orsi, Editor of the quarterly and Professor of History, California State University, Hayward. Volume 1, *Contested Eden: California before the Gold Rush,* coedited by Ramón A. Gutiérrez, Professor of Ethnic Studies and History at the University of California, San Diego, and published in 1997/98, dealt with the social, economic, cultural, political, and environmental patterns of Native American, Spanish, and Mexican California through 1848. The present volume, coedited by James J. Rawls, member of the history faculty at Diablo Valley College, examines the pioneer industry of gold mining, its inception and development, and its impact on the state, the West, and the national and world economies. Volume 3, to be coedited by Kevin Starr, State Librarian of California, will focus on the Gold Rush and the migration and settlement of peoples, cultures, organizations, and institutions. Volume 4, to be coedited by John Burns, former California State Archivist and State Historian and currently historical consultant with the California Department of Education, will investigate the inception of government and politics—statehood, early constitution-building, law, bureaucracy, and civil rights.

The California Historical Society's issuing of these major sesquicentennial publications is made possible through the contributions of all the Society's members, as well as a host of direct and indirect supporters. Chief among the helping agencies are the Mericos Foundation of South Pasadena, which has provided a generous grant specifically for the Sesquicentennial Series, the University of California Press, the California State Archives, and California State University, Hayward, which furnishes ongoing support for editing the quarterly.

Many individuals have also shared their time, knowledge, energy, and resources. The Historical Society's particular appreciation goes to Lynne Withey, associate director of the University of California Press, who has been an indispensable part of the project from the beginning; Kathleen MacDougall, project editor of this volume at the Press, whose understanding, precise editing, and care for the manuscript lightened our burden immeasurably; Mrs. Johan Blokker of the Mericos Foundation, whose belief in and support of the Sesquicentennial project has made it possible; Dr. Norma Rees, President, and Dr. Frank Martino, Vice President and Provost, of California State University, Hayward, who have provided generous assistance for the Sesquicentennial Series and the general editing office of *California History;* James J. Rawls, who but for his youth and vigor would long ago have been anointed the "dean" of California historians and whose partnership in editing this volume and many other services over two decades mark him as a true friend of the California Historical Society; Anthony Kirk, illustrations editor, who applied his unequaled knowledge and appreciation of California iconography to discover, edit, caption, and interpret a stunning series of images, in many cases never before published; and Marlene Smith-Baranzini, associate editor of *California History* and true partner-editor in every facet of the Sesquicentennial Series. Other important contributors include graduate assistants Josh Paddison and Peter Orsi; Liz Ginno and Judith Faust, members of the library faculty at California State University, Hayward; and Larry Campbell, Patricia Keats, Katherine Holland, Emily Wolff, Bo Mompho, Scott Shields, Kathryn Kowalewski, Gail Miller, Jennifer Schaffner, Judith Deaton, and other members of the loyal, dedicated, and professional staff of the California Historical Society, San Francisco.

Finally, our thanks also go to all the individuals and institutions who made it possible to use images from their collections in this work or who provided other valuable assistance. Although space precludes listing all their names, special mention should be made of Dace Taube, curator of the California Historical Society/Title Insurance and Trust Photo Collection, Department of Special Collections, University of Southern California Library; Peter Blodgett and Jennifer Watts, the Huntington Library; Richard Ogar, William Roberts, Jack von Euw, Susan Snyder, and Walter Brem, the Bancroft Library; Ellen Harding and Gary Kurutz, the California State Library; Janice Driesbach and Laura Benites, the Crocker Art Museum; Carl Ryanen-Grant, the Oakland Museum of California; Bill McMorris and Susan M. Haas, the Society of California Pioneers; Robert Chandler, Wells Fargo Bank History Department; Mary Haas, Fine Arts Museums of San Francisco; Alison Poulsen, the Autry Museum of Western Heritage; Claudia Jew, the Mariners' Museum, Newport News, Virginia; Darlene Dueck, the Anschutz Collection, Denver, Colorado; Joshua Ruff, the Museums at Stony Brook, New York; Annie Brose, the National Museum of American Art, Smithsonian Institution; Mary Sluskonis, Museum of Fine Arts, Boston; and Claudine Chalmers, Oscar and Trudy Lemer, Everett Lee Millard, and W. Bruce Lundberg.

Michael McCone
Executive Director,
California Historical Society

Richard J. Orsi
Professor of History,
California State University, Hayward
Editor, *California History*

1

A Golden State

An Introduction

James J. Rawls

On January 24, 1848, a thirty-two-year-old Virginian named Henry William Bigler recorded in his diary one of the most fateful sentences in American history: "This day some kind of mettle was found in the tail race that looks like goald first discovered by James Martial, the Boss of the Mill." Thus was first recorded, in a scrawl barely legible, the momentous discovery of California gold by that eccentric master carpenter James Wilson Marshall working at Sutter's Mill on the South Fork of the American River. As news of the discovery spread across the country and around the world, California was transformed. Hundreds of thousands of Argonauts—a name derived from Jason's followers in search of the Golden Fleece of classical mythology—rushed to what would soon become the Golden State, hoping to find for themselves a fortune in that precious "mettle." Their coming was the foundational event not only for the economic history of California, but for much of its social, cultural, and political history as well.[1]

For an event of such importance, it is striking that we know so little of the exact circumstances of the discovery itself. Marshall was never entirely sure of the date. He later speculated that he had made the discovery "on or about the 19th of January."[2] Several other accounts, including Bigler's diary entry, contradict Marshall. One dubious version, preserved by historian Hubert Howe Bancroft, takes the credit from Marshall altogether. It casts a Native American mill worker, one "Indian Jim," in the role of discoverer. According to this account, the Indian discovered a nugget "as large as a brass button" that he gave to a white worker, who in turn showed it to Marshall.[3] Such discrepancies should not be surprising. As Rodman Paul reminds us, "the difficulty is that no one anticipated, few witnessed, and fewer still recorded the event. . . . The participants in the gold discovery were simple people who had little education and felt little incentive to keep written records."[4]

John Sutter's sawmill on the South Fork of the American River, where on a chilly January morning in 1848 James Marshall caught the glint of gold in the recently deepened tailrace and, stooping to gather the flakes—none larger than a grain of wheat—changed the course of history. The figure in the foreground of the daguerreotype, taken by Robert Vance about 1850, is thought to be Marshall. *California Historical Society, FN-30892.*

The background of the gold discovery stretches back through geologic time to the very creation of California. According to the theory of plate tectonics, the subduction of the Pacific Plate beneath the western edge of the North American Plate generated enormous heat. Within this molten crucible, metal-rich compounds dissolved into solutions that were injected into fissures of rocks being formed above. Different combinations of minerals precipitated to form deposits of various metals.[5] Thousands of veins of gold thus were created in the granitic core of California's primordial mountains. Over eons, erosion tore loose tiny particles of gold and washed them into rivers and streams, where they lodged on sandbars or behind stones. There the particles lay undisturbed until that portentous day in January 1848.

The first people to live in California may well have known of the gold, but apparently they regarded it with little interest. Those who came later were gold-possessed. Spanish explorers and conquerors were drawn ever onward through the Americas by the lure of tales of magnificent wealth. Somewhere up ahead, they believed, were the fabled Seven Cities of Gold and El Dorado, "the Gilded Man," whose loyal subjects covered him with gold dust every morning and washed it off every night. Even the name "California" was identified with these golden dreams. Before Spaniards discovered this land, García Ordóñez de Montalvo's early sixteenth-century novel *Las Sergas de Esplandián* described a place that he called California, a mythical island "very near the Terrestrial Paradise" upon which the only metal to be found was gold. In the 1530s, Spaniards gave the name to the region along the coast north and west of Mexico.[6]

Gold in the Americas, of course, was no myth. Gold worth billions of pesos was taken from the mines of Spain's Latin American colonies. Great mining centers boomed at Potosí and Zacatecas, at Huancavélica and Pachuca.[7] Gold was even discovered in Mexican California, in 1842 at Placerita Creek, about thirty-five miles northwest of the pueblo of Los Angeles. Although gold from the Placerita strike was the first ever sent from California to the U.S. mint, the deposits proved to be inconsequential and attracted little attention. In one of the great ironies in American history, Marshall's discovery came within days of the signing of the Treaty of Guadalupe Hidalgo on February 2, 1848. Mexico thereby ceded sovereignty to about half its national territory, including gold-rich California, just as the value of that territory was poised to appreciate enormously.

Like ripples in a pond pulsing outward from a skipping stone, the news of Marshall's discovery circled the globe. Everywhere the reception of the news followed a similar pattern. At first, reasonable people responded with incredulity. Reports of nuggets as large as misshapen billiard balls and hens' eggs were dismissed as tall tales. How could there possibly be as much gold in California as such wild rumors suggested? Only as the rumors were confirmed by subsequent reports did reasonable people find themselves possessed by a gold mania. Their intense excitement was compounded by a determination to make up for the time they had lost in doubt.[8]

News of the discovery first appeared in March in San Francisco's two fledgling newspapers, the *Californian* and the *California Star*. But the reports failed to stir any immediate excitement. Monterey resident James H. Carson later recalled that during April and May a few local inhabitants left for the mines, but only after having "put the whole golden report down as 'dod drat' humbug." Carson remained an "unbeliever" until May 10, when he saw with his own eyes a sack of gold nuggets, some truly as large as hens' eggs. Then came the moment of Carson's conversion. "There was before me proof positive that I had held too long to the wrong side of the question." His description of what happened next is a classic account of the contagion that began raging out of control:

> I looked on for a moment; a frenzy seized my soul; unbidden my legs performed some entirely new movements of Polka steps—I took several—houses were too small for me to stay in; I was soon in the street in search of necessary outfits; piles of gold rose up before me at every step; castles of marble, dazzling the eye with their rich appliances;

— *Faut-il être dindon, pour croire de pareils canards!*

"You'd have to be turkey to believe such ducks!" runs the caption beneath a cartoon in the April 12, 1849 issue of the Parisian paper *Le Charivari,* making a lively play on the word *canards*—literally "ducks," but colloquially "a false report" or "hoax," especially as circulated by the press. Despite the well-intentioned skepticism of the artist, thousands of Frenchmen purchased stock in gold mining companies, at five francs a share or more, and countless others made the voyage themselves. In 1853 a San Francisco journal claimed that over thirty thousand Frenchmen resided in the Golden State. *California Historical Society, FN-30966.*

thousands of slaves, bowing to my beck and call; myriads of fair virgins contending with each other for my love, were among the fancies of my fevered imagination. The Rothschilds, Girards and Astors appeared to me but poor people; in short, I had a very violent attack of the Gold Fever.[9]

The promise of great wealth, obtained quickly and easily, had a universal appeal. Few could resist its allure. In a phrase made famous by historian J. S. Holliday, "the world rushed in," and California soon became home to the nation's most ethnically diverse population. Included among the gold diggers were Native Americans, working either as laborers for white miners or as independent agents. Colonel Richard B. Mason reported in August 1848 that of the four thousand miners then at work in the gold fields, more than half were Indians.[10] Spanish-speaking Californios also joined the rush for gold, often taking with them Indian laborers from their ranchos. Historian Leonard Pitt has estimated that in 1848 about 1,300 Californios were actively looking for gold.[11] Thousands of other Latin Americans came north to the mines from Mexico, Peru, and Chile.[12] By 1850 the Mexican population in the Southern Mines—in Calaveras, Tuolumne, and Mariposa counties—was about 15,000.[13] From the west came gold seekers from the Pacific Islands and Asia. Place-names such as Kanaka Creek in Sierra County and Trinity County's Kanaka Bar remind us also of the early presence of Hawaiians in the gold country.[14] Australians settled in camps throughout the diggings and formed in San Francisco a loosely knit community known as "Sydney Town."[15] Chinese sojourners, numbering 25,000 in 1852, represented a tenth of the state's non-Indian population; in some mining counties nearly one out of three residents was Chinese.[16] Hundreds of thousands of other Argonauts came from Europe and from the eastern United States. Among these, by the late 1850s, had come 2,500 African Americans, including individuals enslaved and free.[17] "Everybody, speaking all the languages of the world, it seemed, had come in search of gold."[18]

From whatever direction the Argonauts came, they faced enormous difficulties getting to California. Those from the eastern United States followed three main routes to the gold fields. Sea routes were the most popular at first. Sailing around Cape Horn was a voyage of 18,000 nautical miles and took five to eight months. Violent storms off the Cape posed a constant danger to even the most experienced mariners; the fierce gales, recalled one seaborne Argonaut, "produce long, huge swells, over which the ship mounts with a roll, then plunges into the abyss again as if never to rise."[19] Sailing to Central America and crossing the Panamanian isthmus considerably reduced the travel time but exposed travelers to the risk of contracting malaria, yellow fever, and other tropical diseases. Ultimately most California-bound Argonauts traveled by various overland routes through the American heartland. This journey of 2,000 miles took at least three or four months and meant crossing incredibly difficult terrain.[20] Young Sallie Hester, traveling overland with her parents

Bolts of lightning split the dark, roiling clouds over the Great Plains in a drawing by
J. Goldsborough Bruff, captain of the Washington City Company, which departed the
Missouri frontier for El Dorado in late spring of 1849. Several miles past the Platte River
a tremendous storm broke over the wagon train, with rain soon turning to hail as the
temperature plummeted forty degrees. "Hail-stones of extraordinary size," wrote Bruff,
"not only cut and bruised the men, whose faces and hands were bleeding, but [they] also
cut the mules." *Courtesy Huntington Library, San Marino, Calif.*

in 1849, recorded in her diary the rigors of making it across the unbroken deserts of
the Southwest: "The weary, weary tramp of men and beasts, worn out with heat and
famished for water, will never be erased from my memory."[21] The biggest killer on
the overland trail was disease, responsible for nine out of every ten deaths. Cholera
was by far the greatest scourge, but scurvy, typhoid fever, and dysentery also took
their toll. Drownings while fording swollen rivers contributed to the mortality rate,
as did fatal accidents caused by the careless or reckless use of firearms.[22] Following
the accidental death of a ten-year-old boy, Lucia Williams wrote to her mother
that "for many days we could not forget this agonizing experience. It hung over us
like a black shadow. It took all the joy out of our lives."[23]

Arriving in California brought expressions of relief from those who survived the
journey. Charles Glass Gray, a young Forty-niner from New Jersey, celebrated his arrival in San Francisco by sleeping in a bed for the first time in seven months. In his

diary he wrote that he was relieved to be off the trail at last, "for I have suffer'd enough already I think."[24]

Was the trip worth it? Between 1848 and 1854, the peak year of production, the Argonauts harvested nearly $350 million in gold from California.[25] The average daily take was $20 per miner in 1848, at a time when skilled artisans in the eastern United States were earning a daily wage of $1.50 for twelve hours of work.[26] But the cost of living in California was far higher than in the East. A loaf of bread that sold for five cents on the Atlantic seaboard cost fifty to seventy-five cents in California.[27] An entire dinner at a New York restaurant could be had for a quarter or a half-dollar in 1849; the bill of fare in a contemporary eatery in San Francisco listed a leg of mutton for $1.25 and "Fresh California Eggs" at $1.00 apiece.[28] More discouraging still was the shifting ratio between the number of gold seekers and the amount of gold being found. By the end of 1848 about 6,000 miners had obtained $10 million worth of gold. Three years later the output was more than $80 million, but the number of miners had swelled to 100,000.[29] Those who prospered in the Gold Rush—men like Levi Strauss, Domingo Ghirardelli, John Studebaker, and Philip Danforth Armour—were entrepreneurs who learned well the axiom that the main chance for success lay not in mining gold but in mining the miners.

One of the most acute observers of the Gold Rush was Louise Amelia Knapp Smith Clappe, author of *The Shirley Letters,* written along the Feather River in 1851 and 1852. "Gold mining is Nature's great lottery scheme," she wrote on April 10, 1852. "A man may work in a claim for many months, and be poorer at the end of the time than when he commenced; or he may 'take out' thousands in a few hours. It is a mere matter of chance. . . . And yet, I cannot help remarking, that almost all with whom we are acquainted seem to have lost."[30] Historian Oscar Lewis has estimated that fewer than one out of twenty California gold seekers returned home richer than when they left.[31] The frustration of those who failed found expression in the names of their ramshackle mining camps, places like Poverty Hill, Skunk Gulch, and Hell's Delight.[32] Among the many plaintive gold-rush ballads was "The Lousy Miner," first published in John A. Stone's *Original California Songster* (1855).[33] The opening stanza sets us straight:

> It's four long years since I reached this land,
> In search of gold among the rocks and sand;
> And yet I'm poor when the truth is told,
> I'm a lousy miner,
> I'm a lousy miner in search of shining gold.

And the final refrain is one of bitter disappointment:

> Oh, land of gold, you did me deceive,
> And I intend in thee my bones to leave;

William Redmond Ryan, an English-born artist who mined for a spell in the autumn of
'48, caught the labor of his fellow fortune hunters along the Stanislaus River in a drawing
that appeared in his *Personal Adventures in Upper and Lower California, in 1848–9,* published in London in 1850. Rich though the diggings were, Ryan seldom washed more
than four to six dollars a day, and, soon tiring of the hard labor and the "oppressive and
injurious" dampness of the river canyon, he turned his back on the mines and took himself
to Monterey. *California Historical Society, FN-30974.*

> So farewell, home, now my friends grow cold,
> I'm a lousy miner,
> I'm a lousy miner in search of shining gold.

Frustrated ambitions were vented in an almost unending round of ethnic hostilities on the California mining frontier. Scapegoats were eagerly sought, identified
with lightning speed, and dispatched with little regret. The antagonism between
white miners and California Indians was especially intense. Whites advocated and
carried out a program of genocide that they called "extermination," and in the
process thousands of California Indians were killed.[34] San Francisco's *Alta California* reported in April 1849 that the white miners were "becoming impressed with the
belief that it will be absolutely necessary to exterminate the savages before they can
labor much longer in the mines with security."[35] Three years later a miner in the

Auburn area reported that mining activity there had been suspended because of Indian hostilities. The miners organized several armed parties "determined to exterminate these merciless foes, or drive them far from us." After an attack on a nearby Southern Maidu village—in which thirty natives were killed outright and those wounded were knifed to death—the miners resumed their search for gold.[36]

Foreign miners fell victim to xenophobic violence as well as to nativist legislation. Accounts of beatings, floggings, and lynchings of foreign miners appear as a bloody litany throughout the literature of the Gold Rush. Many of the mining codes, adopted in the more than five hundred California mining districts, barred Mexicans, Asians, or other immigrants from staking claims. The California legislature in 1850 enacted a foreign miners' license tax requiring miners who were not citizens of the United States to pay a fee of twenty dollars a month. The tax was aimed primarily at newcomers from Mexico, many of whom were experienced miners and skillful in locating good claims. Thomas Jefferson Green, the author of the tax, once boasted that he could "maintain a better stomach at the killing of a Mexican" than at the crushing of a body louse.[37] The tax, coupled with threats of violence, led to the exodus of ten thousand Mexican miners from California in the summer of 1850. Two years later the legislature adopted a new foreign miners' license tax, setting the fee at three and later four dollars a month. Subsequent legislation made ineligibility for citizenship the main definition of those to whom the tax applied, ensuring that it would be collected primarily from the Chinese (who were barred by race from becoming naturalized citizens). The tax remained in effect until 1870 and produced nearly a quarter of the state's annual revenue.[38]

Historian Malcolm J. Rohrbough has captured the essence of these events in the simplest terms: "The California Gold Rush was about wealth."[39] It was the expectation of great wealth that drove hundreds of thousands of Argonauts rushing to the gold fields. Their presence led to an economic boom that transformed California in countless ways. The Gold Rush also produced a kind of mass hysteria in which greed predominated and ethnic conflict was all too frequent. Philosopher Josiah Royce, born in the gold-rush town of Grass Valley, recognized the power of the forces set loose: "All our brutal passions were here to have full sweep, and all our moral strength, all our courage, our patience, our docility, and our social skills were to contend with these our passions."[40]

Popular understanding of the Gold Rush has evolved in remarkable ways over the past century and a half. The earliest accounts, of course, were the diaries and letters of the Argonauts themselves. Found here is a familiar trajectory of emotions as the miners pass from hopeful anticipation to the painful acceptance of the harsh realities of life in the diggings. Early published accounts of the Gold Rush often examined themes of myth and reality, expectation and disappointment. See, for example,

The Forty-niner Thomas Drew, one of the thousands of bold, confident young Americans who rushed west to reap the golden harvest when news of the wonderful discovery first swept across the land. *Courtesy Society of California Pioneers.*

William Shaw's *Golden Dreams and Waking Realities* (1851), George Payson's *Golden Dreams and Leaden Realities* (1853), and the acerbic Hinton Rowan Helper's *Land of Gold: Reality Versus Fiction* (1855).

Two indispensable guides to the abundance of published and unpublished first-hand accounts are Marlin L. Heckman, *Overland on the California Trail, 1846–1859:*

A Bibliography of Manuscript and Printed Travel Narratives (1984) and Gary F. Kurutz, *The California Gold Rush: A Descriptive Bibliography* (1997). Among the best of these eyewitness narratives is J. S. Holliday's editing of William Swain's diary and letters, published as *The World Rushed In: The California Gold Rush Experience* (1981). Holliday set himself the task of consulting every available gold-rush diary and letter from 1849 and 1850 to provide the larger context; thus Swain's story is truly emblematic. Within six months of his arrival in California, Swain admitted that his expectations had not been fulfilled. He reported that 90 percent of the miners were downhearted and discouraged as "their bright day-dreams of golden wealth vanish like the dreams of night."[41]

Later memoirs and fictionalized accounts, appearing in the decades after the Gold Rush, tended to view the mining frontier through a romantic haze. Understandably, the aging Argonauts wished to put the best possible spin on their youthful exploits. Bret Harte and other local colorists produced nostalgic tales such as "The Luck of Roaring Camp" and "Tennessee's Partner," which conformed perfectly to the way the grizzled veterans of the Gold Rush preferred to remember those glorious "days of '49."[42] Images of heroic pioneers, stouthearted and triumphant, invariably were in the ascendancy in popular celebrations of gold-rush anniversaries. In 1898 California's Golden Jubilee began on January 24 with a procession through the streets of San Francisco witnessed by a crowd of two hundred thousand. Henry William Bigler, then in his eighty-second year, was thrilled to be among those whom the crowd pressed forward to see.[43] The apotheosis was complete by 1948, when Californians observed the centennial of the gold discovery. Gordon Jenkins and his orchestra recorded a "musical narrative" that unabashedly celebrated the Gold Rush as a part of the national legendry.

> There's gold in California,
> Gold out California way.
> Streets are paved with it,
> Fortunes are made with it,
> Even golden razors
> So you can get shaved with it.

Contributing to the general acclaim was a steady stream of scholarly studies of the gold-rush experience. Among the earliest accounts written by an academically trained historian was Charles Howard Shinn's *Mining Camps: A Study in American Frontier Government* (1885). Shinn praised the democratic genius of the Argonauts who managed to fashion codes of law and to establish legal institutions in the wilds of the gold country. His sympathies were clearly with the European Americans; to him their meting out of justice was fair and praiseworthy. He elegized the miners' popular tribunals as "the folk-moot of the Sierra."[44] Most scholarly accounts over the

Painted in 1884 by the German American artist Oscar Kunath, *The Luck of Roaring Camp* portrays a poignant moment in Bret Harte's story of the same name. Pressing forward in single file, the rough, bearded miners of the district troop into the rude cabin of the recently deceased Cherokee Sal to gaze on her orphaned infant, Thomas Luck, neatly tucked into a candle box. In the years that had passed since Harte first mined the rich vein of local color and began publication of his popular tales, Americans across the country had increasingly come to regard the Gold Rush with nostalgia, seeing it as a romantic moment in the westward course of empire. *Courtesy Fine Arts Museums of San Francisco, Gift of Mrs. Annette Taussig in memory of her husband, Louis Taussig, 26562.*

next half-century continued to celebrate the Gold Rush and all that it seemed to represent. Only occasionally did a more critical perspective appear, such as Josiah Royce's often reprinted account of California history from 1846 to 1856. First published in 1886, Royce's book, subtitled *A Study of American Character,* saw in the Gold Rush intimations of "both the true nobility and true weakness of our national character." Royce excoriated Bret Harte for his "perverse romanticism" and unconscionable willingness to sentimentalize the miners' brutal habits. Turning an unflinching gaze upon the lynching of Mexicans and the wholesale murder of California Indians, Royce could only conclude: "All this tale is one of disgrace to our people."[45]

The scholarly study of the Gold Rush took a great leap forward around the time of the centennial. Rodman W. Paul's *California Gold: The Beginning of Mining in the Far West* (1947) was the first serious attempt to analyze the Gold Rush as an economic enterprise. Paul emphasized the growing complexity of mining organizations and mining technology, and stressed the importance of the California experience for subsequent mining frontiers elsewhere in the nation and world. Like Royce, Paul sought to clear away the "thick haze of romantic legend and mythology [that] has settled over the California mining scene." He ended his account with a plea to understand the Gold Rush in multicultural terms: "In California at least a dozen nationalities and half that number of racial strains made major contributions to the progress of mining, and the great state which flourishes today upon America's western border stands as a lasting monument to the effectiveness of their joint efforts."[46] This same larger perspective informed the other major work of urbane scholarship that appeared at the time of the centennial, John Walton Caughey's *Gold Is the Cornerstone* (1948), a comprehensive overview of the economic, political, and cultural consequences of the gold discovery. Caughey acknowledged the environmental havoc wreaked by the miners, the appalling record of ethnic discord, and the failure of many Argonauts to strike it rich. "Nevertheless," he concluded, "there are tangible proofs that gold was the touchstone that set California in motion on the course that made her what she is today, and that her gold did things for the West at large and the Pacific basin that otherwise would not have been done for a generation or perhaps at all."[47]

In recent decades scholars have brought to the study of the Gold Rush a host of new questions and new methods of analysis. Social historians, for example, have begun analyzing masses of data from manuscript censuses, tax lists, town directories, and probate records. From these data, historians have extracted information about the age, sex, ethnic origin, occupation, family size, and mobility of the residents of particular towns or communities. Ralph Mann, author of *After the Gold Rush: Society in Grass Valley and Nevada City, 1849–1870* (1982), brought the methods of the new social history to the study of two mining camps on the California frontier. Confirming many of the earliest anecdotal accounts, Mann concluded that the miners' prospects for instant wealth were quite dim. The heady days of placer mining may have seemed to represent a great chance for making a fortune, but it was only after industrialization had ended frontier conditions that most miners became solvent. Opportunities for upward mobility thus were less than imagined and perhaps even less than in the older, more established, more economically stable areas of the country.[48]

Other historians have borrowed from literary criticism the technique of content analysis to produce systematic analyses of gold-rush diaries. John Mack Faragher, in *Women and Men on the Overland Trail* (1979), evaluated fifty diaries according to a set of predetermined values to determine the importance of gender in the perception and reality of the westering experience. David Rich Lewis, author of a prize-winning 1985 essay in the *Western Historical Quarterly,* took a similar approach in analyzing forty-four diaries of young men on the trail to California. Lewis concluded that aggression and social conflict were parts of the "core experience" of the Argonauts. John Phillip Reid, in his studies of *Law for the Elephant: Property and Social Behavior on the Overland Trail* (1980) and *Policing the Elephant: Crime, Punishment, and Social Behavior on the Overland Trail* (1997), presented a more orderly portrait of the trail, emphasizing the remarkable persistence of law-abiding habits among those who were heading west.[49] Likewise Roger D. McGrath, author of *Gunfighters, Highwaymen and Vigilantes: Violence on the Frontier* (1984), found that criminal and lawless behavior affected only a few specialized groups.

The role of women in the Gold Rush has attracted a growing number of scholars in recent years.[50] The most comprehensive account is JoAnn Levy's *They Saw the Elephant: Women in the California Gold Rush* (1990). Levy portrayed women responding vigorously and positively to the challenges of life on the overland trail and in the mining camps. Especially valuable is her portrait of the "working women" of California who engaged in a wide variety of economic enterprises. Freed from the bonds of domesticity, gold-rush women enjoyed a greater freedom than they had known back home.[51] Jacqueline Baker Barnhart, author of *The Fair but Frail: Prostitution in San Francisco, 1849–1900* (1986), reexamined one of the most common stereotypical roles of western women. She analyzed the prostitutes of San Francisco not as deviants or victims, but as a group of professional workers. She placed them within the tradition of gold-rush entrepreneurship, noting that most prostitutes came to California seeking economic opportunity and that many were willing to leave lucrative jobs working for others to open businesses of their own.[52]

Much of the most recent scholarship on the Gold Rush has been by practitioners of the "New Western History." Emphasizing the importance of racial and ethnic minorities, the New Western historians have produced a considerable library of monographs and synthetic accounts. The multicultural aspects of the Gold Rush take center stage in such general histories of the West as Patricia Nelson Limerick's *Legacy of Conquest* (1987) and Richard White's *"It's Your Misfortune and None of My Own"* (1991). More focused on the California experience are Tomás Almaguer, *Racial Fault Lines: The Historical Origins of White Supremacy in California* (1994) and Lisbeth Haas, *Conquests and Historical Identities in California, 1769–1936* (1995). Typical of the approach of the New Western historians is Albert L. Hurtado's *Indian Survival on the California Frontier* (1988), a book that focuses not on the process of Indian decline but rather on the adaptation and resistance strategies that permitted a remnant of the native people to survive. For a convenient summary of the latest scholarship, see *Peo-*

ples of Color in the American West (1994), edited by Sucheng Chan, Douglas Henry Daniels, Mario T. Garcia, and Terry P. Wilson.

The present volume is a collection of essays that focus on the economic aspects of the Gold Rush. Each essay, written with the general reader in mind, offers an overview of a particular topic and provides some sense of the state of recent scholarship. The essays reflect the excitement of new work being done in the field, presenting new directions in interpretation, areas of inquiry, and methods of analysis.

The first essay, Ronald H. Limbaugh's study of gold-rush technology, demonstrates the diverse origins of the mining equipment and methods used by the Argonauts. From around the world, miners brought older technologies that they adapted and modified for use in California. Local hybrids emerged, as did innovations, most notably hydraulic mining and stamp milling, in a process that marked California mining as "a regional variant if not a separate species." Driving this dynamic process was the power of material ambition, "a common trait found in all Argonauts regardless of race, class, or national origin." So it is, according to Limbaugh, that the legacy of the Gold Rush lives on today "in the quest for riches in the form of good jobs, good living, personal fulfillment—the same things California Argonauts sought 150 years ago."

The San Francisco *Alta California* observed in the autumn of 1851 that "the miners are beginning to discover that they are engaged in a science and a profession, and not in a mere adventure."[53] This prescient observation could serve well as an epigraph for Maureen A. Jung's essay on the rise of corporate enterprise in the Gold Rush. As the Argonauts headed to California, they organized simple partnerships and joint-stock companies. But rapid technological advances in the 1850s—most notably the rise of river, quartz, and hydraulic mining—required far greater capital resources. To meet the growing need for capital, large-scale corporations soon became the dominant form of economic organization, and speculation in mining securities became a regional obsession. The mining corporations played a key role in the economic development of California and the West, but they also had their downside. "Corporate power," Jung reminds us, "won out over individual rights, as insiders manipulated share prices, bilked investors, and drained companies. These activities diverted funds from more productive investments, injured workers' livelihoods, and damaged the economy as a whole."

Daniel Cornford's essay on labor and capital, surveying the rise of corporate organization from the perspective of the miners, complements well the work of Maureen Jung. Cornford's approach reflects the interests of the new social historians, going far beyond the anecdotal testimony of individual miners to analyze basic questions of status and mobility. Acknowledging the pioneering work of Rodman

A mining company, which includes several Indians, pauses from its labors to pose for posterity, probably at Taylorsville, in present-day Plumas County, about 1850. Although the popular image of the Argonaut is often that of the solitary prospector, the economic imperatives of mining required gold seekers to labor together relatively early, either in voluntary associations or, increasingly, as employees of corporate entities. These miners have diverted a stream with a dam and begun their raid on the auriferous Tertiary gravels beneath the riverbed. *Courtesy Huntington Library, San Marino, Calif.*

Paul and the more recent contributions of Ralph Mann, Cornford concludes that upward mobility eluded most Argonauts. The lucky few struck it rich, but the earnings of the average miner "declined sharply from 1848 onward." It is in this context of declining fortunes that Cornford notes the diversity of the gold-rush population and the emergence of ethnic hostilities. He speculates on the origins of xenophobia and racism in the Gold Rush, citing instances of both legal and extra-legal discrimination against immigrant and nonwhite miners. In tracing the development of a labor movement in the California mines, a movement that did not emerge until the ascendancy of hardrock mining in the 1860s, Cornford gives special credit to the role of Cornish immigrants. He concludes that the "proletarianization" of the California miners reflected the steady decline in their economic position and the consequent growth in social tensions between labor and capital.

Like several other essayists in this volume, Raymond F. Dasmann distances himself from the popular celebrations of "the days of '49" as he begins his account of the environmental changes wrought by the Gold Rush. He notes that the native flora and fauna of California already had been impacted severely by European settlement prior to 1848 and that environmental degradation would have continued even without a Gold Rush. Such was the story of California's grizzlies, sea otters, fur seals, tule elks, and pronghorn, as well as its forests and perennial native grasses. Yet the Gold Rush clearly had an "accelerating effect" on the activities that affected the environment. "It was the Gold Rush," Dasmann observes, "that set off the destructive, furious search for the yellow metal that later brought the moving of mountains and filling of valleys." The tortured landscape left behind stands today as "a monument to greed."

Restraining the passions of the Gold Rush is the topic of Donald J. Pisani's essay on mining and American resource law. His thesis is stated in the opening sentence: "The California Gold Rush profoundly influenced the evolution of property law in the American West." Paralleling Ronald Limbaugh's discussion of adaptive technology, Pisani acknowledges that mining codes did not originate in California but were introduced from many other mining frontiers. Nevertheless, out of the peculiar conditions of California came principles of law that later "became the foundation for mining on the public domain throughout the American West." As conflicts over water usage emerged between miners and farmers, further precedents were established that were adopted in other states. Pisani also notes that the speculative spirit of the miners influenced economic activities generally; the same "obsession with profit" characterized both California mining and agriculture. Raymond Dasmann's perspective on the environment here is reinforced, for Pisani concludes that the Gold Rush "strengthened the assumption that nature existed solely for profit." The legacy of California mining is a mixed one: it "produced great wealth, but it came at a high price."

Duane A. Smith's essay expands the range of California's contributions to the American West and beyond. In the spirit of Rodman Paul's early multiculturalism, Smith demonstrates not only the cosmopolitan origins of California's mining frontier but also its worldwide impact. In addition to technology and mining law, California exported capital, manpower, expertise, and a colorful panorama of mining legends and lore. The influence of California was first seen in Nevada, and later in Colorado, Idaho, Montana, and on mining frontiers around the world. Smith also reminds us that although exports like hydraulic mining devastated the landscape, they also gave rise to powerful counterforces of environmental awareness and protection. From the mining enthusiasms of California came a boisterous materialism and also a legacy of optimism—the notion that "over the next mountain, in the next canyon, would be El Dorado."

Anthony Kirk's interpretive chapter, "Seeing the Elephant," introduces a folio of evocative paintings and drawings of gold-rush scenes, most of them contemporaneous to the events themselves. Many of the images selected by Kirk portray the hardships endured by the Argonauts on their trek to California, as well as the hard times they encountered once in the land of their dreams. Kirk concludes that "few Argonauts gathered the golden harvest they set out so confidently to reap." The sense of excitement and drama present in many of these images is often alloyed with an undertone of bitter disappointment and painful regret.

The next four essays—by David J. St. Clair, Larry Schweikart and Lynne Pierson Doti, Lawrence James Jelinek, and A. C. W. Bethel—consider the impact of the Gold Rush on other contemporary economic activities in California. David St. Clair examines manufacturing and industry, raising the question of whether the Gold Rush had a positive or negative effect on the pace of their development. Historians long have disagreed on this vital issue. Maureen Jung argues that mining corporations were a catalyst for the growth of subsidiary industries, but the corporations also tended to divert funds from more productive uses. St. Clair comes down squarely on the side of those who see the Gold Rush as a stimulus to California industrialization. He demonstrates that California manufacturing grew rapidly during the gold-rush years for several reasons: the great boom in population led to an increased demand for consumer goods; industries linked to mining expanded to provide needed products and services; and the infrastructure developed for the mineral extraction industry was eminently transferable to other sectors. A spirit of innovation and flexibility thus was generated in the Gold Rush that became the hallmark of California's entrepreneurial dynamism. "Perhaps the greatest legacy of the Gold Rush," St. Clair concludes, "was not its ability to attract gold miners, but its ability to attract entrepreneurs who seized the opportunities that gold offered."

Larry Schweikart and Lynne Pierson Doti discuss the role of banking in the gold-rush economy. After surveying the regional financial landscape prior to 1848, they affirm that the gold discovery changed fundamentally the way Californians did business. Developing in a region where "hard money" was in abundant supply and at a time when antibanking sentiment was virulent, financial institutions in the Golden State had serious obstacles to overcome. Schweikart and Pierson Doti reveal how those obstacles were surmounted and explain the ways the Gold Rush informed the early economic development of the state. "Banking and the financial sector," they argue, " . . . evolved in often distinctive ways because of the gold-rush economy."

Lawrence James Jelinek reaches a similar conclusion in his essay on ranching and farming during the Gold Rush. The old Mexican ranchos boomed temporarily following the gold discovery and then entered a period of steep decline. Open-range grazing gave way to breeding and fattening ranches, and land ownership became

The banking house of James King of William, located on the corner of Montgomery and Commercial streets in San Francisco, 1854. Founded by the Georgetown, D.C., native who appended the "of William" to distinguish himself from others of that name, the bank was one of the earliest established in California. *Courtesy Wells Fargo Bank.*

concentrated in the hands of a few highly successful agrarian entrepreneurs. Cultivation of crops, on the other hand, was brought to a "near standstill" in the early years
of the Gold Rush, as people and capital moved into mining, but later boomed to
meet the needs of a rapidly expanding population. Wheat farming on a massive
scale led to the rise of an itinerant and multiethnic agricultural work force, what
Carey McWilliams called California's "peculiar institution." Viticulture and the development of orchards followed the wheat boom as California agriculture became
more diversified. State support for farming developed with the realization that gold
alone "could not permanently underwrite a healthy economy."

The Gold Rush was also a time of far-reaching developments in transportation,
as A. C. W. Bethel demonstrates in his catalog of California conveyances. Bethel
surveys the various modes of transportation that brought the Argonauts to California, as well as the evolution of intrastate pack trains, freight wagons, riverboats,
stagecoaches, and railroads. The rapid growth of the gold-rush population and its
distribution throughout the state's interior stimulated the development of California transportation. Bethel's findings support the conclusion of David St. Clair that
the mining of gold produced an infrastructure, including an array of transportation
options, that facilitated growth in other economic sectors.

The final essay summarizes the overall economic significance of the Gold Rush.
Gerald D. Nash ties together the observations of all the other essayists, concurring
that "the Gold Rush helped to trigger momentous economic changes. In the language of economists, it served as a multiplier—an event that accelerated a chain of
interrelated consequences, all of which accelerated economic growth." Nash briefly
notes the dimensions of that growth in manufacturing and industry, banking and
finance, agriculture and transportation. He also emphasizes the worldwide
ramifications of the Gold Rush, tracing its impact on the peoples and economies of
Latin America, Europe, the Pacific, and Asia. Nash's conclusion is far-sweeping: "In
many ways, the California Gold Rush precipitated a veritable economic revolution
in the state, the nation, and the world. Production of precious metals affected price
levels, labor, wages, capital investment, the expansion of business, finance, agriculture, service industries, and transportation." Yet there was more. Nash also reminds
us of the psychological and philosophical dimensions of the Gold Rush, for surely
this epoch-making event "touched a deep-seated nerve in the human psyche." Forces
were unleashed, for good or for ill, that would transform California forever into a
Golden State.

NOTES

1. Diary of Henry William Bigler, January 24, 1848, Society of California Pioneers, San
Francisco.

2. Quoted in *California Heritage: An Anthology of History and Literature,* ed. and comp. John and LaRee Caughey (Itasca, Ill.: F. E. Peacock Publishers, 1971), 191.

3. Hubert Howe Bancroft, *History of California,* vol. 6 (San Francisco: The History Company, 1886), 33–35. See also the discussion in James J. Rawls, "Gold Diggers: Indian Miners in the California Gold Rush," *California Historical Quarterly* 40 (Spring 1976): 28–45.

4. Rodman W. Paul, *The California Gold Discovery: Sources, Documents, Accounts, and Memoirs Relating to the Discovery of Gold at Sutter's Mill* (Georgetown, Calif.: Talisman Press, 1966), 18.

5. See John McPhee, *Assembling California* (New York: Farrar, Straus & Giroux, 1993).

6. An excerpt appears in Caughey, *California Heritage,* 49–50.

7. John Francis Bannon, Robert Ryal Miller, and Peter Masten Dunne, *Latin America* (Encino, Calif.: Glencoe Press, 1977), 170–71.

8. See Ralph P. Bieber, "California Gold Mania," *Mississippi Valley Historical Review* 35 (June 1948): 3–28.

9. Quoted in Caughey, *California Heritage,* 195.

10. Rawls, "Gold Diggers," 31.

11. Leonard Pitt, *The Decline of the Californios: A Social History of the Spanish-Speaking Californians, 1846–1890* (Berkeley: University of California Press, 1970), 50.

12. See Edwin A. Beilharz and Carlos U. Lopez, *We Were 49ers! Chilean Accounts of the California Gold Rush* (Pasadena, Calif.: Ward Ritchie Press, 1976), and Jay Monaghan, *Chile, Peru, and the California Gold Rush of 1849* (Berkeley: University of California Press, 1973).

13. James J. Rawls and Walton Bean, *California: An Interpretive History,* 7th ed. (New York: McGraw-Hill, 1998), 130.

14. Erwin G. Gudde, *California Place Names: The Origin and Etymology of Current Geographical Names* (Berkeley: University of California Press, 1974), 161. See also John E. Baur, "When Royalty Came to California," *California History* 67 (December 1988): 244–65.

15. See Jay Monaghan, *Australians and the Gold Rush: California and Down Under, 1849–1854* (Berkeley: University of California Press, 1966), and David Goodman, *Gold Seeking: Victoria and California in the 1850s* (Stanford: Stanford University Press, 1994).

16. Sucheng Chan, *Asian Californians* (San Francisco: Boyd & Fraser, 1991), 5–6, 27–28. See also Rodman W. Paul, *Mining Frontiers of the Far West, 1848–1880* (New York: Holt, Rinehart and Winston, 1963), 35.

17. Rawls and Bean, *California,* 141. See also Rudolph M. Lapp, *Blacks in Gold Rush California* (New Haven: Yale University Press, 1977).

18. Louis B. Wright, *Culture on the Moving Frontier* (Bloomington: University of Indiana Press, 1955), 128.

19. Quoted in Oscar Lewis, *Sea Routes to the Gold Fields: The Migration by Water to California in 1849–1852* (New York: Ballantine Books, 1971), 64.

20. David Morris Potter, ed., *Trail to California: The Overland Journal of Vincent Geiger and Wakeman Bryarly* (New Haven: Yale University Press, 1967), 231.

21. Quoted in JoAnn Levy, *They Saw the Elephant: Women in the California Gold Rush* (Norman: University of Oklahoma Press, 1992), 17.

22. Robert W. Carter, "'Sometimes When I Hear the Winds Sigh': Mortality on the Overland Trail," *California History* 74 (Summer 1995): 146, 152, 155.

23. Quoted in ibid., 155.

24. Thomas D. Clark, ed., *Off at Sunrise: The Overland Journal of Charles Glass Gray* (San Marino, Calif.: Henry E. Huntington Library and Art Gallery, 1976), 154, 157.

25. Rodman W. Paul, *California Gold: The Beginning of Mining in the Far West* (1947; reprint, Lincoln: University of Nebraska Press, 1967), 345.

26. Ibid., 349; Malcolm J. Rohrbough, *Days of Gold: The California Gold Rush and the American Nation* (Berkeley: University of California Press, 1997), 3.

27. Andrew Rolle, *California: A History* (New York: Thomas Crowell, 1969), 229–30.

28. "Bill of Fare," 1849, Wells Fargo Bank History Room, San Francisco.

29. Rawls and Bean, *California*, 101.

30. Louise Amelia Knapp Smith Clappe, *The Shirley Letters: Being Letters Written in 1851–1852 from the California Mines* (Berkeley, Calif.: Heyday Books, 1998), 113.

31. Lewis, *Sea Routes to the Gold Fields*, 229.

32. Rolle, *California*, 225; Rawls and Bean, *California*, 103.

33. An 1868 edition of the *Songster* is in the California State Archives, Sacramento. See also Richard A. Dwyer and Richard E. Lingenfelter, eds., *The Songs of the Gold Rush* (Berkeley: University of California Press, 1964), 155.

34. Sherburne F. Cook, "The American Invasion, 1848–1870," in his *The Conflict Between the California Indian and White Civilization* (Berkeley: University of California Press, 1976), 5–13, 111. See also James J. Rawls, *Indians of California: The Changing Image* (Norman: University of Oklahoma Press, 1984), 171–202.

35. San Francisco *Alta California* (April 26, 1849), quoted in Rawls, *Indians of California*, 177.

36. Silas Weston, *Four Months in the Mines of California: Or, Life in the Mountains* (Providence, R.I.: Benjamin T. Albro, 1854), 8–10, quoted in Rawls, *Indians of California*, 178.

37. Quoted in Pitt, *Decline of the Californios*, 60.

38. Rawls and Bean, *California*, 130, 135–36.

39. Rohrbough, *Days of Gold*, 283.

40. Josiah Royce, *California, from the Conquest in 1846 to the Second Vigilance Committee in San Francisco: A Study of American Character* (1886; reprint, New York: Knopf, 1948), 175.

41. J. S. Holliday, *The World Rushed In: The California Gold Rush Experience* (New York: Simon & Schuster, 1981), quoted in James J. Rawls, "Great Expectations: William Swain, J. S. Holliday & *The World Rushed In*," *California History* 41 (Fall 1982): 167.

42. See the discussion in Paul, *California Gold*, 334–35, and John Walton Caughey, *The California Gold Rush* (Berkeley: University of California Press, 1975), 288–89; originally published as *Gold Is the Cornerstone*.

43. M. Guy Bishop, ed., "'Many Wanted to Know Which Was Mr. Bigler': Henry Bigler's Account of the 1898 California Golden Jubilee," *California History* 49 (Fall 1990): 284–92.

44. Charles Howard Shinn, *Mining Camps: A Study of American Frontier Government* (New York: Harper & Row, 1965), 105, 125, 176.

45. Quoted in Kevin Starr, *Americans and the California Dream, 1850–1915* (New York: Oxford University Press, 1973), 156, 162.

46. Paul, *California Gold*, 337, 341.

47. Caughey, *California Gold Rush*, 293.

48. Ralph Mann, "Frontier Opportunity and the New Social History," *Pacific Historical Review* 53 (November 1984): 463–91, and also his "The Decade After the Gold Rush: Social Structure in Grass Valley and Nevada City, California, 1850–1860," *Pacific Historical Review* 46 (November 1972): 484–504.

49. David Rich Lewis, "Argonauts and the Overland Trail Experience: Method and Theory," *Western Historical Quarterly* 16 (July 1985): 285–306.

50. See, for instance, Julie Roy Jeffrey, *Frontier Women: The Trans-Mississippi West, 1840–1880* (New York: Hill & Wang, 1979); Joan M. Jensen and Darlis Miller, "The Gentle Tamers Revisited: New Approaches to the History of Women in the American West," *Pacific Historical Review* 49 (May 1980): 173–212; Sandra L. Myers, ed., *Ho for California! Women's Overland Diaries from the Huntington Library* (San Marino: Henry E. Huntington Library and Art Gallery, 1980); Sandra L. Myers, *Westering Women and the Frontier Experience 1800–1915* (Albuquerque: University of New Mexico Press, 1982); Linda Peavy and Ursula Smith, *Women in Waiting in the Westward Movement* (Norman: University of Oklahoma Press, 1994); Glenda Riley, "Women on the Panama Trail to California, 1849–1869," *Pacific Historical Review* 55 (November 1986): 531–48.

51. Levy, *They Saw the Elephant*, 91–107.

52. Jacqueline Baker Barnhart, *The Fair but Frail: Prostitution in San Francisco, 1849–1900* (Reno: University of Nevada Press, 1986), 25–39. Similar conclusions appear in Marion S. Goldman, *Gold Diggers and Silver Miners: Prostitutes and Social Life on the Comstock Lode* (Ann Arbor: University of Michigan Press, 1981).

53. San Francisco *Alta California* (September 23, 1851), quoted in Paul, *California Gold*, 66.

2

Making Old Tools Work Better

*Pragmatic Adaptation and Innovation
in Gold-Rush Technology*

Ronald H. Limbaugh

As any American with a newly purchased computer can attest, rapid technological change is both inevitable and unpredictable in modern, urban-industrial societies. Patterns of rapid change seem inherently modernist and international at first glance, a twentieth-century by-product of economic competition, social upheavals, and the clash of arms around the globe. They also appear to be confined to the most economically advanced nations or regions, those having long passed the frontier or formative stage of development.

This brief study of the Gold Rush provides a broader historical view of technological change. It looks at changing patterns of technology in one region on the fringes of Euro-American industrial civilization, initially isolated but rapidly internationalized and altered in ways neither predictable nor invariably progressive. What it finds are similar forces at work, and similar consequences, whether in postmodernist California, 150 years beyond its Argonaut heritage, or in frontier California during the 1840s and 1850s. The legacy of the Gold Rush lives still in cities and industries that benefited from mining technology, and in the attitudes, lifestyles, and material culture of modern Californians.

While historians traditionally have emphasized the cultural roots of technological change, recent trends in historiography indicate how profoundly the "new" history has been influenced by related disciplines, especially the fields of historical archaeology and geography. Since the 1980s, historians of the American frontier are inclined to view technological change and innovation as a product not only of cultural eclecticism and pragmatic adaptation, but also of the region's material environment. Dianne Newell's study of the Canadian frontier in Ontario, for example, found that innovative technology "was typically cast on a small scale, tailored to local sources of fuel, built from cheap materials available locally—notably wood—and easy to maintain."[1] Farther west, environmental differences help explain why mining and milling in northern Mexico and the American Southwest relied primarily on semi-arid technology, while northern California's relative abundance of water and timber produced a regionally distinctive technology widely copied but not widely successful outside its most optimal geographic boundaries.

Recognizing the importance of the physical setting as an influence on technological innovation, however, is not to endorse any theory of environmental determinism, a discredited idea among modern geographers as well as historians. Much closer to the mainstream scholarly view is Peter J. Hugill's cautious assertion that "environmental conditions influenced society's range of choices."[2] In California during the mid-nineteenth century, culture, pragmatism, and the regional environment combined to produce complex and dynamic patterns of change in mining technology.

AMERICAN MINING TECHNOLOGY AT MIDCENTURY

The Gold Rush came at an optimal time for American technological development. For the first time in history, the Western world at mid-nineteenth century united science and technology in a revolutionary merger that provided a powerful stimulus for material growth.[3] The next fifty years saw a tremendous change in the mining industry as the industrial revolution spread worldwide, stimulating the demand for minerals, transportation, consumer goods, new sources of power, and capital.

These prospects for rapid technological change were not that apparent at midcentury, however. Before the late 1840s, traditional European mining technology and equipment prevailed.[4] Spain had brought to Mexico in the sixteenth century a technology inherited from the Romans in antiquity and from the Germans in the Middle Ages.[5] The global stock of metals was in short supply, with gold production nearly moribund, silver mining in decline, and only a few base metals available, mainly iron, copper, lead, and tin, which were controlled by Europeans, particularly the British.[6] In the early decades of the nineteenth century, prospectors had located gold in Georgia and the Carolinas, copper in Michigan's Upper Peninsula, and lead and zinc along the Mississippi in Illinois, Wisconsin, and Missouri, but those strikes failed to attract much attention outside their immediate regions, and the technology for mineral extraction was crude even by midcentury European standards.

That was soon to change. Britain prepared the way in the 1830s by loosening its export barriers, making legal the exportation of machinery Americans had long been in the habit of smuggling into the States. By 1841 licenses from the British could be acquired for "nearly everything except spinning and weaving machinery."[7] A few years later the Irish potato famine and the decline of tin mining in Cornwall had profound long-range repercussions on California mining. By midcentury, California was in position to benefit from British policy changes as well as from its domestic "distresses."[8]

[Published at the WIDE WEST OFFICE, 184 Clay Street, San Francisco.]

HOW THE CALIFORNIA MINES ARE WORKED.

An engraved letter sheet, after a drawing by the famed artist-Argonaut Charles Nahl, depicts the range of mining techniques practiced in the early years of the gold fever. In the foreground a miner washes a pan of sand and gravel, intent on catching a glint of "color," while his companions labor with a cradle, *left,* and a long tom. Behind them other miners tunnel into the earth or wash for gold with a line of sluices. *California Historical Society, FN-04130.*

CULTURAL STIMULUS TO TECHNOLOGICAL INNOVATION

Technology and culture go hand in hand, and California culture at mid-nineteenth century was predominately American, despite the cosmopolitan flavor of the mining camps after the great trek of 1849. Foreign immigration was large during the early statehood years, but historians have tended to exaggerate its size and impact. The foreign-born population never was in the majority. It peaked in 1860 at 39 percent, having climbed from 24 percent in 1850. By the 1870 census the foreign-born element had dropped to 37 percent, and it continued to decline thereafter.[9]

With a two-thirds majority and an ethnocentric chip on their shoulders, Americans at midcentury imposed on California the mainstream values of a highly materialistic, expansionist, overly optimistic society. From the streets of Boston, Philadelphia, and New York, and from the farms and river cities of the trans-Appalachian heartlands, they ventured forth with a robust spirit of individualism and self-worth, an aggressive nationalism, a self-righteous defense of their religious and moral beliefs, and an abiding faith in their own political and social institutions. Unlike the Australian gold rush, which came when Australia was still a colonial province with a pastoral elite in control and with no middle class, the California rush attracted

Americans who were experienced in developing and sustaining local government and social institutions.[10]

Caught up in the heady spirit of Manifest Destiny and Jacksonian egalitarianism, Americans in the late 1840s and early 1850s brought to the Far West an "emotional dynamism" that was both progressive and materialistic. Their material ambitions reflected a common trait found in all Argonauts regardless of race, class, or national origin. H. J. Habakkuk's remark about Europeans applies equally well to other gold seekers: those who left for California had a personal desire to improve by "ensuring, through hard work, that they did in fact better themselves."[11]

The federal role in California mining was no less important than the power of democratic idealism. For a half-century prior to the Gold Rush, expansionists and visionaries had postulated a continental empire, a land of small farmers and individual entrepreneurs, aided and abetted by government but left for individual or corporate development without federal intervention or control. This Jacksonian image of democratic capitalism had an important ally in Christian morality and ideology. Historian John F. Kasson found a vital midcentury linkage between religious values and technological progress. When Lyman Beecher, Presbyterian theologian and father of Harriet Beecher Stowe, said Christianity was important "in safeguarding American technology," his message brought a provocative response from the nation's most prominent Unitarian orator, Edward Everett. He replied that "the converse was true. . . . Technology stood as the great benefactor of the public good, and he who impeded the progress of modern inventions threatened all."[12]

Even government could not stand in the way of progress by the thousands of "expectant capitalists" who ventured west in search of fortune. Unlike Canadian or Australian mineral rushes, where government made an effort, not always successfully, to regulate the use of public resources, gold seekers in California had a free hand, helping themselves to land, timber, water, and minerals, with government aiding and abetting the privatization at public expense. Before 1878, for instance, mining interests used thousands of acres of timber lands not legally open to settlement except under homestead and preemption laws. Even those restrictions were ignored by early sawmill owners and miners, who openly cut any timber they wanted on federal lands.[13]

GOLD-RUSH TECHNOLOGY AND AMERICAN PRAGMATISM

The massive scale and diffusion of placer deposits in the Sierra foothills gave California a distinctive advantage in nineteenth-century America's race for riches. No other region in North America offered such golden opportunities for so many ordinary people, people without specialized knowledge or skills. The California Gold Rush was both first and biggest in sheer numbers of people involved. It was also the most important, for it accelerated the pace of American urban-industrial development and continental conquest.[14]

American gold seekers carried west a technology based on practical application and experience. Engineering as a profession was still in infancy at mid-nineteenth century; those who called themselves engineers were usually pragmatic, seat-of-the-pants technicians and mechanics with little formal education. They stood in sharp contrast to engineers from Europe, especially continental Europe, which had an engineering legacy grounded in theoretical science and mathematics.[15] Lofty in their traditions and training, some European scientists derided American practical engineering, arguing that the "Yankees" were "blundering along" in gold and silver metallurgy and would continue to do so until they studied at European schools like Freiburg in Germany or the London School of Mines. Some Americans agreed. J. Ross Browne, a Californian and the nation's first commissioner of mining statistics, considered the lack of trained American mining engineers a national disgrace: "Our mines and mills are practically managed by foreign experts; we furnish the labor and mechanical ingenuity, but they furnish the scientific skill."[16] His successor, Rossiter Raymond, took a more balanced view, noting wryly that many Americans puffed the superiority of American methods over the rest of the world. "The truth lies between these extremes," he concluded. Both he and Browne called for a national school of engineering, but Congress responded instead with the land-grant college act, leaving the job of training technicians up to the states.[17]

Whatever the need, it was practical miners in the gold-rush era who responded to technological challenges by adapting existing machines and methods to local conditions. Before 1851 the massive scale of surface placer deposits gave practically anyone a chance to mine without the necessity of elaborate equipment or experience. Only after depleting the high-grade shallow gravels did California mining begin to develop more sophisticated technologies. But even then the change was more innovative than revolutionary. As Browne said in 1868, "with all the genius and enterprise of the American people, no important discovery in the way of machinery for mining was made which had not been long in use in South America, Mexico, or Europe."[18] The Washoe pan process, for instance—the first practical method for reducing Comstock silver ores—was an American hybrid, a modification of milling processes used for centuries in Mexico and Germany.[19] By the late 1860s the hallmarks of American mining technology were ingenuity and innovation, rather than originality and invention. Even former scoffers were impressed. Rossiter Raymond's 1869 *Report* noted with pride that European metallurgists were now coming to the United States to learn from Americans, rather than the other way around.[20]

Technological innovation in gold-rush California, however, was not distinctively American. The notion that Yankees were more ingenious than people from other lands is an ethnocentric stereotype born out of the excessive nationalism of the nineteenth century. In truth, adapting common tools and methods to local conditions was standard procedure in frontier communities regardless of ethnic or cultural differences. In Canada, for example, frontier Ontario fashioned new techniques from old "whenever it was practical to do so."[21]

In California, those who were actively engaged in seeking gold used whatever tools and methods were at hand, regardless of origin. To excavate and wash bedrock gravels, the first miners along the American River used ordinary picks and shovels, household butcher knives, tightly woven baskets made by native Americans, and frying pans. By the summer of 1848 Georgians, Hispanic Californians, and perhaps transplanted Europeans with placer experience, had introduced sheet-iron pans and wooden *bateas* (bowls), wooden rockers (cradles) and riffle boxes, and dry-washing and winnowing techniques with blankets and hides.[22] A Georgian "was said to have introduced the sluice box on Laird's Hill about April 1850," but this claim is disputed by evidence that it was in use earlier.[23] The sluice was actually an ancient device, used as early as Roman times, although California miners may have reinvented it without being aware of its antecedents.[24] Like its cousins the long tom and the rocker, it employed the power of gravity to concentrate heavier eroded gold from lighter sands and gravels. When mercury ("quicksilver") was available and cheap enough for low-budget operators, miners added it to sluice boxes to "amalgamate" finer gold particles, flour gold, or "dust" that tended to wash away. Amalgamation was another ancient process brought to Mexico by Spaniards in the sixteenth century and to California by both Mexican and Georgian miners.[25] Mercury-coated riffle bars in the bottoms of sluice boxes "captured" gold if it was bright and clean and "free-milling," or not locked up in sulfide compounds or tellurides. "Clean-up" was a simple matter of scraping up the amalgam and heating it on a shovel in an open fire at first, or later in a retort, until the mercury vaporized, leaving behind the "sponge" of gold, which could then be melted and poured into bars for delivery to the mint.

In the Southern Mines, those south of the Mokelumne River, where the influence of Hispanic immigrant miners was stronger, the Spanish *batea*—a wooden bowl hollowed out of a single block—was at first widely used in the placer diggings, but it soon gave way to the flat-bottomed iron pan preferred by Americans.[26] More influential was dry-washing, or winnowing, a method used extensively by Mexicans in the Southern Mines, where, prior to the organization of water companies, water was scarce in summer and fall. A French traveler in 1848 watched Sonorans between the American and Cosumnes rivers using this technique to extract six or seven ounces of gold per day from dusty gravels.[27] Experienced Mexican placer and hardrock (quartz) miners made other important contributions to California technology until they were chased out after 1850 by jingoistic Americans using both legal and de facto forms of discrimination.[28]

Chinese miners demonstrated considerable ingenuity in adapting and altering

Placer miners pose with the tools of their trade, gold pans and rockers, in what are possibly dry diggings, to judge by the buckets carried by one of the Argonauts. The rocker, or cradle, first appeared in California in the summer of 1848, employed at Coloma by miners from Georgia, who had long experience with its use in their native state. More efficient than the pan, it usually required the combined labor of two or three men—one to shovel and dig, one to load the hopper with sand and gravel, one to ladle the water and rock the cradle. *Courtesy Bancroft Library.*

European and American placer techniques. They were particularly adept with the pan and rocker, continuing to rely on these portable tools long after they were abandoned by others.[29] The image of the Chinese and his rocker became so pervasive in the mining West that some Americans thought the machine was a Chinese invention, even though Isaac Humphreys, a Georgia miner, took credit for introducing it in California. It was used extensively at Mormon's Bar near Coloma and in the ravines and gulches along the American River before the Chinese arrived.[30] But Chinese quickly made the rocker their own. By the 1850s, Chinese models were being manufactured in China and exported back to the United States for sale to new arrivals from the Celestial Kingdom.[31] Historical archaeologists in recent years, after examining numerous Chinese mining sites in the West, have concluded that even as Chinese miners retained cultural identities through an international trade network that supplied them with traditional Chinese commodities, they were receptive to technological innovation. Thus, as Michael Ostrogorsky puts it, "ethnicity became secondary to technology in determining frontier lifeways, rather than the reverse."[32]

One ancient device distinctively Asian in design, however, saw widespread application and adaptation in the placer camps. This was the Chinese chain pump, a continuous belt of water-lifting pallets, initially foot-powered, that could be used to de-water flooded claims and boggy ground adjacent to a river or stream, or to divert water from a low-lying stream to a nearby sluice or riffle box. Used extensively in river mining, it was widely adapted and quickly altered, growing both in size and capacity, the Asian ancestor of the bucket-line dredge.[33]

Starting with simple, universal designs, practical miners fashioned and re-fashioned mechanisms suitable for specialized needs and adapted to regional conditions. Whenever possible they converted hand- or foot-power to water-power or steam, the most available forms of cheap energy in California before the 1890s. At Mokelumne Hill, for example, William Highly in 1860 built a homemade pump for lifting water thirty feet above a flume, using two water wheels, each twenty feet in diameter, placed so that the same water turned both wheels.[34] Other practical engineers erected "flutter wheels," sometimes forty feet in diameter, that lifted water in buckets or barrels attached to paddle wheels rotating in the stream's flow.[35]

By the early 1870s, high-pressure water wheels of the California-built Pelton and Knight designs were beginning to revolutionize the power-generating needs of the industry. In districts where water was abundant, Pelton-type wheels were cheaper than steam engines and much more efficient for powering air compressors, pumps, and line shafts. Some innovators even experimented using these "hurdy-gurdy" wheels to power machine drills underground.[36]

THE LEGACY OF CALIFORNIA'S GOLD-RUSH TECHNOLOGY

Granted the accelerated pace of development in the West following the international rush of 1849, what were the long-range consequences for California mining technology? John Hittell, California's first regional historian, admitted that western miners were eclectic rather than original. Even so, he continued, their lack of originality "does not deprive the miners of the Sacramento basin of their right to high credit; for although the general principles might have been elsewhere applied at an earlier time, it was here that the inventions were brought to their highest state of efficiency, that they were universally adopted, and that they were adapted to the peculiar circumstances of every locality."[37]

Writing in 1861 about the state's brief mining history, Hittell had the advantage of both his personal observation and a ten-year perspective. By that date California had moved beyond the egalitarian era. Mining was no longer dominated by individual entrepreneurs or small partnerships in search of high-grade shallow placers. By the late 1850s a new era of industrial mining had dawned, an era characterized by corporate organization and consolidation, substantial capital investment, increased professionalization of management and engineering, hired miners working for wages instead of partners working for profits, and new technologies designed to mine lower-grade massive deposits.

Generally, these industrial conditions applied only to the major mines, whether placer or hardrock. On a different scale entirely were the smaller producers, the true heirs of the Gold Rush. Most mines were still in the hands of small-time operators or companies, the "mom and pop" units in the industry. Working with less capital investment, fewer men, smaller properties, and often with antiquated methods and equipment, their numbers were large but the volume of their production modest in comparison to the major producers. Technology made slow progress in these smaller mines for a variety of reasons, some of which had to do with the high cost of change, but mostly because the focus was on high-grade ore extraction, rather than operations that required modernized mass-mining techniques. Dianne Newell's analysis of conditions in frontier Ontario might equally apply to frontier California: in both places high-grade ores, usually close to the surface, were profitable to work without employing expensive new equipment or new technologies.[38] Even after the mines deepened and lower-grade deposits opened, some operators remained in business as long as they could, hoping for another bonanza and financing operations with production revenue when possible, or with "Irish dividends"—stock assessments—when not. Often the mine ended in failure and foreclosure, only to start up again with a new source of ore and a new cycle of intermittent production and decline. Though such operations dotted California throughout its mining history, they generally remained economically insignificant and technologically limited.

California miners may not have been the heroic architects of western technology that John Hittell described in 1861, yet his praise is not wholly unwarranted. By that time, two components of the industry, hydraulic mining and stamp milling, had been indelibly marked with regional distinction.

HYDRAULIC MINING: A CALIFORNIA ORIGINAL

Because of "our peculiar circumstances and conditions," wrote Rossiter Raymond in 1869, the United States has "developed some distinctively American processes." One was hydraulic mining, "native and peculiar to this country," a technology distinctly Californian in design and application.[39] Historians have quibbled about whether it was really "new" or merely another example of adaptive innovation,[40] and have even disputed the place of origin and the originators.[41] The details of its genesis should not obscure the larger significance of its contribution to mining. It was truly a "breakthrough technology,"[42] a revolutionary process using the destructive power of high-pressure water to exploit thick, deeply buried placer deposits at the lowest possible cost. It proved the effectiveness and profitability of working lower-grade ores with mass-mining techniques.

The need for new placer technology became apparent as early as 1850. Cornish miners in Nevada County, following gravel leads that indicated the presence of deep gravels laid down by ancient river channels, sank short vertical shafts to bedrock, then drifted along the channel to locate the "pay streak." Pocket mining, or "coyoting," a common practice among prospectors and small operators in the early 1850s, expanded into drift mining or "tunneling," designed to exploit the richer gravels deposited in a complex series of Tertiary streambeds, buried fifty to two hundred feet or more below the surface.[43]

Drift mining was both dangerous and expensive, requiring more experience and skill than surface placering as well as a greater outlay of capital for underground development and timbering. It was also inefficient, requiring miners to remove tons of barren rock and gravel before reaching pay dirt.[44] In hilly localities, where there was abundant water and adequate drainage, some companies resorted to "ground sluicing." This was an inexpensive way to strip off shallow "overburden," or barren material above bedrock, simply by washing it away with a large volume of swift-running water and allowing the cracks and crevices in the rocky underlay to serve as natural riffle bars for capturing loose gold. Most of the finer particles washed away with the barren sands, but enough gold was caught by this means to make ground sluicing a popular and cheap method of moving massive amounts of material. Philip R. May characterized it as the "essential preliminary technique" to hydraulic mining, since it demonstrated both the earth-moving potential and the economic feasibility of mass-mining by hydraulic action.[45] All that remained was to devise means and methods to increase the velocity and cutting-power, and control the direction of the stream flow.

Hydraulic technology advanced incrementally and differentially, with local inventors working independently to design and patent components. Edward E. Matteson is credited with devising the first successful nozzle. A Rhode Island native and Forty-niner, he added a three-quarter-inch nozzle made of sheet brass to a rawhide hose attached to a barrel set on a stump thirty feet above him, using it for the first time in March 1853 to undercut a steep, high bank that he had been ground sluicing with a stream of water.[46]

Matteson's homemade device was a great success, but as Randall Rohe points out, hydraulic technology could not keep up with demand. Canvas replaced rawhide by 1853, but it was expensive, prone to rot, and unable to withstand the increased pressures demanded by hydraulic operators. Iron pipe eventually replaced not only the hydraulic hose but most of the wooden flumes that had mushroomed in the

[Published at the WIDE WEST OFFICE, 181 Clay Street, San Francisco.]
CALIFORNIA MINING.—GROUND SLUICING.

A half-dozen miners combine their labor in ground sluicing, turning a stream of water to wash over a bank of earth and assist them in cutting down to the pay dirt of the gold-laden gravels resting on the bedrock below. Used extensively beginning in 1851, the technique was a precursor to hydraulic mining. *Courtesy Huntington Library, San Marino, Calif.*

1850s, as hydraulic water companies devised elaborate and expensive delivery systems to supply the mines. Nozzles were fitted to iron "monitors," which also expanded in size, capacity, and maneuverability. Gooseneck swivels and knuckle joints provided both horizontal and vertical movement of these powerful water cannon, rock-filled boxes counterbalanced the water velocity and volume, and solid tripods and pivots added stability and support. By the 1870s, hydraulic monitors, or "giants," came in a variety of shapes and sizes, some weighing a ton or more. Most were designed and built by local technicians in machine shops and foundries both in San Francisco and in regional mining and supply towns.[47]

Aside from the systems for water delivery and discharge for washing down the banks, hydraulicking was a relatively simple and ancient technology that relied on traditional gravity methods. Except for the largest boulders, all the material washed down by hydraulic operators passed through long strings of sluice boxes on its way downstream, leaving huge pits behind and tons of debris clogging the streams and rivers below. Like their shallow-placer-mining colleagues, hydraulic miners relied on amalgamation for recovery of values. Clean up and retorting recovered most of the mercury, but invariably a small percentage escaped, leaving a troubling legacy of pollution for later generations. More immediate was the devastation imposed on

A slender stream of water plays against a high bank at Michigan Bluff, Placer County,
in a daguerreotype made in the spring of 1854, one of the earliest known photographs
of hydraulic mining. It was from such simple and innocent beginnings that the giant cast-
iron monitors of the 1870s evolved. These water cannons, with bores of six to ten inches,
could throw a powerful jet of water several hundred feet and tear away whole hillsides in
an afternoon. *Courtesy Wells Fargo Bank.*

farmers and merchants and families in the Central Valley by the periodic floods
that washed millions of tons of hydraulic debris downstream, filling in riverbeds and
smothering farms and towns. After a decade of lawsuits, the federal courts in 1884
dealt a near-fatal blow to this branch of the industry in California by requiring that
miners impound all hydraulic tailings.

For nearly three decades, hydraulic mining dominated northern California as had
no other form of mineral extraction. But as historian Robert Kelley put it, in the
confrontation wrought by two clashing technologies, mining and agriculture, Californians chose "grain" over "gold."[48] Yet hydraulicking was the first effective technique for mass-mining of lower-grade deposits, and as such it set important precedents for the industry. It also stimulated the development of significant ancillary
industries in California, particularly systems for impounding and diverting water,

both for irrigation and urban use. The legacy of hydraulic mining lives on today in California, a state still embodying, as some have contended, the characteristics of a "hydraulic society."[49]

DEVELOPMENTS IN CALIFORNIA HARDROCK TECHNOLOGY

A later but still vital technological component of the California Gold Rush was hardrock, or lode, mining. It began in 1849, rose quickly between 1850 and 1852, then collapsed, rising again later in the decade and eventually dominating the industry. But hardrock mining's path to commercial viability was tortuous, filled with geologic, technological, and economic pitfalls that took many years to overcome.

As early as the spring of 1849, prospectors near Mariposa found pockets of high-grade gold ore among the quartz outcrops along a mineralized fault zone eventually traced for nearly two hundred miles. Miners called it the "Mother Lode," and popular literature today has often confused it with the more productive foothill deposits farther north in Nevada County, where California hardrock mining had its longest and most lucrative stand. But the initial excitement, overlaid with geologic ignorance and economic impetuosity, focused on the Southern Mines, where the outcrops were most extensive. Enthusiastic mine promoters imported European machinery at great expense, overbuilding the surface plant before understanding the size and nature of the orebody—a management mistake all too common in early American hardrock mining. After two or three years of effort, underwritten primarily by naive British investors relying on dubious field reports prepared by inexperienced and self-serving operators, the bubble burst. The mines shut down, the surface plants were abandoned, and investment capital dried up, leaving a sour taste for hardrock mining that took years to overcome.[50] A contemporary British observer, writing from Mariposita in the fall of 1852, recorded the frustration by noting that the "character of the country has yet to be ascertained, and it will not be found out by the guesser or mere prospector, but by the man of practice and experience. At present all is guess, and hope, and chance."[51] Rossiter Raymond later attributed the failure to "errors of judgment" rather than to "gross mismanagement," pointing out that Old World mining methods were inapplicable in California because of differences in ore character, labor costs, scarcity of materials, and climate.[52]

To remedy the situation, as Rodman Paul, the late dean of modern California mining historians, has written, a few practical miners, burned by the initial failures, inaugurated the "real beginning" of hardrock mining in California in the early 1850s, when they "set out to teach themselves in the fields of geology, mineralogy, engineering, and mechanics."[53] Building practical experience meant adapting available technologies to local conditions, the same pragmatic approach already seen in the gold-rush placer camps. California miners had much to learn. Their collective experience with hardrock mining was minuscule in comparison to immigrants from older hardrock districts, both in the United States and abroad. But early quartz mining was relatively simple because only the shallow deposits were worked. Before the 1860s California mines rarely reached levels below three hundred feet, the maximum depth of groundwater. Above that level, gold deposits containing sulfides, or "sulphurets," were subject to the natural processes of oxidation, leaching, and erosion, leaving a zone of "enrichment," higher in grade and easier to mine and mill than the deeper, unoxidized sulfide deposits. Thus, smart early mine operators kept to the shallow, weathered deposits and used simple methods. From more experienced underground miners from England, Germany, Mexico, and the lead and copper mines east of the Mississippi, they learned the basic techniques for opening a mine by vertical shaft or horizontal adit, advancing the heading by drilling and blasting, drifting and crosscutting to locate the most promising leads, draining and ventilating, timbering, and hauling and hoisting ore and waste.[54]

As the mines deepened, more complex technology was needed. Except for the occasional use of donkeys, mules, or horses to pull ore cars, before the 1860s most of the underground work was hand-powered and labor-intensive. Two-man "double-jack" drilling crews were required to set an effective charge with black powder, since drill holes had to be large in diameter. Dynamite needed smaller holes and fewer workers to handle but did not come into practical use until the late 1860s and early 1870s, and even then its use varied from district to district. In Grass Valley mines, where Cornish crews predominated, for instance, black powder and double-jacking remained the prevailing technology until 1869, when managers tried to introduce dynamite. The effort set off a nine-week strike ending in a compromise that kept out dynamite for another three years but opened the mines to single-jacking. Other districts lacking strong Cornish labor representation made a smoother transition to newer technology.[55]

Machine drills eventually replaced hand-drilling, but the change was slow and uncertain. The availability of innovations did not mean they were readily or widely adopted. Air-powered piston drills were not practical for underground work until the 1870s, and the rock dust they kicked up made them dangerous, especially in quartz mines high in silica. Furthermore, the early machines were awkward and expensive to install, requiring a new surface plant, at least two operators, and more space underground than many mines had available. Some historians have argued that labor resistance retarded the introduction of machine drills, although that view has been challenged by more recent scholarship, which has demonstrated that in some mines, at least, the issue was not health or jobs but basic economics. To financially pinched mine managers, the question often was not whether a new machine would work but whether it would help reduce operating costs. Thus machine drills were not widely used in the West until they were smaller, cheaper, more efficient, more durable, and safer. The real era of machine drilling did not begin until after water-cooled Leyner percussion drills were introduced in the late 1890s.[56]

Technological innovation also depended to some extent on the size and ethnicity of the work force. As John Rowe has observed, Old World technology reflected Old World attitudes and labor practices. In Cornwall, for example, with more workers than jobs available, mining machinery was used primarily to do work that animals and men could not perform; in America, with fewer workers and therefore higher labor costs, machines were designed to replace manual labor. The quality and durability of Cornish machinery also reflected the solid legacy of the Cornish mining heritage and the pride of its craftsmen. In contrast, American machinery was cheaper, less well built, and more easily replaced—a reflection of the newness and speculative nature of American mining—with owners and investors "all the more ready to scrap efficient but slow machines for novelties which promised vaster and quicker returns."[57]

In the mines of the northern Sierra, where the Cornish influence was strongest, Old World technology was reflected in both mining and milling methods. "Cousin Jacks" dominated the drilling crews, and Cornish foremen supervised underground operations. The first Cornish pump in California was installed at the Gold Hill mine in 1855, and the first ore-crushing stamp mills in the district were of Cornish design, although they soon gave way to the improved California mills.[58] Cornish methods also prevailed in the milling cycle. Finely ground mill pulp was discharged into long wooden troughs lined with coarse wool blankets especially made for the purpose. Every fifteen minutes the blankets were carefully removed and washed in amalgamation tanks to recover minute particles of metallic gold. The blanket-washing process, a technology used in Cornwall for centuries, was one of the distinguishing features of what became known as the "Grass Valley System."[59]

The Cornish presence was welcomed by mine and mill managers, many of whom were themselves Cornish, commissioned by English investors counting on their countrymen to protect their mutual interests.[60] Underground and in the surface plants, Cornish mining and milling skill was highly regarded, no less so by their own countrymen. In 1852 W. E. Gill, a Cornish miner from Truro, described his California experiences to a hometown newspaper: "Here some ability must be displayed in separating the gold without a loss, and here John [Bull] respectfully takes leave of Jonathan [Yank]. The latter is evidently a better huxter than a mining engineer."[61] Another Cousin Jack in Michigan, commenting on Cornish resistance to the introduction of dynamite, remarked that "Cornishmen are good miners, and good mine managers—they ought to be—but they are just as apt as others to conclude that what they do not know is not worth knowing."[62]

Along the Southern Mines of the Mother Lode, as in the placer districts, the technology reflected a strong Hispanic heritage. Mexicans were in great demand at first. They brought with them a four-hundred-year hardrock legacy, though their mining methods were less popular than their milling technology.[63] As Otis Young has observed, with some hyperbole, the Hispanic legacy profoundly influenced American milling. "Until the late 1880's," he wrote, "the western mining frontier depended so heavily upon Spanish milling methods that it is almost correct to say that millmen used little else but Spanish techniques hooked up to steam engines."[64] "Almost" is the great qualifier in this statement, especially as it applies to northern California, since that region produced ores distinctly different from those in the Southwest and Mexico, requiring different milling methods.

The most important Spanish technique to California millmen was the *arrastra*, a shallow, rock-lined circular pit where hand-sorted and broken ore could be ground and amalgamated by drag-stones powered by horse, mule, or waterwheel when sufficient water was available. Simple to construct and operate, using local materials widely available, it was the only successful milling tool for quartz miners in the early days. The Chilean mill, which crushed ore under millstones rolling over a stone patio or iron pan, was also used to a limited extent, and the principle was later employed in rotary grinders such as the Huntington mill, a widely used, medium-sized secondary crusher of California origin.[65] But traditional "Chili mills" and "rasters" were too small and slow for American miners, who needed a higher volume of production to meet lode mining's heavy capital expenditures and labor costs.[66] *Arrastras* continued to be used, mostly for reprocessing tailings, right into the twentieth century, but for bulk secondary crushing Americans turned to the stamp mill.

THE CALIFORNIA STAMP MILL

Pulverizing ore by mortar and pestle was an ancient technique. Prospectors used small mortars to test quartz outcrops during the Gold Rush, but the same principle had been used long before to develop a mechanical crusher common in European mills. Agricola claimed it had been invented in the late fifteenth or early sixteenth centuries, and found it in use in the mining districts of Germany and Switzerland.[67] Otis Young, emphasizing its southwestern connections, claimed the Spanish *maza*, or water-powered mill, a device using a single wooden pestle, or "stamp," and a square stone mortar, was "evidently a progenitor of the 'California' gravity stamp mill."[68] Rodman Paul believed stamp-mill technology arrived in the Far West by way of the American South, where it was in place in Georgia, Carolina, and Tennessee by the 1830s and 1840s.[69] Others claim the honor for Cornwall, noting that Cornish miners brought hardrock milling methods to California at least before 1855.[70]

Whatever their origin, imported mills were inadequate to meet California needs. German and Mexican mills used wood for pestle stems and mortar boxes, both subject to warping or leaking when wet and too flimsy for heavy use. Cornish and

The interior of a quartz mill at Grass Valley, Nevada County, the leading center of hard-rock mining, as illustrated in the October 1857 issue of *Hutchings' California Magazine*. To the rear stand two four-stamp batteries, or mills. The cast-iron "stampers," or pestles, weighing from six hundred to a thousand pounds, were raised by the revolving horizontal driveshaft and then fell with tremendous force to crush fist-sized pieces of ore to powder. *California Historical Society, FN-30967.*

Spanish mills had iron stems, split at the lower end and welded onto a cast iron shoe. Stamp heads in these older models were square and wore unevenly as the shoe dropped constantly on the same spot. The mortars were open at the bottom and mounted on stone plates or bedrock. Ore was broken and fed by hand to each stamp, which crushed dry and unevenly with an ear-shattering noise, accompanied by billowing clouds of silica dust.[71]

American millmen, working with these erratic imports, engineered pragmatic alterations whenever necessary, borrowing ideas and designs freely. The result by the 1860s was a regional hybrid, the "California improved stamp mill." The standard unit consisted of a mechanical jaw crusher for breaking rock, an automatic feeder, a five-stamp battery with fine-tooled, interchangeable parts, a heavy iron mortar, and an apron over which the pulp flowed on its way through the milling circuit. Most California mills used primary crushers manufactured in San Francisco from designs by Eli Whitney Blake, an authentic Connecticut Yankee who invented the machine in the 1850s for road construction work.[72] Gravel-sized ore mixed with water and fed into the mortar was ground between cast-iron shoes fitted onto the stamp heads and cast-iron dies attached to the mortar floor. Shoes and dies were easily removed for repair or replacement. A wooden bull wheel powered by water or steam in the early days, and electricity after 1890, turned a camshaft that lifted and rotated tappets connected to each stamp in a sequence designed to spread the wear and the pulp evenly. The mortar, a cast-iron box weighing several tons, came in various shapes and sizes to meet individual milling requirements.[73]

California gold mills, unlike silver mills in Colorado and the Southwest before the 1890s, usually wet-stamped, adding mercury along with water and reagents to the mortar box during the grinding process to improve recovery.[74] Wet-stamping in battery eliminated the dust problem and lowered the noise to a muted thunder, still too loud for millmen to talk normally but less harmful to the psyche, if not to the hearing. More important to millmen, wet-stamping helped to equalize the pulp, to keep it flowing in wave-like pulses through the mortar screens, and to clean the gold for better amalgamation. In mills that preferred dry-stamping, the improved California design closed the battery "as tightly as possible" and added a blower to move the dust into settling chambers, sometimes with the aid of steam.[75]

By the 1860s the California mill had become the standard design in the mining West, regardless of the type of ore, the size of the orebody, or the financial condition of the mine or mill. Single, five-stamp batteries found their way to remote mining camps throughout the West as well as overseas. In the larger mining districts west of the Rockies, twenty-, forty-, and sixty-stamp mills were not uncommon. Most of this complex equipment, along with hundreds of other types of mining and milling machinery and parts, was produced in San Francisco. More than forty foundries, machine shops, and iron works operated in the city by the mid-1860s—contributing to

A horse-drawn wagon moves slowly past the Miners' Foundry and Machine Works on First Street, just north of Folsom, in San Francisco, about 1865. The iron working industry had its origins in the American West less than a mile from here, when in the summer of 1849 James Donahue rigged up a simple charcoal forge for a smithy. With the rise of hydraulic and hardrock mining, the demand for castings soared, and the foundries and machine shops of San Francisco quickly earned a national reputation for fabricating superior mining machinery. *Courtesy Society of California Pioneers.*

San Francisco's status as the industrial capital of the West during the Gold Rush and for nearly a half-century beyond.[76]

East of the Rockies, ironworks in Chicago and other cities also began building California-type mills, usually modified to meet regional conditions. Colorado's complex silver ores, for example, much higher in sulfides than simpler California gold ores, needed deeper mortars, a longer and slower drop, lighter stamps, and a finer grind for efficient milling.[77]

Before the development of cyanidation and flotation, fine grinding was usually a curse for the millman who depended on gravity separation to treat gold and silver ores. The finer the grind the more likely the prospect of "sliming" the ore and "flouring" the mercury if battery amalgamation was used. "Slimes" were particles of mixed ore and "gangue," or nonmetallic waste, crushed and ground so fine that gravity had little effect. Most slimes could not be captured by ordinary gravity-separation processes and were thus lost in the tailings. California stamp mills were prone to sliming if not carefully monitored. But they lasted well into the twentieth century, economically and efficiently working away even in the major mills long after more effective ball and rod mills were available. As one practical engineer, a member of the Technical Society of the Pacific Coast, commented in 1900, "some one will probably invent a better machine than the California quartz mill for crushing rock and catching gold. It has its faults, and yet its much-condemned sliming tendency is too often the fault of the millman. It is simple, relentless and conscientious, with fewer faults than cling to many of its operators."[78]

GOLD-RUSH TECHNOLOGY AND EMERGING PROFESSIONALIZATION

Gold-rush technology was characterized by a frontier phalanx of enterprising amateurs altering or upgrading traditional techniques to meet local conditions. These were practical men—miners, millmen, blacksmiths, self-taught engineers, and other artisans—working independently at the job site or nearby on innovations designed for specific tasks. They were responsible for bringing hydraulic mining, drift mining, and stamp milling to the peak of perfection, and were behind many of the other machines and methods associated with the mining industry in nineteenth-century California.

Alongside them gradually emerged another technological prototype, the professional engineer, but it was a long struggle. Gold-rush miners and their followers generally believed that experience was the only sure path to pay dirt. Educated engineers or geologists were thought too theoretical, too unfocused and impractical, to work in the field either as prospectors or managers. Most professional engineers before 1870 were foreigners, trained in European schools—another mark against them in the minds of Americans still brimming with the fervent nationalism of the Jacksonian era.[79]

As the mining industry stabilized and expanded by the 1860s and 1870s, and as new investment capital came into California after the Civil War, new technology and science also entered. Deeper mining required more complex geological knowledge and more sophisticated machinery and methods. Investors wanted better information, the advice of experts, before risking their money. As the industry changed, so did the older ways of thinking. Mine managers and millmen, once resistant to science, now became more receptive, especially if science had practical application. The result was an increasing opportunity for professionals in the mining industry.[80]

One manifestation of this changing view was the clamor for a statewide geological survey. In the early 1850s, the legislature had appointed a state geologist, John B. Trask, but he was an "enthusiastic amateur," unequal to the task. In the waning years of the Gold Rush, renewed calls for a systematic state survey led to the 1858 appointment of Josiah D. Whitney as director. He was a professional geologist trained at Yale and in Europe, with a distinguished record. Expecting a thorough analysis of ore deposition in California, however, the mining interests were disappointed in the results. Over a thirteen-year period, Whitney and his professional staff produced and published a compendium of California natural history rather than a catalog of mineral resources. The volumes were little immediate help to the regional mining industry, but, as Rodman Paul has noted, the California Survey was the training ground for many geologists who went on to do important work at both federal and state agencies.[81]

At the federal level, some geologists first found jobs in a national agency organized at the urging of U.S. Senator Cornelius Cole of California and the mining interests that backed him. They proposed a national mining bureau to gather data on specific mining regions and operations. The result was congressional legislation in 1866 that established the office of U.S. Commissioner of Mining Statistics under the Treasury Department. The ten annual reports issued during the agency's brief existence by commissioner J. Ross Browne, a Californian, and his successor Rossiter Raymond were filled with technical information gathered by an excellent field staff and are still valuable today as an important source of historical data on mining west of the Rockies.[82] Raymond and Browne also contributed occasionally to the *Mining and Scientific Press*, a San Francisco serial that for sixty years reported comprehensive technical and economic news. Historian H. H. Bancroft called it "the leading journal on all matters connected with mining."[83]

In the 1870s the Treasury Department's Office of Mining Statistics was superseded by the U.S. Geological Survey, the agency ultimately responsible for gathering and disseminating information on American science and technology. Beginning in 1879 with the production of topographical maps, then moving to the classification of public domain lands, within a decade the Geological Survey was providing many services directly benefiting the mining industry, including "topography, geology, paleontology, chemistry, illustrations, mineral resources, library, irrigation, and engraving geologic maps."[84]

More directly beneficial to California mining was the State Bureau of Mines, established in 1880 by the legislature at the behest of mining interests. Headed by a state mineralogist appointed by the governor, the bureau was empowered to collect and preserve mineral specimens and detailed information on mining and milling methods, cultivate mining and metallurgical education, make on-site inspections, and prepare detailed reports on mining operations in each district throughout the state. With dedicated professional staffing, the bureau soon proved its worth by inaugurating a series of informative reports, bulletins, and technical leaflets that continue to the present day.[85]

Another result of the interest in professionalization was the first state efforts to provide technical education. Taking advantage of the federal Morrill Act (1862), giving public lands to the states for educational purposes, the California legislature in 1865 first proposed an "Agricultural and Mechanical Arts College." Under pressure from mining interests the lawmakers soon revised the title to "Agricultural, Mining, and Mechanical Arts College," and added a sentence emphasizing "the application of mechanical arts to practical agriculture in the field and mining." Opening in 1868, the new college, renamed the University of California, took years to graduate its first geologists and engineers. In the meantime eastern and European schools supplied the state with trained personnel.[86]

The presence of immigrant and later home-educated professionals increased the potential for rapid technological advances in California mining and milling, but the rate of change was differential, erratic, and unsystematic. Each sector of the industry independently moved forward, or sometimes backward, depending on local circumstances and personnel. In gold milling, for example, the Grass Valley System was widely adopted in California, but by the 1870s millmen could choose among a variety of techniques, each claiming advantages in cost and efficiency. The choice depended essentially on the type and grade of ore to be processed, matters that required professional training in mineralogy and metallurgy. G. F. Deetken, the man credited with perfecting the Grass Valley System, developed an elaborate procedure that began with fine-crushing and amalgamating in the stamp battery, then discharging the pulp onto blankets to catch the "fines," cycling the slimes and sands through several amalgamating tanks and tables for additional concentration to separate gold from gangue, and finally subjecting the concentrates to heating and chlorinating. But his system was designed for ores relatively low in sulfides. Ores with heavier sulfide content required much different treatment. In the 1880s, M. P. Boss of San Francisco patented a continuous milling process for both gold and silver ores. Touted as less expensive because it saved water and required fewer men to operate, it was also designed to improve the recovery of slimes and floured mercury. The key to this technique was coarse grinding in battery with the "least amount of water requisite to carry the pulp through the screens." Dispensing with blanket troughs and washing tanks, the Boss process discharged pulp into a series of grinding pans with automated mercury feeders, then settlers, and finally through a concentrating circuit. At the California mill in Virginia City, Nevada, completely revamped after the "Big Bonanza" days, the mill tailings were discharged into a series of tailings sluices "extending down the canyon" toward Dayton.[87] Cyanidation eventually replaced both these systems, but it came slowly to California, not making real headway until after 1900, a decade after it was introduced. By that time almost all California mines were deeper, working in lower-grade ore often higher in sulfides, which were ineffectually treated using only gravity-separation technology.

CONCLUSION

By the 1870s, California mining still retained vestiges of the gold-rush era but had reached the status of a modern industry. As Rodman Paul has written, it began as an adventure, changed into a business run by practical miners, and finally evolved into an industry in which the "dominant figure" was not the "honest miner" of the foothills but the "financier" and the "highly paid consultant or superintendent who made of mining a science and a profession."[88] This transition to modern mining came not through sweeping technological changes like a rising tide, but by piecemeal, step-by-step movement, mostly forward but often erratic and sometimes lateral or even backward. California mine managers occasionally had a conservative streak, resisting technology that cost money even if it improved efficiency or mine safety. William H. Storms, a California state mining inspector, deplored such parsimony. He publicly condemned the "antiquated" and "objectionable" methods employed by such men as Alvinza Hayward, who opened huge stopes where ore was removed without adequate timbering in order to return quick profits despite the danger.[89]

California mining had distinctive features that marked it as a regional variant if not a separate species. Though the Gold Rush lasted only a few years, it built a foundation for technological progress and urban-industrial development that continues today. The Golden State's timber and water abundance gave it advantages over drier districts and stimulated advances in peripheral technology such as dam and bridge design, dredging and excavating, and hydroelectric generation. Its massive gold deposits made it different from mining regions in the western interior, which had a different geology and a later development. Nowhere else was there such great opportunity for small-scale entrepreneurial mining as in California, which took longer to pass through the pioneer stage than other mineralized regions of the world. Industrial mining eventually arrived, bringing with it rapid technological advances based on adaptive design and pragmatic innovation, and reducing most of the work force to hired hands guided by professional managers. Yet small-scale entrepreneurial mining lingered on into the twentieth century, providing a psychological link to the Gold Rush and a cultural continuity that ties the past to the present. Today's recreational miners, whether with gold pans or suction dredges, still seek instant riches in the chilly waters of foothill streams. But there is also another form of wealth-seeking in the cities and industrial zones of coastal California, where much of the wealth generated by gold mining eventually came to rest. The legacy of the Gold Rush lives on in the quest for riches in the form of good jobs, good living, personal fulfillment—the same things California Argonauts sought 150 years ago.

NOTES

1. Dianne Newell, *Technology on the Frontier: Mining in Old Ontario* (Vancouver: University of British Columbia Press, 1986), 148.

2. Peter J. Hugill, *World Trade since 1431: Geography, Technology, and Capitalism* (Baltimore: Johns Hopkins University Press, 1993), xix.

3. Lynn White, Jr., "The Historical Roots of Our Ecological Crisis," *Science* 155 (March 10, 1967): 1203–7.

4. Newell, *Technology on the Frontier*, 13.

5. Otis Young, *Western Mining: An Informal Account of Precious-Metals Prospecting, Placering, Lode Mining, and Milling on the American Frontier from Spanish Times to 1893* (Norman: University of Oklahoma Press, 1970), 55–58.

6. Newell, *Technology on the Frontier*, 1–2.

7. H. J. Habakkuk, *American and British Technology in the Nineteenth Century: The Search for Labour-saving Inventions* (Cambridge: Cambridge University Press, 1967), 96–97.

8. Thomas A. Bailey, *A Diplomatic History of the American People*, 3rd ed. (New York: Appleton-Century-Crofts, 1946), 859.

9. Doris M. Wright, "The Making of Cosmopolitan California: An Analysis of Immigration, 1848–1870," *California Historical Society Quarterly* 20 (1941): 73–74.

10. Jermone O. Steffen, "The Mining Frontiers of California and Australia: A Study in Comparative Political Change and Continuity," *Pacific Historical Review* 52 (1983): 428–40.

11. Habakkuk, *American and British Technology*, 220.

12. John F. Kasson, *Civilizing the Machine: Technology and Republican Values in America, 1776–1900* (New York: Viking Press, 1976), 46–47.

13. Nathan L. White, "The Interrelationship between the Gold Mining Period in Sierra County, California, and the Development of the Sierra County Lumber Industry" (M.A. thesis, University of the Pacific, 1961), 76–89.

14. These achievements were regarded as unmitigated triumphs by nineteenth-century historians such as Hubert H. Bancroft and John Hittell. Modern scholars are more distant, more objective, and more critical in evaluating the consequences. See, for example, works by Donald Worster, Malcolm Rohrbough, Richard White, Carlos Schwantes, and Patricia Limerick.

15. Edwin T. Layton, "Mirror Image Twins: The Communities of Science and Technology in 19th Century America," *Technology and Culture* 12 (1971): 573; John B. Rae, "The 'Know-how' Tradition: Technology in American History," *Technology and Culture* 1 (1960): 141; Young, *Western Mining*, 79–80; Terry S. Reynolds, "The Engineer in 19th Century America," in *The Engineer in America: A Historical Anthology from Technology and Culture*, ed. Terry S. Reynolds (Chicago: University of Chicago Press, 1991), 7–8.

16. J. Ross Browne, "Report of J. Ross Browne on the Mineral Resources of the States and Territories West of the Rocky Mountains," in U.S. Treasury Dept., *Reports on the Mineral Resources of the United States* (Washington, D.C.: Government Printing Office, 1868), 8–9.

17. Rossiter W. Raymond, "Metallurgical Processes," in *Statistics of Mines and Mining in the States and Territories West of the Rocky Mountains,* part 5 (Washington, D.C.: Government Printing Office, 1870), 727; Browne, "Report," 8–9.

18. Browne, "Report," 8.

19. Raymond, "Metallurgical Processes," 727.

20. Ibid.

21. Newell, *Technology on the Frontier,* 148. Donald Macleod found similar circumstances in Nova Scotia, where mine promoters and engineers by the 1880s "generally sought to acquire new mill technology soon after its first appearance, normally copied it in part only, took indigenous needs into account in implementing it, and modified it extensively to meet local requirements." Donald Macleod, "Miners, Mining Men and Mining Reform: Changing the Technology of Nova Scotian Gold Mines and Collieries, 1858 to 1910" (Ph.D. thesis, University of Toronto, 1981), 229.

22. Joseph Libbey Folsom, *A Letter of Captain J. L. Folsom Reporting on Conditions in California in 1848* (San Francisco: Grabhorn Press, 1944), 11–12; Henry De Groot, "Six Months in '49," *Overland Monthly,* 1st ser., 14 (1875): 316; Henry W. Bigler, *Bigler's Chronicle of the West; The Conquest of California, Discovery of Gold, and Mormon Settlement as Reflected in Henry William Bigler's Diaries,* ed. Erwin G. Gudde (Berkeley: University of California Press, 1962), 98–99, 108; Thomas A. Rickard, *Man and Metals. A History of Mining in Relation to the Development of Civilization* vol. 2 (1932; New York: Arno Press, 1974), 729; John W. Caughey, *Gold Is the Cornerstone* (Berkeley: University of California Press, 1948), 12–13, 26.

23. Philip R. May, *Origins of Hydraulic Mining in California* (Oakland: Holmes Book Co., 1970), 35–36.

24. Browne, "Report," 118–19; Young, *Western Mining,* 55–66.

25. Young, *Western Mining,* 91–98.

26. Georgius Agricola, *De re Metallica,* trans. Herbert and Lou Henry Hoover (1912; first Latin edition, 1556; reprint, New York: Dover, 1950), 156–57; Rodman W. Paul, *California Gold: The Beginning of Mining in the Far West* (1947; reprint, Lincoln: University of Nebraska Press, 1967), 111–13; Young, *Western Mining,* 109.

27. Jacques A. Moerenhout, *The Inside Story of the Gold Rush,* trans. Abraham P. Nasatir, Special Publication 8 (1848; San Francisco: California Historical Society, 1935), 22.

28. Leonard Pitt, *The Decline of the Californios: A Social History of the Spanish-Speaking Californians, 1846–1890* (Berkeley: University of California Press, 1966), 60–67.

29. Randall Rohe, "Chinese River Mining in the West," *Montana* 46 (Autumn 1996): 17.

30. Excerpt from correspondence to New Orleans *Crescent City,* datelined Monterey, Calif., August 26, 1848, in J. Quinn Thornton, *Oregon and California in 1848* (New York, 1849), 312–15; *The Miners' Own Book, Containing Correct Illustrations and Descriptions of the Various Modes of California Mining,* introduction by Rodman W. Paul (1858; San Francisco: Book Club of California, 1949), 28–29; Moerenhout, *Inside Story of the Gold Rush,* 17–18.

31. Randall Rohe, "Chinese Small-Scale Mining in the American West 1848–1900" (paper delivered at the eighth annual conference, Mining History Association, Houghton, Michigan, June 6, 1997).

32. Michael Ostrogorsky, "The Influence of Technology on Social Typology and Change in the Western American Mining Frontier" (Ph.D. diss., University of Idaho, 1993), 21–23.

33. William Blake, "The Mechanical Appliances of Mining," in *Statistics of Mines and Mining in the States and Territories West of the Rocky Mountains,* part 4 (Washington, D.C.:

Government Printing Office, 1870), 602; Young, *Western Mining*, 114; Rohe, "Chinese River Mining in the West," 14–15; Robert Temple, *The Genius of China: 3,000 Years of Science, Discovery, and Invention* (New York: Simon & Schuster, 1989), 56–57.

34. Richard F. Epstein, *Old Mok [Mokelumne Hill]: The Story of a Gold Camp* (San Francisco: Dry Bones Press, 1995), 73.

35. Blake, "Mechanical Appliances of Mining," 600–602; Rohe, "Chinese River Mining in the West," 14–15; Young, *Western Mining*, 114, 271.

36. Rossiter W. Raymond, "Condition of the Mining Industry—California," in *Statistics of Mines and Mining in the States and Territories West of the Rocky Mountains* (Washington, D.C.: Government Printing Office, 1873), 40–44; Edward B. Preston, "California Gold Mill Practices," California State Mining Bureau *Bulletin* 6 (September 1895): 31.

37. John S. Hittell, *Mining in the Pacific States of North America* (San Francisco: H. H. Bancroft and Co., 1861), 37.

38. Newell, *Technology on the Frontier*, 142.

39. Raymond, "Metallurgical Processes," 727.

40. See, for example, May, *Origins of Hydraulic Mining in California*, 16–20; Young, *Western Mining*, 129.

41. For the conflicting claims of local origin, see Charles Waldeyer, "Treatment of Gold-bearing Ores in California," in *Statistics of Mines and Mining in the States and Territories West of the Rocky Mountains* (Washington, D.C.: Government Printing Office, 1873), 390n; Paul, *California Gold*, 152; May, *Origins of Hydraulic Mining in California*, 45–46.

42. Newell, *Technology on the Frontier*, 18.

43. Paul, *California Gold*, 147–50.

44. Ibid., 147–51.

45. May, *Origins of Hydraulic Mining in California*, 29–31.

46. Paul, *California Gold*, 153–54; May, *Origins of Hydraulic Mining in California*, 45. Matteson made another significant contribution to the mining industry in 1860 by devising a hydraulic derrick to lift heavy boulders (ibid., 50).

47. Randall Rohe, "Hydraulicking in the American West: The Development and Diffusion of a Mining Technique," *Montana* 35 (1985): 20–24; Paul, *California Gold*, 293–94.

48. Robert L. Kelley, *Gold vs. Grain: The Hydraulic Mining Controversy in California's Sacramento Valley* (Glendale, Calif.: A. H. Clark, 1959).

49. Donald Worster, "Hydraulic Society in California: An Ecological Interpretation," *Agricultural History* 56 (1982): 503–15.

50. Paul, *California Gold*, 130–32.

51. Thomas Allsop, *California and Its Gold Mines, Being a Series of Recent Communications from the Mining Districts, Upon the Present Condition and Future Prospects of Quartz Mining . . .* (London: Goombridge & Sons, 1853), 85.

52. Raymond, "Condition of the Mining Industry," 19.

53. Paul, *California Gold*, 132.

54. Ibid., 132–33.

55. Richard E. Lingenfelter, *The Hardrock Miners: A History of the Mining Labor Movement in the American West, 1863–1893* (Berkeley: University of California Press, 1974), 83–90; John Rowe, *The Hard-Rock Men: Cornish Immigrants and the North American Mining Frontier* (Liverpool: University of Liverpool Press, 1974), 120–24.

56. Larry D. Lankton, "The Machine under the Garden: Rock Drills Arrive at the Lake

Superior Copper Mines, 1868–1883," *Technology and Culture* 24 (January 1983): 13–34; Raymond, "Condition of the Mining Industry," 41–43; Blake, "Mechanical Appliances of Mining," 557–69; Young, *Western Mining*, 206–11.

57. Rowe, *The Hard-Rock Men*, 285–86.

58. Ibid., 118–20.

59. G. F. Deetken [Dutken], "Treatment of Gold-Bearing Ores in California," in *Statistics of Mines and Mining in the States and Territories West of the Rocky Mountains*, chap. 11 (Washington, D.C.: Government Printing Office, 1873), 323; J. G. Player-Frowd, *Six Months in California* (London: Longmans, Green, 1872), 104.

60. Newell, *Technology on the Frontier*, 45.

61. W. E. Gill, October 29, 1852, quoted in Rowe, *The Hard-Rock Men*, 109–10.

62. Excerpt from the *London Morning Journal*, November 1871, in printed letter from "Miner," Keweenaw County, Michigan, October 9, 1872, as quoted in Raymond, "The Burleigh Drill," in *Statistics of Mines and Mining in the States and Territories West of the Rocky Mountains* (Washington, D.C.: Government Printing Office, 1873), 488.

63. For problems with Spanish "rat-hole" mining, see Young, *Western Mining*, 79–83.

64. Ibid., 55.

65. Ibid., 71–72; Thomas Egleston, *The Metallurgy of Silver, Gold, and Mercury in the United States*, vol. 2 (New York: John Wiley & Sons, 1890), 458–59.

66. Browne, "Report," 8; Blake, "Mechanical Appliances of Mining," 683.

67. Agricola, *De re Metallica*, translator's note, p. 281.

68. Young, *Western Mining*, 71–72.

69. Edmund Newton, D. B. Gregg, and McHenry Mosier, "Operations at the Haile Gold Mine, Kershaw, S.C.," U.S. Bureau of Mines *Information Circular* 7111 (Washington, D.C.: Government Printing Office, May 1940), 2; Paul, *California Gold*, 132–33, 136–37.

70. Rowe, *The Hard-Rock Men*, 118–20. Dianne Newell, in her study of frontier Ontario, pointed out that Cornish stamps originated in Saxony and were introduced to Cornwall in the seventeenth century, long before coming to California. See Newell, *Technology on the Frontier*, 25.

71. Guido Kustel, *Nevada and California Processes of Silver and Gold Extraction for General Use and Especially for the Mining Public of California and Nevada* (London: Trubner & Co.; San Francisco: Frank D. Carlton, 1868), 66–71; Paul, *California Gold*, 136–37; Young, *Western Mining*, 195–98.

72. Blake, "Mechanical Appliances of Mining," 647; Young, *Western Mining*, 195; Newell, *Technology on the Frontier*, 26; Risdon Iron and Locomotive Works, *Gold Milling Machinery Catalog No. 12* (San Francisco: Risdon Iron Works, 1903).

73. Blake, "Mechanical Appliances of Mining," 657; Rossiter W. Raymond, "Mining Machinery," in *Statistics of Mines and Mining in the States and Territories West of the Rocky Mountains*, chap. 19 (Washington, D.C.: Government Printing Office, 1873), 475; Paul, *California Gold*, 136–37.

74. Egleston, *The Metallurgy of Silver, Gold, and Mercury*, vol. 2, 439.

75. Kustel, *Nevada and California Processes*, 85–86.

76. Lynn R. Bailey, *Supplying the Mining World: The Mining Equipment Manufacturers of San Francisco, 1850–1900* (Tucson: Westernlore Press, 1996), vii–viii, 20, 28–29.

77. Blake, "Mechanical Appliances of Mining," 472, 657; Ostrogorsky, "Influence of Technology," 80–82, 103.

78. Dana Harmon, "Stamp Milling of Free Gold Ores," reprinted from *Journal of the Association of Engineering Societies* 25 (December 1900): 9.

79. Clark C. Spence, *Mining Engineers & the American West: The Lace-boot Brigade, 1849–1933* (New Haven: Yale University Press, 1970), 25, 70–71.

80. Paul, *California Gold*, 302–3.

81. Ibid., 302–6.

82. Ibid., 306–7.

83. Hubert Howe Bancroft, *History of California*, vol. 7 (*The Works of Hubert Howe Bancroft*, vol. 24) (1888; reprint, Santa Barbara: Wallace Hebberd, 1970), 644.

84. U.S. Dept. of the Interior, "The United States Geological Survey: Its Origin, Development, Organization, and Operations," USGS *Bulletin 227* (Washington, D.C.: Government Printing Office, 1904), 10–11.

85. Bancroft, *History of California*, vol. 7, 643–44.

86. Ibid.; Paul, *California Gold*, 308–9.

87. Egleston, *The Metallurgy of Silver, Gold, and Mercury*, vol. 2, 544–47.

88. Paul, *California Gold*, 310.

89. Ibid., 195–96.

3

Capitalism Comes to the Diggings

From Gold-Rush Adventure to Corporate Enterprise

Maureen A. Jung

Mention the stock market, the rise of the modern economy, or the growth of corporations, and most people think of the New York Stock Exchange and railroads in the eastern states. When it comes to U.S. business history during the nineteenth century, relatively little attention has focused on California or the growth of mining corporations. Recent historians have rarely examined the role of corporations and the growth of stock exchanges in the mining West, apart from Marian V. Sears's rare volume, *Mining Stock Exchanges 1860–1930*, published in 1973.[1] California's unique contribution to the history of corporations has been neglected, in part, because of the long-standing interest in the more romantic, individualistic, and unorganized aspects of the Gold Rush. Thus, we still think of the Gold Rush as an adventure undertaken by individuals, although historians have recognized for more than a century that most emigrants traveled to California as members of companies.[2] Despite the importance of companies to the subsequent development of California's economy, we know relatively little about the pioneer firms that organized the Gold Rush. Similarly, we know little about the gold-field mining companies and corporations that superseded them. Few company records survive to tell the story. Apart from occasional mentions in diaries and letters, newspaper articles, government reports, and corporate filings, few reliable sources exist.[3] Still, if we examine such records from an organizational perspective, we can begin to construct a history of California's mining companies and their role in a larger transformation: the development of the modern corporate economy that emerged in California during the decades following the Gold Rush. This process was characterized by three developments: the rise of business corporations, the widespread ownership and trade in corporate securities, and the formation of stock exchanges to organize investment.[4]

While railroads drove economic expansion in the eastern United States, mining

A company of miners at Lincoln poses for the pioneer California daguerreotypist William Shew sometime in the early 1850s. Even before the emergence of the heavily capitalized corporations that came to dominate mining in the Golden State, fortune hunters formed associations to undertake large-scale operations, such as turning a river out of its bed to expose the rich sand and gravel below. *Courtesy Bancroft Library.*

was the first industry in the West to widely adopt the corporate form of organization. Despite a history of animosity toward business corporations in the early nineteenth-century United States, a speculative boom occurred in California mining between 1851 and 1853. Dozens of mining corporations were formed. They attracted investment capital from the East Coast and even from Europe. During the 1850s, California mining was quickly transformed from individual adventure to an industry organized by corporations and worked by wage laborers. Although the early mining corporations succeeded in attracting outside investment, few produced profits or paid dividends. Disappointed investors quickly abandoned the California mines, which for years would have trouble attracting outside capital.

In 1859, however, interest in mining corporations surged once again. Discovery of gold and silver on the Comstock Lode triggered a mining industry boom in which thousands of corporations were formed. This sudden growth fueled public interest and promoted widespread trade in mining securities, as California became the first site of broad public stock ownership and intense share trading. Such investments funded important advances in mining and initially revived California's stagnant economy. During the 1860s and 1870s, however, corporate insiders used the securities market as an organizational mechanism to wrest control over mining properties. Corporate power won out over individual rights, as insiders manipulated share prices, bilked investors, and drained companies. These activities diverted funds from more productive investments, injured workers' livelihoods, and damaged the economy as a whole. For all the imperfections of this system, however, these mining corporations played a central role in California's economic development and in the advance of the mining West.

BUSINESS ORGANIZATIONS PRIOR TO THE GOLD RUSH

Mining was a minor industry in the agriculture-dominated eighteenth century, though small-scale mines operated in several eastern and north-central states before the Revolutionary War. While a few corporations for mining and other purposes were established by 1800, most people in the United States viewed government-chartered business corporations with suspicion.[5] State laws made incorporation for private profit a difficult process, which initially required passage of a special legislative act; they also placed severe restrictions on corporate size and span of operations.[6]

Partnerships were the dominant form of commercial enterprise in this country for much of the nineteenth century, adequately serving business interests from "small country storekeepers to the great merchant bankers."[7] Larger business ventures often organized as joint-stock companies, a type of group partnership. Joint-stock companies offered two distinct advantages over traditional partnerships: ownership interest was divided into shares and the death or withdrawal of one partner did not end the partnership.

Unlike corporations, which were rooted in state authority, partnerships were based on individuals' freedom to associate, to pool their energies and capital for mutual advantage. This freedom was understood as a "right of business bodies, not . . . a privilege to be granted or withheld" by government rules.[8] Partners participated in company operations on an equal footing. They maintained direct control over their ownership interests and often voted on company decisions. By contrast, corporate shareholders possessed only indirect, limited control over their investments—the ability to sell their shares, should they find a willing buyer. Despite the advantage of greater control, however, partnerships had one great drawback: each partner was fully liable for debts incurred by the company, an onerous burden in large-scale ventures.

Large-scale businesses such as railroads, mines, banks, and insurance companies

pressed the state legislature for broader rights, including the ability to organize under general incorporation laws. Gradually legislatures relented, extending the term
of life allowed corporations and limiting shareholder liability.[9] Such changes gave
corporations several distinct advantages over partnerships, which also made corporate stock a more attractive investment. Nonetheless, early shareholders were vulnerable to assessment calls when company management decided additional investment was necessary. Shareholders who neglected to pay the levied assessment
forfeited their stock, and ownership reverted to the company.

As statutory limitations gradually loosened, growth in the number of corporations
aroused public concern and stimulated popular support for government regulation of
corporations and corporate securities.[10] For decades, people viewed corporations as
monopolies, as economic historian Clark Spence put it, "enemies of individual enterprise."[11] It is not surprising, then, that entrepreneurs formed relatively few corporations in the eastern states prior to the Civil War. Between 1800 and 1843, for example, total incorporations in six eastern states reached 3,249, only seventy-one of
them formed under general incorporation laws, the rest by special charter.[12] The
Panic of 1837 sharply curtailed incorporations, as thousands of banks and businesses
failed. The ensuing depression continued well into the 1840s.

ORGANIZING THE GOLD RUSH:
PIONEER MINING COMPANIES

Although rumors of the gold discovery in California reached the East Coast in
mid-1848, it was President James Polk's December message to Congress that riveted
public attention. He affirmed the rumors were true. There was gold in California, on
public land, and free for the taking. Many men resolved to hurry to the gold fields,
acquire a quick fortune ("strike it rich"), and return home to establish a respectable
business. Across the country, men organized partnerships and joint-stock companies
and made plans to seize their riches. Dozens of elaborately organized companies
were ready to sail before a month had passed. On January 24, 1849, the New York
Herald listed forty-seven companies, with a total of 2,499 members, ready to leave.[13]
A few days later, the *Herald* reported that while a few impetuous individuals had already left for the gold fields alone, most men planned to travel as members of companies. In what was surely an exaggeration, the newspaper stated that already 10,001
companies had "sprung up like mushrooms—all a lot alike," and listed thirty-two articles typically adopted by such companies.[14]

Like other partnerships, equality was the organizational principle upon which
these companies were founded. Members of the Perseverance Mining Company of
Philadelphia, for example, vowed to "pursue such business in California, or else
where, as shall be agreed upon by a majority of its members, and that the expenses

of the company shall be mutually borne and the profits equally divided. . . . We hereby pledge ourselves, to support and protect each other in case of emergency and sickness, and in all cases to stand by each other as a band of brothers."[15]

Members usually elected officers and voted to determine company actions. Members of larger companies also worked together under an agreed-upon division of labor. While not all companies published formal articles of agreement or printed membership shares, members shared a unity of purpose. They joined together to improve their chances of success as they journeyed to a distant and, to them, unknown land to engage in mining, an occupation about which almost all were entirely ignorant.

Company organizers were often community leaders, who solicited members by newspaper advertisement, handbill, or word of mouth.[16] Members, often from a single locale, commonly had to forswear alcohol, strong language, and gambling. Company size varied greatly, from as few as three to over one hundred members. Share prices in the companies also varied widely, from as little as $50 to more than $2,000. After formation, members met regularly to plan their California expedition. Money collected through the sale of company shares went to purchase and outfit a ship or buy wagons and mules or oxen for the journey. Companies traveling by sea frequently bought supplies intended for sale in California. Many took along elaborate mining contraptions they later found to be useless. Not surprisingly, companies from eastern seaboard states were more likely to sail to California around Cape Horn or via the Isthmus of Panama, while those from the western states (Wisconsin, Illinois, Arkansas, and Missouri) usually traveled overland by wagon train or pack mule.

Despite all their careful plans and businesslike approach, few gold-rush adventurers were prepared for the planning and provisioning necessary on a journey that could last six months or more. Few anticipated the adventure ahead, or the ordeals and downright tragedies so many of them would face. The story of the Gold Rush unfolds in the changing landscape of companies struggling against their environments and among themselves, whether they circled Cape Horn, crossed Panama, or traversed the continent. They faced inestimable odds, and few companies survived the journey intact. Of those that did, most voted to disband shortly after arrival in California. While some men set out alone for the diggings, many chose to travel with a partner or small band of companions as they began their search for fortune. Although most pioneer mining companies were short-lived, they served as important models for companies the adventurers established in the diggings.

REORGANIZING THE GOLD RUSH: MINING COMPANIES IN THE GOLD FIELDS

In the absence of established cities and towns, mining districts became the basic political unit in California's gold fields. Although they initially had no legal standing,

Handbill of the California Emigration Society, Boston, advertising passage
to California "in a first-rate Clipper Ship." Published in 1856, it promoted the
economic opportunities to be found in the new El Dorado. On the verso, notice
was made of mining companies offering wages of "$4.00 per day and board to
steady workmen," testifying to the transformation of gold mining from individual
adventure to corporate enterprise. *Courtesy Huntington Library, San Marino, Calif.*

codes were framed by the miners of each locale, which regulated both social behavior and mineral rights within the district. So fundamental did these miners' codes become to the regulation of mining that both state and federal governments refused to intervene for nearly two decades. While miners' codes varied across California's mining districts, two elements were central to nearly all of them: discovery and work. The man who "discovered" or "claimed" an area, then marked it and recorded the location, acquired its mineral rights. To retain these rights, the codes required miners to work their claims steadily, as many as twenty days per month in some districts. Most of the early codes limited claim size to what a single person could mine alone, initially 100 to 150 square feet. Size limits and work requirements effectively prevented absentee ownership and the monopoly of mining claims, both of which were strongly opposed by most miners.[17] It is no surprise, then, that in his study of western mining camps, historian Charles Shinn judged that buying, selling, and speculating in mining claims were activities that were probably foreign concepts to the early gold-rush miners.[18] Individual rights were paramount. As miner Samuel Upham observed, "no chartered institutions have monopolized the great avenues to wealth. . . . everyone has an equal chance to rise. . . . Neither business nor capital can oppress labor in California."[19] Equality of ownership was the principle underlying the mining codes.

Within this context, working miners, a majority of the early population in the mining districts, viewed one another in a particular light. "All men who had or expected to have any standing in the community were required to work with their hands, labor was dignified and honorable," wrote early California historian Theodore Hittell, "the man who did not live by actual physical toil was regarded as a sort of social excrescence or parasite."[20]

Yet things changed quickly in the gold fields. By April 1850, John Banks, a former member of the Buckeye Rovers, an Ohio company, described what typically happened in each new mining camp. Newcomers arrived steadily, forming "almost one continuous stream of men. Every place is snatched up in a moment. This canyon is claimed to its very head, nearly 20 miles, each man being allowed but 20 feet."[21] As the number of gold seekers outpaced the number of claims discovered, and as the technology and capital needed to work the diggings exceeded the resources of individual miners, they formed partnerships and joint-stock associations and worked together. California historian and philosopher Josiah Royce referred to this organizing tendency as a unique attribute of the American character, "a natural political instinct," yet it was based on practical experience.[22] As gold-rush traveler and miner J. D. Borthwick observed, despite the "spirit of individual independence" many Americans proclaimed, "they are certainly of all people in the world the most prompt to organize and combine to carry out a common object. They are trained to it from their youth in their innumerable, and to a foreigner, unintelligible caucus-meetings, committees, conventions, and so forth."[23] To men already accustomed to working together for mutual advantage, forming companies to pursue mining operations seemed an obvious alternative. Indeed, the miners had little choice, as earnings fell steadily through the early 1850s. Estimated at about $20 per day in 1848, miners' daily wages dropped from about $16 in 1849 to $10 in 1850 and to $8 or less in 1851, and down to about $3 a day between 1856 and 1860.[24] At the same time, another change took place. Between 1848 and about 1850, miners' "wages" referred to earnings from a day of mining, whether the individual worked on his own account or was employed by a company.[25] By 1851 fewer men mined "on their own hook," and the term took on its modern connotation: the earnings of wage laborers.

Mining underwent a transformation. From individual adventure and competition, mining operations began to resemble factories in the eastern states and Europe, with distinct divisions of labor and differential pay scales. While competition over claims increased and miners' wages fell, easily acquired gold was fast depleted. On July 15, 1851, San Francisco's leading newspaper, the *Alta California*, appeared pessimistic about prospects for the industry: "Now we hear of the complete exhaustion and abandonment of many of the diggings." Miner John Banks felt the stress acutely: "We have left our claim like hundreds of others. . . . Misery loves company; we have plenty. . . . Men are frightened, some starving, confused, not knowing what to do, where to go. . . . Prospecting is a necessity and a dangerous business."[26]

Technological advances, such as the rocker, the sluice box, and the long tom, permitted miners to work more efficiently. By instituting a division of labor, miners were able to exploit their claims more systematically than was possible working alone. While the work was rigorous, costs were relatively low given the labor-intensive methods of placer mining. Gold-field mining companies, mostly partnerships and joint-stock companies, shared many similarities to the pioneer mining companies in which so many had emigrated. Both were voluntary associations in which members participated equally or proportionally in the labor, costs, and profits, if any. Members exercised voting rights on company decisions, worked under an elected foreman, and operated on the principle of joint shares.[27] Claims turned over quickly, as miners made a discovery, swarmed in to exploit it, and moved on. Mining partnerships and companies formed quickly and could be dissolved just as quickly when things went wrong, as they often did. Rampant rumors sent miners scrambling from one reputed bonanza to the next. A few lucky souls struck pay dirt, but most struggled, subsisting on whatever came to hand.

Though many gold-rush adventurers returned home with empty pockets, others applied themselves to solving the technical and organizational problems of mining for gold. To solve the major obstacles to finding, extracting, and processing gold, miners developed three new large-scale approaches to mining during the early 1850s: river, quartz, and hydraulic mining. Each approach had its own particular set of costs. In river mining operations, supplies and building materials for flumes, dams, and ditches

Miner Prospecting, a hand-colored lithograph designed and drawn by Charles Nahl and August Wenderoth, illustrates the archetypal California gold seeker of romance and legend. The two artists, who spent the summer of 1851 mining at Rough and Ready in Nevada County, portrayed the heavily armed and well-outfitted Argonaut as solitary, self-reliant, and resourceful. Published in San Francisco in 1852, the print contributed to the popular image of the gold hunter that has endured for a century and a half. *Courtesy Bancroft Library.*

River mining, about 1852. A dam has been constructed upstream, diverting the watercourse into a flume, visible on a diagonal cutting across the daguerreotype image. The large water wheels powered by the flume turn huge driveshafts, connected by leather belts to pumps, which keep the exposed riverbed dry. Though highly speculative, river mining was widely practiced, the first of the large-scale entrepreneurial enterprises pursued in the diggings. In 1853 several companies working independently spent three million dollars turning twenty-five miles of the Yuba out of its bed. *Courtesy Bancroft Library.*

consumed money. Similarly, hydraulic operations required huge quantities of water delivered to the mine site, while quartz mining involved extracting gold through deep shafts, then crushing and processing the ore, all expensive undertakings, particularly when the technology available then allowed for the recovery of so small a percentage of the gold. While technology presented formidable challenges to the miners, lawsuits over disputed claims and water rights became increasingly common. For years to come, law and water developed as subsidiary industries to mining.

Fighting lawsuits, building flumes and ditches, and developing large-scale quartz mining operations all required capital. Despite rising gold production during 1850 and 1851, the large number of men and the growing difficulty of extracting the gold led to changes in social relations in the gold fields and transformed the organization of mining operations. Until 1851, most money invested in California mines was produced by the miners themselves. With the changes and experiments with new technology and high interest rates on borrowing, the need for outside investment was apparent if the industry was to grow. At the same time, some observers viewed the organization of joint-stock companies and corporations as a positive sign that more stable industrial organization was emerging to displace the turbulent era of gold-rush adventurers. Felix P. Wierzbicki, who described his tour of the gold fields in a widely quoted pamphlet, *California as It Is & as It May Be, Or a Guide to the Gold Region*, predicted that "When this gold mania ceases to rage, individuals will abandon the mines; and then there will be a good opportunity for companies with heavy capital to step in; there will be enough profitable work for them; and it is then that the country will enter on a career of real progress, and not until then."[28]

LAUNCHING A MARKET FOR CORPORATE SECURITIES

As some miners struggled to advance industrial mining and establish a scientific approach to mine operations, others turned their attention to the financial side of corporate organization. The most immediate, and notorious, manifestation was a speculative boom in quartz mining that rocked the state's economy between 1851 and 1853. California miners formed corporations, hoping to raise funds by selling corporate stock. To be successful, however, they had to overcome the legacy of suspicion attached to corporations and corporate securities.

California's state constitution followed the lead of several other states with regard to corporations. Chapter 128 of the state's legal codes, "An Act Concerning Corporations," was a general corporation law passed by the state legislature in April 1850. It permitted companies to incorporate without seeking approval of a special act of the legislature, although it prohibited bank corporations altogether. The law held shareholders "individually and personally liable" for a proportional share of corporate debts. In other words, those who invested in corporations were required to pay assessments levied by corporate management when additional funds were needed to keep the company afloat. These were not ideal conditions under which to attract investors, yet the need for outside investment was clear, if the mining industry was to revive and expand.

Until the rise of quartz mining, outside investors showed scant interest in California mining companies. River mining companies grew primarily through investments from and efforts by company members. Additional labor by the partners often compensated for a company's lack of ready cash. Quartz mining, the high technology of its day, was altogether different. Outsiders recognized quartz mining as a complex, capital-intensive activity that required sophisticated machinery and the application of scientific processes to free gold from the quartz. Quartz mining captured the imaginations of miners and outside investors alike, and heightened interest in the trail of gold. The discovery of what appeared to be rich quartz deposits in Nevada County stimulated a rush to locate quartz claims in 1851. In the picturesque language of Edwin F. Bean, who compiled the 1867 Nevada County history and directory, "prospectors were running over the hills in every direction" in search of likely spots to stake claims.[29]

Though few miners knew anything about quartz mining or processing, this lack of knowledge failed to inhibit their enthusiasm for organizing new ventures. As some miners transformed their companies into corporations and began to market shares to the public, many others sold or abandoned their claims, recognizing not only the technical problems, but also the difficulty of raising the money necessary to develop a quartz mine.

Just as newspapers sold the Gold Rush to adventurers in 1849, corporate promoters used the press to attract investors. They had to convince the public that mining was no longer a reckless adventure but instead was an industry conducted by sober businessmen with practical experience. Promoters contributed newspaper articles, wrote letters to editors, and served as sources for the press, and the papers responded with optimism. As the San Francisco *Morning Post* reported on October 13, 1851, "quartz mining in this country is no longer an experiment." In addition to marketing through newspaper advertisements, some promoters produced elaborate stock prospectuses for potential investors to examine.

Such promotional efforts paid off, if only temporarily. While no one knows with certainty the number of mining companies formed during the 1850s, the number of mining corporations can be estimated with some accuracy from copies of articles of incorporation filed with the California secretary of state.[30] Table 3.1 shows the number of corporations formed each year in California during the 1850s. Predictably, in a decade during which mining companies accounted for 75 percent of incorporations, the very first corporation was a mine: the California State Mining & Smelting Company. Organized and operated in Santa Clara County, this company incorporated with $100,000 in capital stock.[31] California's second corporation, the Mariposa Mining Company, was quite different. With $1 million in capital stock, the sheer size of the company must have been mind-boggling to many early investors. Incorporated by seven San Francisco residents, who conducted company business from the city, mining operations took place in Mariposa County, on land leased from John C. Frémont.[32] Company prospects seemed bright, and in 1851 Mariposa Mining Company securities were traded on both the London and Paris stock exchanges.[33] In a departure from earlier practices, its company organizers were not working miners. They held interests in other mining corporations; at least two acted as attorneys; and the company was closely linked with a leading San Francisco bank association, Palmer, Cook & Company. Despite such connections, the Mariposa Mining Company was unable to solve the technical problems related to quartz processing. Like

TABLE 3.1

Corporations Formed in California, 1850–1859, by County and Type

County[a]	1850	1851	1852	1853	1854	1855	1856	1857	1858	1859	Total
Amador					2	6	4	3	3		18
Butte		1	9	1	5	18	18	18	12	5	87
Calaveras			3		8	2	4	5	6	4	32
El Dorado		1	5	4	6	1	1	5	1	1	25
Mariposa	1	2			2	1	1	2	2		11
Nevada		17	16	1	1	2	2	5	2	4	50
Placer			1	2	1	1	2	3	2	4	16
Sacramento		1	4	5	2	2	3		1		18
San Francisco		2			2	6	2	1	4	1	18
San Joaquin						1	3	3			7
Shasta			2	2	2						6
Sierra			1	3	3	2	1	2	2	3	17
Tuolumne			6	2	3	7	20	25	11	5	79
Yuba		2	2		3	3	1	5	1	1	18
Other[b]	1		4	4	4	4	7	2	3	1	30

Type

	1850	1851	1852	1853	1854	1855	1856	1857	1858	1859	Total
Total mining & water corps.[c]	2	26	53	24	44	56	69	79	50	29	432
Total nonmining corps.[d]	1	1	11	17	26	24	12	18	14	20	144
Total corporations formed	3	27	64	41	70	80	81	97	64	49	576

SOURCE: Records of Incorporation and Articles of Incorporation, 1850–1859, California State Archives, Sacramento. Empty cells indicate no known corporations formed. Only "for profit" corporations are included in this tabulation.

a. Refers to the county in which the company was incorporated, as specified in the articles of incorporation.

b. Includes ten counties in which fewer than six corporations were formed and nine incorporations with no county specified.

c. Includes all companies with mining or water operations specified in the articles of incorporation.

d. Includes all companies not formed for mining or water operations. Major groups include 30 road or bridge companies, 28 wharf and shipping companies, 21 railroads, 13 gas companies, and 11 manufacturers.

The Mount Ophir Mill, located at the town of the same name, a half-dozen miles west of the county seat of Mariposa, within the boundaries of the extensive land grant acquired by John C. Frémont. In 1858, the year before Carleton E. Watkins took this photograph, there were twenty-four steam-driven stamps in operation at Mount Ophir. All that remains today of this once-vital mining center are a few crumbling ruins and colorful memories of days of gold. *California Historical Society, FN-24671.*

so many early mining companies, it was also plagued by lawsuits. Mariposa's legal disputes over mineral and water rights spanned a number of years and a variety of succeeding companies.

Just as California's legal profession developed in tandem with mining, banking also evolved as a subsidiary industry. Members of the leading bank associations were frequently aligned with the leading mining corporations. The linkage was natural. The banks handled both transportation and deposit of the gold produced in the mines. They frequently provided short-term loans for mining companies and often served as trustees on corporate boards.[34]

Table 3.1 shows that promoters formed twenty-six mining corporations in California during 1851, the first year of the quartz boom. Capital stock in these companies ranged from $100,000 to $1 million. While there is no way of knowing how much money was actually paid in to these corporations, it is clear that investors overall poured millions into mining corporations. Nevada County was the center for quartz mining during these early years. Thirty-three mining corporations, 42 percent of the total organized during the boom years of 1851 and 1852, were located in Nevada County. Along with the corporations, stamp mills to crush the quartz were also built, and, by November 1851, eight mills operated around the clock in Nevada County, and seven more were under construction.[35]

Though Nevada County miners worked hard to develop quartz mines and mills, most of the early attempts were failures. The first mill builders found to their dismay that their ore-crushing stamps wore out after just a few months. Others had trouble importing machinery, and much of the machinery that arrived at the mines was worthless in actual operation. Once again, many sold out or abandoned their mining claims after exhausting both money and hope. In the fall of 1851, for example, John A. Collins & Company completed a ten-stamp mill that operated around the clock. Capable of crushing 100 tons of ore per day, this mill was considered one of the finest built to that date. Before the year was out, however, Collins & Company sold out to the Grass Valley Gold Mining Company, a corporation formed on July 25, 1851, with $100,000 in capital stock and the option of increasing to $250,000, should additional capital be needed. All five founders of the corporation listed San Francisco as their residence.[36]

Relying on advantageous relationships with the press, letters and stories about the company appeared not just locally, but also in New York City. Company president Jonas Winchester was a former business associate of Horace Greeley, publisher of the New York *Tribune*. For a time in 1850 and in 1851, Winchester lived in New York City to promote interest in quartz mining and to advance the sale of his company's stock. During this time, he also assisted James Delavan, secretary of the Rocky-Bar Mining Company, who also journeyed to New York to promote his company. Both men wrote often and authoritatively on the subject of California mining, usually neglecting to reveal their financial interests and occasionally omitting to mention their names. On March 9, 1850, for example, a letter published in the *Tribune* and signed "J.W." reviewed the prospects for quartz mining in California. "With capital, machinery, and a proper scientific knowledge of mining, which must be rapidly introduced," the author wrote confidently, "you need not fear the supply of gold being less than thirty to fifty millions a year in this generation."[37] That same year Delavan anonymously published *Notes on California and the Placers: How to Get There and What to Do Afterwards*, an entertaining description of a trip to the gold fields and travel in the mines, which included an admiring account of the Rocky-Bar Mining Company and its rich prospects, without mentioning the author's affiliation with the company.[38] Such publicity efforts attracted public attention as well as investors, as more California mining companies chose incorporation to raise capital and increase the scope of their operations.

In 1852, the number of mining corporations formed in California nearly doubled, to a total of fifty-three. On January 1, 1852, trustees of the Grass Valley Mining Company voted to increase the company's capital stock to $250,000. The same day, four of these trustees joined John Collins and formed another corporation, the Manhattan Quartz Mining Company. Horace Greeley himself was listed as secretary and treasurer of the company, while Collins served as president. To attract investors, each company issued an elaborate stock prospectus. By that time, the Grass Valley Mining Company held more than four hundred mining claims, while the Manhattan held sixty-four, a significant departure from the earlier principle of one claim per miner. Each prospectus quoted from the law, from published articles, letters, and reports, and cited production figures as evidence of the soundness of their undertaking and the lucrative dividends investors could anticipate. According to the Manhattan Company prospectus, "shareholders [will] reap a golden harvest."[39]

Investors contributed millions to California mining operations between 1850 and 1853. Increasingly, investors from afar—Sacramento, San Francisco, New York City, Boston, and abroad—purchased stock in California's mines. Foreign corporations were also formed to undertake mining operations in California. British investors, for example, sank nearly $10 million into shares of California mining corporations, and, by 1853, British promoters organized thirty-two corporations in London to mine for gold in California.[40]

Though dozens of California and foreign corporations successfully attracted investment capital, developing efficient ore-processing methods and machinery proved to be a more intractable problem. At the same time, lawsuits also consumed a significant proportion of the gold produced. Few of these early corporations paid out even a single dollar in dividends, provoking widespread disillusionment and an almost immediate reaction: the collapse of outside investment in California mining in 1853. Thereafter, through the end of the decade, California mining corporations had trouble raising investment capital.

Nonetheless, California miners continued to form corporations and to invest their own capital in mining operations, frequently buying out earlier works and attempting to run them more efficiently. The end of California's first wave of corporate mining speculation was not the end of mining corporations, by any means. As Table 3.1 shows clearly, the number of mining corporations grew throughout the 1850s, accounting for fully three-quarters of California's corporations formed during the decade. The growth of corporate mining meant fundamental changes in the gold fields that did not escape notice of the press. On June 11, 1858, Sacramento's *Daily Union* described this transformation as a "complete revolution" in "the methods and means applied to mining," leading to the concentration of mine ownership among "men of means who have employed others to mine for them."

Despite widespread company failures and continued uncertainty about the industry, the boom of 1851 through 1853 illustrated an important business principle: incorporation was a means for channeling investment dollars into mining company operations. In that sense, these corporations served as a force for stability and a catalyst for growth for mining and its subsidiary industries, particularly in the long run. In the short run, however, they proved destabilizing, funneling money into ill-conceived ventures and diverting funds from more productive uses.

For the remainder of the decade, outside investors shunned California mining corporations. Meanwhile, gold production fell steadily from its peak in 1852 at $81 million to $46.8 million in 1859. The California economy languished at the end of the decade, seemingly awaiting the next big strike that would stimulate manufacturing and boost commerce. Suddenly it happened: in 1860, a wave of new mine incorporations propelled rapid expansion of the California economy.

ORGANIZING A CORPORATE ECONOMY

The restructuring of mining that began during the early 1850s was completed with the rise of corporate mining on what came to be known as the Comstock Lode in Nevada (then part of Utah Territory) during the 1860s. Miners who crossed the Sierra from California had prospected the area for nearly a decade, barely eking out a living. Then, in June 1859, a party of prospectors discovered a rich ore deposit containing gold and silver.[41] Quickly forming a company, the partners worked their claim. News spread fast, and miners from throughout the West, especially Californians, swarmed to the Comstock. Problems emerged quickly. The mining codes adopted on the Comstock, modeled after California's, ensured that conflicts would develop over claim boundaries and guaranteed that lawsuits would follow. This was hardly surprising in an area that stretched less than three miles, where nearly seventeen thousand claims were quickly recorded.[42] A lively trade in mining claims developed immediately. In his detailed study of the Comstock Lode for the U.S. Geological Survey, Eliot Lord noted that "without and within doors a fever of speculations raged without check. Sales of claims for money were comparatively rare, but barters were incessant. . . . Paper fortunes were made in days."[43]

The original claimholders, lacking both the knowledge and the capital to develop large-scale quartz mining operations, sold out. The buyers included some familiar names: Judge James Walsh, Joseph Woodworth, and George Hearst, all from Nevada County, California.[44] After forming a partnership, the Ophir Mining Company, they undertook the first systematic mining operations on the lode. Before long, they sent a shipment of ore to San Francisco for assay. On November 16, 1859, the San Francisco *Alta California* reported that the ore revealed an estimated $1,595 in gold and $4,791 in silver per ton, fabulously valuable by California standards. And California standards prevailed on the Comstock. Initial ore assays helped create the impression that the Comstock mines would prove rich beyond belief and produce for centuries, similar to the fabled mines of Mexico, Bolivia, and Peru.

As California miners and financiers bought up Comstock properties and established corporations, speculation in mining claims quickly gave way to speculation in mining stock. On April 28, 1860, Hearst and his partners incorporated their mine in California to create the Ophir Silver Mining Company. With $5.04 million in capital stock, the Ophir was the largest corporation in the West. Others quickly followed suit. By the end of 1860, thirty-seven additional Comstock mines were incorporated in California, which triggered a wave of incorporations never before seen in this country. More than one thousand mining companies were incorporated in California that year.[45]

All this activity attracted intense interest, as more and more people hoped to make money in mining stock. While some hoped for more reliable financial reporting, most appeared more interested in the speculative prospects of mining securities.[46] The increase in transactions and opportunities for the collection of brokerage commissions led to the formation of the San Francisco Mining Stock and Exchange Board on September 1, 1862. Although founders of this exchange were branded in the press as the "Forty Thieves," the organization prospered. By 1864, six new mining stock exchanges were formed in San Francisco, and nine in the vicinity of the Comstock Lode, along with exchanges in Sacramento, Stockton, and Marysville.[47] Meanwhile, the number of mining corporations skyrocketed; 2,933 were formed in 1863 alone, 84 percent of them gold and silver mines.[48] California banking historian Ira Cross concluded that "especially during 1863 did it become the normal, expected thing for any party possessing a small mining claim to organize a corporation of large proportions and to sell the stock at astounding prices to a gullible and speculative public."[49] Securities of the Comstock corporations dominated the market. Strangely enough, stock speculation increased, due largely to the production of a single mine, the Gould & Curry.[50] Few of the other mines produced profits or paid dividends. Yet, as miners on the Comstock Lode wrestled with technical problems of extracting and processing the complex amalgam of gold and silver found there, financiers and promoters developed sophisticated new methods of organizing companies and manipulating stock transactions. By comparison, California mines continued to have difficulty attracting investments.[51] California's gold mines were much smaller operations. They required far less operating capital than the gold and silver mines on the Comstock Lode and offered fewer opportunities for speculation on the stock market. As Table 3.2 shows, California gold production continued to decline into the 1860s, after which it remained relatively steady, between $15 and $24 million through 1878. While gold and silver on the Comstock Lode did not exceed California's gold output until 1873, the annual transactions on the San Francisco Mining Stock and Exchange Board alone exceeded $100 million a year between 1871 and 1877.

TABLE 3.2

Annual Mining Production in California and Nevada, along with Total Sales of Securities at the San Francisco Mining Stock and Exchange Board, 1863–1877 (in millions of dollars)

Year	California Gold[a]	Comstock Gold & Silver[b]	SFMSEB Mining Stock Transactions[c]
1863	23.5	12.4	15.5
1864	24.1	16.0	25.8
1865	17.9	16.0	49.2
1866	17.1	12.0	32.8
1867	18.3	13.7	66.3
1868	17.6	12.4	115.9
1869	18.2	7.5	69.1
1870	17.5	8.0	51.2
1871	17.5	10.2	127.9
1872	15.5	12.2	189.2
1873	15.0	21.7	146.4
1874	17.3	22.5	260.5
1875	16.9	25.8	220.2
1876	15.6	31.6	225.8
1877	16.5	36.3	119.7
1878	18.8	19.6	n.a.

a. SOURCE: William B. Clark, *Gold Districts of California* (Sacramento: California Division of Mines and Geology, 1963), 4. Numbers are rounded to the nearest hundred-thousand.

b. SOURCES: Eliot Lord, *Comstock Mines and Miners* (Washington, D.C.: U.S. Geological Survey, 1883), and Grant H. Smith, "The History of the Comstock Lode, 1850–1920," *University of Nevada Bulletin* 37 (July 1943).

c. SFMSEB refers to the San Francisco Mining Stock and Exchange Board. SOURCE: Assembly Committee on Corporations, "Majority Report," in California Legislature, *Appendix to the Journals of the Senate and Assembly*, vol. 4 (Sacramento: State Printing Office, 1878), 3–11. These numbers reflect sales only at the SFMSEB and so understate the total amount of mining stock transactions by an estimated 40 percent, according to the committee's report, which ended with the 1877 figures.

Following the practices adopted a decade earlier, corporate promoters on the Comstock Lode issued elaborate prospectuses that they distributed far and wide. They also enlisted the press in campaigns to sell stock to the public, and with huge success. For the first time in the history of the United States, stock market participants represented a broad cross-section of social classes.[52] San Francisco's *Mining and Scientific Press* observed that it was the rare person who did not own at least a share or two of mining stock.[53] According to the publication, "the market extends everywhere; the buyers and sellers of stock include the millionaire and the mendicant, the modest matron and the brazen courtesan, the prudent man of business and the gambler, the maidservant and her mistress, the banker and his customer."[54]

As had been the case a decade earlier, close ties developed between banks and mining corporations. Banks managed mining corporation accounts, arranged payrolls, made short-term loans, lent money for the purchase of mining stock, and accepted mining stock as collateral on loans.[55] When production dropped at the Comstock mines, San Francisco banker William C. Ralston and his agent, William Sharon, stepped in to take control. Indeed, close relations between the leading bank on the West Coast, San Francisco's Bank of California, and the Comstock mining corporations lent an air of respectability to mining stock transactions. At the same time, it gave Sharon and Ralston direct access to financial information on local businesses, which they used to advance their own interests.

Enacting a liberal lending policy, Ralston and Sharon lent money to independent mills, but then starved them of ore to process. Without income from ore processing, mills were unable to repay their loans, and Ralston and Sharon gained control over most mills in the area, which they then consolidated as a single corporation, the Union Mill and Mining Company. They held onto these shares, rather than distributing them through the stock market.[56] At the same time, they extended their control over both mines and mine suppliers, which continued to operate as formally distinct corporations.[57] Relying on advance knowledge about progress in the mines, Ralston, Sharon, and their allies, known as the "Bank Crowd," fed rumors to the press and timed assessment calls and stock sales to drive prices up or down according to their plans. According to early historian John S. Hittell, "every trick that cunning could devise to make the many pay the expenses, securing to the few the bulk of the profit, was practiced on an extensive scale."[58]

This broad control, even backed by the financial power of the Bank of California, could not guarantee perpetually growing production at the Comstock mines, however. Nor did it prevent the rise of rival groups to challenge the control wielded by Ralston and his allies. Twice during the 1870s, successful campaigns were waged through the stock market to wrest control of particular mines.[59] Alvinza Hayward and John P. Jones broke away from the Bank Crowd and gained control of the Crown Point and Savage mines. At about the same time, four Irish immigrants soon known

Mount Davidson, on the far western reaches of Nevada, looms above a
miner at the lower dump of the Gould & Curry Mine in 1865. Although
the Comstock Lode entered into decline that year, its fortunes would revive
in the early 1870s, when the Silver Kings struck the "Big Bonanza," the
massive veins of silver and gold buried deep beneath the windswept heights
of Mount Davidson. Financed in large by California capital, the mines not
only produced enormous quantities of high-grade ore but sparked volatile
trading in silver stocks on the San Francisco exchanges. *Courtesy Huntington
Library, San Marino, Calif.*

as the "Bonanza Firm"— John W. Mackay, James G. Fair, James C. Flood, and
William S. O'Brien—formed a formal partnership and pooled their money for stock
operations. The resulting growth in stock transactions fueled the formation of a
new wave of mining corporations.[60] By 1873, they controlled five mining companies:
Hale & Norcross, Gould & Curry, Consolidated Virginia, California, and Kentuck.[61] The rival campaigns waged through the stock market produced a staggering
volume of transactions, peaking in 1874 at more than $260 million, more than ten
times the total production of gold and silver from the Comstock that year. Before the

fight to control the Comstock was over, Ralston was ruined. Though Sharon and the Bank of California survived, the activities of the Bonanza Firm exacted a heavy toll on the broader economy.

Following the pattern adopted by the Bank Crowd, the Bonanza Firm not only purchased all major suppliers to their mines, they also established an "independent" mill, the Pacific Mill and Mining Company, a corporation that they wholly owned. Such arrangements were so common that, in a trial closely watched throughout the mining West, the Bonanza Firm successfully countered shareholders' complaints of fraud by pleading that the practice represented industry custom.[62]

By the end of the 1870s, the era of the fabulous Comstock was nearly at its end. The mines had been gutted. In 1877, even as the Bonanza Firm's mines produced millions in gold and silver, the mining stock market collapsed, and California's economy sank into depression. The California Assembly Committee on Corporations concluded:

> Where there should be universal prosperity and happiness, there is widespread poverty and suffering. Thousands of comfortable homes and many millions of dollars earned by the patient toil of the industrious masses, have been swept away by disastrous investments in mining shares. Undoubtedly the stock market has been a chief factor in producing the present destitution of the people. Its baneful effects have been felt in every neighborhood and almost every family in the State.[63]

CONCLUSION

Much of the scholarship on the rise of corporations during the nineteenth century has focused on elements of internal organization and competition within free and unregulated market arenas. Organizations are treated as distinct entities, independent from one another and dependent for survival on the efficient use of market resources.[64] My research into the rise of mining corporations and their interrelations across markets presents a very different view.

As mining corporations proliferated in California during the early 1850s, a new pattern of economic power emerged. Direct individual control over investment capital was displaced by indirect control and the loss of decision-making power, as the power of corporate insiders expanded. During the 1860s, the sudden wave of mining incorporations stimulated by the development of the Comstock Lode created the opportunity for insiders to manipulate information, along with legal and financial resources. In effect, these powerful actors used mining corporations as tools to advance their own plans and fortunes to the detriment of the underlying economy.

As mining advanced east and north from California, miners carried with them the techniques, practices, ideas, and organizing strategies—as well as the problems—

that emerged during the Gold Rush and were institutionalized during the era of the Comstock Lode in the 1860s and 1870s. Mining, which continues to be a risky undertaking, still carries the burden of its speculative past.

NOTES

1. Marian V. Sears, *Mining Stock Exchanges, 1860–1930* (Missoula: University of Montana Press, 1973).

2. See for example, Hubert Howe Bancroft, *History of California,* vol. 6 (San Francisco: The History Company, 1888), 120; see also 120–21, n. 16, and 144, n. 1.

3. Such sources are discussed in Maureen A. Jung, "Documenting Nineteenth-Century Quartz Mining in Northern California," *American Archivist* 53 (Summer 1990): 406–18.

4. Maureen A. Jung, "The Comstocks and the California Mining Economy, 1848–1900" (Ph.D. diss., Department of Sociology, University of California, Santa Barbara, 1988).

5. See for example, Joseph S. Davis, *Essays in the Earlier History of American Corporations* (Cambridge: Harvard University Press, 1917), and Oscar Handlin and Mary Handlin, "Origins of the American Business Corporation," *Journal of Economic History* 5 (May 1945): 1–23.

6. Clark C. Spence, *The Sinews of American Capitalism: An Economic History* (New York: Hill and Wang, 1964), 134. See also Lawrence M. Friedman, *A History of American Law* (New York: Simon & Schuster, 1985), 177–201, 511–31.

7. Alfred D. Chandler, *The Visible Hand: The Managerial Revolution in American Business* (Cambridge: Harvard University Press, 1977), 36.

8. Shaw Livermore, *Early American Land Companies: Their Influence on Corporate Development* (New York: Octagon Books, 1966), 296.

9. Friedman, *A History of American Law,* 190–91.

10. Gerald D. Nash, "Government and Business Relations: A Case Study in State Regulation of Corporate Securities," *Business History Review* 38 (Summer 1964): 141–62.

11. Spence, *Sinews of American Capitalism,* 134.

12. William C. Kessler, "Incorporation in New England: A Statistical Study, 1800–1875," *Journal of Economic History* 8 (May 1948): 47. The six states include Massachusetts, Connecticut, Rhode Island, New Hampshire, Maine, and Vermont.

13. New York *Herald,* January 24, 1849.

14. Ibid., January 29, 1849.

15. Recorded by Perseverance Mining Company member Samuel Upham in his *Notes on a Voyage to California Via Cape Horn, Together with Scenes in El Dorado in the Years 1849–50* (Philadelphia: Samuel Upham, 1878), 105.

16. On the joint-stock companies, see Octavius T. Howe, *The Argonauts of '49* (Cambridge: Harvard University Press, 1923); R. W. G. Vail, *Bibliographical Notes on Certain Eastern Mining Companies of the California Gold Rush, 1849–1850* (Princeton: Bibliographical Society of America, 1949).

17. Joseph W. Ellison, "The Mineral Land Question in California, 1848–1866," *Southwestern Historical Quarterly* 30 (July 1926): 9–15. See also John Walton Caughey, *The California Gold Rush* (Berkeley: University of California Press, 1975), 229–31.

18. Charles H. Shinn, *Mining Camps: A Study in American Frontier Government* (1884; New York: Knopf, 1948), 224.

19. Upham, *Notes on a Voyage,* 307.

20. Theodore H. Hittell, *History of California,* vol. 3 (San Francisco: Stone and Company, 1879), 174.

21. Howard L. Scamehorn, ed., *The Buckeye Rovers in the Gold Rush* (Athens: Ohio University Press, 1965), 116.

22. Josiah Royce, *California, from the Conquest in 1846 to the Second Vigilance Committee in San Francisco: A Study of American Character* (1886; New York: Knopf, 1948), 217.

23. J. D. Borthwick, *Three Years in California* (New York: The Book League of America, 1929), 347.

24. These estimates of miners' wages are developed in Rodman W. Paul, *California Gold: The Beginning of Mining in the Far West* (Cambridge: Harvard University Press, 1947), 120. Bancroft's estimates are quite similar, though slightly lower for 1852; *History of California,* vol. 6, n. 5, p. 639.

25. Paul, *California Gold,* 121.

26. Scamehorn, *Buckeye Rovers,* 133–34.

27. For detailed description from a careful observer and mining company president, see Daniel B. Woods, *Sixteen Months at the Gold Diggings* (New York: Arno Press, 1973). On pp. 144–48, he presents articles of agreement for the Hart's Bar Draining and Mining Company, organized in May 1851 as a joint-stock company, and notes that such "mining associations enjoy all the privileges and immunities of corporate bodies."

28. Felix P. Wierzbicki, *California as It Is & as It May Be, Or a Guide to the Gold Region,* ed. George D. Lyman (1849; reprint, San Francisco: Rare Americana Series, 1933), 34. This was the first book written in English published in California.

29. Edwin F. Bean, comp., *History and Directory of Nevada County* (Nevada City: Daily Gazetteer Book and Job Office, 1867), 149.

30. Records of Incorporation, vols. A and B, 1850–1859, California State Archives, Sacramento.

31. Ibid., vol. A, 1.

32. Ibid., vol. A, 2.

33. Bancroft, *History of California,* 666.

34. It was common practice for a banker to serve as a mining corporation's treasurer.

35. *California Express,* November 12, 1851.

36. Grass Valley Gold Mining Company, *Charter* (New York: Printing Office, 1852).

37. John Cumming, ed., *The Gold Rush Letters of Dr. James Delavan from California to the Adrian, Michigan, Expositor, 1850–1856* (Mount Pleasant, Mich.: Cumming Press, 1976), viii.

38. Delavan's book, published by H. Long and Brother, was advertised in the New York *Tribune* on March 1, 1850, its author identified only as "One Who Knows." See also Carl I. Wheat, "The Rocky-Bar Mining Company: An Episode in Early Western Promotion and Finance," *California Historical Society Quarterly* 12 (March 1933): 65–77. Appended to this article is a complete copy of the 1850 stock "Circular" Delavan wrote to promote the Rocky-Bar Mining Company.

39. Manhattan Quartz Mining Company, *Facts Concerning Quartz and Quartz Mining: Together with the Charter* (New York: W. L. Burroughs, 1852), 24.

40. Leland Hamilton Jenks, *The Migration of British Capital to 1875* (New York: Knopf, 1927), 46.

41. The story of the Comstock Lode is told by many. See, for example, Eliot Lord, *Comstock Mines and Miners* (Washington, D.C.: U.S. Geological Survey, 1883); Grant H. Smith, "History of the Comstock Lode, 1850–1920," *University of Nevada Bulletin* 37 (July 1943); Charles Howard Shinn, *The Story of the Mine as Illustrated by the Great Comstock Lode of Nevada* (Reno: University of Nevada Press, 1980); and George D. Lyman, *Ralston's Ring* (New York: Charles Scribner's Sons, 1937) and also his *The Saga of the Comstock Lode: Boom Days in Virginia City* (New York: Charles Scribner's Sons, 1934).

42. Smith points out that 20 percent of the production on the Comstock Lode through 1866 was spent in litigation; "History of the Comstock Lode," 61.

43. Lord, *Comstock Mines,* 73.

44. Smith, "History of the Comstock Lode," 16.

45. Ira B. Cross, *Financing an Empire: A History of Banking in California* (San Francisco: S. J. Clarke, 1927), 238.

46. John Wallin Carlson, "History of the San Francisco Mining Exchange" (M.A. thesis, Department of Economics, University of California, Berkeley, 1941), 6. See also Clyde Garfield Chenoweth, "The San Francisco Stock Exchange and Its History" (Ph.D. diss., Department of Economics, Stanford, 1941). For the recollections of a stock exchange member, see Joseph L. King, *History of the San Francisco Stock and Exchange Board* (San Francisco: Joseph L. King, 1910).

47. Sears, *Mining Stock Exchanges,* 10.

48. San Francisco *Mining and Scientific Press,* January 30, 1864, 74.

49. Cross, *Financing an Empire,* 238.

50. John S. Hittell, *A History of the City of San Francisco and Incidentally of California* (San Francisco: A. L. Bancroft, 1878), 340.

51. Ibid., 333.

52. Shinn, *Story of the Mine,* 144–45.

53. February 16, 1863.

54. Quoted in Shinn, *Story of the Mine,* 145.

55. Cross, *Financing an Empire,* 398; Cecil Gage Tilton, *William Chapman Ralston, Courageous Builder* (Boston: Christopher Publishing House, 1935), 135; Paul, *California Gold,* 185–86.

56. Lord, *Comstock Mines,* 246–47; Shinn, *Story of the Mine,* 164–65; Smith, "History of the Comstock Lode," 49–51, 180–81. Although Smith states that both Ralston and Sharon remained in the background while others served on corporate boards and carried out their bidding, an examination of articles of incorporation and annual reports from the companies reveals that Ralston served as treasurer of the Gould & Curry Silver Mining Company in 1860, 1861, and from 1865 to 1872. During the same period, he was also treasurer of the Ophir and Savage mines. In 1869, Sharon was treasurer of the Belcher mine; he also served as a trustee of the Consolidated Imperial Silver Mining Company from 1868 to 1872, while the Bank of California was listed as its treasurer. While complete lists of corporate officers for all the Comstock mines no longer exist, those that remain show that both men occupied key positions within these corporations.

57. Smith, "History of the Comstock Lode," 50–51.

58. Hittell, *History of the City of San Francisco,* 343.

59. See for example, Oscar Lewis, *Silver Kings: The Lives and Times of Mackay, Fair, Flood, and O'Brien, Lords of the Nevada Comstock Lode* (Reno: University of Nevada Press, 1986).

60. The San Francisco *Bulletin* noted on May 7, 1872, that "the excitement in mining stocks and mining claims during the past few months has been without a precedent in the history of our mines. Mining incorporations have been multiplied like the leaves of autumn. . . . Yet it is noteworthy that out of 150 claims offered to the public through the stock boards, only four are paying dividends."

61. Lord, *Comstock Mines,* chaps. 14, 15; Smith, "History of the Comstock Lode," chaps. 11, 13, 14; Lyman, *Ralston's Ring,* chap. 22; and Lewis, *Silver Kings.*

62. Lewis, *Silver Kings,* 247–48; Lord, *Comstock Mines,* 330. See also Squire P. Dewey, "The Bonanza Mines of Nevada: Gross Frauds in Management Exposed," pamphlet reprinted in *Speculation in Gold and Silver Mining Stocks* (1879; reprint, New York: Arno Press, 1970), 61.

63. Assembly Committee on Corporations, "Majority Report," in California Legislature, *Appendix to the Journals of the Senate and Assembly,* vol. 4 (Sacramento: State Printing Office, 1878), 8.

64. See for example, Chandler, *The Visible Hand.*

4

"We all live more like brutes than humans"

Labor and Capital in the Gold Rush

Daniel Cornford

DEMYTHOLOGIZING GOLD-RUSH LABOR

Few events in the history of the United States have been as glamorized by historians as the California Gold Rush. From the late nineteenth century to the present, most historians have portrayed it as both a heroic and dramatic epic and as a giant step toward the fulfillment of the nation's Manifest Destiny that presaged the full-fledged exploration and development of the Far West.

Even Carey McWilliams, hardly an ardent nationalist and indeed a man who devoted much of his scholarship to exposing the darker side of California's history, subscribed to much of the historical drama and mythology associated with the Gold Rush. Writing fifty years ago, he described the event "as one of the most extraordinary mass movements of population in the history of the western world." McWilliams argued that it was not simply the scale of the California Gold Rush that made it unique. It was "the first, and to date [1949] the last, poor man's Gold Rush in history." Influenced particularly by the anecdotes of men making fortunes in the early years, McWilliams described the Gold Rush as "the great adventure for the common man" and wrote of "this exceptional mining frontier [that] made for a real equality of fortune." He was not referring simply to the early years, however. McWilliams maintained that in California "unlike in other western mining states, the free miner remained, at least until 1873 or later, the foundation of the whole system." According to McWilliams, the placer mining of this period exemplified "democracy in production."[1]

The fact that even Carey McWilliams wrote about the Gold Rush and the Argonauts' experience in such neo-Turnerian language is testimony to the power of myth to influence historians' judgment. Traditional accounts have treated the Argonauts rather narrowly as adventurers who either failed or succeeded at the diggings; important aspects of the miners' larger social and labor history were thus overlooked

Hard work and perseverance bring success to a gold hunter in an illustration to *The Idle and Industrious Miner,* a moralistic poem attributed to William Bausman. Published in Sacramento in 1854, with wood engravings after designs by Charles Nahl, the allegorical tale contrasts the disparate rewards attending vice and virtue. Despite the vivid imagery of author and illustrator, good fortune in the diggings sprang more from good luck than from good work habits. "Gold mining," as the witty Dame Shirley wrote her sister, "is Nature's great lottery scheme." *California Historical Society, FN-30967.*

or treated in an incidental fashion. This is particularly true of the period from the mid-1850s to the 1870s, when gold mining was still important to the California economy but the rush years were over. With a few exceptions, not until relatively recently have historians of the Gold Rush begun to separate myth from reality in their work on the social history of the era.[2] Because California and western historians were captivated by the myth and drama of the period, they were tempted to rely on the abundance of excellent anecdotal sources: diaries, memoirs, and letters, in particular, and, to an extent, newspaper accounts.[3] They used these sources at the expense of examining more objective statistical evidence to be gleaned from such sources as, among others, manuscript census data, passenger ship records, and reports and data generated by governmental agencies.

As Malcolm Rohrbough observes,[4] Rodman Paul's *California Gold* (1947) was the first "modern" study of the California Gold Rush in that it made extensive use of quantitative sources as well as the more traditional ones.[5] While not totally neglecting social and labor history, Paul's work focused primarily on the business and technological history of California gold mining. The advent of the new social history during the 1960s eventually spawned a greater interest in the social history of California and the American West by a new generation of historians making much greater use of more objective statistical sources than their predecessors. Despite a few excellent works, however, we still lack a sufficient body of work on the social history of the Gold Rush to fill many of the gaps in our knowledge, and to definitively affirm, modify, or rebut some of the conclusions of the traditional accounts.

Notwithstanding these limitations, this essay examines the history of miners and their work during the gold-rush era (1848–1870), gleaning information from both old and new research on the subject. It explores questions central to understanding the labor history of this period: What impelled the mass migration of 300,000 people to California between 1848 and the mid-1850s? What were the living and working conditions of the miners? How and why did the Gold Rush generate episodes of nativism and racism that presaged and bedeviled the history of the Golden State far into the twentieth century? In particular, this essay explores how, between 1848 and 1870, the Argonauts were transformed from individual prospectors seeking (and sometimes obtaining) nuggets of gold from superficial placers into wage laborers employed by heavily capitalized hydraulic and quartz mining concerns in working conditions very much akin to those experienced by eastern workers in mid-nineteenth-century American factories. Rodman Paul noted this development in his seminal work fifty years ago, but several more recent studies of mining and miners in the American West, and, most notably, Ralph Mann's detailed study of Nevada City and Grass Valley during the gold-rush era, have significantly enhanced our knowledge.[6]

The proletarianization of the California mining labor force reflected a steady decline in the fortunes of most miners and large disparities in wealth and earnings between miners, merchants, and professional people in emergent towns such as Grass Valley and Nevada City. By the late 1860s, the result was growing social tensions between labor and capital. Influenced to a significant degree by the success of the Comstock Lode mining unions a few years earlier, miners conducted the first ma-

Nevada City in 1852, a rough, raw mining town built on the banks of Deer Creek, where gold was found in the autumn of 1849. The rich placer deposits sparked a tremendous rush, and soon the surrounding hills were covered with tents, brush shanties, and rude cabins. By late 1850 the population had reached six thousand. That year several prospectors wrested a four-hundred-pound lump of gold from the earth, but within the decade, miners were laborers and wage earners, working for others rather than for themselves. *Courtesy California State Library.*

jor strikes in the California mining industry. They also founded the Golden State's first mining unions and resisted many of the concessions demanded by a new class of mining entrepreneurs.

WHY THEY WENT

While mythology and hyperbole surround the California Gold Rush, it would be no exaggeration to say that it was one of the largest *occupational* migrations of labor in American history. The number of people engaged in mining skyrocketed from 4,000 in 1848 to about 100,000 by 1852 and stayed at that number until the late 1850s.[7] An even better indication of the importance of mining is obtained by calculating the proportion of the work force engaged in mining. In 1850, almost 75 percent of all employed men in California (57,797 of 77,631) were miners.[8] As late as 1860, when mining had declined in importance in absolute and relative economic terms, the federal census data reveals that miners still made up 38 percent of the California work force (82,573 of 219,192).[9]

Historians have yet to explain convincingly why some people succumbed to the lure of gold and others did not. Undoubtedly, people with some previous experience of mining were eager to employ their skills in California. They included base-metal miners from the British Isles, especially Cornwall, and men from the gold and silver regions of such countries as Mexico, Chile, and Peru, as well as some who had participated in the earlier gold rushes in North Carolina and Georgia and the lead mining boom in the upper Mississippi Valley.[10] But these miners made up a relatively small fraction of the migrants.

Insofar as generalizations can be made about the forces that propelled this mass migration, historians have pointed to improvements in transportation, the expansion of global trade networks in the mid-nineteenth century, and the emergence of a "mass" press in many countries that was only too eager to stir up gold fever. For example, news of the Gold Rush reached Cornwall before it arrived in northern Michigan.[11] Historians have also argued that the discovery of gold in California coincided with the continuing decline of agriculture in many parts of the northeastern United States, and that other workers were increasingly faced with the prospect of working for a subsistence existence in the burgeoning factories and workshops of America's major cities. Whether they were struggling to maintain a farm or working a twelve-hour day for not much more than a dollar a day in a textile or shoe factory, some found the lure of gold irresistible.[12]

Other historians, such as David Goodman, have maintained that the wide acceptance of ideas associated with a pervasive laissez-faire political ideology in the mid-nineteenth century played an important role. Moreover, according to Goodman, an emergent "equalitarian republicanism" reconciled an ideology of self-aggrandizement with the growing imperial aspirations of the nation. In short, the ideology of laissez-faire legitimated, even encouraged, the single-minded pursuit of wealth at all costs and thus made many people susceptible to gold fever.[13] It is, however, dangerous to explain the exodus to California in mechanistic terms of the stages of American (or world) economic development and associated ideologies.[14] As one of the leading historians of the California Gold Rush has observed with reference to an earlier era of American history, "the agrarian frontiers shared with the mining frontiers a persistent American restlessness, an equally pervasive addiction to speculation and a desire to exploit virgin natural resources under conditions of maximum freedom."[15]

In all likelihood a person's propensity to emigrate to California had as much to do with mundane practicalities as it did with the forces of national or world economic development. Proximity to ports and sources of transportation in general was almost certainly a significant factor. As important was the ability of the prospective Argonaut to raise sufficient capital to make the journey and to become established in the diggings. In 1848 and 1849 the cost of the ocean voyage from the East Coast via either Cape Horn or the Isthmus of Panama ranged from $300 to $1,000. Overland travel required approximately $300.[16] Although the journey could be completed for $300, this was a significant, even prohibitive, sum for many farmers and workers in the East whose annual income rarely exceeded this amount. Even if pooling capital in joint-stock companies and borrowing money from family networks helped offset financial obstacles to migration,[17] probably only a small portion of ordinary workers and farmers caught in an emergent industrial revolution could avail themselves of the opportunity of joining the Gold Rush. Few of those who came were among the abject poor.

There is, of course, less uncertainty about the motivation of the Argonauts. Although, as David Goodman has pointed out, people like Henry David Thoreau and more traditional elements of society, such as the church, had some grave reservations about such single-minded pursuit of wealth and its consequences, these people were in a minority.[18] As Ralph Mann succinctly put it, "the California Gold Rush was not an aberration in nineteenth century American history, nor were the Forty-Niners alienated from the values of their time."[19] The Gold Rush promised "opportunities and experiences approved by their society—even identified by it as uniquely American."[20] In the words of another historian, the event represented "an image of instant success available through hard work; an affirmation of democratic beliefs under which the wealth would be available to all."[21] To those who felt guilt at leaving their families or had some reservations about the pursuit of wealth for its own sake, qualms could be allayed by the ethnocentric belief that they were also serving the higher purpose of fulfilling the nation's Manifest Destiny. In an address to the Society of California Pioneers in 1860, Edmund Randolph was enraptured at the thought of

> California in full possession of the white man, and embraced within the mighty area of his civilization! . . . We see in our great movements hitherward in 1849 a likeness to the times when our ancestors . . . poured forth by nations and in never-ending columns from the German forests, and went to seek new pastures and to found a new kingdom in the ruined provinces of the Roman Empire.[22]

While the pursuit of wealth was undoubtedly the migrants' predominant motivation, one of the great paradoxes of the Gold Rush is that the attainment of this end required almost unprecedented levels of cooperation between strangers, such as the formation of joint-stock companies for the journey and similar ventures at the diggings to build dams, sluices, tunnels, and the like. But the longer-term impact of this spirit of cooperation should not be exaggerated. One miner put it this way: "The people have been to each other strangers in a strange land. Absorbed in this eager pursuit of wealth, they have not taken time for the cultivation of those affinities which bind man by a higher and holier tie than mere interest."[23] He stressed that the expectation of most miners that their visit to California would be a temporary one resulted in an "almost total lack of social organization."[24] Under these circumstances, it is hardly surprising that, even as independent miners were reduced to the status of modestly paid wage laborers employed by hydraulic and quartz mining companies, collective activity in the form of strikes or unions was late in arriving in the California mining industry.

DIFFERENT LABOR SYSTEMS, DIVERSE GOLD SEEKERS

Not all miners, even in the early phase of the Gold Rush, were freewheeling independent entrepreneurs. As Susan Johnson has put it, "work in the diggings proceeded according to a dizzying array of systems that included independent prospecting and mining partnerships as well as altered Miwok gathering practices, Latin American peonage, North American slavery, and, later, Chinese indentured labor."[25] In the case of African Americans, a significant number of free blacks joined the Gold Rush. Some were seamen deserting vessels arriving from New England ports, while others made their way to California as employees or servants of overland joint-stock companies. But just as commonly, African Americans arrived in California as slaves to their gold-seeking masters. Rudolph Lapp estimates that 962, or approximately 50 percent of the African Americans in California in 1850, were slaves.[26]

We will never know precisely how many of the at least 15,000 Mexicans (10,000 from the province of Sonora alone) came as unfree laborers sponsored by *patrones*. Leonard Pitt asserts that "the north Mexican patrons themselves encouraged the migration of peons by sponsoring expeditions of twenty or thirty underlings at a time, giving them full upkeep in return for half of their gold findings in California."[27] The *patrón* system was also responsible for bringing a certain (unknown) proportion of miners to the diggings from Chile and Peru.

The Chinese did not arrive at the diggings quite as early as the Mexicans and South Americans. In 1850 there were only 500 Chinese miners in California, and 1,000 Chinese people in the entire United States.[28] However, in 1852 alone, 20,000 Chinese people entered California, most of them en route to the mining counties. By one contemporary estimate there were 20,000 Chinese miners in California by 1855.[29] Many of the first Chinese migrants were merchants able to pay their way from China. Others were not so fortunate. Most of the Chinese who emigrated to the United

American and Chinese miners work a claim at the head of Auburn Ravine with a line of sluice boxes in 1852. Woods Dry Diggings, as Auburn was originally named, was one of the earliest mining camps in California, established in May 1848 when Claude Chana and a party of Indians discovered gold in the ravine. Chinese merchants contributed to the growth of the town, and several of their old wooden shops, dating to the year of this daguerreotype, still stand on Sacramento Street. *Courtesy California State Library.*

States did not experience the exploitation of the notorious "coolie" system, which bound workers to sign contracts agreeing to work in a foreign land for a specified time in return for their passage. Instead, most Chinese workers paid for their passage by what Sucheng Chan calls the "credit-ticket system," whereby Chinese middlemen paid the passage of emigrants in advance. In return, the emigrants contracted to pay their debts after arrival, with the prospect that the emigrants could keep their earnings after debts were paid.[30] While more research is needed to determine more precisely what proportion of Chinese emigrants arrived under the credit-ticket system, historian Elmer Sandmeyer asserts with confidence that "the evidence is conclusive that by far the majority of Chinese who came to California had their transportation provided by others and bound themselves to make repayment."[31] Indeed, the consensus of other historians is that the labor of indebted passengers was sold through Chinese subcontractors to Chinese mining companies, although some describe the labor system and working conditions of these Chinese as akin to debt peonage.[32]

In part, as Leonard Pitt has argued, the "free labor" preferences of white Americans contributed to the xenophobia and racism that most foreign miners (as well, of course, as Native Americans and Californios) encountered.[33] But there were other reasons why white American-born miners often had no compunction about expelling foreign miners, especially racial minorities, from the diggings and from mining towns. First, the American miners, conscious of the fact that access to gold was limited, resented the fact that the mining experience of peoples from Mexico, Chile, and Peru often made them more successful prospectors. Second, the belief in Manifest Destiny, reinfused by the United States's victory in the Mexican-American War, led many Americans to presume that they had priority at the diggings. Third, even while hostility and violence were also directed at white foreign nationals such as the French and Australians, the depths of racist ideology cannot be overemphasized. Indeed, as more and more historians have demonstrated, racist ideology was a crucial building-block in the making of white working-class consciousness.[34] Finally, as wage labor became more and more common in the mines, the disillusioned American Argonauts resented the competition of cheaper "foreign" labor. This contributed to the expulsion of many Native Americans in the early gold-rush years and was a source of tension between white and Chinese miners throughout the 1850s, 1860s, and 1870s.[35]

In general, minorities suffered most from extra-legal forms of violence, but in the early 1850s white miners had the political clout to impose "legal" forms of discrimination on their rivals. This came in the form of two foreign miners' tax measures that were passed by the state legislature. The first, enacted in 1850, required miners who were not citizens of the United States to pay a licensing fee of $20 a month. Targeted particularly at Mexicans, this measure led to violence and the eventual departure of about 10,000 Mexican miners to their homeland in 1850.[36] The protests of many American merchants who lost customers as a result of the measure led to its repeal in 1851, but the influx of Chinese in 1852 prompted the passage of another act that provided for a tax of $3 per month, later raised to $4.[37]

While not a target of foreign miners' taxes, Native Americans suffered extreme violence at the hands of Argonauts from many nations. California Indian labor played a particularly important role in the early gold-rush years. The best estimate is that by the summer of 1848 perhaps half of the 4,000 miners were Indians. Even before the Gold Rush, Anglo-Americans and other immigrants in Hispanic California were quick to imitate the Mexican system of Indian labor exploitation. A group of pioneers such as John Sutter and John Bidwell simply moved their Indian labor force from their ranchos to the mines. There were reports of individual whites employing up to one hundred Indians at the diggings.[38]

Not all Indians worked for whites. Some were independent miners who bartered their gold dust with merchants on increasingly favorable terms as they came to appreciate the value that the white man attached to it. But the Indian presence as independent and employed miners was short-lived. As Albert Hurtado and others have shown, newly arriving white miners from Oregon and other parts bitterly resented the advantage that ranchero employers of Indians had. Starting in 1849, and using indiscriminate and extreme violence, they drove most Indians from the mines. The 1852 state census showed that, with the exception of the southern mining counties, Indians made up a relatively small proportion of the population of the mining counties. Outside the southern mining counties, they constituted less than 10 percent of the population in every mining county but one. In these counties, probably only a small proportion of the Indians still present worked in the mines, and in most cases, historians agree, they usually worked for white miners. In the Southern Mines the Indians' numerical superiority prevented whites from driving them out during the early 1850s, but in time "attrition caused by disease, gradual displacement, and only occasional fighting would make the south a white man's country."[39]

LIFE AND LABOR AT THE DIGGINGS

Unquestionably, the ability to employ slaves, peons, or indentured labor gave some miners an advantage. However, the circumstances of the early gold-rush years made, to some extent, for the appearance of a degree of equality, or at least equality of opportunity, among the majority of miners. In the period where superficial placer mining predominated, most miners had access to the capital necessary for such mining. Furthermore, some early mining tools, such as the cradle, which required more than one person to operate, fostered a spirit of unity and cooperation among miners. But, most importantly, success at the diggings in the early years was as much a matter of luck as anything else. As Dame Shirley succinctly put it, "gold mining is Nature's great lottery scheme."[40]

The fact also that miners dressed almost identically helped blur class distinctions. "Their heavy boots, sturdy trousers, checked shirts, large belt, slouch hat, and gloves formed a uniform worn by miners up and down the Sierra that made them indistinguishable from one another," says historian Malcolm Rohrbough in his recent study.[41] Moreover, he adds, the miners "wore their uniforms with pride. Their dress was a badge of members in a large fraternity and it established their status as workers."[42] In addition, the miners' hostility to other occupational groups, such as merchants, teamsters, boardinghouse keepers, doctors, and lawyers, on whom they depended at times, reinforced the miners' identity of themselves as workers.[43] One observer at a boardinghouse for miners summarized the situation as follows: "The wondrous influence of gold seem to have entirely obliterated all social distinctions."[44]

The sheer hard labor entailed in most forms of early placer mining also contributed to weakening class identities. Rodman Paul describes the work as "most

The Forty-niner Solomon Yeakel set out for the new El Dorado at the age of twenty-one, crossing the Plains and the Rockies to seek his fortune. Like most Argonauts, Yeakel returned home rather than settle in California. He later enlisted in the Pennsylvania Volunteers and fought at the Battle of Bull Run. *Courtesy Bancroft Library.*

nearly akin to ditch digging."[45] In 1848 and 1849, most independent miners worked the diggings as individuals or with their families. By 1850, as placer mining required a cradle and the building of dams and sluices, miners formed themselves into companies of four to eight men. While usually the tasks were rotated, the labor was grueling. Work was often performed in ice-cold water generated by the melting snow, even while in the sun's glare summer temperatures not uncommonly reached 100 degrees. The workday generally began at 6 A.M. There was a break around noon for a couple of hours to escape the worst of the sun and eat lunch, then work resumed until sunset. The physical exigencies of mining may be gauged from the fact that by one estimate, even in 1849 when the yields were good, miners needed to wash an average of 160 buckets a day to acquire one ounce ($16) of gold.[46] "You can scarcely form any conception of what a dirty business this gold digging is and of the mode of life which a miner is compelled to lead," wrote one miner. "We all live more like brutes than humans."[47] The seasonal nature of the work added to the miners' sense of urgency. In the Northern Mines, work was possible most years only from July through late November. Heavy rains and snow made work impossible for the rest of the year. One option for miners was to move during winter and spring to the Southern Mines and engage in the "dry diggings." However, stresses Rodman Paul, while "the yield of the dry diggings during the winter months was often large . . . the period of effective operations was short, and the chances were extremely dependent up on the weather," especially a sufficient flow of water during the spring months.[48]

The almost complete absence of women at the diggings forced men to learn a wide range of domestic skills, including sewing, washing, and, of course, food preparation. Some men had acquired these skills on the overland trail, but many had not, and not until the advent of boardinghouses and an assortment of domestic-related service industries in mining towns were the majority of miners relieved of such chores.

In 1850, less than one-tenth of the population of California was female, according to the census, and in the mining counties women made up only 3 percent of the inhabitants.[49] While they made up 30 percent of the California population by the 1860s, they continued to be as small a proportion of the population in the mining counties as they had been in 1850. Small wonder that even in established mining towns such as Grass Valley and Nevada City only one in ten men was married in 1860, and among miners only one in twenty-five was betrothed.[50]

This small female population engaged in a variety of occupations. In 1848, American families and migrant families, especially from Sonora, encamped near the diggings and undoubtedly women panned for gold. However, there is little evidence that women participated in the diggings in significant numbers for very long.[51] Yet the female population of the mining counties engaged in a wide range of occupations. Some women worked as prostitutes in the mining towns,[52] while others were

RIVER MINING.

Having dammed the river and turned its torrents into a flume, miners burrow deep into its bed, laboring with picks and shovels to win the riches of ancient Tertiary deposits. Beginning work at dawn, laboring six or even seven days a week, often in icy waters or under a burning sun, Argonauts occasionally lost all sense of time in an exhausting round of never-ending physical exertion. "Digging for gold," as one miner put it, "is the hardest work a man can get at." *California Historical Society, FN-04135.*

employed in the entertainment industry as dance hall girls and singers. But women also worked in many other occupations that do not fit the popular stereotypes of female employment during the Gold Rush. Ralph Mann's study of Grass Valley and Nevada City provides us with the most definitive evidence. Mann's data show that the townswomen from these two cities engaged in fifteen different occupations. In both places, two-thirds of employed women cared for boarders. Women also worked as servants, seamstresses, dressmakers, shopkeepers, cooks, bakers, washerwomen, boardinghouse operators, and by 1870 in a few cases, as schoolteachers.[53]

There is a lack of consensus about the quality of the miners' diet. Some overlanders and miners such as William Swain ate well and found food a major compensation for their many other drudgeries.[54] While lines of supply in the early gold-rush years were not always reliable, historian Joseph Conlin asserts that "grocers reached most camps before the prostitutes did."[55] Nevertheless, in the early years the basic diet of meat, bread, or biscuits washed down with tea or coffee was not always supplemented with fresh fruit and vegetables. The very high price of food sometimes caused the miners to cut corners on their diets, and a few unfortunate ones may have starved. Rodman Paul concludes that in 1849, and for some of 1850 at least, partially as a result of dietary deficiencies, "many suffered from diarrhea, dysentery, scurvy, and other debilitating diseases," although, he argues, the situation quickly improved during the 1850s.[56]

The primitive dwellings that were hastily erected in clusters as close to the diggings as possible did not contribute to the health of miners but instead abetted the spread of disease. Some early miners built log cabins, but most lived in rudimentary canvas tents that they usually abandoned during the winter.[57] As the 1850s progressed, the situation improved, as mining towns such as Grass Valley and Nevada City sprang up with regular boardinghouse facilities. However, before 1870 a majority of miners in both places lived in cabins,[58] and in more isolated areas miners continued to occupy fairly primitive cabin dwellings until much later.[59]

Accidents at the mines were commonplace from the outset, but as mining became more technologically advanced, the potential for serious accidents increased.[60] The growing use of tunneling and gunpowder, in particular, took its toll. While the issue of gunpowder contributed to the first major labor strike in the California mines, the legislature showed little interest in passing any protective legislation for miners during the nineteenth century. In this respect California was hardly atypical. In the most recent book on the history of occupational safety, Mark Aldrich, after describing a fatal mining accident in West Virginia in 1898, concluded that "most managers, and probably most Americans, if they thought about these matters at all, would have deemed such deaths individual tragedies for which the company bore little, if any, responsibility."[61]

By any standard, miners were highly itinerant workers. In the space of the five-month mining season, miners might explore several different claims. They might move within their mining region or between the northern and southern mining areas. They might also depart for another rush such as the Comstock rush of 1859 or the short-lived rush on the Fraser River in British Columbia in 1858. Winter forced many miners into the towns of Marysville, Sacramento, Stockton, and, of course, San Francisco, where many searched for work. But even during the mining season, poverty, disillusionment, or the need to reprovision caused miners to move back and forth between the diggings and the cities. By the early 1850s, the appearance of well-equipped stores and full-fledged mining towns in some areas eliminated some of the causes of transience.

Mann's study, however, indicates that even as mining camps evolved into well-developed towns, rates of geographical mobility remained high throughout the period between 1850 and 1870. Mann found that in both Nevada City and Grass Valley only 3 percent of the miners recorded in the 1850 census were still there in 1860.[62] During the 1860s, the persistence rate of miners was not much higher. Only 5 percent of those appearing in the 1860 census for Nevada City could be found in the census of 1870, while the persistence rate for Grass Valley was only 6 percent.[63] If the communities of Grass Valley and Nevada City are taken as a whole, only one in ten of

Seated before a rude cabin roofed with canvas, a solitary Argonaut plays his flute, filling the evening air at Boston Flat with music, in a daguerreotype by H. M. Bacon. In addition to enduring hard labor and bad food, homesickness and disease, the Argonauts often spent their nights and dreary rainy days under the most miserable of conditions. "We all," as one miner wrote his sister in 1850, "live more like brutes than humans." *Courtesy Society of California Pioneers.*

the population of both towns continued their residence between 1860 and 1870. While the turnover rate in many other American towns and cities was high, especially on the frontier, Mann's comparative data indicates that the turnover of populations in Grass Valley and Nevada City was exceptionally high. Even turbulent San Francisco experienced a persistence rate of 25 percent between 1850 and 1860. Persistence rates for other studied frontier communities have varied from 25 to 60 percent over the course of a given decade.[64]

Historians studying social and geographic mobility have long pondered the relationship between the two without drawing definitive conclusions about why some people settled down and others did not. High rates of geographic mobility may indicate that people were "pushed" from communities by limited opportunities for advancement. Alternatively, it may show that people were pulled away from their communities by the prospect, and actuality, of greater opportunity. The higher rates of persistence of people with professional or high-paying occupations leads most historians to believe that itinerant workers were, in general, more likely to be pushed than pulled.

Perhaps this was not the case with the Argonauts, eternal optimists ready to move on to the next site on the flimsiest of rumors. Whether hopes and expectations were borne out by reality, however, is quite another question. Moreover, it must be noted, increasingly during the 1850s, the miners' status was changing from independent prospector to permanent wage laborer.

FROM ARGONAUTS TO WAGE LABORERS

The glory days of the lucky, individual Argonaut were very short-lived. By the early 1850s, even the expedient of pooling capital with fellow Argonauts barely enabled most miners to retain a vestige of their independence. Increasingly, during the 1850s, miners were forced to work as wage laborers for large corporations often employing several hundred men. Although reliable statistical data is not available, it would be safe to say that by the late 1850s, a substantial majority of miners were wage laborers. While the corporations probably employed a significant number of the early Argonauts who remained at the diggings, they also began to hire a large number of men with considerable experience in mining, especially from the British Isles. In short, in the space of a few years the noble and adventurous Argonaut had been reduced to the status of a proletarian working for wages and in conditions not much better than factory workers in the East.

Unquestionably, some miners, especially those arriving between 1848 and 1850, struck it lucky. The majority, however, did not, and "wages," defined either as earnings from the work of individual prospecting or wage labor, declined sharply from 1848 onward. Conceding the lack of totally comprehensive and reliable data, Paul estimates that the miner's "wage" declined from $20 per day in 1848 to $10 per day in 1850, to $5 per day by 1853, and to $3 per day in the late 1850s.[65] Notwithstanding the fact that the decline in wages was offset by a decline in the cost of living, it appears that the miners' real wages declined significantly between 1848 and 1860.

Mann's detailed statistical data also support such a conclusion. He found that in Grass Valley and Nevada City only one out of ten miners reported owning real estate or personal property at the time of the 1860 census. By contrast, one-half of the two towns' businessmen reported over $1,000 in real estate and personal property.[66] Small wonder that Mann concluded that "in a disproportionate number of . . . cases the man was a propertyless miner. . . . No longer living in camps, hoping to strike it rich, they now dealt in embryonic industrial slums, hoping for a living wage. The gap between miners and the rest of society was more than spatial; they were much less likely to own their own homes, have families, or accumulate possessions."[67] While by 1870 things had improved for a relatively small core of more skilled miners, 75 percent or more of them in both towns still reported no personal or real estate.[68]

How had it come to pass that the ever-optimistic Forty-niners, hopeful of finding their fortunes, or at least enough money to buy farms back East, had been reduced to such lowly status and economic standing? By the early 1850s, external and inexorable forces were impinging on the miners' chances of succeeding as individual prospectors. After the easy pickings from the superficial placers had been exhausted, more elaborate and capital-intensive technologies had to be employed to extract gold. Initially, Argonauts were able to pool their capital and labor to acquire and use rockers and to build dams and sluices necessary to the more advanced forms of placer mining. If the miners' capital was not sufficient, local merchants often subscribed to the joint-stock companies.[69] However, during the 1850s, the scale of hydraulic mining projects increased, necessitating a growing reliance on both wage labor and external capital.

In 1853, it was reported that nearly twenty-five miles of the Yuba River had been diverted at a cost of $3 million.[70] A single construction project could, by the mid-1850s, cost as much as $120,000, and as many as 260 men might be employed on it.[71] The scale that hydraulic mining assumed may be gauged from the following statistics. By 1857, 4,405 miles of canals, ditches, and flumes had been constructed at a cost of about $12 million.[72] With investments on this scale by the late 1850s, "the new owners were what contemporaries called 'capitalists,' and the operation of this process sometimes meant a transfer of control from the working men in the foothills to the business and financial men in the cities."[73] Or, as Ralph Mann put it "for many men the fortunes of the mining company became the fortunes of the company that employed them."[74]

Also requiring large investments of capital, and threatening the independence of miners, were the quartz mines of the early 1850s. These mines attracted a significant amount of eastern and English capital.[75] As early as 1851, there were twenty quartz mines in operation in Grass Valley and Nevada City,[76] and by 1852 Grass Valley residents claimed that the Gold Hill mine had yielded $4 million in gold.[77] The quartz companies employed men for $100 a month and found plenty of Argonauts willing to sacrifice their independence.[78]

While the quartz mining boom of the early 1850s fell far short of investors' expectations,[79] hardrock mining became more widespread and stable during the late 1850s. In 1855 there were only thirty-two quartz mines in the state, but by 1857 there were as many as 150 and a larger number of stamp mills and *arrastras* for extracting the gold from the quartz.[80] By 1870, quartz mining accounted for 31 percent of the dollar value of all gold mined in California.[81] Quartz mining became well established

A flume carries water for hydraulic mining at Smartsville, Yuba County, about 1865.
Beginning with the rise of hydraulicking in the mid-1850s, an enormous water-delivery
network arose in the Sierra Nevada, and by the end of the decade nearly seven thousand
miles of flumes, canals, and ditches had been constructed to serve mining companies in
the Golden State. *Courtesy Society of California Pioneers.*

in some towns like Grass Valley, where by the 1860s as many men were employed in
quartz mining as in hydraulic mining.[82] Mann suggests several reasons for the expansion and success of quartz mining in Nevada County. First, many entrepreneurs
and miners acquired much invaluable technical knowledge from their experience of
quartz mining at the Comstock Lode. Second, there was a large supply of capital
from the eastern states and Europe to finance this expansion. Third, an increasing
influx of skilled Cornish miners, in particular, furnished the expertise to work these
mines profitably.[83]

THE MINERS FIGHT BACK: STRIKES AND UNIONS

Not until the late 1860s, and with the ascending importance of quartz mining, did anything resembling a "labor movement" emerge in California mining. Prior to 1869, when the first union was formed and the first major labor strike occurred, strikes appear to have been sporadic.[84] Why were there so few strikes in the gold mines and why did it take over twenty years for the first labor union to appear? First, even as the days of the independent prospector came to an end and the era of wage labor began, miners continued to be itinerant. This was not conducive to strikes and certainly not to the building of unions, especially among workers, a substantial majority of whom saw their stay in California as temporary. Like many disgruntled workers in other industries with a highly mobile work force, miners tended to strike with their feet and simply move on to the next camp or mine. Second, the relative isolation of the work setting made it hard for miners to coordinate a strike effort or to build a union. Furthermore, in these isolated settings workers could not call on the support of the community, a factor that was crucial to the success of later strikes and unions. Third, deep-seated ethnic, racial, and national animosities among the diverse workers were inimical to the waging of strikes and the building of unions. Fourth, until the 1860s, absentee mine ownership was uncommon. Quite often the owner was also a manager and therefore, in the eyes of the worker, a fellow member of the "producing classes," and one who often risked considerable capital to put men to work. Finally, while a vibrant labor movement had existed at times during antebellum America (especially during the Jacksonian era), the movement was episodic and the majority of American workers had had no experience of strikes or trade unions.

It is significant that strikes and unions in California gold mines occurred after the first successful organizing wave by hardrock miners at the Comstock Lode in Nevada and that the major conflicts occurred at quartz mines employing a relatively large number of miners. Many California miners joined the Comstock rush in the early 1860s, and many returned within a few years. In some cases these returning men played a key role in sparking strikes and building unions in California. At the very least, historians are agreed that the success of the labor movement in the Comstock mines was a major influence in spurring the development of labor militancy and unionism among hardrock miners all over the American West.[85]

Experienced Cornish workers played a particularly important role in the development of western mining and also in the building of a labor movement. By the third quarter of the nineteenth century, immigrants from the British Isles comprised approximately half the work force in many of the hardrock mining centers of the West, such as Grass Valley.[86] They were roughly evenly divided between Irishmen and non-Irishmen, most of whom were from Cornwall. The Cornish miners had been encouraged to emigrate because of the serious decline of the centuries-old regional tin industry. Sometimes they emigrated to other regions of the United States to mine coal or other ores before coming to California; sometimes they migrated directly.

Exceptionally clannish, the Cornish had a fierce pride in their long-standing craft traditions and skills. Indeed, no group of miners was more prized for their skill by mining employers than were the Cornish in the latter half of the nineteenth century. It was in some ways ironic that the Cornish should be thrust into the vanguard of the union movement among miners in the West. The Cornish did not bring with them any traditions of trade unionism from the British Isles, but rather a tradition of fierce individualism. What thrust the Cornishmen into the forefront of the western mining labor movement was the fact that soon after their arrival new mining technologies began to threaten their craft traditions and workplace prerogatives.

The cause of the first major strike in the California gold mines, which occurred in Grass Valley in 1869, is illustrative.[87] A series of issues, including Sinophobia, demands for higher wages, and the objection of Cornish miners, in particular, to the use of dynamite and new drilling practices, precipitated the strike. By 1870, three-quarters of all adult men in Grass Valley were foreign born, and slightly over half of these were British, most Cornish.[88] The Cornish miners were accustomed to working in pairs as "double-handed" drillers. One would wield the hammer while the other held and twisted the drill bit. By the 1860s, some employers saw this as a wasteful use of labor and advocated single-handed drilling. Employers also began to insist that miners use dynamite, or "giant powder," as it was called, instead of the less powerful and volatile "black powder." The Cornish miners insisted that this new gunpowder produced noxious fumes and refused to use it. The situation was further complicated and inflamed by mining employers' threats to hire Chinese workers as single-handed miners using the new explosives. All this occurred in the context of a situation where quartz miners' wages had been reduced to three dollars per day or less, and in which mine owners were trying to crack down on the practice of high-grading. High-grading was the name given to the miners' habit of privately helping themselves to promising lumps of quartz, apparently a common practice before the 1860s.

The catalyst for this first strike was the decision of one mine in Grass Valley to change over exclusively to the use of dynamite and to allow only single-handed drilling. In April 1869, other mining employers followed suit, and soon several hundred miners went on strike in protest. The miners decided to form a "branch league" of the Comstock unions and asked the Nevada miners to send them an organizer. The striking miners resolved not to use the new powder or allow single-handed drilling, and they pledged that no one would work underground for less than three dollars per day. The employers attempted to hire scabs, but with very little success.

Faced with the solidarity of the miners, who had much community support, most mine owners accepted the union's terms by July, and within a few months the union boasted seven hundred members.[89]

Further conflict between labor and capital was not long in spreading. The quartz mines of Amador County were one locus of discontent.[90] Again many issues were involved in the dispute, but when one company cut wages to two dollars a day, the "Amador War," as it became known throughout the state, was on. The miners formed themselves into the Amador County Laborers' Association, which soon claimed four hundred members. Like the miners of Grass Valley, the Amador men were determined not only to improve their wages, but also to exclude, as far as possible, the employment of Chinese in the mines.

By 1871, as the strike dragged on, the Amador War had become a state issue. The attempt of California governor Henry Haight to use the state militia to break the strike was almost comically inept and ineffective. With the exception of negotiating a daily minimum wage of three dollars for surface and mill workers, the union eventually won all its demands.[91]

Several other major mining strikes occurred in the early 1870s. While California gold miners' opposition to giant powder weakened, as it did everywhere, the labor movement in the California mines was, like the Comstock unions, effective not in bringing about great improvements in miners' conditions, but at least in holding back employers' attempts to further erode the miners' working conditions and prerogatives during the late 1860s and 1870s. Richard Lingenfelter attributes their success to the "internal solidarity of the unions and their strong support within the community," as well as to the fact that a significant group of miners now felt a sense of permanence in their communities.[92]

Little study has been devoted to California gold miners after the 1870s that might reveal whether their unions retained power. It seems likely, however, that the gradual decline of the California gold industry eroded the strength of the miners' position. In the early years of the twentieth century, miners in most western states obtained the eight-hour work day, but not in California. Mark Wyman quotes the president of the Tuolumne Miners' Union, who in 1900 said that, as far as miners were concerned, California "was the poorest organized state in the West."[93] He added that miners had not won employer agreement to limitations of the workday or bans on compulsory hospital fees. Finally, in 1909, the state passed an eight-hour-day law for miners.[94]

It seems likely that the decline in California gold mining weakened the hand of the miners in the last quarter of the nineteenth century. Miners simply no longer had the numbers to intimidate scabs and the state militia, or to influence the state legislature in the way that miners were able to do in many other western hardrock states. Instead, if we are to believe Rodman Paul, many California gold miners, both quartz and hydraulic ones, eked out an existence during the late nineteenth century in rather isolated company towns where their power was limited.[95] Whatever the case, Paul's judgment is sound when he asserts that "within the short span of twenty-five years California mining had passed through a cycle that commenced with what economists call 'home crafts' and ended with what socialists term 'proletarian industry.'"[96]

NOTES

I would like to thank Jeffrey Stine for his helpful comments on an earlier draft of this article.

1. Carey McWilliams, *California: The Great Exception* (New York: Current Books, 1949), 26–29.

2. The best, and most recent, overview of the historiography on the California Gold Rush is in Malcolm J. Rohrbough, *Days of Gold: The California Gold Rush and the American Nation* (Berkeley: University of California Press, 1997), 295–300.

3. For a good assessment of these traditional sources on the history of the Gold Rush, see ibid., 300–304.

4. Ibid., 298.

5. Rodman W. Paul, *California Gold: The Beginning of Mining in the Far West* (Cambridge, Mass.: Harvard University Press, 1947).

6. Ralph Mann, *After the Gold Rush: Society in Grass Valley and Nevada City, California, 1849–1870* (Stanford: Stanford University Press, 1982). Also offering new insights into the California Gold Rush is the recently published book by Walter T. Durham, *Volunteer Forty-Niners: Tennesseans and the California Gold Rush* (Nashville: Vanderbilt University Press, 1997).

7. Paul, *California Gold*, 43, and Rodman W. Paul, *Mining Frontiers of the Far West, 1848–1880* (New York: Holt, Rinehart and Winston, 1963), 16.

8. U.S. Bureau of the Census, *Seventh Census of the United States, 1850*, vol. 1, p. 976. Unfortunately, and partly because of the upheaval caused by the Gold Rush, the 1850 census is not fully reliable. For a discussion of this problem, see Paul, *California Gold*, 23–25. Likewise, the California state census of 1852 is flawed in some respects. See Dennis E. Harris, "The California Census of 1852: A Note of Caution and Encouragement," *Pacific Historian* 28 (Summer 1984): 59–64.

9. U.S. Bureau of the Census, *Eighth Census of the United States, 1860*, vol. 1, p. 35. Unlike in 1850, the table of occupations did not confine itself to enumerating only employed men, but, as will be shown later in this essay, few women were miners.

10. While the southern gold rushes of the earlier nineteenth century paled by contrast to the California Gold Rush, comparisons between the two are interesting and instructive, and there is a growing historical literature on the southern gold rush. See Otis E. Young, "The Southern Gold Rush, 1828–1836," *The Journal of Southern History* 48 (August 1982): 373–92. See also David Williams, *The Georgia Gold Rush: Twenty-Niners, Cherokees, and Gold Fever* (Columbia: University of South Carolina Press, 1993). This book contains a useful bibliography. On gold-rush migrants from Chile and Peru, see Jay Monaghan, *Chile, Peru, and the California Gold Rush of 1849* (Berkeley: University of California Press, 1973). The gold-rush emigration and experience of people from the Mexican province of Sonora is discussed in

M. Colette Standart, "The Sonoran Migration to California, 1848–1856: A Study in Prejudice," *Southern California Historical Quarterly* 58 (Fall 1976): 333–57. On emigration from Cornwall and the Cornish in America, see John Rowe, *The Hard-Rock Men: Cornish Immigrants and the North American Mining Frontier* (Liverpool: University of Liverpool Press, 1974).

11. Rowe, *The Hard-Rock Miners,* 96.

12. See David Douglas Clinton, "Laboring for the Golden Dream: Labor in Gold Rush San Francisco" (Ph.D. diss., University of California, Santa Barbara, 1991), 73–74, 180–81. For data on wage comparisons, see U.S. Department of Labor, *History of Wages in the United States from Colonial Times to 1928* (Washington, D.C.: Government Printing Office, 1934). See also Rohrbough, *Days of Gold,* 2–3.

13. David Goodman, *Gold Seeking: Victoria and California in the 1850s* (Stanford: Stanford University Press, 1994).

14. See Susan Lee Johnson, "'The Gold She Gathered': Difference, Domination, and California's Southern Mines, 1848–1853" (Ph.D. diss., Yale University, 1993); see chap. 2 for analysis of the factors spurring emigration from both within and without the United States. She cautions historians (p. 100) not to be too deterministic about the factors that in particular impelled migration from the eastern United States.

15. Paul, *Mining Frontiers of the Far West,* 41.

16. Estimates of the cost of the journey vary considerably. In part this reflects inadequate data, and also the fact that the cost of passage varied enormously according to the date and circumstances of travel. In addition, it is not always clear whether estimates included food for the passage and the cost of capital equipment and other supplies necessary for mining. In general, the costs of the voyage by sea declined after 1848–49.

17. On forming joint-stock companies and using families' funds to finance the migration, see Rohrbough, *Days of Gold,* 39–45. For a detailed discussion of the formation of joint-stock companies to finance the voyage by sea, see James P. Delgado, *To California By Sea: A Maritime History of the California Gold Rush* (Columbia: University of South Carolina Press, 1990).

18. Goodman, *Gold Seeking.*

19. Mann, *After the Gold Rush,* 1.

20. Ibid.

21. Rohrbough, *Days of Gold,* 2.

22. Quoted in Goodman, *Gold Seeking,* 28.

23. Quoted in J. S. Holliday, *The World Rushed In: The California Gold Rush Experience* (New York: Simon & Schuster, 1981), 370.

24. Ibid.

25. Johnson, "The Gold She Gathered," 292. The historical literature has not examined this issue in very great detail and we shall probably never know what proportion came to the diggings as unfree laborers of some kind. The sporadic evidence would seem to indicate that a relatively small number were unfree laborers. If, however, one includes wage laborers in one's definition of "unfree," the proportion becomes somewhat larger.

26. Rudolph M. Lapp, *Afro-Americans in California* (San Francisco: Boyd and Fraser, 1987), 4–6. See also Rudolph M. Lapp, *Blacks in Gold Rush California* (New Haven: Yale University Press, 1977).

27. Leonard Pitt, *The Decline of the Californios: A Social History of the Spanish-Speaking*

Californians, 1846–1890 (Berkeley: University of California Press, 1970), 54; Tomas Almaquer, *Racial Fault Lines: The Historic Origins of White Supremacy in California* (Berkeley: University of California Press, 1994), 69. On the bringing of unfree labor from Latin America to the Gold Rush, see Monaghan, *Chile, Peru and the California Gold Rush*, 53, 61, 109, 127, 131.

28. Ping Chiu, *Chinese Labor in California: A Economic Study* (Madison: State Historical Society of Wisconsin, 1967), 12. On the forces that impelled Chinese emigration to the United States there are many works, but see Sucheng Chan, *This Bittersweet Soil: The Chinese in California Agriculture, 1860–1910* (Berkeley: University of California Press, 1986); June Mei, "Socioeconomic Origins of Emigration: Guangdong to California, 1850–1882," in *Labor Immigration Under Capitalism: Asian Workers in the United States Before World War II*, ed. Lucie Cheng and Edna Bonacich (Berkeley: University of California Press, 1984); and Yong Chen, "The Internal Origins of Chinese Emigration to California Reconsidered," *Western Historical Quarterly* 28 (Winter 1997): 521–46.

29. Paul, *California Gold*, 43.

30. See Chan, *This Bittersweet Soil*, 21. Chan defines emigrants who obtained passage to the United States via the credit-ticket system as "semifree."

31. Elmer Sandmeyer, "The Bases of Anti-Chinese Sentiment," in *Racism in California*, ed. Roger Daniels and Spencer C. Olin, Jr. (New York: Macmillan, 1972), 80.

32. David V. DuFault, "The Chinese in the Mining Camps of California: 1848–1870," *Southern California Quarterly* 41 (Summer 1959): 155–70. James J. Rawls and Walton Bean, *California: An Interpretive History* (New York: McGraw Hill, 1993), 126.

33. Pitt, *Decline of the Californios*, 56.

34. This argument was made powerfully and convincingly in Alexander Saxton's book, *The Indispensable Enemy: Labor and the Anti-Chinese Movement* (Berkeley: University of California Press, 1971). It was a position adopted by many subsequent California historians, especially of the labor movement. More recent work views racism and the development of a white working-class consciousness as by no means exclusively a California phenomenon. To cite but two of the works: David R. Roediger, *The Wages of Whiteness: Race and the Making of the American Working Class* (London: Verso, 1991), and Alexander Saxton, *The Rise and Fall of the White Republic: Class Politics and Mass Culture in Nineteenth Century America* (London: Verso, 1990).

35. We still lack a definitive explanation of why Chinese miners were expelled from some communities but not others. In some towns the expulsion took place in the early 1850s, but in others attempts were not made until the 1870s. On the persistence and role of the Chinese in California and western mining see Randall E. Rohe, "After the Gold Rush: Chinese Mining in the Far West, 1850–1890," *Montana: The Magazine of Western History* 32 (Summer 1982): 2–19, and also his "Chinese River Mining in the West," *Montana: The Magazine of Western History* 46 (Autumn 1996): 14–29. On strong anti-Chinese sentiment in California mining communities during the 1870s, see Richard E. Lingenfelter, *The Hardrock Miners: A History of the Mining Labor Movement in the American West, 1863–1893* (Berkeley: University of California Press, 1974), and Mann, *After the Gold Rush*.

36. See Richard Henry Morefield, "Mexicans in the California Mines, 1848–53," *Southern California Quarterly* 35 (March 1956): 37–46. Also very useful on nativism and racism in the Southern Mines is Johnson, "The Gold She Gathered."

37. On the first foreign miners' tax, see Richard H. Peterson, "The Foreign Miners' Tax of 1850 and Mexicans in California: Exploitation or Expulsion?" *Pacific Historian* 20 (Summer 1976): 265–71.

38. On Native Americans in the Gold Rush, see James J. Rawls, "Gold Diggers: Indian Miners in the California Gold Rush," *California Historical Quarterly* 55 (Spring 1976): 28–42; Albert L. Hurtado, *Indian Survival on the California Frontier* (New Haven: Yale University Press, 1988); and George Harwood Phillips, *Indians and Indian Agents: The Origins of the Reservation System in California, 1849–1852* (Norman: University of Oklahoma Press, 1997), esp. chap. 3.

39. Hurtado, *Indian Survival,* 117. For a breakdown of the Indian population by mining county in 1852, see 111.

40. Louise A. K. S. Clappe, *The Shirley Letters: Being Letters Written in 1851–1852 from the California Mines* (Salt Lake City: Peregrine Smith, 1970), 123.

41. Rohrbough, *Days of Gold,* 152.

42. Ibid.

43. Ibid.

44. Quoted in ibid., 19.

45. Paul, *Mining Frontiers of the Far West,* 26.

46. For descriptions of hard labor in the mines see Paul, *California Gold,* 56: Paul, *Mining Frontiers of the Far West,* 26; Rohrbough, *Days of Gold,* 137–39; and Holliday, *The World Rushed In,* 395–97.

47. Quoted in Holliday, *The World Rushed In,* 360.

48. Paul, *California Gold,* 113–14.

49. Rohrbough, *Days of Gold,* 94.

50. Mann, *After the Gold Rush,* 98.

51. See Rohrbough, *Days of Gold,* 9, 180–81. In her book *A Mine of Her Own: Women Prospectors in the American West, 1850–1950* (Lincoln: University of Nebraska Press, 1997), Sally Zanjani searches out examples of women miners but with a notable lack of success in California. Using manuscript census data, Ralph Mann found that in 1860 only one women in Grass Valley and one in Nevada City described her occupation as "miner," and none did in 1870; *After the Gold Rush,* 244. One of the more recent works on women in the Gold Rush, with a useful bibliography, is JoAnn Levy, *They Saw the Elephant: Women in the California Gold Rush* (Norman: Oklahoma University Press, 1992).

52. Sucheng Chan argues, on the basis of good evidence, that a substantial majority of Chinese women in rural northern counties in 1860 and 1870 were prostitutes; *This Bittersweet Soil,* 389.

53. Mann, *After the Gold Rush,* 108–15, 244.

54. William Swain is the principle subject and writer in Holliday's *The World Rushed In.*

55. Joseph R. Conlin, *Bacon, Beans, and Galantines: Food and Foodways on the Western Mining Frontier* (Las Vegas: University of Nevada Press, 1986), 107. This book contains much information about diet and eating in gold-rush California and on the western mining frontier in general.

56. Paul, *California Gold,* 87. See also Rohrbough, *Days of Gold,* 142–44.

57. Paul, *California Gold,* 72–75, and Mann, *After The Gold Rush,* 15–17.

58. Mann, *After the Gold Rush,* 240. It is possible, however, that residents of boarding-houses were more likely to be undercounted by the census enumerator.

59. Paul, *California Gold,* 317–18.

60. A point stressed by Rohrbough, *Days of Gold,* 182–83, and Mann, *After the Gold Rush,* 191–92.

61. Mark Aldrich, *Safety First: Technology, Labor, and Business in the Building of American Work Safety, 1870–1939* (Baltimore: Johns Hopkins University Press, 1997), 2. See also Alan Derickson, *Workers' Health, Workers' Democracy: The Western Miners' Struggle, 1891–1925* (Ithaca: Cornell University Press, 1988). Not until long after the gold-rush era (1848–1870) did the state and federal government begin to compile records of accidents in the mining industry and other occupations.

62. Mann, *After the Gold Rush*, 227

63. Ibid., 262.

64. See ibid., 212, 266.

65. Paul, *California Gold*, 120.

66. Mann, *After the Gold Rush*, 84–85. The unequal distribution of wealth was not unique to mining towns or counties. In his study of wealth distribution in twenty-six northern California counties, Robert Burchell found some variation but, in general, a very skewed distribution of wealth. Robert A. Burchell, "Opportunity and the Frontier: Wealth-Holding in Twenty-Six Northern California Counties, 1848–1880," *Western Historical Quarterly* 18 (April 1987): 177–96.

67. Mann, *After the Gold Rush*, 106.

68. Ibid., 230.

69. Paul, *California Gold*, 60–64.

70. Ibid., 127.

71. Ibid., 129.

72. Ibid., 164.

73. Ibid., 166.

74. Mann, *After the Gold Rush*, 29.

75. San Francisco capital seems to have been slow and reluctant to invest in the California gold mines until at least the late 1860s. For a discussion of this, see Paul, *California Gold*, 296–302.

76. Rohrbough, *Days of Gold*, 201.

77. Mann, *After the Gold Rush*, 26.

78. Rohrbough, *Days of Gold*, 202.

79. Paul, *California Gold*, 145.

80. Ibid., 143–44.

81. Calculated from the U.S. Bureau of the Census, *Ninth Census of the United States, 1870*, vol. 3, *Statistics of the Wealth and Industry of the United States*, 760. The usually reliable Rodman Paul deprecates the importance of quartz mining in the 1860s and uncharacteristically does not provide good supporting evidence.

82. Paul, *California Gold*, 260.

83. Mann, *After the Gold Rush*, 139–50.

84. References in the secondary literature are very rare. Mann mentions only one instance of a strike in Grass Valley or Nevada City; *After the Gold Rush*, 91. It is, of course, possible that many small strikes were not recorded, or if recorded in such places as newspapers, have not been gleaned by researchers. In his book *California Gold*, Paul claims (p. 324) that in the latter half of the 1850s "there had been many so-called 'strikes.'" But he provides no evidence or citations to support this assertion.

85. Lingenfelter, *The Hardrock Miners;* Mark Wyman, *Hard Rock Epic: Western Miners and the Industrial Revolution, 1860–1910* (Berkeley: University of California Press, 1979); and

Ronald C. Brown, *Hard-Rock Miners: The Intermountain West, 1860–1920* (College Station: Texas A&M University Press, 1979).

86. Mann, *After the Gold Rush,* 86.

87. Lingenfelter provides a good account of this strike and several other subsequent ones in his book *The Hardrock Miners* (pp. 81–103). Mann, *After the Gold Rush* (pp. 183–94) also provides an account of the strike. Mann states that while the strike began in Nevada City "both the strike and the Sinophobia centered in Grass Valley" (p. 183).

88. Mann, *After the Gold Rush,* 142.

89. Lingenfelter, *Hardrock Miners,* 88.

90. See ibid. for a good account. Paul, *California Gold,* also provides useful narratives of some of the major strikes of this period (pp. 325–33).

91. Lingenfelter, *Hardrock Miners,* 100.

92. Ibid., 103.

93. Wyman, *Hard Rock Epic,* 224.

94. Ibid., 224–25.

95. Paul, *Mining Frontiers of the Far West,* 92.

96. Paul, *California Gold,* 333.

5

Environmental Changes before and after the Gold Rush

Raymond F. Dasmann

The celebration of the Gold Rush has been an occasion for fun and games for many Californians—dressing up in pioneer costumes, marching in or cheering for parades, consuming alcohol, and other diversions. There is a nostalgia for an earlier time, one seemingly without the pressure of laws, rules, or community restrictions, when one could do as one pleased and, if lucky, suddenly become wealthy. Indeed, those who flocked to the gold fields were often betting their lives on "getting rich quick," and it is not surprising that a gambling hall was one of the first structures to be built in the new gold towns, usually in combination with a saloon and brothel.

In reading the accounts of those who were there in 1849 and later, most often one seeks in vain for descriptions of the countryside, the natural world, or the wild animal life. There was no obvious concern for the environment. Anything that stood in the way of the gold seeker was pushed aside or destroyed, whether a grizzly bear or a mountain. Ruthless exploitation with no thought for tomorrow was the basis for the way of life in gold-rush times.

The start of the Gold Rush was obviously related to the 1848 discovery of gold in the gravels of the American River near Sutter's Fort in what is now the Sacramento metropolitan area. The heavy influx of people began in 1849, but when did it end? In terms of population movement, it has really never ended, since the tens of thousands who came in 1849 hardly compare to the half-million or more who arrived in each of some recent years. In terms of environmental damage, it has not ended at all.

It is tempting to blame the Gold Rush for starting the process of severe environmental damage in California, in what had previously been a place where nature thrived, little disturbed by humans. Unfortunately this simplistic view would not be correct. California in 1849 had already experienced serious environmental changes resulting from human activity. Extensive open-range livestock grazing introduced by

Powerful jets of water play across a scene of astounding environmental destruction at the Malakoff Diggings, Nevada County, in a picture by the famed California photographer Carleton Watkins. The big hydraulic-mining monitors began their work here in September 1870 with water carried by a system of ditches and flumes stretching forty-seven miles into the mountains and constructed at a cost of three-quarters of a million dollars. By the time operations ceased in the 1880s, the North Bloomfield Gravel Mining Company had carved out a canyon more than a mile long and six hundred feet deep in places. *Courtesy California State Library.*

Spaniards and Mexicans had resulted in modification of native grasslands, from a long-established and highly productive perennial bunchgrass community to one dominated by introduced (exotic) annual grasses of Mediterranean origin. Russian, Aleut, and American poachers had also hunted populations of sea otters and other marine mammals to near extinction. One could say there had been a cattle rush starting in the late eighteenth century with the coming of Spanish settlers and a fur rush starting in the late eighteenth and early nineteenth century, well before the more well-known Gold Rush. Certainly the Gold Rush directly caused even more severe damage to streams, rivers, their watersheds, and flood plains, and undoubtedly it accelerated the damage to grasslands, wildlife, forests, and other natural communities. But the damaging processes were already in place and those states that experienced no Gold Rush, such as Oregon, were to experience similar changes, although at a slower rate.

Still there is little doubt that, in terms of natural balances, California before the

Gold Rush was a more idyllic place than it was to be after that event. Perhaps the greatest indicator of the health of the environment was the abundance and diversity of wildlife, since wild animals do not thrive without a healthy habitat. The habitat for California wildlife was all of the forests and woodlands, prairies and marshlands, mountains and valleys, and rivers and seashores of the state.

WILDLIFE CHANGES

In the pyramid of life that comprised the natural world of California there is little doubt that the large predators were at the top. For them to thrive, there must be an abundance of prey, and for these to thrive, there must be an abundance of the plant foods that sustain them. Thus if you see an area where the predators seem fat and happy, you can suspect that all is well with the total environment. In California when the Spanish settlers first arrived in 1769, there was certainly an abundance of what was then the top predator on land, the grizzly bear.

It would be wrong to say that the grizzly was a bad-tempered animal. At times it could be quite cheerful and content in its bearish way. But it was easily and unpredictably offended. Then, it would fly into a rage and might tear the offender apart. The Indians had deep respect for the large bears and usually managed to coexist with them peacefully. So, too, did James "Grizzly" Adams, a colorful and loquacious gold-rush era hunter who roamed the wild country of California with his two tamed grizzlies, raised from cubs and taught to tolerate humans. His accounts, although not always trustworthy, confirm the relative abundance of bears throughout California. Adams also reported on the presence of true wolves, along with the ever-abundant coyote. On one occasion he encountered a female jaguar, with a cub, in the Tehachapi Mountains.[1]

All early accounts of conditions in California before European hunting began to seriously impinge on the wildlife and wild country indicate that California Indians and wild animals lived in relative harmony. It was not that Indians did not hunt. They did, and indeed depended on deer, elk, pronghorn, and other species for part of their food supply. But they did not kill for profit and had deep respect for the animals on which they depended. In consequence, animals that are now wild and wary, such as mountain lions and black bears, were then relatively tame and not quick to flee from human presence. A view of this relationship was provided by pioneer Hale Tharp, as told by Walter Fry and Toby Whyte:

> There were about 2,000 Indians then living along the Kaweah River above where Lemon Cove now stands. . . . The Indians told me that I was the first white man that had ever come to their country. Few of them had ever seen a white man prior to my arrival.

The famed hunter James Capen Adams and his pet grizzly Ben Franklin, as portrayed by Charles Nahl. Few Californians maintained Adams's complex and imaginative relationship with bears, preferring simply to slaughter them for food or sport. "The California Grizzly," remarked a writer for *Hutchings' California Magazine* in 1858, "is exceedingly ferocious, and powerful; and unless treated to a deadly bullet, it is a hard customer to manage in an encounter." From Theodore H. Hittell, *The Adventures of James Capen Adams, Mountaineer and Grizzly Bear Hunter of California* (1860). *California Historical Society, FN-30962.*

There was an abundance of game. Deer were everywhere, with lots of bear along the rivers, and occasionally a grizzly bear. Lions, wolves, and foxes were plentiful.

During the summer of 1858, accompanied by two Indians, I made my first trip into the Giant Forest. When we arrived at Log Meadow there were a great many deer and a few bear in the meadow, and the animals paid little attention to us. The deer came around our camp, and some of the bears sat upright in order to get a good look at us. I shot a small buck for camp meat. The shot did not seem to frighten the other deer or any of the bears.[2]

More striking was the testimony of a Chumash elder, Grandfather Semu Huaute, who refers to a wilderness north of Santa Barbara: "You know, daughter, before the Spaniards came to California, the bears and us used to gather berries together. The bears were real friendly. We got along real well. We could talk to each other, and we had a good understanding. When the Spaniards came, they found it pretty easy to shoot the bears. After that the bears wouldn't go berrying with us any more."[3]

The Spaniards hunted bears and, although the grizzly population increased greatly in the countryside because of the new food supply—Spanish cattle—they succeeded in controlling the bears' numbers somewhat around the missions and pueblos. But it was the dispersion of people into the wild country in the gold-rush days, first as prospectors, then as miners, finally as settlers, that led to the massive depletion of wildlife. Of course the grizzly, who challenged people and often attacked, was one of the first to go. One indicative example was Humboldt County, where, according to the settlers, grizzlies were obnoxiously abundant. Early pioneer Calvin Kinman had counted forty grizzlies from one high hill in the Mattole country, but probably the last bear to live in the region was killed in 1868. In Santa Cruz County, grizzlies were also common until 1886, when the last one was reported dead. In the Sierra, they lasted longer, but the last grizzly seen, but not killed, was in Sequoia National Park in 1925.[4]

The fate of the grizzly and other animals illustrates the Gold Rush's adverse effects on the land animals of California and their habitats. However, offshore the same depletion and near extermination of marine mammals occurred. There, the decimation began even before the advent of mining, without the influence of tens of thousands of gold seekers. Two aquatic animals—the sea otter and the beaver—were the targets of the fur rush beginning more than a century before the Gold Rush. The sea otter was abundant along the California coast, particularly around San Francisco and Monterey bays and the Channel Islands. Perhaps 300,000 or more swam in the offshore waters. Unfortunately for the otters, they had a dense, warm brown coat with a silvered frosting of guard hairs. This came to be regarded as highly desirable among fur wearers in Moscow, Peking (Beijing), and elsewhere among the world's elite.

The trouble started in 1740, when the Russian government sent Vitus Bering to explore the northern Pacific toward Alaska. In the Aleutian Islands, the native Aleuts brought him large numbers of otter skins, which on the return of his expedition proved to be highly popular in Russia and China, and by the late 1700s, Russian ships were hunting the animal along the California coast.[5] The Spanish exploitation of sea otters, probably using Chumash hunters, began before 1785, when the first government regulations on the trade were issued. Between 1786 and 1790 alone, nearly 10,000 skins were exported from Mexico to Asia via the Manila galleons. The Russians, partly to improve their access to the fur trade, established bases at Fort Ross in 1812 and in the Farallon Islands, from which they went forth with their Aleut hunters to kill sea otters. One hunting party in San Francisco Bay in 1811 massacred 1,200 otters. The French also played a minor role; in 1786 the expedition of Jean-François de Galaup, Comte de La Pérouse obtained 1,000 skins, which they sold in China for $10,000. The price went up from $10 to $60 a skin by the 1790s. Americans became involved in the early 1800s and were still active by gold-rush times. The best known American hunter, George Nidever, was particularly busy in the Channel Islands and offshore in Baja California from 1834 to 1855.[6] By gold-rush times the otters were becoming scarce, and prospecting held a greater allure for the hunters. Nevertheless, the otter population had been reduced to perhaps thirty-two survivors by the time it was given full protection in 1911.

It was not only sea otters that suffered from this marine carnage. The Alaska fur seal was greatly reduced; and the Guadalupe fur seal was pushed to near extinction and, along with the elephant seal, survived only on Guadalupe Island in Baja California. As I wrote in an earlier work,

> Few people realize even today, with the current interest in whales, how many kinds of sea mammals occur in California waters. There are twenty-six species of cetaceans, the whales and dolphins, seven species of seals and sea lions, and one sea-going otter. . . . Just as great herds of elk and antelope [pronghorn] moved across the plains of the Central Valley, in pre-European days, so also did great herds of sea mammals travel above the plains of the continental shelf, moving up the slopes of the islands and occasionally down into the depths of the submarine canyons. The abundance and variety of these sea mammals were greater than those of their terrestrial counterparts.[7]

The marine mammals under greatest hunting pressure were those that came upon the shore to rest or breed, but even the truly marine species did not escape. By the early 1800s, whaling ships from New England were in California waters chasing after right whales and sperm whales. Shore-based whaling started in 1851 and concentrated on gray and humpback whales. But all of the great whales were under attack, and with most, numbers were quickly reduced to the point of endangering the survival of the species.

The mammal that contributed more than its share to the fur rush was not a marine or coastal-waters species but an inhabitant of fresh water—the golden beaver. This large rodent reached its greatest abundance, not in the forests of the Sierra or the coast, but in the Central Valley and particularly the marshlands where the Sacramento and San Joaquin rivers came together to flow into the San Francisco Bay. Unlike its relatives of the Great Lakes forests and Rocky Mountains, the golden beaver did not usually build large dams or lodges that protruded above the water surfaces. Usually, beaver dens were dug into the river banks and the entrances were below the water line. Since beaver are mostly active at night, an abundance of beaver in a river may not be noticeable.

Beaver trappers reached California in 1826, when a party led by Peter Skene Ogden of the Hudson's Bay Company came south from Fort Vancouver in Canada in the same year that the American trappers Jedediah Smith and James O. Pattie led parties from their bases near the Great Salt Lake and Santa Fe. Skene and Smith were particularly successful and took thousands of beaver between 1826 and 1828. They were to be followed by enough others to greatly reduce beaver numbers before the Gold Rush, when most hunters gave up trapping in the search for what was hoped to be an easier source of wealth, but eventually other fur bearers suffered the beaver's fate. According to Joseph Grinnell and his coauthors, "After the first period of rapid depletion, the second half of the nineteenth century brought an extension of trapping to the remaining and less conspicuous fur bearers in California. Thus the exhaustion of this resource [beaver] was extended to include nearly all the kinds of fur animals."[8]

The grasslands and marshlands of California were home to abundant tule elk when the first Europeans arrived. Dale McCullough of the University of California, Berkeley, has done the most complete study of these animals and has estimated their aboriginal numbers at 500,000.[9] Richard Henry Dana in his *Two Years Before the Mast* described "hundreds and hundreds" of these animals on the Marin headlands, which he watched when his sailing ship anchored in San Francisco Bay in 1835.[10] Missionary-explorer Pedro Font noted the abundance of elk in the San Francisco peninsula and east bay in 1775 and 1776.[11] Early American settler William Heath Davis reported seeing as many as three thousand elk "that swam from Mare Island to Vallejo and back," and John Bidwell wrote of elk "by the thousand" in the Napa and Santa Clara valleys in 1841.[12] It was the tule marshes and grasslands of the Central Valley, however, that supported the greatest numbers of elk, and it was there that they made their last stand.

The Gold Rush touched off the slaughter of elk because of the demand for meat in the burgeoning mining camps, towns, and cities, coupled with a shortage of beef or mutton. For a time, market-hunting of elk, deer, and pronghorn, along with waterfowl and other game, became a lucrative livelihood for those who preferred shoot-

Egg pickers gather the harvest on one of the Farallon Islands, some thirty miles off the Golden Gate, in 1880. The wild rush west of thousands of gold seekers created an enormous demand in California not only for game, but also for fish and fowl and eggs. Between 1850 and 1856 the Farallone Egg Company alone brought over three million eggs—chiefly those of the common murre—to the San Francisco markets. *California Historical Society, FN-30975.*

ing to grubbing for gold. While there is little doubt that market-hunting depleted elk populations, it was the spread of agriculture, and the corresponding destruction of elk habitat, that really led to their near extinction. With agricultural demands came the drainage of the tule marshes, the canalization of rivers, and the fencing of farmlands. Meanwhile, great herds of domestic cattle, sheep, horses, and other livestock competed with elk for the forage produced on lands not suited to crops. In the words of T. S. Van Dyke,

> As the swamps began to be drained and the cover burned off, and roads made through the drying ground, it was again the same old story of the white man. By 1875 the antelope were a curiosity on the great plains, where so many thousands lately glimmered through the dancing heat, while the elk were almost as rare in the great tule swamps

that so lately seemed inaccessible. By 1885 only one band was left, and that was on the immense (half-million acre) ranch of Miller and Lux in the upper part of the valley, some twenty miles from Bakersfield.[13]

Van Dyke visited the last herd in 1895 and found that only twenty-eight animals had survived despite the protection provided by Henry Miller. From these and perhaps only one other pair of elk reported by Game Warden A. C. Tibbets in 1895, the present population of tule elk, now numbering over two thousand, descended, but genetic diversity has been lost.

The near extermination of elk was matched by that of the pronghorn. The antelope-like grazers roamed the sea coast from Monterey to the Los Angeles basin, and the interior from the upper limits of the Sacramento Valley south into Baja California and east into the Great Basin and the Mojave Desert. But the pronghorn were animals of the grasslands, not adapted to forest, chaparral, or tule marshes. Thus, unlike the elk or black-tailed deer, they had no place to hide from the hunters. Their keen eyesight and fast running speed were no match for firearms, and they were rapidly wiped out from their main center in the Central Valley, the coastal areas, the desert fringes. Only in the northeastern corner of the state, in the sagebrush plains, did pronghorn survive. One could blame their decline on gold-rush mining, and it was, no doubt, a contributing factor, but it was the resultant lack of government protection and popular support for conservation, combined with the spread of pastoralism and agriculture, that were the main causes.

GRASSLAND CHANGES

Radical changes in California's grasslands began to take place more than seventy years before the Gold Rush. With the coming of the Spanish missionaries in 1769, new elements were added to California's broad spectrum of animal life: cattle, sheep, goats, horses, and donkeys, as well as domestic fowl. These exerted a heavier pressure on the grasslands and oak savannahs of the state, which were already supporting, presumably at a carrying capacity level, great herds of elk, pronghorn, deer, and bighorn sheep. Even without any other element of change, this increased pressure of grazing alone would have changed the nature of the grasslands in favor of those species less preferred by, and of lower nutritional value for, domestic livestock. At the height of the mission period in the early decades of the nineteenth century, some 400,000 cattle and 300,000 sheep were added to the half-million elk and no doubt greater numbers of pronghorn and deer in the grasslands of the state.[14] Many wild herds of cattle and horses had strayed from missions and ranchos into the San Joaquin Valley, but most of the managed herds were in the coastal mountains and valleys from San Diego to Sonoma. Added to this pressure on the native grasses was the sometimes devastating effect of California's climatic cycles of flood and drought years, as well as the cessation of grassland-burning by Native Americans.

Perhaps of even greater consequence was the Spaniards' introduction of foreign species of grasses and forbs. These exotic species of Mediterranean origin were well adapted to California's climate, and equally important, to heavy grazing pressure. They were, for the most part, annuals, able to ride out drought in seed form and germinate when rains finally came.[15]

Before the Gold Rush, introduced species of grasses were certainly well established in the more southern areas, but probably not as much in those northern parts of the state with higher rainfall and less pressure from introduced livestock. In 1841 John Bidwell traveled through the Central Valley in the spring. He wrote of the clear atmosphere, the plains brilliant with flowers, the luxuriant herbage. Historian Rockwell Hunt wrote that "When Bidwell entered California in 1841, and for several years thereafter, wild game abounded and in such variety that even the most moderate and restrained description, were it not already familiar everywhere, would excite the absolute incredulity of the critical listener."[16] Similarly, in the spring of 1844, John Charles Frémont traveled through the San Joaquin Valley to Walker's Pass in the southern Sierra. He described

> a level region covered with grass with an occasional grove of live oaks to lend variety. There were fields of blue lupine, several feet in height, which interspersed with the profusion of golden poppies, added to the pleasure of the travelers. They saw several bands of elk and antelope . . . also bands of wild horses were numerous, particularly on the west side of the river.[17]

However, cattle herds were built up in the 1850s to meet the demands of an increasing gold-rush population, with a peak of over three million head reached in 1862. Grazing pressure intensified and became more widespread, only to face the floods of 1862 and severe drought of 1862–1864. Cattle numbers crashed to a low of a half-million by 1870. Sheep were more adaptable than cattle, and their numbers increased to 5.5 million by 1875. With sheep came heavy pressure on wet high mountain ranges, to which they were driven when grazing and summer drought had depleted lower-elevation ranges. John Muir, who worked as a sheepherder in the late 1860s, recorded the devastation of the meadows: "Sheep, like people are ungovernable when hungry . . . almost every leaf that these hoofed locusts can reach within a radius of a mile or two from camp has been devoured. Even bushes are stripped bare."[18] Scientist William Brewer kept a journal, and during the great drought he also described a similar scene on May 30, 1864:

> We came onto San Luis de Gonzaga Ranch, at the eastern end of the pass. Our road lay over the mountains. They are perfectly dry and barren, no grass—here and there a

gaunt cow is seen, but what she gets to eat is very mysterious. All around the house it looks desolate. Where there were green pastures when we camped two years ago, now all is dry, dusty bare ground. Three hundred cattle have died by the miserable water hole back of the house, where we get water to drink, and their stench pollutes the air.

The ranch contains eleven square leagues, or over seventy six square miles. In its better days it had ten thousand head of cattle, besides the horses needed to manage them. Later it became a sheep ranch, and two years ago, when we camped here, it fed sixteen thousand sheep besides some few thousand cattle. Now, owing to the drought, there is no feed for cattle, and not over one thousand sheep, if that, can be kept through the summer.[19]

Heavy grazing, drought, and fire suppression in the 1850s and later took their toll on the rangelands, with the result that annual grasses of Mediterranean origin now dominate in California, and relatively few sites are still covered by native perennial bunchgrasses.

FOREST CHANGES

California's forests were not subject to heavy pressure, except locally, until relatively recently. In Spanish and Mexican times there was only a limited demand for wood for building. The Gold Rush brought its influx of people and a demand for housing. Redwood forests were cut down in the hills surrounding the San Francisco Bay and southward in the Santa Cruz Mountains. Around the gold camps and the new towns, forests soon disappeared. Historian Ralph Mann has written of this for the Grass Valley and Nevada City mining towns:

The towns had been located among hills once laden with the most magnificent forests imaginable but now the ridge between the towns, like the hills for miles around, was denuded. The mines and mills required vast amounts of fuel and lumber, and by the late 1860s the great American plan of cutting down every tree was beginning to cause concern. Timber lands had been pre-empted, wood had to be hauled great distances, and prices were high.[20]

Following on the Gold Rush, the Comstock silver mines in Nevada caused removal of the pine forests on the Sierra east of Lake Tahoe. Away from the Mother Lode country, the ancient sequoia were cut down, apparently just because they were there, in the Converse Basin of what was to be Sequoia-Kings Canyon National Park. They were left lying on the ground.[21]

The first mechanical sawmill to be built in Hispanic California was in the Santa Cruz Mountains in 1822, but by that time the Russians at Fort Ross may have been exporting redwood lumber to Hawaii and elsewhere. The practice was well established by 1827, when Fort Ross was visited by the French explorer Duhaut-Cilly. By the Gold Rush, lumber was shipped in large quantities from Eureka to San

In 1856, when the pioneer San Francisco lithographers Charles Kuchel and Emil Dresel drew the town of Downieville on stone, the surrounding hills had been stripped nearly bare of trees. Established in 1849 on a fork of the Yuba River, the camp grew rapidly, its vigorous mining economy creating a huge need for lumber and fuel. Today, a century and a half later, Downieville is one of the most picturesque of the old mining communities, and grand forests once again cover the rugged slopes. *California Historical Society, FN-16040.*

Francisco, resulting in the inevitable removal of the old-growth forests surrounding Humboldt Bay. All of these efforts had devastating local effects, but at least some forest lands, unlike the grasslands, were to receive federal protection, starting with Yosemite Valley in 1864, to be followed after 1890 by the establishment of national forests and national and state parks throughout the wooded areas of the state.[22]

HYDRAULIC MINING

Today, motorists driving along the Tyler Foote Crossing Road off Highway 49 on San Juan Ridge in the Sierra foothills will encounter some strange scenery. Mostly, they will drive through second-growth ponderosa pine forest, much of which is heavily invaded by manzanita or Scotch broom. Settlement is sparse, but there are enough houses, old and new, to indicate the area is inhabited. It is a long way from wilderness, but semi-wild forest vistas are common. Occasionally bears pass through, and coyotes sing at night. Mountain lions are present, usually unseen, along with numerous bobcats, foxes, raccoons, and skunks. Deer do not abound, but there are quite a few. Human society there is somewhat two-layered, the old timers (before 1960) and the various immigrants of the 1960s and 1970s—call them hippies if you will, although most dislike the appellation. Then there are some newcomers, long-distance computer-commuters from Sacramento and points west who are usually well-heeled and build expensive houses. Visitors to the district are shocked to suddenly encounter a moonlike landscape, where the land has been turned upside down and its leached underpinnings revealed. Hills of washed gravel appear stark white in contrast to the red soils of the ponderosa forest. Between some of the gravel ridges there are ponds or marshy areas. At first look the land appears totally barren, but then you notice a few dwarfed pine trees and some green growth in the marshes. It is not, after all, moonlike, but clearly a desert where none should be.

These "diggins," as they are called, extend on up the course of Shady Creek and Tyler Foote to the Malakoff Diggins State Park, where they have been preserved as a historical landmark. They are part of the heritage from the gold seekers of the "days of '49"—a heritage of ruined land. Technically, they were not diggings. Nobody shoveled them. Instead, they date to the hydraulic mining period after 1860, when miners directed powerful jets of water to wash hillsides away and into sluices where the heavy gold could be separated. All the lighter particles, from sand to clay, along with larger rocks and wood, were washed downstream to eventually clog the rivers and help cause the major Sacramento River flooding of the 1860s and later. When the damage landed almost on the steps of the State Capitol, the legislature still took no effective action to outlaw hydraulic mining. Those downstream from the Sierra foothills were left with the residue.

Charles Nordhoff, in his book *California . . . for Travellers and Settlers*, published in 1873, watched the process of hydraulic mining and described it as follows:

Water brought from a hundred or a hundred and fifty miles away and from a considerable height is fed from reservoirs through eight, ten or twelve inch iron pipes through . . . a nozzle, five or six inches in diameter, is thus forced against the side of a hill one or two or three hundred feet high. The stream when it leaves the pipe has such force that it would cut a man in two if it should hit him. Two or three and sometimes even six such streams play against the bottom of a hill, and earth and stones, often of great size, are washed away until at last an immense slice of the hill itself gives way and tumbles down.

At Smartsville, Timbuctoo and Roses Bar (near Marysville) I suppose they wash away into the sluices half a dozen acres a day, from fifty to two hundred feet deep, and in the muddy torrent which rushes down at railroad speed through the channels prepared for it, you may see large rocks helplessly rolling along . . . the gold is saved in long sluice boxes, through which the earth and water are run, and in the bottom of which gold is caught by quicksilver. . . .

But, in order to run off this enormous mass of earth and gravel, a rapid fall must be got into some deep valley or river. . . . At Smartsville, for instance, the bed which contains the gold lies above the present Yuba River, but a considerable hill, perhaps two hundred and fifty feet high, lies between the two, and through this hill each company must drive a tunnel before it can get an outfall for its washings.

. . . of course the acres washed away must go somewhere, and they are filling up the Yuba River. This was once, I am told by old residents, a swift and clear mountain torrent; it is now a turbid and not rapid stream, whose bed has been raised by the washings of the miners not less than fifty feet above its level in 1849. It once contained trout, but now I imagine a catfish would die in it.

. . . as you journey . . . toward the Yosemite, after you leave Murphy's every foot almost of the soil, for mile after mile, has been at some time turned over by the gold seekers. River beds have been laid bare and the adjoining bottoms searched. The earth all the way to the foothills was removed, and as you near Columbia you see immense fields made up of nothing but rocks and boulders sticking their barren, water worn heads into the landscape, with deep pits between them.[23]

If hydraulic mining had not been stopped, the gold hunters might well have washed all the soil and loose rock from the Sierra into the Central Valley. As it was, enough debris was washed down the rivers to cause serious damage. The especially heavy rains of 1861–62 brought the first severe flooding induced by hydraulic mining to the Sacramento Valley, as the once-clear streams dumped their loads of silt and debris (slickens). A vast lake covered the southern Sacramento Valley, including the grounds of the State Capitol. William Brewer, who was in California during the flood and the following drought, wrote in January 1862 that "The Central Valley of the state is under water—the Sacramento and San Joaquin valleys—a region 250 to 300 miles long and an average of at least twenty miles wide." In September he wrote from the area of Red Bluff:

Although the channel of the Sacramento is insufficient to carry off all the water of wet winters, yet it is rapidly filling up, each year increasing the difficulty. Previous to 1848 the river was noted for the purity of its water, flowing from the mountains as clear as crystal; but, since the discovery of gold, the "washings" render it as muddy as the Ohio in spring flood—in fact it is perfectly "riley," discoloring even of the waters of the

K Street in Sacramento during the great flood of January 1862. The unprecedented rains that fell from the skies beginning late the previous year overwhelmed river channels choked with mining debris and turned the Central Valley into an inland sea. The city of Sacramento responded by strengthening its levees and raising its streets above the high water mark, as much as ten feet in some instances. *Courtesy California State Library.*

great bay into which it empties. . . . Last winter's floods alone are supposed to have raised the bed of the river at Sacramento six or seven feet at least.[24]

Despite the complaints of valley landholders, hydraulic mining continued. In 1875, Marysville was virtually destroyed by Yuba River flooding, and great damage was wrought by the Bear and Feather rivers. Still, the political influence of the mining companies was so great that it took many lawsuits and sessions of the state legislature and Congress before any action was taken, and even then early regulations were ineffectual. Finally, in 1884 the U.S. Circuit Court in San Francisco granted a perpetual injunction against hydraulic mining. Although many small miners continued to fight in Congress, the influence of farmers in the valley had grown greater than that of miners in the hills.[25]

Along Tyler Foote Crossing Road and Highway 49, towns like North Columbia and North San Juan, which thrived to serve the miners, faded away. The population of North San Juan dwindled from 10,000 to a few hundred. One would think that with such a monument to greed as the "diggins," California would have learned a lesson. But mining companies never give up, and still propose to re-enter the ruined lands to scrape up any gold that was missed in the nineteenth century. The setback experienced by the miners in the 1884 court decision was more than compensated by the Mining Act of 1872, which gave miners essentially carte blanche to mine where they pleased on public lands. Despite many efforts to repeal this law, it remains on the books and affects California today.

The Gold Rush can be held responsible for the damage done by mining, even if much of it took place well after the original rush, after many of the Forty-niners had made their slow, crestfallen way home, without gold. It was the Gold Rush that set off the destructive, furious search for the yellow metal that later brought the moving of mountains and filling of valleys.

EVALUATION

There is enough damage to be charged to the Gold Rush without adding to it environmental changes that preceded it or would have gone on in its absence. Undoubtedly the greatest harm resulted from hydraulic mining, but mostly because the damage persisted far beyond the mining period. Beyond that, the Gold Rush had, at worst, an accelerating effect on activities that would have occurred, but at a slower pace, such as grazing, draining of wetlands, logging, and hunting. The changes in grasslands that were still localized in 1849 became much more widespread and severe because of rapidly growing numbers of people and much greater demand for meat, milk, wool, hides, and other livestock products. Some of these changes were further accelerated by the recurrent droughts that were a normal part of California's climate. Areas visited by William Brewer in 1861 and noted as rich pastures were devastated and barren when revisited in 1864 when the severe drought was in progress. These disturbed areas were quickly colonized by the exotic, aggressive annuals brought in during Spanish colonization.

The increase in population started by the Gold Rush also stimulated an increased demand for housing, which in turn caused stepped-up logging in the more accessible forest stands. But the towns and cities would have grown eventually without the Gold Rush, and the demand for wood also. It is dubious that government intervention and control during a slower-paced period of growth would have been much help in saving the old-growth forests, when such regulations are still relatively ineffective today.

Without the Gold Rush, the spread of agriculture would have happened in any event, and with it, the drainage and clearing of tule marshes, the construction of irrigation canals, and the damming of rivers, and with that the loss of waterfowl and fish habitat. The construction of the transcontinental railroads had more effect by far on the demand for farm products than did the Gold Rush. The Homestead Act and other government policies intended to encourage settlement brought the movement of people into every habitable area of the state by the end of the century.

The devastation of wildlife began long before the Gold Rush, and it was more the increase in population and spread of people into the far reaches of California after the Gold Rush that brought the demise of the grizzly, jaguar, and wolf and the near extermination of elk, pronghorn, condors, and other species. But in reach of the mining camps and towns, wildlife had small chance for survival.

There was a "window of opportunity" for more balanced resource usage between the breakdown of Spanish/Mexican control and the creation of the new state of California. The Gold Rush easily closed that window and gained for the miners unlimited license to create environmental havoc. It is fortunate that the supply of accessible gold was limited and not more widely distributed throughout the state, or California would be known for its barren diggings instead of its mountain forests and golden hills.

NOTES

1. Theodore H. Hittell, *The Adventures of James Capen Adams* (New York: Charles Scribner, 1911). "Grizzly" Adams roamed around California in gold-rush times. This volume is based on interviews with Hittell. Although Adams was known for tall tales, his accounts of wildlife have most often proved reliable.

2. Walter Fry and Toby Whyte, *Big Trees* (Stanford: Stanford University Press, 1930), 10–11, 17–23. Fry and Whyte wrote of the experiences of Hale Tharp, who was the first European encountered by the Potwisha Indians along the Kaweah River. He established a ranch in the Three Rivers area and was one of the first to visit the "Big Tree" (*Sequoiadendron giganteum*) forests in what is now Sequoia-Kings Canyon National Park.

3. Joan Halifax, *The Fruitful Darkness* (San Francisco: Harper San Francisco, 1993), 97–98. Semu Huaute's description was told to Joan Halifax.

4. Joseph Grinnell, J. S. Dixon, and J. M. Linsdale, *Fur Bearing Mammals of California* (Berkeley: University of California Press, 1937), 68–94. Although the two volumes of this work are primarily a natural history and biological account of the larger mammals sought by

fur traders, they are also a source of historical information on the distribution, abundance, and behavior of the larger species of furbearers.

5. Grinnell et al., *Fur Bearing Mammals*, 5–10.

6. W. H. Ellison, *The Life and Adventures of George Nidever* (Berkeley: University of California Press, 1936).

7. Raymond F. Dasmann, *California's Changing Environment* (San Francisco: Boyd and Fraser, 1981), 15.

8. Grinnell et al., *Fur Bearing Mammals*, 10.

9. Dale R. McCullough, *The Tule Elk, Its History, Behavior and Ecology*, University of California Publications in Zoology, vol. 88 (Berkeley: University of California Press, 1969), 17–27.

10. Richard H. Dana, Jr., *Two Years Before the Mast* (New York: Harper and Bros., 1840; New York: Doubleday, 1949), 76.

11. Herbert Eugene Bolton, *Font's Complete Diary: A Chronicle of the Founding of San Francisco* (Berkeley: University of California Press, 1933), 361, 382; Bolton translates Father Pedro Font's *Diary of an Expedition to Monterey by Way of the Colorado River, 1775–1776*.

12. Rockwell D. Hunt, *John Bidwell, Prince of California Pioneers* (Caldwell, Idaho: Caxton Printers, 1942), 76.

13. T. S. Van Dyke, "The Deer and Elk of the Pacific Coast," in Theodore Roosevelt et al., *The Deer Family* (New York: Macmillan, 1902).

14. Lee T. Burcham, *California Rangeland* (Sacramento: California Division of Forestry, 1957).

15. George W. Hendry, "The Adobe Brick as an Historical Source," *Agricultural History* 4 (July 1931): 110–22.

16. Hunt, *John Bidwell*, 76.

17. Herbert Bashford and Harr Wagner, *A Man Unafraid, The Story of John Charles Fremont* (San Francisco: Harr Wagner Publishers, 1977), 132–33.

18. John Muir, *My First Summer in the Sierra* (Boston: Houghton Mifflin, 1911), 54–55.

19. William H. Brewer, *Up and Down California in 1860–1864* (Berkeley: University of California Press, 1974), 508.

20. Ralph Mann, *After the Gold Rush: Society in Grass Valley and Nevada City, California, 1849–1870* (Stanford: Stanford University Press, 1982), 137.

21. Fry and Whyte, *Big Trees*, 18–23.

22. C. Raymond Clar, *California Government and Forestry* (Sacramento: California Division of Forestry, 1959), 8, 16, 30, 64.

23. Charles Nordhoff, *California . . . for Travellers and Settlers* (Berkeley: Ten Speed Press, Centennial Printing, 1873–1973), 95, 100–102.

24. Brewer, *Up and Down California*, 243.

25. Ralph J. Roske, *Everyman's Eden: A History of California* (New York: Macmillan, 1968), 410–12.

6

*"I am resolved not to interfere,
but permit all to work freely"*

The Gold Rush and American Resource Law

Donald J. Pisani

The California Gold Rush profoundly influenced the evolution of property law in the American West. In theory, Congress held the public domain in trust for the benefit of all citizens of the United States. In practice, the public lands bought or taken from Indians or other nations now belonged to those Euro-Americans with sufficient wit, energy, zeal, and capital to exploit them. California was the first state admitted to the Union that contained large deposits of precious metals, and its experience set an important precedent: mining on the public domain would be open to all. The national government imposed neither charges nor regulations on the Argonauts who swarmed into California during the late 1840s and 1850s. The miners were trespassers on government land, yet *they* decided who would be granted access to the gold and under what conditions. They also decided who would be allowed to use the water needed to work the mineral claims, laying the foundation for the legal doctrine of "prior appropriation," which eventually spread to agriculture with enormous implications for the history of the arid and semi-arid American West.

MINING AND AMERICAN RESOURCE LAW
BEFORE THE GOLD RUSH

In the United States, mineral law grew out of the same assumptions and values that shaped land law. In medieval Europe, land ownership imposed a set of obligations and relationships that defined and ordered society. With the Enlightenment, theories of the English philosopher John Locke, among others, freed property from class and state, making it the bedrock of individual freedom and autonomy. In the second of Locke's *Two Treatises on Government* (1690), property became a God-

123

Miners with Rocker and Blue Shirts, a handsome and striking hand-tinted daguerreotype
made about 1852, probably by George H. Johnson. In theory the federal government held
the public domain in trust for all citizens of the republic. But in practice the Argonauts
seized it for their own enrichment, controlling its use through a self-administered system
of mining codes that prevailed far in advance of any constitutionally authorized body of
laws. *Collection of W. Bruce Lundberg.*

given, transcendent natural right that preceded human society and the social contract; it was no longer the gift of kings, queens, nobles, or even Parliament. The concept of property derived from a set of interlocking assumptions: God had given the
earth to human beings in common, but had created it for the rational and industrious, not for the slothful and impecunious. Human beings had a right to life or self-
preservation, which, in turn, dictated the right to a subsistence. To make the earth
useful, there had to be a method of appropriation. Since human beings "owned"
themselves, by extension they also had a right to their own labor. Therefore, the primary value of land derived from the labor that went into fencing, plowing, planting,
or draining it. Property was created only when human beings produced something
from the raw materials God had provided.[1]

In the United States of the late eighteenth and nineteenth centuries, law, politics, economics, and anthropology reinforced Lockean thinking. In his *Commentaries*, published in the United States in 1772, the English jurist William Blackstone noted that "so great is the regard of the law for private property, that it will not authorize the least violation of it; no not even for the general good of the whole community."[2] Adam Smith bolstered Lockean thought by emphasizing the virtue and wisdom of rational self-interest. He also anticipated Frederick Jackson Turner's frontier thesis by arguing that human societies evolved through distinct stages that corresponded to modes of subsistence: hunting, grazing, agriculture, and, ultimately, commerce. Later, the marriage between anthropology and Social Darwinism added a new element to the American concept of property. Most anthropologists regarded property held in common, or by the state, as more "primitive" than individual rights—which were widely assumed to be more efficient and less wasteful. The monopolization of natural resources by private corporations or the state stifled economic opportunity, undermined civic virtue, and promoted the growth of bureaucracies that threatened liberty.

Those who settled on the public lands of the United States carried Lockean ideas to the vast frontier of the American West. Usually ignoring all prior Indian land use and property rights, the first Euro-Americans to enter a region assumed a paramount right defined by chronological priority and continuous, "beneficial" use. Then, as now, priority was used to ration scarce items. Yet the public domain was so large that it simultaneously encouraged monopoly as well as equal access. "There was room enough for all," the historian Ernest Osgood wrote decades ago, "and when a cattleman rode up some likely valley or across some well-grassed divide and found cattle thereon, he looked elsewhere for range." In eastern Montana and central Wyoming, cattlemen even advertised their claims in newspapers. "I, the undersigned," one announcement read, "do hereby notify the public that I claim the valley, branching off the Glendive Creek, four miles east of Allard, and extending to its source on the South side of the Northern Pacific Railroad as a stock range.—Charles S. Johnson." In theory, only Congress could dispose of the "open range," but many territories and states enacted laws upholding the exclusive usufructuary rights (to use and the profits from that use) of the first stockmen on the scene.[3]

Squatter clubs, commonly called "claims' associations," reinforced the assumption that unimproved government land—again, usually ignoring prior Indian settlement—was not property. Where government land had not been surveyed—and surveys rarely kept pace with settlement—federal preemption laws gave actual settlers a claim to their homestead. But even the general Preemption Act of 1841 did not eliminate the need for such associations. In theory, the claimants had to be beyond the reach of formal legal institutions. Trespassers drafted constitutions, elected governing councils, established arbitration procedures to prevent or mitigate disputes, and pledged to prevent bidding by those who did not belong to their club. The first residents, it was argued, should have the right to purchase government land at the minimum price of $1.25 per acre once the surveyors caught up with them—without interference from "claim jumpers" or those who came later. The claims clubs assumed that the public domain existed to aid individual opportunity and the economic development of the frontier rather than the economy of the nation or the financial needs of the central government. Most clubs also welcomed small-fry land speculators by permitting the first settlers to purchase an additional 80 to 160 acres and to sell all or part of their "occupancy right."[4]

The values that drove American land policy also dictated mineral policy. Most of the states' old colonial charters had contained outright grants of minerals, but they also reserved a share to the English Crown (usually 20 percent of all precious metals). During the American Revolution, mining was seen as a way to help pay off the war debt, and the Land Ordinance of 1785 reserved to the federal government one-third of all gold, silver, lead, and copper taken from the public lands. The major land acts of the first half of the nineteenth century excluded mineral lands from entry. In 1807 Congress authorized leasing the lead mines in Indiana Territory—the site of the only extensive mining undertaken in the United States before the California Gold Rush—for terms of up to five years. Military needs dictated this decision, and the leases were administered by the War Department, which began collecting a 10 percent royalty in 1822. Many miners refused to secure a permit, and the actual production of lead was four times that reported to the War Department. Nearly one million acres of mineral lands had been reserved by the 1840s, but the public lands had not been classified and plenty of mineral land became private property before it was subjected to leasing. Beginning in 1834, and especially after the Panic of 1837, the price of lead plummeted and rental fees dried up. The War Department, moreover, lacked a sufficient number of agents to police the frontier. Even so, the cost of administration and litigation far exceeded the revenue returned to the central government.[5]

In the mid-1840s, the commissioner of the Land Office and President James K. Polk called for an end to leasing, a practice that had prompted extensive litigation and was highly unpopular on the frontier. To add insult to injury, in the years from 1841 to 1844 leasing returned only about 25 percent of the cost of administering the system. Polk wanted to sell the mineral lands and require purchasers to pay a small royalty to the government. "It was better to realize something on these lands [through outright sale]," historian Roy Robbins has written, "than to have them appropriated illegally by settlers, or to have them plundered by trespassers and thus rendered unfit for sale. Undoubtedly the pressure of western protest against continuing the leasing system also influenced the government to recommend the change. The State of Michigan in 1846 took a firm stand against the perpetuation of a system of 'patroonery' on her territory, and insisted that all mineral lands be sold and rendered taxable by her." The lead-bearing lands in Illinois, Wisconsin, Michigan, and Arkansas went on sale in 1846 and the copper and lead mines in the Lake Superior District of Wisconsin and Michigan in 1847.[6]

GOLD IN CALIFORNIA

Those who flocked to California at the end of the 1840s carried with them strong ideas about the nature of property, the right of American citizens beyond the pale of law to govern themselves, and the power of American citizens to make their own rules concerning the acquisition and use of public lands—including those containing mineral deposits. Nevertheless, Congress had authorized the sale of lead and copper lands. Would it now authorize the sale of gold-bearing land to the highest bidders?

This was the question that faced the U.S. Army in California when gold was discovered in January 1848. In February 1848, Colonel Richard Mason, the military governor of California from 1847 to 1849, abolished all Mexican mining laws and customs. In July, he visited the gold camps and considered selling the mineral land in twenty- to forty-acre plots, or charging miners a license fee of $100 to $1,000 for the privilege of working claims. But Mason had only 660 soldiers under his command, and martial law would have been intolerable to the Argonauts. If used to govern the mineral region, Mason fretted, his troops might desert and turn to mining themselves. Nor could he be sure that his system would prevent a handful of capitalists from monopolizing the best land. "It was a matter of serious reflection with me," Mason wrote, "how I could secure to the government certain rents or fees for the privilege of procuring this gold; but upon considering the large extent of the country, the character of the people engaged, and the small scattered force at my command, I am resolved not to interfere, but permit all to work freely."[7]

California was technically not even a part of the United States when the Gold Rush began. Initially, alcaldes (mayors) ruled over most settlements, including some mining camps, but the miners soon took matters into their own hands. The principles of equal opportunity, home rule, antimonopoly, preemption, and priority rights were customs of the American frontier with deep roots in logic and experience. Mexican institutions and values emphasized conciliation and accommodation to the detriment of contract, and they regarded community stability as a higher good than individual property rights. Mining camp codes, by contrast, were more concerned with the allocation of natural resources to individuals than with creating a moral society.[8]

The miners made great use of the essential premise of the English common law: that universal custom had as much legal sanction as formal statutes. Two common-law principles were particularly important. First, when two or more people trespassed on land owned by a third, the first to enter and use the land had a superior claim to all others (except the legal owner); second, all trespassers were limited to "reasonable use." These principles helped lay the foundation for priority rights on the public domain.[9]

Mining camp codes did not originate in California,[10] but within the United States no previously discovered mineral regions were as extensive as those in California, which by the 1860s contained about five hundred mining districts. Regulations varied from camp to camp, but they had much in common. Those miners who were the first to locate the precious metals had spent money and energy demonstrating that gold was available; all subsequent work depended on their efforts and ingenuity. Much of mining was trial and error, so the second or third wave of Argonauts to enter a mining district did not face the same economic risks or obstacles. Those first on the scene also founded towns and built roads, creating the economic context in which profitable mining could take place. Therefore, they were granted a "right of discovery"—usually a larger claim or two claims—as well as chronological priority.

The mining codes regulated the size of claims, the process of filing and marking them, and the necessity for continuous work for the claim to remain valid. Since the land was owned by the federal government, claims conferred usufruct rights rather than absolute ownership. Depending on the richness of the gold deposits, they could be as small as one hundred square feet or several times that large, but they were generally limited to the amount of land one man could work. The land laws of the United States permitted farmers to acquire far more land than they could work; the mining laws did not. The codes also provided a process for arbitrating disputes by an alcalde, council, or jury—often with a right of appeal from the arbitrator or arbitrators to the entire mass of miners within a district—and proclaimed that no compensation need be paid for the privilege of mining to either the state or federal governments. Many miners expressed disdain for formal law, and thus some districts banned lawyers—or at least prohibited them from practicing their trade.[11] In February 1850, the California Senate's Committee on the Judiciary noted that it was a "popular doctrine" that common sense was "entitled to higher consideration than the reflection and ripe experience of the most profound jurist. . . . In short, reduced to its simplest terms . . . the proposition is, that the man who is entirely ignorant of a multifarious subject, is more competent to form a just and correct judgment concerning it, than the man who has made it the business of his life to comprehend it in theory and understand it in its minute and practical details."[12]

FREE MINING

The California legislature sanctioned "free mining" at the beginning of 1851. In 1850 the alcalde of Marysville, Stephen J. Field—who was destined to become chief justice of the California Supreme Court in 1857 and to serve the longest term in the his-

"Bogue Ejecting the Squatters," one of the illustrations by Charles Nahl that enliven the pages of *Old Block's Sketch-Book*. This collection of charming and humorous tales of gold-rush California was published in 1856 by Alonzo Delano, who, like Nahl, had earlier tried his hand at mining. Although disputes over claims were generally resolved through arbitration according to the dictates of local custom and code, miners occasionally relied on direct action to secure their rights. *California Historical Society, FN-30963.*

tory of the U.S. Supreme Court, from 1863 to 1897—ran for the legislature from Yuba County, which at that time also contained what would become Nevada and Sierra counties. The immense county was 100 miles long and 50 miles wide, with a scattered population of 25,000. Most miners were far removed from the county seat and institutions of government.

Late in his life, Field recalled that one of his campaign planks in 1850 was "giving greater jurisdiction to the local magistrates, in order that contests of miners respecting their claims might be tried in their vicinity. As things then existed the right to a mule could not be litigated without going to the county seat. . . . I was in favor of legislation which would protect miners in their claims, and exempt their tents, rockers, and utensils used in mining from forced sale [by the federal government]." The 1851 law he sponsored provided that "in actions respecting 'Mining Claims,' proof shall be admitted of the customs, usages, or regulations established and in force at the bar, or diggings, embracing such claim; and such customs, usages, or regulations, when not in conflict with the Constitution and Laws of the State, shall govern the decision of the action." Simple as it was, this law became the foundation for mining on the public domain throughout the American West. Field claimed that mining camp law symbolized "that love of order and system and of fair dealing which are the prominent characteristics of our people." The laws were framed, he insisted, "to secure to all comers, within practicable limits, absolute equality of right and privilege in working the mines." Field, of course, exaggerated. The mining camp codes did not always welcome "all comers" or promote "fair dealing." The California legislature enacted many laws pertaining to the mineral lands, including foreign miners' taxes that permitted some miners to discriminate against others and provided for eviction from the mining districts if not paid.[13]

California's courts quickly adopted the principle of free mining, though not without confusion. Miners could not abridge the rights of the United States, but they limited competition and prevented the monopolization of the mines by the state or private corporations. In 1853, in a bizarre appeal to English precedent, the California Supreme Court proclaimed the state's sovereignty over all mineral lands in California. Those who favored the decision hoped that the mines could be taxed to pay state expenses. The ruling met strong opposition from within the mining districts, where critics charged that the court had been bribed by capitalists who hoped to take from the state what they could not persuade Congress to give them. Critics also feared that since the case would inevitably be overturned by the U.S. Supreme Court—which it was—it would weaken rather than strengthen mineral claims.[14]

In his annual message to Congress in December 1850, President Millard Fillmore echoed President Polk's suggestion that the mineral lands be sold at auction in small parcels. But by the time he addressed Congress a year later, Fillmore feared the consequences of such a policy. Now he recommended that the gold fields of California "be permitted to remain as at present, a common field, open to the enterprise and industry of all our citizens, until further experience shall have developed the best policy to be ultimately adopted."[15]

Congress said little more about the mineral lands during the 1850s, but large hydraulic mining companies proliferated in California during the first half of the 1860s, and friends of corporate mining feared that English and Scots investors would refuse to sink more money into the mines until Congress *formally* approved free mining. Moreover, at the end of the Civil War, western miners faced several financial threats. Congress might auction off the mineral lands to help pay off the national debt incurred by the war, an alternative favored by the secretary of the treasury. Or it might retain title to these lands, levy a production or transportation tax, or extend the 1861 income tax to miners. (By the end of the war, the income tax produced almost one-fifth of all federal revenue, but given the transient nature of miners the cost of administering such a tax system would have been high.) In 1865, Congressman George Julian of Indiana introduced a new bill to sell the mineral lands. Similar legislation was introduced in the U.S. Senate, but Congress refused to act—in large part because California's delegation predicted that revolution would result. Miners bombarded Congress with petitions urging the rejection of the Julian bill.[16]

In 1865, the U.S. Supreme Court acknowledged that free mining enjoyed "implied sanction" and had contributed "largely to the prosperity and improvement of the whole country."[17] Nevertheless, since the Constitution explicitly granted Congress the authority to regulate and dispose of the public lands, the high court could not make policy. In 1866, the disposition of the mineral lands again came before Congress. Debate focused on a bill introduced by Senator William Morris Stewart of Nevada, who, along with Senator John Conness of California, had led the opposition to Julian's plan in the previous session of Congress. Stewart spoke for the vast capital that had been poured into the Comstock Lode, but he played on public sympathy for the individual miner: "I assert . . . that the sand plains, alkaline deserts, and dreary monuments of rock and sagebrush of the great interior, would have been as worthless today as when they were marked by geographers as the Great American Desert, but for this system of free mining fostered by our own neglect, and matured and perfected by our generous inaction." Since the principal asset securing the national debt was land, and since increasing the production of gold would drive up the value of that land, Stewart also argued that free mining would do more to reduce the national debt than would selling the mineral claims.[18]

Congress adopted Stewart's bill in 1866, and it became the foundation of mining on the public domain. It confirmed the status quo and extended the rules established in California's gold camps to the rest of the West. It ensured that mineral lands within the public domain would remain open to "all," that the rules governing their use should be dictated by the miners themselves and ratified by the state, territorial, and federal governments, and that miners who wished to secure clear title to their claims could do so for $5 an acre. The 1866 law applied only to shaft mining, but in 1870 Congress extended the opportunity to purchase claims to placer miners, at $2.50 per acre. A third mining law, adopted in 1872, completed the formal process of turning control over precious metals to the miners, counties, and states.[19]

HYDRAULIC MINING

The extent to which these laws contributed to the growth of hydraulic mining is uncertain, but they did nothing to restrain that growth. Hydraulic mining flourished only in those parts of California blessed with abundant surface water. The Argonauts could not have washed away mountains of topsoil to get at ancient stream beds except on California's remote and mountainous public domain, where no substantial industries competed with mining and no traditional riparian water rights prevented diverting water from natural channels. North of the Feather River, thick volcanic deposits covered rich Tertiary gravels, but in the Southern Mines the Tertiary deposits were far smaller. The most profitable hydraulic mines were located on the ridge running between the South and Middle forks of the Yuba River, ten to twenty miles northeast of Nevada City. There, the mining communities of French Corral, Birchville, Sweetland, North San Juan, Columbia Hill, Lake City, North Bloomfield, Relief Hill, and Moore's Flat flourished. By the 1860s, Nevada was the leading mining county in California. As early as 1864, one observer reported that "so great has been the quantity of ground washed away, that many of the ravines are covered with a depth of twenty feet and upwards of tailings from the sluices." Nevada County's gaping hydraulic mines were as much as a mile long and exposed walls of earth five hundred feet high.[20]

In 1861, a thicker canvas hose, reinforced with iron hoops, tripled the velocity of water that miners could direct against the earth. Eight-inch nozzles produced a force great enough to kill the hapless miner who ventured into the water's path.[21] After the drought of 1862–1864, corporations consolidated most of the smaller companies. English capital poured into hydraulic mines, in part because of high profits, in part because of the promises of geologists like Benjamin Silliman of Yale, who reassured potential investors: "It is proven by the most ample testimony that the ancient gold bearing gravel of California contains an inexhaustible store of gold diffused with wonderful uniformity throughout the mass, and, in the aggregate, far exceeding the entire product which the golden State has yet sent into the commerce of the world." This, coupled with Silliman's promise that investors could expect a 20- to 25-percent annual return for an "indefinite time to come," won plenty of financial support.[22]

The hydraulic mines of Nevada, Sierra, and adjoining counties produced great wealth for decades after the Gold Rush, but the mining industry became more and more localized. In the 1860s and 1870s, it faced a serious challenge from the expansion of wheat farming in California's Central Valley. The flood of 1862 washed huge quantities of debris into the Yuba River, and thence into the valley. Marysville, at the confluence of the Feather and Yuba rivers, became a walled city, surrounded by levees as high as chimney tops. As the years passed, the Sacramento, Feather, and Bear rivers, as well as the Yuba, filled with silt, which affected navigation and commerce as far away as Suisun, San Pablo, and San Francisco bays. Thirty thousand acres of prime alluvial farmland became choked with mud from mining sites in the foothills. Once mining had been supreme, but by the 1870s, agriculture played an increasingly prominent role in California's economy.[23]

The mining debris controversy became a prominent issue in California politics, prompting the first debates over flood control in the Sacramento Valley.[24] In 1884, Judge Lorenzo Sawyer of the U.S. Circuit Court permanently enjoined the mining companies from damaging the property of Central Valley residents. Ironically, he used the same argument for equality of opportunity that had once justified free mining. "It

"Piping the bank" near the community of French Corral, hard by the South Fork of the Yuba River in the richest of all the hydraulic mining districts of California, about 1865. Despite the compelling aesthetic of the photographer's powerful composition, hydraulicking was a terribly destructive technology, laying waste to rolling hills, devastating streams, and covering downstream farmland with "slickens." "It is impossible," wrote an observer, "to conceive of anything more desolate, more utterly forbidding, than a region which has been subjected to this hydraulic mining treatment." *Courtesy Society of California Pioneers.*

is by protecting the most humble in his small estate against the encroachments of large capital and large interests," Sawyer proclaimed, "that the poor man is ultimately able to become a capitalist himself. If the smaller interest must yield to the larger . . . all smaller and less important enterprises, industries, and pursuits would sooner or later be absorbed by the large, more powerful few; and their development to a condition of great value and importance, both to the individual and the public, would be arrested in its incipiency."[25] Shaft, or hardrock, mining survived, but never again would the mining industry exercise the political clout it enjoyed in the 1850s and 1860s.[26]

An impoundment dam choked with hydraulic mining debris forms the subject of one of a series of photographs by John A. Todd that were introduced as evidence in the celebrated case of *Woodruff* v. *North Bloomfield Gravel Mining Co.* Ruling for the plaintiff in 1884, U.S. Circuit Court Judge Lorenzo Sawyer effectively brought an end to hydraulicking in the Golden State—a landmark decision in the first environmental pollution battle in the American West. *California Historical Society, FN-29933.*

RESOURCE LAW AND THE CORPORATION

The future was on the side of agriculture, but it was not on the side of "the most humble in his small estate." In the late 1840s and early 1850s, free mining provided reasonably equal access to wealth—except to certain groups of "foreign" miners. But during the 1850s, as corporations increasingly dominated mining, the law changed from encouraging economic democracy to protecting capital. Perhaps the best example was the legal permission to "follow the vein." In Mexico, England, and other European countries, miners could only dig within the boundaries of their claims, and initially California's mining camp codes limited hardrock miners to part of a vein, often one hundred feet. As early as 1852, however, Nevada County modified its laws to encourage miners to follow a vein downward to any depth and in any direction, even if they tunneled under an adjoining claim. The new laws were designed to protect investors from financial loss when only the tail end of an outcropping was located within their claim. Not surprisingly, this innovation spawned many lawsuits. In an attempt to reduce litigation, the 1872 Congress specified that only those miners who located the highest point of a lode—the "apex"—should be allowed to follow the lode under adjoining claims.[27]

The 1872 law promoted rather than quieted legal conflict. Locating the apex of a vein that snaked through the earth was difficult, and the fact that many veins are not continuous made the problem even more complicated. Was a discontinuous vein part of the original vein or an entirely new mineral deposit? The historian Otis Young has explained how this law opened the door to legal blackmail: "At its rock-bottom worst, apex litigation began when a would-be plaintiff had, or arranged to obtain, title to property adjacent to that of a prosperous mine. He next hired a geologist to 'discover' that a shoot of the high-grade lode cropped out on his own property and to theorize somehow that the tail of the shoot wagged the dog of the lode. The next step was to retain a high-powered attorney, one who specialized in apex litigation on a contingency-fee basis, to bring suit against the prosperous mine. The attorney then filed a brief on the law side of the appropriate court, swearing that the plaintiff either had priority of discovery (thus entitling him to the whole) or at worst was entitled to receive lucrative remedies for the damages he was suffering from the depredations of a soulless corporation. The hope, of course, was that the defendant mining company would settle out of court for a substantial sum, irrespective of the facts, in order to be rid of a dangerous nuisance."[28]

Both sides in such a contest hired as many expert witnesses as they could find and afford, so more than a few geologists spent their entire careers as expert witnesses. In one five-year period, lawsuits in Nevada courts cost about 20 percent of the entire output of the Comstock mines. "No industry in any country," Clark Spence has wisely concluded, "was ever subject to as much or as complicated legal activity as mining in western America."[29]

WATER LAW

The prior appropriation principle of water rights was to placer mining what the apex law was to lode mining. As enforced in courts within the eastern United States, riparian rights granted those who owned land bordering a stream the exclusive right to use water from that stream on their property. Such rights were "correlative" rather than absolute. They could be defined only in relationship to each other, not as absolute grants of specific quantities of water. Riparian owners could divert water to meet domestic needs or to water livestock. They could even reduce the flow of a stream, *if* their diversions were "reasonable." However, no commercial use of water, such as irrigation, could materially reduce the flow of a stream—at least not if the other riparian owners complained.[30]

Prior appropriation granted the first to use water the right to carry it anywhere, and use it for any purpose, as long as that use was "beneficial." The principle was simple, but the law took shape gradually. During the 1850s, many mining camps prohibited water diversions that injured one group of miners at the expense of another. They demanded the consent of those working placer deposits adjoining a stream before water could be turned from its natural channel. In addition, mining camp codes often prohibited the construction of diversion dams that backed up water onto claims above the dam, reserved the use of water in a creek or ravine exclusively to miners within that watershed, and prohibited miners from claiming surplus water for speculative purposes. Not all mining camps adopted formal rules related to water use because most preferred the arbitration of disputes to cut-and-dried edicts. Nevertheless, when the arbitration process broke down, miners dynamited ditches, chopped down wooden diversion dams, and tore down or burned flumes. Most often, lawyers, and later historians, ignored these conflicts, preferring to portray the mining districts as models of grassroots democracy rather than communities torn between individual and corporate enterprise. Only after mining passed from an activity engaged in by individual miners or miners organized in small groups to large hydraulic mining corporations—for which the miners worked as hired hands—did prior appropriation calcify into doctrine. Its triumph was due more to changing technology and capital requirements than to the fact that it made more sense in arid or semi-arid climates.[31]

It was one thing for *miners* to claim water by prior appropriation for their own use, quite another for *entrepreneurs* who did not engage directly in mining to claim water and form companies to sell it. Monopoly and outside control were two of the deepest fears in the mining camps. At first, priority rights applied to the age of claims, not to the age of water rights; water use was incidental. Eventually, however, the cost of carrying water farther and farther from existing streams proved overwhelming, and once the miners permitted the creation of autonomous water companies, the genie could not be stuffed back into the bottle. Heavily capitalized, the companies demanded an exclusive market. In October 1853, a group of miners at Yankee Jim's in Placer County wrote to the *Placer Herald* warning that the new ditch companies would soon destroy the rights of actual miners: "They [the water companies] tell us that we are to be harassed and embarrassed with endless and perplexing law suits, that will cost more than all the claims are worth, and they further tell us, that the price of water will not be reduced. . . . Thus has crept into our midst a tyrant in the form of a lamb, and has gradually assumed the form of a two horned beast, whose right horn is bread, and the left horn water, and the community [sic] are gored into surfdom [sic]."[32] The miners were caught in a dilemma: without water, they could not find gold; with it, they became the subjects of powerful corporations whose headquarters were scattered from San Francisco to Scotland.

The office of the Coyote and Deer Creek Water Company near Nevada City in 1852, the year following completion of its ditch, which brought water to the dry diggings of the district. Among the earliest water companies in California, it was later one of hundreds that became part of the Pacific Gas and Electric hydroelectric system. *Courtesy California State Library.*

Contradictory decisions issued by the California Supreme Court from 1853 through 1858 or 1859 reflected the diversity of mining. In the hydraulic mining districts, prior appropriation quickly predominated. But in some camps, small-scale placer mining survived throughout the 1850s, and there a species of riparian rights persisted. Other camps tried to balance both legal principles. District judges were elected, and they responded to local opinion. Personal safety and the widespread hostility to formal institutions of law left them little choice. In addition, mining communities paid far more attention to their own regulations than to court judgments. The state supreme court had little power to enforce its decisions during the 1850s, and judges worried that Congress might overturn any decision that did not fairly represent the aspirations and needs of the miners.[33]

The success of prior appropriation was cultural as well as economic. In the California of the 1850s, fear of concentrated power and the demand for home rule reinforced the traditional American disdain for bureaucracy and centralized planning.

Prior appropriation did not require an expensive government bureaucracy to administer, nor did it require the legislature to pass elaborate statutes. It let the economic actors themselves set public policy, as they had dictated the land policy of the United States since the 1780s. It was based on thoroughly familiar principles, and no institution of government had to decide who would have access to water, where it would be used, or for what purpose. Prior appropriation assumed that when disputes arose they were better left to the courts, which, of course, represented the interests of litigants rather than the public as a whole. Only in the second half of the nineteenth century would the private corporation replace government as the chief instrument of tyranny in the minds of most Americans. It took nearly a decade for prior appropriation to triumph in the mining districts and even longer to take hold in agriculture. In the 1850s and 1860s, irrigation was largely confined to southern California. In that part of the state, the principle of community control over water, inherited from the Mexican period, prevailed. That system recognized a right to irrigate certain tracts of land, but no absolute grants to specific quantities of water. Then, in the 1870s, the Southern Pacific Railroad built through the San Joaquin Valley and over the Tehachapi Mountains into Los Angeles, and land and water companies proliferated. In the 1850s and 1860s, the valley had been devoted to cattle ranching and dry farming, but now irrigation communities grew up around Fresno, Modesto, and Bakersfield. Parts of the valley had been included in Mexican land grants and had never been part of the public domain. Therefore, passage of the Desert Land Act in 1877—which mandated prior appropriation on government lands and excluded all other water rights—had no effect in much of California. The increase in irrigation and a drought at the end of the 1870s resulted in conflict between those who held traditional riparian rights and those who claimed the right to divert water under prior appropriation. Simultaneously, the region south of the Tehachapis experienced a population boom and the systems of community control—which held water in common for the community—came to be seen as impediments to speculation in land and to economic growth.[34]

Prior appropriation was no more rational or efficient than riparian rights, nor was it better suited to all parts of the arid and semi-arid West. In California, the courts allowed riparian owners to irrigate, and riparian rights were well suited to California in the years before large storage reservoirs made massive diversions possible. In the 1870s and 1880s, technology restricted irrigation to the land adjoining streams. That land was alluvial and highly productive. It was also the cheapest to irrigate and allowed the maximum amount of water to seep back into the stream. Moreover, since riparian rights were correlative—with no existence apart from each other—they could be expanded or contracted according to fluctuations in the water supply. The major "weakness" of the riparian right was that it did not promise an absolute quantity of water. As capital looked for new investment opportunities in the

1870s and 1880s, as it poured into speculative land and water companies, it demanded that prior appropriation be extended to irrigation.

At the end of the 1870s, several contests over agricultural water rights reached the California Supreme Court. The court consistently ruled that riparian rights took precedence outside the public domain.[35] The land and water companies hoped to persuade the legislature or state supreme court to abandon riparian rights, as the courts had in other western states. In 1886, a special session of the legislature accomplished little, but the biggest battle came from 1881 to 1886, after Henry Miller, Charles Lux, and other riparian claimants in Buena Vista Slough at the end of the Kern River filed suit against James B. Haggin and his associates in the Kern County Land and Water Company to block diversions under prior appropriation near present-day Bakersfield. The plaintiffs argued that nature intended the Kern River to stay in its natural channel and that the value of their land depended on the water remaining there. No one, they insisted, had the right to claim water for nothing and carry it a great distance to dry land when doing so destroyed the property rights of downstream riparian owners. The court decided that abolishing riparian rights would replace one monopoly with another, forcing those whose water rights had been confiscated to purchase water from those who had taken it away, but there was surprisingly little enthusiasm for state ownership or regulation of water rights.[36]

Ultimately, the "California Doctrine," which embraced both riparian and appropriative rights, stood in stark contrast to the "Colorado Doctrine," which recognized prior appropriation exclusively.[37] Kansas, Montana, Nebraska, the Dakotas, Oregon, Texas, Washington, and Oklahoma followed California, and Utah, Wyoming, Arizona, New Mexico, and Idaho followed Colorado. With the exception of Montana, all states that accepted the California Doctrine contained both humid and arid sections. Diverse climates and economies help explain how water rights evolved in the West. Still, whether the evolution of western water law would have followed the same course had mining not preceded agriculture is a tantalizing and enormously significant question.

Most legal scholars and historians have lauded prior appropriation as a fair and equitable way to distribute a scarce water supply. Walter Prescott Webb proclaimed that "history . . . makes clear the necessity of . . . prior appropriation." In 1935, Carey McWilliams lauded appropriation as "the fairest and most economical and the fullest use of an inadequate water supply," and in 1953 Wallace Stegner declared it "an essential criterion" in an "irrigating country."[38] With most of California's best water lawyers enlisted on the side of prior appropriation, the possibility that the riparian doctrine or the system of community control in southern California had anything to offer Californians eager to build stable communities of small farmers was all but forgotten by the end of the nineteenth century. Yet, there was a dark side to prior appropriation. In large parts of the Central Valley, it permitted a handful of agricultural corporations to dominate the water supply. Instead of efficiency, it promoted waste, as each claimant used as much water as possible to "stockpile" the largest future supply. It also led to expensive and protracted litigation, as the earliest water users claimed far more water than they could use. Finally, because rights acquired under prior appropriation could be condemned only at great cost, it prompted the construction of expensive new water projects in the twentieth century. The easiest answer to water shortages was to augment the existing supply, not to reallocate it or place restrictions on its use.

CONCLUSION

When the Public Lands Commission surveyed western mining in 1880, it observed that the "California common law," to use the commission's phrase, had become the law of mining west of the Missouri River. California miners had scattered throughout the West, carrying with them the legal principles worked out in the 1840s and 1850s.[39]

Some historians have argued that free mining resulted more from congressional neglect than from a positive policy choice. California was far removed from the rest of the nation, and slavery and sectional issues preoccupied the central government during the 1850s. Since the public domain still contained plenty of good agricultural land in the Midwest, and since California's arid and semi-arid climate initially seemed unsuited to agriculture, mining represented the state's only hope for economic development.

Nevertheless, the public domain belonged to all the people of the United States, and Congress had good reason to regulate mining on government land. California's mines produced more than $300 million from 1849 to 1854. In each of those years, the gold output matched the federal currency in circulation during the mid-1830s. The dramatic increase in the money supply had far-reaching implications for the American economy. "An era of inflation was thus inaugurated," historian Roy Robbins has written, "which was to have a tremendous effect on the whole country. For every addition of a million dollars in gold three or four million dollars in paper would be issued by existing banks, and it was expected [in the mid 1850s] that a new crop of banks would appear." The massive increase in precious metals inflated the prices of real estate, stocks, and commodities. This was reason enough for Congress to pay close attention to mining developments in California.[40]

Instead, Congress ignored the Gold Rush's financial implications and deferred to the customs of the country. The mining camps have long fascinated students of American history, in part because they can be viewed in two very different ways. On the one hand, they represent the mythical "state of nature." More than a new beginning, they could be seen as a perfect or idyllic state where the essential goodness and rationality of human beings flowered unrestrained by the weight of history, the corruption of flawed institutions, the power of established elites, and the iniquities of laws designed to protect vested interests rather than to ensure equal opportunity. It was a world that permitted a return to "first principles" and the purest form of self-government. Charles H. Shinn, one of the foremost nineteenth-century champions of mining camp law, described the codes as "the only original contribution of the frontiersmen of America to the art of self-government."[41] Here was "popular sovereignty" in action.

The idyllic portrayal of mining camp law came to dominate California history, but not without protest. For example, Josiah Royce thought that the mining camp was closer to Thomas Hobbes's state of nature: a cruel, brutal, and "lawless" place bereft of civilization and beyond the institutions and constraints that tamed the worst impulses in human nature. Royce saw the miner as a squatter who created a smokescreen of "natural rights" to obscure predatory self-interest. The mining camps stimulated the endemic fear of law, judges, and lawyers rooted deep in American culture. Not only did the mining codes encourage ethnic and racial hatreds and "Judge Lynch," they further undermined faith in formal institutions of government, which for decades after the Gold Rush remained weak throughout California and the West.[42]

Long after the formal legal structure had been erected, miners were loath to accept direction from either the courts or legislature. For example, beginning in 1851, fledgling mining companies began to hold conventions to discuss uniform codes. The need for standardization was particularly great in the quartz or shaft mining districts. As litigation over the boundaries, sale, and speculation in claims increased—to name but a few sources of legal action—formal legal institutions began to take precedence. As a result, the state legislature heard shrill protests from the mining districts. Therefore, it refused to authorize a convention to draft a uniform mineral law, believing that no such code could meet the varied conditions in different parts of the state. Laws should come from the bottom up rather than the top down, the lawmakers concluded, and while Nevada, Sierra, and Tuolumne counties adopted uniform quartz mining laws in the late 1850s, the counties that relied on placer mining resisted them.[43]

Mining towns were not so much settlements as temporary encampments, and people who invested nothing more than their labor in a place were likely to treat it with contempt—particularly because they were more often than not disappointed in the search for wealth. The miners denied the right of local governments to tax either mineral claims or the product of the mines to help pay for public services, and when they moved to cities, towns, and farms, they carried with them their suspicions of government and their resistance to any limitation on economic freedom.

Free mining led to the rapid exploitation of easily accessible placer deposits and

When the photographer Carleton Watkins visited the town of Mariposa in 1859, it had a population of perhaps five hundred souls, chiefly miners. Though most Argonauts returned home after the most virulent symptoms of the gold fever had passed, some stayed on—sojourners become settlers—and contributed to the growth of stable communities in the Mother Lode country. In the distance, *left of center,* outlined against the chaparral-clad hills is the Greek Revival county courthouse constructed in 1854. Still in use today, it is the oldest in the state. *California Historical Society, FN-24676.*

a highly transient population. The discovery of the Comstock Lode in western Nevada at the end of the 1850s, and mining strikes in other parts of the West during the Civil War, depopulated large parts of California. John S. Hittell, one of California's most prominent writers in the 1860s, suggested that the state's future depended on the sale of mineral lands. "Ownership makes the people permanent," he observed, "and induces men to get wives and comfortable homes; and permanence and the possession of families and homes make them temperate, economical, industrious and careful of their reputations. Without homes, families and permanent residence, they must be intemperate, idle, wasteful of their money, regardless of their reputations, and without hope of improvement in the future. This is unfortunately the condition of many of the miners of California at the present time." If the mineral lands were sold, Hittell reasoned, California would attract permanent settlers, not vagabonds. Its institutions of government would become more stable, and its wealth would be systematically and efficiently developed. Moreover, until the mineral lands passed into private ownership, California agriculture—the state's true hope for future growth—would languish.[44]

Most miners did not agree with Hittell, but the attitudes and values of the mining camp had a profound effect on agriculture. During the 1850s, the state's best arable land was contained in large Mexican grants. It took a special commission and the courts many years to confirm or deny those grants. Meanwhile, state law favored mining over farming. "The Legislature of our State in the wise exercise of its discretion has seen proper to foster and protect the mining interest as paramount to all others," the California Supreme Court observed in 1855.[45] The logical place to create farms was near markets, and the mining camps provided the largest markets outside the state's cities. Yet a long-established principle of American land law held that preemption did not apply to mineral lands. Those "farmers" who staked out 160-acre farms on government land within the mineral districts were often suspected of using preemption to secure larger mineral claims. Miners routinely invaded farms and destroyed crops, and initially the law required no indemnification.[46]

The extent to which agriculture in the Sacramento Valley was structured by the dominance of free mining is uncertain. Until the court decision against hydraulic mining in 1884, the state's laws did more to encourage the rapid exploitation of mineral wealth than the sustained exploitation of farmland. Not surprisingly, the type of agriculture that grew up closest to the mines was wheat, rather than fruit, nuts, or vegetables—all of which required skill, labor, and a commitment to the land.

Long before Frank Norris published *The Octopus* (1901)—which characterized wheat farming as another form of mining—California agriculture had taken on a distinctively speculative appearance. In 1872, the *Overland Monthly* published an article that compared farming in California and the rest of the nation. In the Golden State, it found, farmers did not work their land steadily; most simply sowed and reaped wheat. They seldom planted trees, leaving their farms with a desolate look. With the exception of wheat and pork, everything eaten on these farms was imported, often from outside California; there were no gardens. No quarters were built for farm laborers, and villages were rare; indeed, many wheat farmers lived in the city and had little or no association with the land. These agriculturalists made no effort to diversify crops and raise rice, oranges, and grapes—which would have permitted them to use the land more intensively and live on it all year around. The article did not mention that free mining had conditioned Californians to look at all land solely in terms of quick wealth. The same lack of attachment to place, the same lack of community, the same shortsightedness, and the same obsession with profit characterized both mining and agriculture, at least until horticulture gained in popularity during the 1870s and 1880s. The family farm never had a chance in California, and the persistent legal and cultural power of the mining industry helps explain why.[47]

Free mining also had a profound effect on California politics. California was a huge state that would have been difficult to govern under any circumstances. But the dominance of mining exacerbated sectional tensions. Conflicts erupted between northern and southern California, between mining and agricultural counties, and between San Francisco—where much of the capital for mining was raised—and flood-prone interior communities, such as Sacramento and Marysville, along the state's major rivers. In the United States, a fundamental constitutional principle was that those who paid taxes should share the burden and benefits equally. But ranchers and farmers in the southern counties—where most land was privately owned—paid relatively heavy taxes while residents of the mining districts paid little. The mining counties had the strongest representation in the state legislature while the counties dominated by agriculture and grazing paid most of the bills—such as the cost of maintaining a judicial system concerned mainly with conflicts over mineral claims.

In 1852 and 1853, the legislature debated the creation of a new state from southern California. In 1859, it actually approved division, and residents of Los Angeles, San Bernardino, San Diego, Santa Barbara, San Luis Obispo, and Tulare counties ratified that decision by a three-to-one margin. Congress refused to ratify the plebiscite, however, and the Civil War made the decision a dead letter. Still, for decades after the golden years of the mining industry had passed, the mining counties enjoyed disproportionate power in the legislature. For example, the 1880 legislature imposed a statewide tax to build restraining dams to capture hydraulic mining debris that washed down into the Sacramento Valley. Southern California claimed that this was yet another scheme to transfer the tax burden from mining to ranching and agriculture.[48]

Even more important, the Gold Rush and free mining strengthened the assumption that nature existed solely for profit. Never had the land been used so ruthlessly, with so little heed of tomorrow. As one observer of hydraulic mining in Montana wrote in 1881, "hydraulic, or even sluice mining is not an aesthetic pursuit; the regions where it is practised may be, before the miner's advent, like the garden of the Lord for beauty; but after his work is completed, they bear no resemblance to anything, except the chaos which greeted the eye of the seer at the dawn of the Mosaic record of the rehabilitation of the earth for the use of man. . . . It is impossible to conceive of anything more desolate, more utterly forbidding, than a region which has been subjected to this hydraulic mining treatment." Historian Duane Smith has written that "all this development did not take place without disturbance—environmental, personal, economic, political, and social. Mining left behind gutted mountains, dredged-out streams, despoiled vegetation, open pits, polluted creeks, barren hillsides and meadows, a littered landscape, abandoned camps, and burned-out miners and the entrepreneurs who came to mine the miners." Only direct injuries to property owners restrained mining. The contamination of water supplies and destruction of fisheries attracted little attention. Free mining produced great wealth, but it came at a high price.[49]

NOTES

1. Lawrence C. Becker, *Property Rights: Philosophic Foundations* (London: Routledge & Kegan Paul, 1977); William B. Scott, *In Pursuit of Happiness: American Conceptions of Property from the Seventeenth to the Twentieth Century* (Bloomington: Indiana University Press, 1977); Ellen Frankel Paul, *Property Rights and Eminent Domain* (New Brunswick, N.J.: Transaction Books, 1987); Andrew Reeve, *Property* (Atlantic Highlands, N.J.: Humanities Press International, 1986); Richard Schlatter, *Private Property: The History of An Idea* (London: G. Allen & Unwin, 1951).

2. W. C. Jones, ed., *Commentaries on the Laws of England*, vol. 1 (San Francisco: Bancroft-Whitney, 1916), 240.

3. Ernest S. Osgood, *The Day of the Cattleman* (Minneapolis: University of Minnesota Press, 1929), 182–83.

4. On early claims associations or clubs, see Allan G. Bogue, "The Iowa Claim Clubs: Symbol and Substance," *Mississippi Valley Historical Review* 45 (September 1958): 231–53; Paul Wallace Gates, *History of Public Land Law Development* (Washington, D.C.: Government Printing Office, 1968), 152–63; and Benjamin Hibbard, *A History of the Public Land Policies* (Madison: University of Wisconsin Press, 1965), 198–208.

5. James E. Wright, *The Galena Lead District: Federal Policy and Practice, 1824–1847* (Madison: State Historical Society of Wisconsin, 1966).

6. Roy M. Robbins, *Our Landed Heritage: The Public Domain, 1776–1970* (Lincoln: University of Nebraska Press, 1976), 151. Also see Robert W. Swenson, "Legal Aspects of Mineral Resources Exploitation," in Gates, *History of Public Land Law Development*, 701–2; and Curtis H. Lindley, *A Treatise on the American Law Relating to Mines and Mineral Lands*, vol. 1 (San Francisco: Bancroft-Whitney, 1914), 66–67.

7. The Richard Mason quote is as reprinted in John F. Davis, *Historical Sketch of the Mining Law in California* (Los Angeles: Commercial Printing House, 1902), 12. Also see Neal Harlow, *California Conquered: War and Peace on the Pacific, 1846–1850* (Berkeley: University of California Press, 1982), 45–47, 297; Joseph Ellison, *California and the Nation, 1850–1869: A Study of the Relations of a Frontier Community with the Federal Government* (Berkeley: University of California Press, 1927), 55–57.

8. For an excellent discussion of the differences between Anglo-American and Hispanic law in pre-gold-rush California, see David J. Langum, *Law and Community on the Mexican California Frontier: Anglo-American Expatriates and the Clash of Legal Traditions, 1821–1846* (Norman: University of Oklahoma Press, 1987). Also see Michael C. Meyer, *Water in the His-*

panic Southwest: A Social and Legal History, 1550–1850 (Tucson: University of Arizona Press, 1984).

9. Samuel C. Wiel, "Public Policy in Western Water Decisions," *California Law Review* 1 (November 1912): 12–13, and Charles W. McCurdy, "Stephen J. Field and Public Land Law Development in California, 1850–1866: A Case Study of Judicial Resource Allocation in Nineteenth-Century America," *Law and Society Review* 10 (Fall 1975): 264.

10. For example, in June 1830, the lead miners of Dubuque, Iowa, gathered and appointed a five-man committee to draft a mining code. See Davis, *Historical Sketch of the Mining Law in California*, 18.

11. On the mining codes, see Rodman W. Paul, *California Gold: The Beginning of Mining in the Far West* (Cambridge, Mass.: Harvard University Press, 1947), 210–39; John Walton Caughey, *The California Gold Rush* (Berkeley: University of California Press, 1975), 228–29; J. Ross Browne, *Resources of the Pacific Slope* (New York: D. Appleton, 1869), 235–47; Gregory Yale, *Legal Titles to Mining Claims and Water Rights in California, Under the Mining Laws of Congress of July, 1866* (San Francisco: A. Roman, 1867), 73–88; Charles J. Hughes, "The Evolution of Mining Law," in *Report of the Twenty-Fourth Annual Meeting of the American Bar Association Held at Denver, Colorado, August 21, 22, and 23, 1901* (Philadelphia: Dando Printing and Publishing, 1901), 330–31.

12. The quote is from "Report on Civil and Common Law," February 27, 1850, in *California Reports*, 1850, 588–89.

13. *Jennison* v. *Kirk*, 98 U.S. 453 (1878), at 457. Many cases decided by the California Supreme Court agreed with Stephen J. Field's interpretation of mining camp law. In particular, see *'49 and '56 Quartz Mining Co.*, 15 Cal. 152 (1860), at 161, and *Morton* v. *Solambo*, 26 Cal. 527 (1864), at 532–33.

14. *Hicks* v. *Bell*, 3 Cal. 220 (1853); Stephen J. Field, *Personal Reminiscences of Early Days in California, With Other Sketches* (Washington, D.C.: Privately printed, 1893), 59, 90, 154–55; Ellison, *California and the Nation, 1850–1869*, 67–69.

15. *Congressional Globe*, 32nd Cong., 1st sess., 1851, appendix, p. 4.

16. For discussion of the Julian bill, see *Congressional Globe*, 38th Cong., 2nd sess., House, February 9, 1865, pp. 684–87. Also see Swenson, "Legal Aspects of Mineral Resources Exploitation," in Gates, *History of Public Land Law Development*, 714–17; and Yale, *Legal Titles to Mining Claims and Water Rights*, 10.

17. *Sparrow* v. *Strong*, 70 U.S. 49 (1865).

18. The quote is as reprinted in Davis, *Historical Sketch of the Mining Law in California*, 13. Also see Russell Elliott, *Servant of Power: A Political Biography of Senator William M. Stewart* (Reno: University of Nevada Press, 1983), 49–55.

19. Albert Hart, *Mining Statutes of the United States, California and Nevada* (San Francisco: A. L. Bancroft, 1877); Paul, *California Gold*, 231–32; Rodman W. Paul, *Mining Frontiers of the Far West, 1848–1880* (New York: Holt, Rinehart and Winston, 1963), 171–72.

20. George Black, *Report on the Middle Yuba Canal and Eureka Lake Canal, Nevada County, California* (San Francisco: Towne & Bacon Printers, 1864), 30 (quote); Philip Ross May, *Origins of Hydraulic Mining in California* (Oakland: Holmes Book Co., 1970), 22; Rossiter W. Raymond, *Mining Industry of the States and Territories of the Rocky Mountains* (New York: J. B. Ford, 1874), 68.

21. Robert L. Kelley, *Gold vs. Grain: The Hydraulic Mining Controversy in California's Central Valley* (Glendale, Calif.: Arthur H. Clark, 1959), 45–46.

22. Benjamin Silliman, *Reports on the Blue Tent Consolidated Hydraulic Gold Mines of California, Limited: Situate on the South Yuba River, Nevada County, California* (London: D. P. Croke, 1873), 23 (quote), 37.

23. The best survey of the hydraulic mining controversy in California is still Robert Kelley's *Gold vs. Grain.* For a more recent summary see Duane A. Smith, *Mining America: The Industry and the Environment, 1800–1980* (Lawrence: University Press of Kansas, 1987), 67–74.

24. On hydraulic mining and flood control in the nineteenth century, see Robert Kelley, *Battling the Inland Sea: American Political Culture, Public Policy, & the Sacramento Valley, 1850–1986* (Berkeley: University of California Press, 1989), 67–246.

25. *Woodruff v. North Bloomfield Gravel Mining Co.,* 18 Fed. 753 (1884), at p. 807.

26. Kelley, *Gold vs. Grain,* 229–42; Donald J. Pisani, *From the Family Farm to Agribusiness: The Irrigation Crusade in California and the West, 1850–1931* (Berkeley: University of California Press, 1984), 162–75.

27. Paul, *California Gold,* 237–38; Lindley, *Treatise on the American Law Relating to Mines and Mineral Lands,* vol. 1, 111–12.

28. Otis E. Young, *Western Mining: An Informal Account of Precious-Metals Prospecting, Placering, Lode Mining, and Milling on the American Frontier from Spanish Times to 1893* (Norman: University of Oklahoma Press, 1970), 229.

29. Clark C. Spence, "Western Mining," in *Historians and the American West,* ed. Michael P. Malone (Lincoln: University of Nebraska Press, 1983), 107.

30. On the nature of riparian rights, see John Norton Pomeroy, *A Treatise on the Law of Water Rights* (St. Paul: West Publishing, 1887), and Joseph K. Angell, *A Treatise on the Law of Watercourses* (Boston: Little, Brown, 1877). Also see Theodore Steinberg, *Nature Incorporated: Industrialization and the Waters of New England* (New York: Cambridge University Press, 1991), and Morton Horwitz, *The Transformation of American Law, 1780–1860* (Cambridge, Mass.: Harvard University Press, 1977).

31. Charles H. Shinn, *Land Laws of Mining Districts* (Baltimore: N. Murray, 1884), 21, 56–58; Jane Bissell Grabhorn, *A California Gold Rush Miscellany* (San Francisco: Grabhorn Press, 1934), facing p. 34; John S. Hittell, *Mining in the Pacific States of North America* (San Francisco: H. H. Bancroft and Co., 1861), 192–95; *Tenth Census of the United States,* vol. 14 (Washington, D.C.: Government Printing Office, 1885), 286, 291, 297; Hughes, "The Evolution of Mining Law," 329; John Heckendorn and W. A. Wilson, *Miners & Business Men's Directory for the Year Commencing January 1ˢᵗ, 1856* (Columbia, Calif.: Clipper Office, 1856), 9. For a case study of one extended conflict over water rights see Donald J. Pisani, "The Origins of Western Water Law," *California History* 70 (Fall 1991): 242–57, 324–25.

32. As quoted in Donald J. Pisani, *To Reclaim a Divided West: Water, Law, and Public Policy, 1848–1902* (Albuquerque: University of New Mexico Press, 1992), 21.

33. Pisani, *From the Family Farm to Agribusiness,* 30–53; Pisani, *To Reclaim a Divided West,* 11–32; Douglas R. Littlefield, "Water Rights During the California Gold Rush: Conflicts over Economic Points of View," *Western Historical Quarterly* 14 (October 1983): 415–34.

34. For an excellent recent survey of the development of water rights in nineteenth-century California see Norris Hundley, Jr., *The Great Thirst: Californians and Water, 1770s–1990s* (Berkeley: University of California Press, 1992), 63–118.

35. See, for example, *Creighton v. Evans,* 53 Cal. 55 (1878); *Pope v. Kinman,* 54 Cal. 5 (1879); and *Anaheim Water Company v. Semi-Tropic Water Company,* 64 Cal. 185 (1883). On water

conflicts in the San Joaquin Valley during the 1870s, 1880s, and later, see Arthur Maass and Raymond L. Anderson, . . . *and the Desert Shall Rejoice: Conflict, Growth, and Justice in Arid Environments* (Cambridge, Mass.: MIT Press, 1978), 157–274.

36. Pisani, *From the Family Farm to Agribusiness*, 209–49.

37. For an overview of these two systems of water law, see Robert Dunbar, *Forging New Rights in Western Waters* (Lincoln: University of Nebraska Press, 1983), 59–85.

38. As quoted in Donald J. Pisani, *Water, Land, & Law in the West: The Limits of Public Policy, 1850–1920* (Lawrence: University Press of Kansas, 1996), 12.

39. Paul, *Mining Frontiers of the Far West*, 169.

40. Robbins, *Our Landed Heritage*, 144.

41. Shinn, *Land Laws of Mining Districts*, 7.

42. Josiah Royce, *California, from the Conquest in 1846 to the Second Vigilance Committee in San Francisco: A Study of American Character* (Boston: Houghton, Mifflin, 1886). Also see Robert V. Hine, *Josiah Royce: From Grass Valley to Harvard* (Norman: University of Oklahoma Press, 1992).

43. Paul, *California Gold*, 214–15, 218, 223.

44. Hittell, *Mining in the Pacific States*, 212.

45. *Fitzgerald* v. *Urton*, 5 Cal. 308 (1855), at 309.

46. Harry N. Scheiber and Charles W. McCurdy, "Eminent-Domain Law and Western Agriculture, 1849–1900," *Agricultural History* 49 (January 1975): 112–30; McCurdy, "Stephen J. Field and Public Land Law Development in California, 1850–1866," 246, 250–51.

47. Anon., "Wants and Advantages of California," *Overland Monthly* 8 (April 1872): 338–47.

48. William Henry Ellison, *A Self-Governing Dominion: California, 1849–1860* (Berkeley: University of California Press, 1950), 167–91; Yale, *Legal Titles to Mining Claims and Water Rights*, 89–98.

49. Smith, *Mining America*, 3, 6, 23.

7

Mother Lode for the West

California Mining Men and Methods

Duane A. Smith

High in the Colorado Rockies, snow hampered the little prospecting party as it moved slowly up a gulch from the Arkansas River. The men dug deep into gravel on this cold morning in April 1860 and called on the oldest and most experienced member of their party to pan the sand. Veteran Forty-niner Abe Lee obliged, while the rest of the group gathered around a fire to warm themselves. The rest of the story became legendary.

Noticing Lee peering intently into his pan, one of the party shouted to him, "What have you got, Abe?" "Oh, boys," he yelled, "I've just got California in this here pan." Thus the gulch and a brand new mining district had a name, California. Abe Lee had never had such luck in California, nor would he again, although he would be around long enough to be marginally involved in the later bonanza Leadville silver rush that occurred only a few miles from his 1860 discovery.[1]

This story was repeated many times throughout the West, as ex-Californians took their skills and experience over deserts and mountains in their search for gold. Abe Lee and his friends were part of a worldwide movement, yet they probably never took the time to consider, or comprehend, the California mining contribution. Nor was it only people, it was everything that could be considered part of mining— from the legend of life in the mining camps to equipment that is still being used.[2]

Fifty years after the 1848–49 rush, Alaska and the Canadian Yukon exploded on the mining scene. Maybe there were not many Forty-niners there, but their legacy arrived and stayed well into the twentieth century with the clanking dredges. Mining historian Clark Spence described it concisely: "Thus Alaska gold dredging was part of a global industry—one that looked to California for inspiration, technology, skilled labor and sometimes capital."[3] The same story, sans dredges, had been repeated scores of times earlier.

California Argonauts pause from working their claim to have their picture taken sometime in the early 1850s. The skills and tools and techniques developed in the mines of the Golden State were carried throughout the American West—and indeed, the world—by prospectors who joined in the successive rushes that for half a century kept alive the dream of a new El Dorado just over the horizon. *Courtesy California State Library.*

Not that Californians were always welcome. In 1853, they were not greeted eagerly to the Australian gold rush. As historian Jay Monaghan explained, "Only a small proportion of the people coming to Australia were Californians. But Californians' bad reputation, lawlessness, revolutionary background, aggression against Mexico, and crusading determination to save the world from mobocracy by force if need be, tainted all Americans, just as the few ex-convicts from Australia had tainted all immigrants in San Francisco from down under."[4] It was a two-way street in many ways. After they returned home, Australians who had gone to California helped open the gold fields in New South Wales. Gold fever is universal.

These three examples display California's worldwide impact, but as California would give to the world, so had the state itself also borrowed from several centuries of worldwide mining experience. The cosmopolitan California rush brought together miners and mining people from throughout Europe, Asia, and the Americas.

Germans, Latin Americans, Cornishmen, Mexicans, Welsh, English, French, Spaniards, Italians, and Chinese, as well as lead miners from Wisconsin and gold miners from Georgia and North Carolina, all contributed. They helped the "pilgrims" learn the basic rudiments of mining. Mining laws, methods, mining and milling equipment, and ideas arrived along with the people in those exciting days of 1848 and 1849. Indeed, had these early Californians but realized it, many methods they used had been described (in Latin) and illustrated in 1556 by a German scholar who wrote under the name of Agricola. To these they added innovations derived from their own experiences, including hydraulicking, dredges, and water laws. This mining heritage was exported to the whole world.[5]

By the mid-1850s, the glory days of "poor man's diggings" of placer gold were beginning to pass in California. The pattern that would be repeated throughout the West had occurred. Companies and corporations now mined on a large scale; it took money to make money in mining. Already, around Grass Valley and Nevada City, hardrock mining, or burrowing into the ground after gold found in combination with other minerals, was taking place. This took skill, equipment, and finances that the average Californians did not have. They stood ready, however, poised to stampede to any new El Dorado that promised to be another California. In the generations that followed, they and their descendants did just that. Off they went, prospecting up nameless creeks, digging into any mountain that looked promising, crossing waterless deserts, and wandering on over the next ridge into any valley that seemed more enticing. With them went California's mining heritage—both placer and hardrock.

The miners themselves often remain nameless. Average folk they were, who caught mining fever and chased their dreams into a lifetime of "might-have-beens" or "used-to-bes," though these cruel epitaphs do not tell the whole story. The itinerant miners opened many parts of the West and the world, built camps and towns, created jobs, encouraged settlement, promoted the places they went, helped finance developments far beyond mining, and did more by their incessant wanderings than they ever have imagined. They changed the course of national and world history only to be buried in forgotten graves near where they toiled so enthusiastically and tirelessly. As early mining historian Charles Shinn wrote in 1884, "the migratory impulse circling outward from Sutter's ruined mill had a meaning for lands outside of North America. It ultimately became of world-wide influence."[6]

Why did they go, when there was still gold in California, though much less than they had dreamed of? Maybe it is most clearly expressed in a song about the rush to Australia. For whatever reason, miners everywhere wrote more songs that concerned California (in whatever way) than all the other mining excitements combined:

> Farewell, old California, I'm going far away,
> Where gold is found more plenty, in larger lumps, they say;
> And climate, too, that can't be beat, no matter where you go—
> Australia, that's the land for me, where all have got a show.[7]

Off they went with "their washboard on their knee."

By the end of the 1850s, the impact of former miners of the Golden State was already clearly shown. California dominated the first decade of mining in the West. Only a few small gold discoveries of local significance, primarily in Washington, Oregon, Arizona, and Nevada, challenged this dominance. Then in the spring of 1858 came news of gold discoveries along the Fraser River in British Columbia. Fraser River fever swept San Francisco and the Mother Lode country.

Perhaps more than thirty thousand rushed to the new El Dorado; we will never know the exact numbers. They commandeered anything that would float and sailed northward. Little mining camps soon sprung up, featuring a high cost of living. They tried California mining techniques only to find the river high because of melting snows; not until September would conditions be favorable. There was gold, just not as much as reports promised, and most rushers soon returned to California discouraged, many losing every penny they had gathered for the trip.[8]

Amazingly, they seemed not to be deterred by this and the earlier Kern River "humbug." The year 1859 witnessed two more major rushes, to Nevada and Colorado, in which Californians and their experience played major roles. Never again would there be such national excitement nor two major mining rushes at one time; considering all that was occurring in the United States that year with the sectional and slavery questions, 1859 would seldom be equaled in American history.

Of the two 1859 rushes, Californians particularly dominated Nevada's Comstock. "Nevada is the child of California," San Francisco's *Daily Alta California* (February 3, 1872) could truthfully boast. Briefly, the early Comstock story ties it completely to California. Since 1850, small placer deposits had been worked along the Carson River drainage, particularly in a place called Gold Canyon. A few Californians from west of the Sierra drifted in and out of the unpromising area, but it remained in the backwater of mining. Finally, with California and Gold Canyon placer deposits declining, prospectors moved into the mountains and early in 1859 found several deposits that they considered to be silver. Traveling over to Nevada City and Grass Valley, they had the ore assayed. The results confirmed their expectations. The ore was indeed rich in silver. They had discovered the famous Comstock silver lode.

Nevada County, one of California's most prosperous mining counties and famous for its progress in quartz and hydraulic mining, buzzed with excitement. Off went the curious, the hopeful, the investors, and many experienced mining men. They

Hardrock miners enter the hoists of the Savage Silver Mining Works on the Comstock Lode, Nevada Territory. Photographed by Timothy O'Sullivan, who illuminated the scene in a pioneering experiment with burning magnesium wire, it is one of several images made in February 1868 at the request of the director of the Fortieth Parallel Survey. O'Sullivan's pictures, which also included views of the Gould & Curry Mine, were the earliest photographs to show the interior of American mines and to document the reality of hardrock mining. *Courtesy Bancroft Library.*

were soon joined by other Californians, who rushed to the once-isolated Nevada diggings (at the time still in western Utah). This was almost exclusively a California rush, since the rest of the country to the east was caught up with the Pike's Peak excitement, which received even more national headlines and obviously was nearer "to the states."

The miners needed every bit of mining and milling experience, financial resources, and general knowledge in their command, because never had Californians seen anything like the Comstock. They had never encountered complex silver ore before or mined under such difficult conditions. Mining costs soared, but so did profits, beyond the best the Forty-niners had ever seen. The Comstock boomed from 1860 into 1864, helping to finance the Civil War effort for the North, and then declined. Never losing faith, a few men kept plunging their mine shafts deeper, and in 1870 the "Big Bonanza" era opened. The Comstock and its principal town, Virginia City, again dominated the mining world. Before the bonanza days ended in the late 1870s, the Comstock made millionaires, created legends, advanced mining and smelting technology, and became the yardstick against which other districts would be measured. Admittedly incomplete production figures credit the Comstock from 1859 to 1881 with $292 million in silver and gold production.[9]

From start to finish, California's contributions proved critical and essential to the Comstock's development and prosperity. Nor was it all a one-sided street, as H. Grant Smith, lawyer and Comstock miner in his youth, explained. The Comstock "lifted California out of a disheartening depression. It rejuvenated San Francisco . . . the entire State shared in the benefits. California was the source for all supplies, from fruit to mining machinery, and every industry thrived." Also, many of the newly enriched Comstock investors were, or would become, San Franciscans.[10]

As much as California benefited, the Comstock gained even more from the relationship. That ever-observant Comstock reporter and writer, Dan De Quille (the pen name for William Wright), chronicled the early impact of Californians in his classic *The Big Bonanza*. They set the stage, kept the district open, and finally discovered the silver and founded the early mines. The early roads into the district all were built with California money, labor, and determination. Californians populated the early Comstock; perhaps ten thousand of them, "of all sorts and conditions," came in 1860 alone. When the Comstock miners ran into problems with the rotten rock and the huge silver veins in 1860, it was a young German mining engineer (who had been in California since 1851), Philip Deidesheimer, working in Georgetown, California, who came up with the square-set timbering system that allowed mining to continue. Square-set timbering would be an important technical feature in mining for years.[11]

Californians touched every aspect of Comstock life. As H. Grant Smith wrote in a romantic vein, "practically all of the men who came to rule the mines, the business, and the politics of Nevada had been youthful, adventurous, romantic California pioneers, and were in the prime of life; men of exceptional ability and resourcefulness, tried by hardship and ripened by experience." California and Nevada pioneer C. C. Goodwin concurred: "California drew to her golden shores the pick of the world, Nevada drew to herself the pick of California."[12] California merchants established Gold Hill's and Virginia City's major stores, operated freighting and stage lines, started newspapers, promoted the region, and even imported the first theatrical companies. They literally infused the spirit and flavor from the mining camps of California into what became the first great mining town in America's history, Virginia City. No California camp captured the attention of the American public like Virginia City did in its glory days of the 1860s and 1870s. Even budding miner and newspaper reporter Samuel Clemens ventured out there and sympathetically and humorously described the city as he experienced it in the 1860s in his classic Comstock account, *Roughing It:* "It claimed a population of fifteen thousand to eighteen thousand, and all day long half of this little army swarmed the streets like bees and the other half swarmed among the drifts and tunnels of the 'Comstock,' hundreds of feet down in the earth directly under those same streets. Often we felt our chairs jar, and heard the faint boom of a blast down in the bowels of the earth under the office."[13] It was those people under Virginia City who benefited mightily from California. The state contributed what experience it had in underground mining, basically from the Grass Valley and Nevada City mines. Mining methods, experienced miners (especially some Cornish), timbering, corporation development, and equipment traveled over the Sierra, even if they did not always meet the specific needs of the Comstock.

Rossiter Raymond, an expert mining reporter and also the U.S. Commissioner of Mining Statistics, devoted a whole chapter of his 1869 report to the manufacture of mining machinery in California. He praised the San Francisco mechanical engineers, foundries, and machine-shops for "successfully meeting" the needs of broader Pacific slope mining: "Their work is characterized by great boldness, independence of precedent, ingenuity and originality; and they to-day furnish some of the best machinery in the world for certain departments of the art of mining. . . . California not only manufactures mills and machinery for the Pacific slope, for Nevada, Idaho, Oregon, Washington, and Arizona, but exports to British Columbia, Mexico, Central America, South America, Colorado, North Carolina, and, to some extent, to Australia." He went on to praise California: "There is no country where so much money and effort has been expended in so short a time in experimenting with, and perfecting, the various machines used in mining."

Raymond elaborated in some detail the types of mills, tools, and machines that California was exporting to the Comstock and other out-of-the-state mining regions. The variety is amazing. These included various hydraulic mining equipment that had been pioneered in California in the 1850s, although the idea dates back at least to Roman times. The hand tools included thirty-one different mining picks and hand-drills and hammers. San Francisco manufactured explosives, including "giant powder," or dynamite, after 1867. Already they were experimenting with rock-drilling machines. Mine cars, rails, pumping engines, wagons, steam engines, hoisting machinery—the list is almost endless.

California stamp mills, according to Raymond, had become world famous, "superior to any other, and are regarded as models to be followed," and the state's manufacturers stood in the forefront of many new milling and smelting machines and ideas. Pans for grinding and amalgamating, copper-plates for saving gold and quicksilver, breakers, and ore-dressing and concentrating machines were a few that

The most famous of all San Francisco foundries and machine shops, the Union Iron Works at First and Mission streets, sometime in the late 1860s. Founded in the Gold Rush by the Donahue brothers, the company established its expertise in the fabrication of mining machinery at an early date. In the 1870s, during the heyday of the Comstock Lode, the works employed nearly two hundred molders and machinists and could pour more than thirty tons of molten iron every two and one-half hours. *Courtesy California State Library.*

manufacturers and foundry men sent throughout the mining world. Raymond did admit that "it may be said there has been a great waste of material and money in the headlong, blundering way in which the progress has been made." The outcome justified the means, however, in his opinion: "the result on the whole is more satisfactory than it would probably have been by this time, if every problem had been the subject of slow and careful deliberation."[14]

Pioneer California industrialist, English-born Andrew Smith Hallidie, for example, made his own contributions—wire rope and the concept of the tram. He arrived in California in 1852 and four years later began manufacturing "metal rope" at American Bar, moving to San Francisco the next year. His cables became famous, and from them came the idea of the "endless moving rope" that proved "to be of practical advantage for freight on open hillsides and in the mines." Certainly by 1871, he was building a tram in Nevada. The *Engineering and Mining Journal* enthusiastically hailed the innovation: "The wire tramway seems calculated to perform work that can scarcely be expected from any railway with two rails, no matter how narrow the gauge." Hallidie later built trams in other western states and mining men hailed them as "the cheapest way to move ores on steep mountain sides."

In the Rocky Mountains, the idea would be developed and improved. California-type trams would eventually be found throughout the world. Noted mining engineer and reporter T. A. Rickard, when he toured Colorado's San Juan mining district in 1903, called them "great spider's webs . . . spanning the intermountain spaces."[15]

California mining produced two products that helped western mining, milling, and smelting. Borax, used in metal fluxing, assaying, and a variety of other ways, was sold throughout the world. Quicksilver (mercury), with its ability to seize upon and amalgamate gold dust, and to a lesser degree silver, proved very important to the placer miner and mill and smelter man. California's New Almaden quicksilver mines were America's most extensive. They shipped quicksilver around the West and overseas, an important contribution to the success of mining, milling, and smelting.[16]

Life at company-run New Almaden was quite different from other California camps, as artist and writer Mary Hallock Foote described in her journal; she pointed out another California contribution, in describing some of the people with whom her engineer husband, Arthur, worked. They were an "unmatchable group on the West Coast who were not only great engineers whom it was an education to work under, but remarkable men, cultivated, traveled, original." These men included James D. Hague, Louis and Henry Janin, Hamilton Smith, and William Ashburner. They gained experience in California mining and traveled throughout the world during their careers. San Francisco was the headquarters for many mining engineers, including Hague.[17] Along with others, like Rossiter Raymond, who has been called "the single most influential person in shaping the development of mining engineering into a respected profession," they were the ones who took mining from the school of "hard knocks" to a professionally guided industry.

British engineer and author J. H. Curle concurred. He wrote in 1905 that "there is to be had in San Francisco about the best scientific and practical mining education in the world." Curle, who pioneered in using the automobile in mining engineering, praised the contributions of these Californians:

> The men who are being turned out from here usually begin their careers on the Mother Lode mines. With this groundwork, and with the practical knowledge they then gain of special branches of mining, as the use of big timbers, close concentration, electric and water powers—and, more than all, the treatment of low-grade ore, where economy is essential—it is not to be wondered at that these men soon become absolutely proficient. And so we find the young California engineer, or mine manager, going to-day to take up well-paid mining positions in Australia and South Africa.[18]

Even the legendary "honey bucket" owed a debt of gratitude to California. The question of human waste and sanitation in the mines had long troubled miners and owners and resulted in at least one California study about disease and sanitary conditions. The use of abandoned rooms, drifts, and other out-of-the-way places was not conducive to good health. One solution advanced was an "underground privy car" that furnished a "practical and economical remedy." The Bureau of Mines eventually published a pamphlet on underground latrines, complete with drawings and instructions on how to make a "honey bucket." It concluded by emphatically stating that, "if the cars are kept clean and are reasonably convenient, the miners should be compelled to use them." Given the independent nature of miners, such advice was probably not always heeded.[19]

The California contribution did not end with machinery. Placer gold did not have to be worked in a milling process; ore coming from the hardrock mines had to be milled or smeltered and the gold and silver saved. This took experiments, skill, equipment, and financial backing. Initially, Nevada mine owners picked out the richest ore and, incredibly, sent it to England (Swansea, Wales) to be smelted. The lower-grade ore awaited local treatment. The solution came with the work of Almarin Paul, veteran California mining man and owner of a quartz mill in Nevada City. Throughout the winter of 1859–60, he experimented with ore. By the spring of 1860, he decided to build a stamp mill to crush the ore on the Comstock. He ordered machinery from San Francisco foundries, purchased lumber, and spent an "extraordinary" amount on transportation expenses. Paul used the California stamp mill that by 1860 offered a "reliable basic model that was capable of enlargement and further improvement to meet Comstock needs." Because the Comstock ore was basically silver and gold, it could be treated much like California gold ores. That gave Paul and other California quartz men a remarkable advantage as they pioneered milling on the Comstock. Improvements and modifications had to be made, and eventually Paul developed what became known as the "Washoe pan process," or the "Washoe pan amalgamation" process. This mechanical and simple chemical process would be transferred throughout the world wherever similar ores were found.[20] That pattern would be repeated with many Comstock ideas, inventions, and techniques, as Comstock miners and mining engineers migrated throughout the West and the world.

Because of these developments, and others that followed in the 1870s, San Francisco emerged as the "queen city" of a vast inland mineral empire. Combined with all of California, it was the source of leadership, supplies, mining equipment, and capital investment for a region that stretched from British Columbia to the northern provinces of Mexico and as far east as the Rocky Mountains.

California money underwrote much of the early Comstock developments, as experienced quartz miners and investors raced eastward to get in on the ground floor. Among the former was George Hearst, who had come west in 1850 and eventually mined at Grass Valley. He was one of the lucky ones who learned "in strictest confidence" of the wonderful silver assays from across the mountains. Hurrying

Montgomery Street, San Francisco, looking north from the Eureka Theater near the intersection with California Street, 1865. Along this thoroughfare stood most of the great financial institutions of the Golden State, which provided capital for investment in countless enterprises throughout the American West. John Parrott's Granite Block, *center*, was constructed in 1852 and over the years housed such leading banks as Adams & Co., Page, Bacon & Co., and Wells, Fargo & Co. *California Historical Society, FN-30961.*

across the range, he purchased one-sixth interest in the Ophir mine, the first bonanza. He sold his California property, borrowed money, and saw it all returned handsomely when the first shipment of silver ore paid $91,000 above smelting and transportation costs. Those Ophir silver bars convinced Californians that the bonanza had been found. They also provided the basis for the Hearst fortune. Before he finished, his investments were strung across the mining West. Hearst's money would help develop both gold in the Black Hills of South Dakota and copper in Butte, Montana.[21]

More legendary were the accomplishments of four Californians, four poor Irishmen who became the "bonanza kings" of the Comstock—John Mackay, James Fair, James Flood, and William O'Brien. Their fight to control the Comstock, a fight among California investors, is one of the epic financial struggles in mining history. All had been miners in California except O'Brien, a small-time San Francisco businessman who eventually became a partner with Flood in a saloon. Mackay and Fair migrated to the Comstock, and ultimately the four teamed up.

The story does not start with them, however. Rather, it begins with William Ralston, the speculative genius who in 1864 helped organize the Bank of California, which soon became the leading financial institution of the Far West. As the Comstock slipped from rich ore into *borrasca* (barren rock) that same year and the next, the bank suffered some serious overdrafts in its Virginia City branch. Ralston sent William Sharon, a shrewd, cynical, mining and stock speculator, to Virginia City as branch manager and agent. Behind these two stood most of the "big names" in San Francisco finance. Sharon recovered the money and became convinced that with some shrewd planning the bank could monopolize the district and reverse the Comstock's fortunes.[22]

After some discussion and disagreement with the bank's board, the effort was started. Sharon's plan was simple in design, complex to carry out. First, he lent money at lower interest to milling, smelting, and mining companies; then, when they could not make a payment, he ruthlessly foreclosed on their properties. The mills and smelters fell first, and Ralston soon acquired a near monopoly and relocated the reduction works to the Carson River, with its water power. To reduce transportation costs, Ralston and Sharon in 1869–70 built the Virginia and Truckee Railroad, which tied into the Central Pacific at Reno. They then moved to control the companies that brought lumber and water to the Comstock. Criticism of the "bank crowd" and its various monopolies became legendary as Comstockers forgot that the bank's heavy investments during these disheartening years gave the district and Virginia City a needed boost and hastened the coming of the revival.

The challenge to Ralston and Sharon came from two groups, the "bonanza kings" and two other Californians, Alvinza Hayward and John Jones. Through a series of stock manipulations and trading, and inside information, the two groups broke the Ralston/Sharon monopoly in the early 1870s and brought in the era of the "Big Bonanza." In the end, both San Francisco and the Comstock benefited, although Ralston went bankrupt.

The four Irishmen gained control of the greatest of the Comstock mines, the Consolidated Virginia, and promptly became multimillionaires. Of them, Comstock historian H. Grant Smith said that "the members of the Firm played a fairer game than any other group in control of Comstock mines." They did more extensive "deep work" than any other group, and "they paid dividends whenever it was possible." Eighty million of the $125 million in dividends paid by Comstock mines came from their mines.[23]

San Francisco emerged as the mining investment and stock center of the Pacific Coast, and its money went throughout Nevada and elsewhere in the mining West. Not always were the investments successful. An interesting story is that of Adolph Sutro, who arrived in California in 1851 and joined the Comstock rush. His dream was to dig a tunnel under the Comstock to drain groundwater from the mines, provide a passageway for ore to the Carson River mills, and supply needed ventilation

The works of the Gould & Curry Mine at Virginia City, one of the many hardrock enter-prises on the Comstock underwritten by California investors, 1865. *Courtesy Huntington Library, San Marino, Calif.*

for the increasingly hot, humid mines. Financial, technical, and political problems slowed him, and although begun in 1869, his tunnel did not reach the Comstock's main mines until 1878. He managed to depart a millionaire, but the tunnel never proved financially successful.[24]

Financial manipulations such as these were not unique to California. California investors became masters of the "game," however, and would be found throughout the West in the years that followed. Companies incorporated in California were a trademark of many western mining districts. The same proved true of the emergence of San Francisco as a mining manufacturing center. California mining equipment would be found everywhere, but especially in the states of Idaho and Nevada, both of which had direct transportation connections and multiple ties to California.

Comstock excitement and success created interest in the rest of Nevada. Prospectors, followed by miners and investors, scurried over desert valleys and mountains searching for the next Comstock. Along with them came more California experience and money. W. Turrentine Jackson observed that California capital moved into the Austin and Eureka districts, two of the most prominent Nevada strikes in the 1860s after the Comstock. Not every district so benefited. Treasure Hill in eastern Nevada, much to the dismay of locals, did not receive much California money. But mining methods developed in California and the Comstock were found there, and everywhere. California newspapers "boomed" each new Nevada discovery, and Californians' interest was whetted by each new "Comstock." "Ho for the Reese River [Austin]," they read, along with Pioche, Tuscarora, Belmont, and places between. For more than two generations, Nevada and California were close mining partners.

Eureka was typical of the pattern that occurred in Nevada. There, California money and experience helped develop transportation, mines, and smelting. San Francisco capitalists purchased the major mines and helped develop the Eureka district into second place in production behind the Comstock. Because this was a lead and silver district, new smelting methods had to be developed, and Eureka emerged as one of the foremost smelting districts in the entire West. Smelting methods developed here went directly to Colorado's Leadville and San Juan mining districts, displaying how California's influence went well beyond its immediate physical and financial impact.[25]

Nor did it stop with the end of the century. Californians were there, along with their money, experience, and machinery, in Goldfield and Tonopah, Nevada, in the early 1900s. They purchased, developed, and speculated in these gold and silver districts and helped one more time to boom Nevada's mining industry. As in 1849 and again on the Comstock, the production of the Tonopah and Goldfield areas, Nevada historian Russell Elliott concluded, "had a pronounced effect on the total gold and silver production of the United States." The Comstock in 1875 accounted for 75 percent of American production; Nevada accounted for 20 percent in 1910.[26]

Colorado's connection to California was not nearly as close as Nevada's. At first, the Pike's Peak gold rush of 1859 completely overshadowed the slower-to-develop and farther-from-the-East excitement at the Comstock. "Pike's Peak or Bust" attracted the attention of the eastern press and easterners. They came in near record numbers that spring—100,000 people, give or take a few—second only to the numbers of 1849. Because Californians became enamored with the potential of the Comstock, and because California investment and manufacturing centers were far away, Coloradans looked to the Midwest, the East, and Europe for support.

Nevertheless, Californians played an important role in the early discoveries of Colorado gold. A group of Cherokees from Indian Territory, en route to the California gold fields in 1850, found a small amount of gold near what would become Denver. Subsequently, having little luck in California's Mother Lode country, they returned home but did not forget what they had found along the Rocky Mountains. In 1858 they returned to the Rocky Mountains, led by William Russell, an experienced Georgia and California miner. The few hundred dollars worth of gold they found became the incident igniting the 1859 rush. "The New Eldorado!!!! Gold in Kansas Territory," screamed midwestern and eastern newspapers, and the rush was on in the spring. It would have been the "hoax" that some people predicted, if other experienced California miners had not found several more promising discoveries during the winter of 1858–59. George Jackson and John Gregory struck gold near present-day Idaho Springs and Central City. While they tried to keep their finds secret, by May 1859 the word was out, and Colorado's mining future leaped from questionable to boom.

Among the "Fifty-niners" who rushed westward were a few Forty-niners whose knowledge of placer mining helped the storekeepers, farmers, and other would-be miners work through the early trials and tribulations of the Pike's Peak country. As Rodman Paul observed, "former Californians and Georgians were their instructors; from these veterans of earlier mining frontiers the inexperienced multitude learned just enough to get started." Unfortunately, however, Colorado's placer deposits were neither as rich nor as large as California's, and within months Coloradans turned to quartz mining. Here, "since so many of the 'Old Californians' of the Colorado rush had in fact left California several years previously, they were not familiar with the technical progress that came with the maturing of mining on the Pacific Coast." Colorado miners were thus doomed to repeat some of the same mining and milling mistakes and other experiences of California.[27]

They were not doomed to repeat everything, however. One of the significant contributions of Californians was the development of the concept of mining districts and mining law. The need to provide a basis for claim ownership and registration, and a fundamental mining law structure, had caused these developments. They wanted nothing costly or detailed, only a system that could be easily understood and function with rudimentary democracy. Again the Californians drew on worldwide experience in addition to their own as they scattered throughout the West taking the ideas with them.

The first mining district, created June 8, 1859, in present-day Gilpin County, Colorado, shows the influence of Fifty-niners and their California experience. The boundaries of the Gregory District were defined, the number of claims an individual could stake limited (to one), the rules for staking and registering claims specified, the rights of companies defined, and the rules for settling disputes in a miner's court (with a three-man jury) described. The costs were small, $1 for registering a claim and $5 each for the secretary and "referees" for "their services" in settling a dispute. These first "laws and regulations" would be expanded at a July 16, 1859, meeting, and later as needed. Out of the experience of Gregory District and scores of other districts throughout the West would eventually come the federal mining laws in 1866, 1870, and finally 1872. Mining Commissioner Raymond hailed the "eminently wise and salutary" 1872 measure. "Doubtless some minor points in the bill would be found to require modification to insure its smooth working. Those may be left to the indications of future experience." William Stewart, the U.S. Senator from Nevada, led a determined battle to help bring this about. A former California miner, lawyer, and mining law expert, Stewart had transferred his career to the Comstock and on to Washington. Raymond congratulated him for displaying both "courage and judgment in its preparation." That 1872 mining law is still the "law of the land."[28]

One of the most significant impacts of California and Colorado on western mining would be the development of water law, the doctrine of prior appropriation, or "first in time, first in right." The use of water was critical to placer operations, and that water could not be turned into the consistency of "liquid mud" by the work of miners higher up the stream. Water conditions affected the rights of quartz miners and mill and smelter men as well. California wrestled with the problem in the 1850s and Colorado faced it soon after the 1859 rush. The Gilpin County meeting of June 8 defined a basic principle—"in all cases priority of claim when honestly carried out shall be respected"—and "resolved" that, for quartz mining purposes, no one could use more than half the water of a stream. A February 1860 meeting produced a series of more detailed sections on water rights, including "that when water is claimed for Gulch and quartz Mining purposes on the same stream neither shall have the right to more than one-half unless there shall be insufficient for both, when priority of claims shall determine" and "that all other questions not settled by the provisions of this act, arising out of the rights of Riparian proprietors shall be decided by or in accordance with the provisions of the Common Law." It would not be until the 1870s in Colorado that finally the water conflicts between mining, agriculture, and urban needs would bring the issue to a head. The Colorado Supreme Court in 1872 laid down the basis for what became the "Colorado System," which was adopted throughout much of the West.[29]

Colorado also used California technology, a point Rodman Paul clearly brought out in his vanguard 1960 essay, "Colorado as a Pioneer of Science in the Mining West." Some of the earliest mining equipment, including simple stamp mills, although they came from Iowa, were manufactured from plans obtained from experienced San Francisco manufacturers. Modifications soon appeared, and California's technological influence diminished after the early 1860s, although in a few cases where similar types of ores were found, machinery and milling practices were almost identical. California- and Nevada-trained mining men and miners continued coming to Colorado in the following decades. As mentioned earlier, along with them came Eureka, Nevada, smelting and other techniques and equipment. Colorado would make its own contributions in the use of electricity, trams, power drills, and particularly in the scientific approach to smelting and mining gained from metallurgists, geologists, and chemists, but Colorado's start reflected California precedents.[30]

California was the "pioneer teacher" for its two most important rivals, Nevada and Colorado. Each state made contributions, along with other western states, to the advancement of the mining industry. "Within a generation, [they] transformed American miners from unskilled operators into mining specialists whose services were sought in all parts of the world." By the turn of the century, Americans and American equipment had moved into the front rank of mining.

Unfortunately, California contributed something else to Colorado: mining speculators and speculation. It might have happened anyway, but the experienced Californians raced to pick up pieces of Colorado's wealth before it was too late. George D. Roberts, a ruthless sort who cut his teeth on California and Nevada mining speculations and the 1872 "diamond hoax" in northwestern Colorado, arrived. Along with George Daly, and some others of his crowd, they worked in booming Leadville and the nearby Ten Mile District. Of Roberts, it has been said that he was "a prosperous San Franciscan with—to be charitable—a shady past," who left in his wake "the shipwrecks of mines, reputations, and fortunes." Before he finished, two famous mines, the Chrysolite and the Robinson, lay in ruins.[31]

In contrast to Roberts, George Hearst helped develop two of the great western mines, Butte's Anaconda and Lead's Homestake. Experienced California miner Marcus Daly, who had also worked at the Comstock and in Utah, had taken Hearst and several of his wealthy California associates to Butte. These investors' money in the early 1880s allowed Daly to spend the funds necessary to develop the Anaconda into one of the country's famous mass-production copper mines using refined smelting techniques. They almost single handedly put Butte on the road to becoming a world famous copper center. A few years previous, during the Black Hills gold rush, the same group had purchased the Homestake claim, near Deadwood. They developed this mine into one of the world's greatest, and established the model company town of Lead.[32]

George Roberts gave California mining investors a bad reputation, but the industry needed the promotion and finance that such people and their contemporaries contributed. As historians Clark Spence and W. Turrentine Jackson have shown, California's mining promoters were active throughout the second half of the nineteenth century in England and Scotland.[33] The record is a mixed one, but that was as much the fault of overenthusiastic, naive, and greedy investors as it was of unprincipled and unscrupulous speculators. Without the promotion and financial support of these men, and a few women, such as Ferminia Sarras, Ellen Cashman, and Laura Swickhimer, mining would not have developed at the pace and to the extent that it did during these years.

Californians would be found in all the western mining states, but not with the impact they had in neighboring Nevada. J. Ross Browne, a contemporary of Raymond and also a well-known writer and mining reporter, observed that, when discoveries were made in Idaho in 1861 and 1862, the region was initially looked upon "as a theater for speculation and as a place for a temporary residence"; therefore, people returned to either the Pacific or Atlantic states with their fortunes. This transitory lifestyle shaped much of the West, at least in the early years of new districts. It was the case in California in 1849, in Colorado in 1859, and in Alaska in 1898. In 1867, however, Browne had hopes that this was changing, that Idaho would attract permanent settlement, and the territory would eventually be able to maintain itself. California, in this instance, contributed agricultural products and also mining knowledge and equipment.

Veteran California prospectors and miners, who helped open the Idaho mines, repeated the process, crossing the mountains into neighboring Montana, a familiar pattern in the West. Browne, however, warned that the California experience could be taken too far. "In California nearly all the gold-bearing veins are quartz, and the prospectors hardly ever prospect for anything else." Gold, he observed, is found in "slate and porphyry" in Idaho. It was a warning well taken, but he also knew that Californians could adjust. "The skill of some prospectors," he reported, "is wonderful in determining the existence and locality of small veins covered deep under the soil."[34]

Idaho had its "golden age" in the 1860s. With California placers declining and Colorado's not matching expectations, Idaho and Montana became the "poor man's diggings." Both regions eventually turned to quartz mining, and corporation control developed there as elsewhere. California money and experience spread to both. The silver mines developed in the 1890s in Idaho's Coeur d'Alene also benefited. Even across the Canadian border, in Rossland and small mining districts such as Sandon and Silverton, California influence reached, albeit generally, and indirectly. Meanwhile, Californians and California-experienced miners scattered throughout the West, chasing their golden and silver dreams as the Forty-niners had done before them. Prospector Henry Wickenburg discovered Arizona's Vulture Mine in 1863, and Ed Schieffelen the Tombstone silver deposits in 1877. These two helped open Arizona to mining, but in the end, despite legendary and romantic contributions, it was the George Hearsts of the West who developed the prospectors' discoveries and profited the most from them.[35]

California placer and hardrock mining might have been in decline by the turn of the century, but California's influence was not. The floating California dredge, for in-

The dredge *Phoenix* at work on the Yuba River, about 1850, as portrayed by William N. Bartholomew. The machine—one of the first—was described by J. Wesley Jones, who traveled west with the artist, as "a Cumbrous arrangement, by which it was designed to drag up sand from the bed of the river, and obtain gold in large quantities." According to Jones, the *Phoenix* was abandoned after it was found to have "dredged more Money from the pockets of the owners than it did gold." Dredging ultimately proved highly profitable, and following the turn of the century the "California dredge" came to dominate the industry worldwide. *California Historical Society.*

stance, became world famous. Californians had been tinkering with the dredge idea since 1850. It was part of their effort to move more gold-bearing gravel with less work and more profit, particularly from river bottoms and banks. These early efforts produced, as dredge historian Clark Spence noted, a "never-ending line of ingenious and sometimes bizarre equipment, with one failure after another consigned to the scrap heap until the late nineties." Finally, by combining ideas from New Zealand and Montana, the "hybrid California-type" dredge appeared, superior to all its ancestors. It became the "standard for a global mining industry and a significant export item."[36]

Basically, the dredge applied the notion of mass production to mining. It offered the low cost and versatility to handle low-grade ores. Mining engineer Arthur Lakes, Jr., described it in 1909: "A gold dredge consists of a floating hull with a superstructure, a digging ladder, [an] endless chain of digging buckets, screening apparatus, gold-saving devices, pumps and stacker. It could be described as a floating mill with the addition of apparatus for excavating and elevating the ore." California set the pace, not only for manufacture, but for use. In 1910, for example, 72 of the 113 dredges operating in the United States dug in California districts. Even more significant was the complete dominance of the California dredge. In 1915, only 11 out of a total of 225 dredges in use throughout the world were not American-made. Even if not manufactured in California, they were based on California's experience. In time, these dredges operated from Nigeria to Korea, from Portugal to the Philippine Islands. By mid-1932, they could be found in the Soviet Union; 22 new California dredges worked in Soviet placer fields. The California dredge had conquered the world. "The California-type dredge, known all over the world, is so efficient that it is being used on every continent where large quantities of low-grade metals are found."[37]

It might have conquered the world, but the dredge did not conquer everyone's heart. As Robert Service watched the device tear up the Klondike, where only a few years before the Ninety-eighters had prospected, he wrote from the viewpoint of one of those pioneers:

> There were piles and piles of tailings where we toiled with pick and pan
> and turning round a bend I heard a roar,
> And there a giant gold-ship of the very newest plan
> Was tearing chunks of pay-dirt from the shore.

It was the triumph of corporations and, as Service observed, "Ah, old-time miner, here's your doom!"[38]

Service was right on both counts: the old days were gone and, tragically, the environment's balance as well. The dredge's "bill of fare was rock and sand; the tailings were its dung." That dung, the piles of washed rock snaking along wherever the dredge dug, can be seen throughout the world. Therein lies another contribution of California. Not only did California pioneer in American mining, it pioneered in environmental awareness, even if that term may have been foreign to the nineteenth century.

Hydraulic mining, using a powerful hose and high water pressure to wash gravel, was carried on extensively in California by the 1870s. While it turned a profit and allowed lower-grade deposits to be worked, it also created major problems. Tailings obstructed the river, causing flooding that ruined agricultural land in the valleys and threatened towns. The issue came to a head in the Feather River Valley and at Marysville, which had been suffering damage from floods and hydraulic debris since the early 1860s. With residents unable to manage the altered river's behavior, and facing even further flood damage despite building higher levees to protect the town and surrounding lands, the dispute entered the federal courts. Local resident Edwards Woodruff sued some of the responsible mining companies, and the case of *Woodruff* v. *North Bloomfield Gravel Mining Co.* forced the industry to defend itself.

It was a contest between the emerging agricultural and urban California versus the mining industry that had created the state.

At the trial, both sides presented economic, social, and emotional arguments, not to mention threats to support their positions. Finally, on January 7, 1884, in a landmark case, U.S. Circuit Court Judge Lorenzo Sawyer, coincidentally a Forty-niner, "perpetually enjoined and restrained" the North Bloomfield Company "from discharging or dumping into the Yuba or its tributaries." As no place existed where the mining companies could profitably dump the tailings, they were forced to cease operation. An era ended that day. Times had changed, but mining methods had not changed with them. The ruling implied that miners no longer represented California's present and future. The industry no longer drew the population or wielded the economic and political power to impose its will. The legal case marked the first skirmish of a war over broad environmental policy that would become heated a century later.[39]

The industry should have taken notice a decade earlier in Oakland. There residents objected to building a smelter in the city. Opposition centered on the offensive fumes, which would "poison our pure air" and render this "beautiful city an undesirable place to live." The city council heard complaints and, finally, on March 6, 1872, declared it would welcome all smelting works except those producing gases that would be harmful to the health of "her inhabitants." No smelter came to Oakland.

California might have "pioneered" in the environmental fight, but California's nineteenth-century miners were no pioneers in cleaning up the environment. For thousands of years, miners had dug into the earth without being challenged, so why should they pay heed now? Nor did other western miners and smelter men show any more interest when they were challenged in Salt Lake City, Denver, and Butte. They "sowed the wind and they shall reap whirlwind."[40]

California was more than the Mother Lode country. It was the mother of western and to a lesser degree, world mining. This was claimed early by the Californians, a product of local boosterism as much as a reflection of the facts. However, outside observers noted the same trend. J. Ross Browne, in his 1866 report as U.S. commissioner for the collection of mining statistics, spent almost the entire first section of it discussing California's contribution to the migration of people, ideas, equipment, and finances in other mining districts. Mistakes had been made, but the future was bright with promise.[41] That optimism was also a heritage of California—over the next mountain, in the next canyon, would be El Dorado.

Those ubiquitous veterans of the Sierra mines, the "old Californians," went everywhere carrying with them their craft of mining. They did more than that, however. They influenced regional life, the life of the mining camp and the town. The materialistic, boisterous, transient conditions of California mining communities would be re-created throughout the mining West. Perhaps Charles Shinn said it best when he wrote more than a hundred years ago that, "out of the [mining] camps of old, powerful currents have flowed into the remotest valley of the western third of the American continent. We may even seek the great cities, whither all currents flow,—New York, London, Paris, Berlin, St. Petersburg."[42]

California exported something else as well, a dream: a legend—"the days of '49." Call it nostalgia for a time passed, or perhaps one that had never really been. Maybe the Forty-niners remembered more than actually happened, but for whatever reason, the Gold Rush has become part of the American heritage, of American folklore. The entire nation felt the pull of the West. The last verse of a popular song, "Old Forty-Nine," concludes:

> But now, alas! Those times have flown,
> We ne'er shall see them more, sir,
> But let us do the best we can,
> And dig for golden ore, sir,
> And if we strike a "decent lead"
> Let's work and not repine, sir,
> But take things easy as they did
> In good old forty-nine, sir.

NOTES

1. Edward Blair, *Leadville: Colorado's Magic City* (Boulder: Pruett, 1980), 6, 7, 12, and 56. In the past generation, mining historiography has come of age. It has evolved from primarily general studies of local interest to well-researched studies of state, regional, national, and finally a start has been made on international histories. Topics and themes have matured and are as unlimited as was, and is, mining's impact. A group of well-trained, enthusiastic young scholars has emerged to "prospect" the veins of mining history. The formation of the Mining History Association, preservation efforts, and new interest within the mining industry have also stirred research and writing. The result of this effort can be seen in the notes that follow.

2. For a fascinating look at mining archaeology, preservation, and history, see *Death Valley to Deadwood: Kennecott to Cripple Creek* (San Francisco: National Park Service, 1990). This collection of the proceedings of the 1989 Historic Mining Conference at Death Valley National Monument also contains an excellent bibliography of western mining history.

3. Clark C. Spence, *The Northern Gold Fleet: Twentieth-Century Gold Dredging in Alaska* (Urbana: University of Illinois Press, 1996), 11.

4. Jay Monaghan, *Australians and the Gold Rush* (Berkeley: University of California Press, 1966), 223; see also chap. 12.

5. Rodman W. Paul, *Mining Frontiers of the Far West 1848–1880* (New York: Holt, Rinehart and Winston, 1963), 19–29; Georgius Agricola (Georg Bauer), *De re Metallica*, trans. Herbert and Lou Henry Hoover (New York: Dover, 1950), vi–xv. William S. Greever, *The Bonanza West* (Norman: University of Oklahoma Press, 1963; reprint, Moscow: University of Idaho Press, 1990), 46–54.

6. Charles Howard Shinn, *Mining Camps* (reprint, New York: Harper Torchbooks, 1965), 292; see also 290–95.

7. Richard A. Dwyer and Richard E. Lingenfelter, *The Songs of the Gold Rush* (Berkeley: University of California Press, 1964), 80.

8. Paul, *Mining Frontiers of the Far West*, 38–39; Daniel P. Marshall, "Rickard Revisited: Native 'Participation' in the Gold Discoveries of British Columbia" (unpublished paper presented at the 1996 Mining History Conference).

9. For a summary of the Comstock, see Greever, *Bonanza West*, Paul, *Mining Frontiers of the Far West*, Dan De Quille, *The Big Bonanza* (originally published in 1876, numerous reprints), and H. Grant Smith, *The History of the Comstock Lode* (reprint, Reno: University of Nevada, 1980).

10. Smith, *History of the Comstock Lode*, 289. Robert W. Cherny, "City Commercial, City Beautiful, City Practical," *California History* 73 (Winter 1994/95): 297–300.

11. De Quille, *Big Bonanza*, chaps. 1–13; Smith, *History of the Comstock*, 19, 23–24, 37–38.

12. Smith, *History of the Comstock*, 30–31; Greever, *Bonanza West*, chaps. 4, 5.

13. Mark Twain, *Roughing It* (Hartford: American Publishing, 1872), 304.

14. Rossiter W. Raymond, *Statistics of Mines and Mining* (Washington, D.C.: Government Printing Office, 1876), 471–73, 475–89, 505–17; Doreen Chaky, "John Henry v. Charles Burleigh's Drill," *Mining History Journal* (1994): 104–7; Otis E. Young, Jr., *Western Mining* (Norman: University of Oklahoma Press, 1970), chaps. 4, 5.

15. Edgar M. Kahn, *Andrew Smith Hallidie* (San Francisco, 1953), 10–11, 13. Hallidie is most famous for the San Francisco cable car system. *Engineering & Mining Journal*, June 20, 1871, p. 385, and August 22, 1903, p. 269. Otis E. Young, Jr., *Black Powder and Hand Steel* (Norman: University of Oklahoma Press, 1976), 108–12.

16. David J. St. Clair, "New Almaden and California Quicksilver in the Pacific Rim Economy," *California History* 73 (Winter 1994/95): 279–80, 291–94.

17. Rodman W. Paul, ed., *A Victorian Gentlewoman in the Far West* (San Marino, Calif.: Huntington Library, 1972), 11–13, 130, 186, chap. 12. For New Almaden, see Rossiter W. Raymond, *Statistics of Mines and Mining* (Washington, D.C.: Government Printing Office, 1874), 379–81; Rossiter Raymond, *Statistics of Mines and Mining* (Washington, D.C.: Government Printing Office, 1877), 458–59; J. Ross Browne and James W. Taylor, *Reports upon the Mineral Resources* (Washington, D.C.: Government Printing Office, 1867), 178–86; St. Clair, "New Almaden and California Quicksilver," 278–95.

18. J. H. Curle, *The Gold Mines of the World* (New York: Engineering and Mining Journal, 1905), 249. Curle concluded by saying "the young Englishman, who has as high a character, and as good brains—but a bad training—wonders why he is being passed over." See also Clark Spence, *Mining Engineers & The American West* (New Haven: Yale University Press, 1970), 127.

19. *Underground Latrines for Mines* (Washington, D.C.: Government Printing Office, 1916), 12–14.

20. Paul, *Mining Frontiers of the Far West*, 64–67.

21. Watson Parker, *Deadwood: The Golden Years* (Lincoln: University of Nebraska Press, 1981), 110–12. For the impact of other California mining men, see Richard H. Peterson's two books, *The Bonanza Kings* (Lincoln: University of Nebraska Press, 1977), and *Bonanza Rich* (Moscow: University of Idaho Press, 1991).

22. Smith, *History of the Comstock Lode*, 48–51; Paul, *Mining Frontiers of the Far West*, 76–79; Greever, *Bonanza West*, 124–30.

23. Smith, *History of the Comstock Lode,* 262–63.

24. Greever, *Bonanza West,* 117–20; Smith, *History of the Comstock Lode,* 107–15.

25. W. Turrentine Jackson, *Treasure Hill* (Tucson: University of Arizona Press, 1963), 151–52; Stanley W. Paher, *Nevada Ghost Towns & Mining Camps* (Berkeley: Howell-North, 1970), 166–72, 181–85; Russell R. Elliott, *History of Nevada* (Lincoln: University of Nebraska, 1973), 102–3, 105–7.

26. Russell R. Elliott, *Nevada's Twentieth-Century Mining Boom* (Reno: University of Nevada Press, 1966), 299–302; Ronald H. Limbaugh, "Making the Most of Experience," *The Mining History Journal* (1994): 9–13. See also Sally Zanjani, *Goldfield: The Last Gold Rush on the Western Frontier* (Athens, Ohio: Swallow Press/Ohio University Press, 1992).

27. See Duane A. Smith, *Colorado Mining* (Albuquerque: University of New Mexico Press, 1977), chaps. 1, 2; Paul, *Mining Frontiers of the Far West,* 111–14.

28. Thomas Marshall, ed., *Early Records of Gilpin County, Colorado 1859–1861* (Boulder: W. R. Robinson, 1920), 10–16; Paul, *Mining Frontiers of the Far West,* 172–73; Rossiter Raymond, *Statistics of Mines and Mining* (Washington, D.C.: Government Printing Office, 1872), 502, see also chap. 18. Charles W. Miller, Jr., *Stake Your Claim!* (Tucson: Westernlore Press, 1991), chaps. 2, 4; Russell R. Elliott, *Servant of Power* (Reno: University of Nevada Press, 1983), 55, 67–69; *The Continuing Vitality of the General Mining Law* (Denver: Colorado Mining Association, 1989), 2–17.

29. Marshall, *Early Records of Gilpin County,* 22; Carl Ubbelohde et al., *A Colorado History,* 7th ed. (Boulder: Pruett, 1995), 190–91.

30. Rodman W. Paul, "Colorado as a Pioneer of Science in the Mining West," *Mississippi Valley Historical Review* (June 1960): 34–50.

31. Stanley Dempsey and James E. Fell, Jr., *Mining the Summit* (Norman: University of Oklahoma Press, 1986), 116–25; Duane A. Smith, *Horace Tabor* (reprint, Niwot: University Press of Colorado, 1989), 118–19, 144–45; Bruce A. Woodward, *Diamonds in the Salt* (Boulder: Pruett Press, 1967), 22, 23, 29, 86; Clark Spence, "I Was a Stranger and Ye Took Me In," *Montana Magazine* (Winter 1994): 43–53; Joseph E. King, *A Mine to Make a Mine* (College Station: Texas A&M University Press, 1977), 91–97, 113–14.

32. Isaac Marcosson, *Anaconda* (New York: Dodd, Mead, 1957), 35–40; Watson Parker, *Gold in the Black Hills* (Norman: University of Oklahoma Press, 1966), 196–97; Greever, *Bonanza West,* 239–40, 307–8; Paul, *Mining Frontiers of the Far West,* 147, 180, 185–86. For a less successful Black Hills operation, see David A. Wolff, "Mining Ground on the Fringe," *Mining History Journal* (1995): 15–26.

33. See Clark C. Spence, *British Investments and the American Mining Frontier, 1860–1901* (Ithaca: Cornell University Press, 1958), and W. Turrentine Jackson, *The Enterprising Scots* (Edinburgh: Edinburgh University Press, 1968).

34. J. Ross Browne, *Report on the Mineral Resources of the States and Territories West of the Rocky Mountains* (Washington, D.C.: Government Printing Office, 1868), 517, 518–19, 522–23, 532; Merle W. Wells, *Gold Camps and Silver Cities* (Moscow, Idaho: Bureau of Mines, 1983), 1–24; Julia Conway Welch, *Gold to Ghost Town* (Moscow: University of Idaho Press, 1982), 9–20. See also Ronald C. Brown, *Hard-Rock Miners* (College Station: Texas A&M University Press, 1979). For women's contributions see Sally Zanjani, *A Mine of Her Own* (Lincoln: University of Nebraska Press, 1997).

35. Jeremy Mouat, *Roaring Days* (Vancouver: University of British Columbia Press, 1995), chaps. 1–3; Veronika Pellowski, *Silver, Lead & Hell* (Sandon: Prospector's Pick Publishing,

1992), 11–20; Duane A. Smith, "The Vulture Mine," *Arizona and the West* (Autumn 1972): 231–35; John Fahey, *Hecla* (Seattle: University of Washington Press, 1990), 3–15.

36. Clark C. Spence, *The Conrey Placer Mining Company* (Helena: Montana Historical Society Press, 1989), 3–11; Spence, *Northern Gold Fleet*, 1–12.

37. Arthur Lakes, Jr., "Gold Dredging Practice in Placers of Breckenridge, Colorado," *Mining Science* 59 (January 12, 1909): 28; Spence, *Northern Gold Fleet*, 10–11.

38. Robert Service, *The Best of Robert Service* (New York: Dodd, Mead, 1953), 56.

39. Robert Kelley, *Gold vs. Grain: The Hydraulic Mining Controversy in California's Central Valley* (Glendale, Calif.: Arthur H. Clark, 1959), 57–58, 76, 240–42; Duane A. Smith, *Mining America* (reprint, Niwot: University Press of Colorado, 1993), 67–72.

40. Smith, *Mining America*, 74–75; also chaps. 3, 4, 5.

41. Browne and Taylor, *Reports upon the Mineral Resources*, 13–36. See also Browne, *Report of the Mineral Resources*, 12.

42. Shinn, *Mining Camps*, 294–95. See also, for example, Rodman W. Paul, *California Gold: The Beginning of Mining in the Far West* (reprint, Lincoln: University of Nebraska Press, 1965), 334–41, chaps. 6, 16, 18; Laurie F. Maffly-Kipp, *Religion and Society in Frontier California* (New Haven: Yale University Press, 1994), 184–85; Duane A. Smith, *Rocky Mountain Mining Camps* (reprint, Niwot: University Press of Colorado, 1992), chaps. 2, 14.

8

Seeing the Elephant

Anthony Kirk

In December 1848—the month President James K. Polk precipitated a mad rush west by publicly declaring that rumors of the discovery of a new El Dorado on the far reaches of the continent were true—a struggling young artist named George Holbrook Baker caught the gold fever. Tossing aside his brushes and closing his New York City studio, Baker hurried home to Boston, where he threw in with eleven other "respectable young gentlemen" to form a mining company, the New England Pioneers. "Armed with proper defensive weapons," the adventurers set out for California in early January, having received the admonition of Reuben Lovejoy "to stick to our 'New England Principles' and not to leave one in exchange for every lump of gold taken out."[1]

Traveling by way of New Orleans, the Pioneers crossed the gulf waters on the schooner *Nancy Bishop* and, after riding muleback from Vera Cruz to Mazatlán, boarded a steamer for San Francisco. By late June, Baker was working a claim on the North Fork of the American River, one of thousands of enthusiastic young Americans eager to gather the golden harvest of this distant, fabled land. The first day, Baker's labor brought him the grand sum of two dollars. The following day, fortune again eluded him, and on the third day of backbreaking toil he was rewarded with exactly forty cents. A miner, Baker philosophized, was "one who endures many hardships, suffers many privations, and ventures his health, in a measure, for the golden hope of gain, and often it amounts only to that, as some return with injured health and empty pockets." On the Fourth of July, after less than two weeks in the mines, Baker packed up and headed off for Sacramento City, "satisfied," as he put it, "with having seen the 'elephant.'"[2]

Popular in the mid-nineteenth century, the expression "seeing the elephant" carried a variety of meanings. Following an exhausting forced march across the dreary

"Seeing the Elephant," a mid-nineteenth-century lithograph designed by Wm. B. Mc-Murtrie. Printed and published by Benjamin F. Butler. *California Historical Society, FN-30610.*

wastes of western Washoe from the Carson Sink to the Truckee River—the road lined with dead and dying livestock, abandoned wagons and provisions—the Forty-niner Lucius Fairchild wrote in his diary that "that desert is truly the great Elephant of the route and God knows I never want to see it again." Like Fairchild, Americans used the phrase to describe a hardship or an ordeal they had experienced. But more often than not, the Argonauts said they had "seen the elephant" only after making it to the diggings and trying their hand at mining, after coming to realize that golden riches could be won only through hard labor and good fortune and that they had been "humbugged" by reports of treasure for the taking. If the expression, as such, conveyed disappointment, it was a disappointment mixed with other power-ful emotions: with the pride of having persevered in the face of countless dangers and difficulties, with the awe of having seen the new country and the mines, with the sat-isfaction of having had a grand and glorious adventure. Many an Argonaut who used the phrase probably had in mind the old tale of the farmer who upon hearing that a circus had come to town excitedly set out in his wagon. Along the way he met up with the circus parade, led by an elephant, which so terrified his horses that they bolted and pitched the wagon over on its side, scattering vegetables and eggs across the roadway. "I don't give a hang," exulted the jubilant farmer as he picked himself up. "I have seen the elephant."[3]

The tremendous excitement associated with the gold discovery was captured on canvas in 1850 by the foremost American genre painter of the age, William Sidney Mount, of Long Island, New York. Reflecting Mount's strong interest in character, *California News* (plate 1) focuses on the emotions aroused by tales of El Dorado. Wonder and awe and delight animate the faces of young and old, male and female, white and black, as all listen spellbound to an account of the far-off diggings printed in Horace Greeley's New York *Daily Tribune*. On the rear wall hang posters adver-tising the departure dates of two California-bound ships, *Loo Choo* and *Sabina,* and the sale of "Gold Diggers Outfits."

A celebrated painter, his pictures widely admired in Europe as well as in America, Mount had little incentive to respond to the excitement sweeping the country, apart from preserving the phenomenon in paint. Financially secure, he was largely immune to the gold fever, and, moreover, at forty-three he was perhaps a bit old to join in the rush, which was not only overwhelmingly masculine in character but youthful as well, the average age of the Argonauts being less than thirty. Numerous other artists, however, *were* caught up in "this extraordinary mania," as the New York *Herald* of Jan-uary 11, 1849 described it, and like George Holbrook Baker, they shut their studios and headed off for the land of gold. None had a reputation to equal Mount's, but many were gifted and successful, and together with the countless amateur draftsmen and country painters who flocked to the diggings, they created an engaging pictorial record of what they saw and of what they did, of what it meant to see the elephant.

Among the thirty thousand or so gold seekers who gathered along the Missouri frontier in the spring of 1849—at Independence, at Council Bluffs, at points between—for the march across the Great Plains was J. Goldsborough Bruff. A deep-water sailor in his youth, a former master's mate in the U.S. Navy, and most recently a draftsman for the U.S. Bureau of Topographical Engineers, Bruff commanded a joint-stock company of more than sixty men from Washington, D.C., and environs. Crossing the wide Missouri the first week of June, Bruff kept up the journal of the expedition he had begun earlier, illustrating many of his experiences with pencil drawings and pastels. Particularly charming is his *Ferriage of the Platte* (plate 2), showing boatmen taking two wagons of the artist's Washington City Company across the river, near its confluence with Deer Creek. Although Bruff and his men made the passage without incident, death by drowning was a surprisingly common occurrence on the California Trail, with the Platte claiming more lives than any other river. In 1849 twenty-eight people lost their lives trying to cross at North Fork, and nearly as many died there the following year.[4]

As the overland migrants massed along the muddy Missouri frontier that spring—a great army of gold seekers impatiently waiting for traveling conditions to improve—the first wave of Argonauts who had set out by sea was already in the mines. The first vessel loaded with fortune hunters departed New York shortly after President Polk confirmed the abundance of gold in California, and in 1849 some forty thousand Americans followed one of the sea routes, which would prove far more popular than the overland trail. John Hovey, a laborer from Lynn, Massachusetts, was in the advance guard, taking passage with forty-three other adventurers in the billet-head brig *Charlotte*, which sailed from Newburyport in January. Once at sea, Hovey opened his journal and painted a handsome, vividly colored image of his ship crossing the bar outside the harbor (plate 3), the beginning of a long voyage around Cape Horn. "This day," he wrote, "we bid adieu to our Dear Native Land, severing the many endearing ties which bind us to our relations and friends, amid the sighs and tears of the fairest portion of mankind and amidst the Cheers and acclamations of about seven hundred male friends who had assembled to witness our Departure for the Golden Land of Cali[fornia]."[5]

For the most part, the Argonauts who followed in Hovey's wake had an easier time of it than the men who traveled the California Trail. The overland route was a journey of more than two thousand miles and some five months, an epic excursion across prairies and mountains and deserts, a test of men and animals, requiring both physical and mental toughness. Those who set out from the Missouri frontier in the greatest migration in the history of the Republic ran a variety of risks. They suffered various diseases, including cholera, which carried away its victims by the score, and such misfortunes as accidental shootings, broken axles, insufficient supplies, and even the occasional Indian attack. By contrast, except for stale water and insect-

infested food, seasickness, or a bully mate and a bad crew, the greatest hardship endured at sea was often boredom, the terrible tedium of half a year under sail. Argonauts able to afford passage on a clipper ship, those noble greyhounds of the seas
that coursed the main at breathtaking speed, could make it to San Francisco in
ninety days. They could also shorten the trip by crossing Central America at the
isthmus and waiting at Panama City for one of the Pacific Mail Steamship Company's side-wheelers to take them to the golden shore.

The German-born artist Charles Nahl chose the Panama route when he set out
for California in 1851, as did the majority of gold seekers by this date. Nahl, who had
arrived in New York by way of Paris two years earlier, was a superb draftsman and
among the most able of the artist-Argonauts. Taking the steamer *Ohio* to Havana in
late March, he boarded the *Falcon* and arrived off the isthmus on April 11. While
waiting to go ashore at Chagres he made a pencil drawing that several years later he
would work up into a sparkling, meticulously detailed oil showing the ship's launch
pulling for shore in the shadow of the storied castle of San Lorenzo (plate 4).
Though the Pacific Ocean lay but sixty miles distant from the pestilent port of
Chagres, the trip took five days, traveling by boat and muleback, and Argonauts
could encounter a variety of dangers—bandits, alligators, poisonous snakes, and
fever among them. Despite the hardships Nahl endured, he was profoundly impressed by the sweltering tropical landscape and later wrote home to tell of rank,
teeming jungles, of "palms softly waving their branches," of the "screams of mon-
keys," of a "full moon over the water reflecting swarming beetles and birds."[6]

When Nahl arrived in San Francisco, he lingered but a single night before hurrying off to the diggings. Most Argonauts spent longer, pausing to prepare their
outfits for the final push to the mines or to seek out new comrades if contention had
splintered the mining company with which they had set out so confidently months
earlier. After a long sea voyage, a half year of terrible food and unbearable monot-
ony, it was difficult, as well, for a young man not to succumb to the attractions of San
Francisco—the streets lined with lively shops and saloons and crowded with a busy,
enterprising, and cosmopolitan people. "The very air is pregnant with the magnet-
ism of bold, spirited, unwearied action," exclaimed the journalist Bayard Taylor,
"and he who but ventures into the outer circle of the whirlpool, is spinning, ere he
has time for thought, in its dizzy vortex."[7]

Evenings in California's magnificent metropolis were particularly enchanting,
and high-minded and stout-hearted was the Argonaut who did not succumb to the
temptation of entering one of the gambling palaces surrounding Portsmouth Square,
where in a blaze of light the pleasures of drink and gaming and "bad, lewd" women
prevailed. The English-born author, adventurer, and amateur artist Frank Marryat,
who arrived in San Francisco in June 1850, caught the barbaric splendor of one of
these saloons in a drawing that was reproduced as a hand-colored lithograph in the

English edition of his *Mountains and Molehills* (plate 5). Dazzled as he entered by the brilliance of the huge chandeliers and mirrors, he delighted in the rich furnishing of the room, the gilded ceiling supported by glass pillars, and the walls "hung with French paintings of great merit, but of which female nudity forms alone the subject." Gold was heaped high upon the monte tables, where "dexterous dealers" turned the cards, and above "the din and turmoil of the crowd" sounded the occasional pistol shot.[8]

Unlike the Argonauts who came by sea, the overland emigrants often needed to rest upon their arrival, weary and ragged as they were from the rigors of crossing endless deserts and high-mountain passes. Placerville was a favored spot to gather their strength if they took the Carson River route, or Johnson's Ranch if they traveled the Truckee Trail, which led past the remains of the "cannibal camp" marking the sufferings of the Donner Party. The eight thousand unfortunate Forty-niners who chose Lassen's Cutoff far to the north, which flourished for a single season and added two hundred miles to the trip, had the hardest time of it. Those in the rear found themselves caught in the mountains dangerously late in the year and forced to abandon wagons and belongings in a race for the sheltering Sacramento Valley.

J. Goldsborough Bruff and his Washington City Company were among the last to travel the "Greenhorn Cutoff," as the Lassen route would come to be called. When the party made the strategic decision to divide, Bruff volunteered to remain with two of the wagons while the others took the strongest mules and went for help. Trapped by heavy snows, Bruff suffered through the winter in a primitive lodge constructed of poles covered with heavy cotton sheets—sharing it for a spell with two companions, one of them a four-year-old boy abandoned by his father—and then stumbled out of the mountains, more dead than alive. Despite the ordeal, Bruff kept up his journal and continued to draw. In mid-December he produced a pastel of the lodge (plate 6) where he endured inflamed and painful eyes, fever, rheumatism, and the most miserable of rations, including, one day, a portion of parboiled raven and several old, weathered deer shanks, which, when broiled, provided him with "more carbon & burnt hairs, than nutritious matter."[9]

Once safe in California, the hardships of the journey behind them, the overlanders swarmed through the mines, joining the Argonauts who had earlier arrived by ship. Among the first artists to visit the diggings was the surveyor and skilled amateur William R. Hutton. Traveling from San Francisco by way of Sutter's Fort, Hutton reached the community of Mormon Island on April 14, 1849, noting in his diary that the miners were still meeting with success in working the old sandbar in the American River where gold had been discovered the previous March. Curiously indifferent to the commotion all around him—more interested in the flora and fauna than in the gold diggers—Hutton arrived at Sutter's Mill the next afternoon, and on the sixteenth he made a fine watercolor drawing of Coloma, the mining camp that had sprung up around the storied site of James Marshall's discovery (plate 7). It was "a pretty place," he thought, and "thriving," too, composed of some twenty to thirty cabins and numerous tents. "High & bare hills on both sides," he wrote in his diary, "the vally narrow & level; full of tall, straight pines, with some oak, yew & Pinus Sinclairii."[10]

In their quest for riches, the Argonauts streamed through the foothills of the Sierra Nevada, trying their luck at Coloma, at Poverty Hill, at Agua Fria, at Humbug Flat, at countless established communities and secluded camps of their own, wherever a pan of sand and gravel washed in a mountain stream showed sufficient "color." The Philadelphia artist William McIlvaine, Jr., who arrived in the gilded summer of 1849, delighted in the scenery he encountered, particularly the rugged canyons of the Southern Mines, which he thought "extremely wild and picturesque." While tramping the diggings, McIlvaine produced a number of watercolors, including one of two miners working their claim along a gently flowing river (plate 8). But despite the serenity of McIlvaine's evocative image, with its picturesque setting and poetic atmosphere, mining was grueling work. Beginning early in the morning, the Argonauts toiled with pick and shovel, with gold pan and rocker—digging deep into the rocky earth, washing shovel after shovel of soil and sand—as the oppressive sun rose higher and higher in the sky. Exhausted, they broke for the midday repast, then returned to their claims in the afternoon to continue the sweaty struggle until sunset brought blessed relief from the drudgery. "Gold," cautioned the Forty-niner Samuel S. Osgood, "cannot be had by any one who sits still, but he must labor hard—hard as the Irishman who carries the hod or the paver who paves the street."[11]

Charles Nahl and August Wenderoth caught the toils of the Argonauts in a painting, *Miners in the Sierras* (plate 9), which shows four men in a lonely mountain canyon working a claim with a long tom. Nahl and Wenderoth, who had traveled together from New York, knew life in the diggings firsthand, having mined in the spring of 1851 with Charles's brother Arthur near Rough and Ready in Nevada County, and their portrayal of the gold diggers is powerful and authentic, wonderfully suggestive of the colossal labor necessary to wrest riches from the earth. Presumably the artists had some experience themselves with the long tom, an elongated evolution of the rocker, which had come into common use the previous year and which allowed three or four men, working together, to increase their efficiency enormously.

The Argonauts who headed west soon after President Polk electrified the nation with word of the new El Dorado often met with surprisingly good luck mining on their own, simply by employing a tin pan to wash golden flakes and nuggets from the sandy loam of a riverbank. The following year, however, good claims became scarce as the shallow placer deposits disappeared. And even before Nahl and Wenderoth started for the land of gold, miners found it imperative to form partnerships and companies in order to make a go of it in the diggings—two or three men to oper-

Plate 1. William S. Mount, *California News*, 1850. Oil on canvas, 21 ½ x 20 ¼ in. *Courtesy Museums at Stony Brook, New York; gift of Mr. and Mrs. Ward Melville.*

Plate 2. J. Goldsborough Bruff, *Ferriage of the Platte,* 1849. Pastels on paper, 8 x 11 ⅜ in. *Courtesy Huntington Library, San Marino, Calif.*

Plate 3. John Hovey, *Brig Charlotte Crossing N[ewbury] P[ort] Bar,* 1849. Gouache and watercolor on blue paper, 7 ½ x 13 ¼ in. *Courtesy Huntington Library, San Marino, Calif.*

Plate 4. Charles C. Nahl, *Boaters Rowing to Shore at Chagres,* 1855. Oil on tin, 9 ¼ x 12 in. Collection of Oscar and Trudy Lemer. *Photograph courtesy Crocker Art Museum, Sacramento.*

Plate 5. Frank Marryat, *The Bar of a Gambling Saloon.* From Frank Marryat, *Mountains and Molehills: or, Recollections of a Burnt Journal,* 1855. *California Historical Society.*

Plate 6. J. Goldsborough Bruff, *W. End of Lodge before the Snow Storm,* 1849. Pastels on brown paper, 11 x 16 ½ in. *Courtesy Huntington Library, San Marino, Calif.*

Plate 7. William R. Hutton, *Sutter's Saw Mill,* 1849. Watercolor and pencil on paper, 6 x 9 in. *Courtesy Huntington Library, San Marino, Calif.*

Plate 8. William McIlvaine, Jr., *Panning Gold, California,* undated. Water-color over graphite on paper, 18 ⅝ x 27 ½ in. *Courtesy M. & M. Karolik Collection, Museum of Fine Arts, Boston.*

Plate 9. Charles C. Nahl and August Wenderoth, *Miners in the Sierras,* 1851–1852. Oil on canvas, 54 ¼ x 67 in. *Courtesy National Museum of American Art, Smithsonian Institution; gift of the Fred Heilbron Collection.*

Plate 10. Unidentified artist, *Washing Gold at Calaveras River,* 1853. Water-color and gouache on paper, 16 ⅛ x 22 in. *Courtesy M. & M. Karolik Collection, Museum of Fine Arts, Boston.*

Plate 11. Henry Walton, *William D. Peck, Rough & Ready, California,* 1853. Watercolor on paper, 11 x 13 ¼ in. *Courtesy Oakland Museum of California.*

Plate 12. Alburtus D. O. Browere, *Goldminers*, 1858. Oil on canvas, 29 x 36 in. *Courtesy Anschutz Collection, Denver.*

Plate 13. Ernest Narjot, *Miners: A Moment at Rest*, 1882. Oil on canvas, 39 ⅜ x 49 ⅜ in. *Courtesy Autry Museum of Western Heritage, Los Angeles.*

Plate 14. Unidentified artist, *The Miner's Dream,* undated. Oil on canvas, 36 x 44 ½ in. *Courtesy Society of California Pioneers.*

Plate 15. Alburtus D. O. Browere, *The Miner's Return,* 1854. Oil on canvas, 24 x 30 in. Collection of Everett Lee Millard. *Photograph courtesy Crocker Art Museum, Sacramento.*

ate a rocker, three or four for a tom, six for two cradles, a dozen for ground sluicing. The increasingly cooperative nature of gold mining, which ultimately evolved into large-scale corporate businesses, is evident in a handsome watercolor executed in 1853 in Calaveras County (plate 10). The work of an unidentified artist, it shows a company of fortune hunters engaged in a river-mining operation, the tall mast of their derrick rising above the rocky outcrop. Although such enterprises could yield incredible riches, they could also result in complete failure or even disaster, with dams and flumes and canals—the work of months—destroyed in an unseasonable storm. As the wise and witty observer who called herself Dame Shirley put it, "Gold mining is Nature's great lottery scheme."[12]

After a day's labor of working a rocker or shoveling pay dirt into a long tom, the miners returned to their camp and prepared the evening meal, with fatigue soon leading them to sleep. For many, the hard, rocky ground was their bed, a canvas tent or rude brush shanty their only shelter. The more industrious Argonauts fitted up snug cabins with comfortable bunks, such as the New York-born artist Henry Walton depicted in his meticulously detailed watercolor *William D. Peck, Rough and Ready, California* (plate 11). Though far from home and loved ones, such accommodations were the setting for many an agreeable evening, with several miners indulging themselves in the simple pleasures of a companionable meal, pipes, and conversation. The same surroundings could, however, be the scene of sorrow and sickness and death, as related by a Forty-niner in a letter rich with imagery and human emotion. "Imagine to yourself," he wrote, "three persons in a lonely cabin situated in a deep ravine, the rain pouring down, a dark night, and nothing to be heard save the pattering rain and the barking of coyotes; one of the three lying in the worst stages of the smallpox, his face and hands almost as black as coal; the sick one in the last hour of his life and the other two sitting by, watching in silence for the last of earth; then you can see us as we passed the night of the fourth of January, 1853, in Dragoon Gulch, California."[13]

As a relief from the drudgery of their long days, the boredom, the frequent disappointment, miners sought out recreation whenever opportunity arose. Alburtus Del Orient Browere, who arrived in California in 1852 from his home in Catskill, New York, produced an animated portrait of miners enjoying a spirited game of cards at day's end (plate 12). The pleasures of cards and tobacco were innocent enough, but many of the men who labored six or seven days a week succumbed to more serious vices. "Gambling, drinking & *houses of ill-fame* are the chief amusements of the country," declared Lucius Fairchild in the summer of 1850, though he was quick to add that he did "not frequent such places." Sunday was invariably the great day to seek out the amusements of town, as all miners attested, often with surprise or shock. "In the morning," wrote Enos Christman of Sonora, "we have public auctions, in the afternoon the bullfight and the circus and Dr. Collier's troupe of

Model Artists, together with numerous fandango rooms, dance houses, and scores of gambling hells."[14] Many Argonauts, by contrast, held fast to traditional values and spent the Sabbath quietly—reading passages from the Bible, washing clothes, writing letters home, soaking up the wild, mountain beauty of their Sierra Nevada home. The talented French-born artist-Argonaut Ernest Narjot ably developed the theme of Sunday as a day of companionable relaxation in *Miners: A Moment at Rest* (plate 13), a painting executed some thirty years after he himself had mined for gold at Fosters Bar on the Yuba River.

Despite high hopes of bright fortune smiling upon them, the freedom and independence of the new country, the lusty pleasures of San Francisco and the mining towns, rare was the Argonaut whose thoughts did not regularly drift homeward to family and loved ones. "I am a stranger in a strange land," wrote William Swain to his wife in February 1850, "with the bonds of friendship, the endearments of the home of youth and the fond ties of kindred all exerting their influences upon me, and like the pole to the needle, they attract all my thoughts and preferences back to the land of my home and family." Etienne Derbec, an astute French observer of life in the mines, declared that homesickness gripped all the miners, and that "when they stretch out at night on the hard earth, their backs broken by the day's labors, they think about the bed on which they used to rest so comfortably." Many of them thought, as well, of the fond embrace that awaited them so far away, as poignantly portrayed in an oil painting by an unknown artist that dates to the age of gold (plate 14). "Oh, Matilda," moaned the Forty-niner David Dewolf in the summer of 1850, "oft is the night when laying alone on the hard ground with a blanket under me and one over me that my thoughts go back to Ohio and I think of you and wish myself with you."[15]

Few Argonauts gathered the golden harvest they set out so confidently to reap. Many returned home after a single unsuccessful season in the mines, satisfied with having seen the elephant, while others stayed on a year or two or more, finding it difficult to overcome their pride and admit defeat. But, ultimately, unless they remained and became Californians, they packed up and headed home—to Pennsylvania or Massachusetts or Iowa or Georgia, to the glad welcome portrayed in Alburtus D. O. Browere's sentimental painting *The Miner's Return* (plate 15), executed in 1854, two years before the artist took himself back to Catskill, New York. For the most part, though, whether they made their "pile" or returned empty-handed, the Argonauts came to glory in the grand adventure of their splendid, vigorous youth. The Forty-niner Richard Lunt Hale appeared in his hometown of Newburyport, Massachusetts, in the spring of 1854, bronzed and bearded, but without the riches he had set out for more than four years earlier at the age of twenty-two. His odyssey had taken him to El Dorado, where he mined on the Yuba River and at Murphys Camp, as well as to Portland and the Oregon Territory. Despite failure, Hale realized "that my experiences had been as valuable to me as the bag of gold I had come home without. The gold might easily vanish, but that which I had gained in pursuing the 'pot of gold at the end of the rainbow' could never be taken away."[16]

NOTES

1. An unidentified Boston newspaper and Reuben Lovejoy are quoted in George H. Baker, "Records of a California Journey," *Quarterly of the Society of California Pioneers* 7 (December 1930): 218, 220.

2. George H. Baker, "Records of a California Residence," *Quarterly of the Society of California Pioneers* 8 (March 1931): 46–47, 48.

3. Joseph Schafer, ed., *California Letters of Lucius Fairchild* (Madison: State Historical Society of Wisconsin, 1931), 34. The story of the farmer, which has appeared in various versions over the years, is taken from Time-Life Books, *The Forty-niners* (New York: Time-Life Books, 1974), 80. Numerous examples of how the Argonauts used the phrase can be found in the Foreword to John Phillip Reid, *Law for the Elephant: Property and Social Behavior on the Overland Trail* (San Marino, Calif.: Huntington Library, 1980), ix–x.

4. John D. Unruh, Jr., *The Plains Across: The Overland Emigrants and the Trans-Mississippi West, 1840–60* (Urbana: University of Illinois Press, 1979), 409. For Bruff's diary, richly illustrated with his drawings, most of which are at the Huntington Library, see Georgia Willis Read and Ruth Gaines, eds., *Gold Rush: The Journals, Drawings, and Other Papers of J. Goldsborough Bruff*, 2 vols. (New York: Columbia University Press, 1944).

5. John Hovey, "Journal of a Voyage from Newburyport, Mass. To San Francisco, Cal., in the Brig Charlott[e]," January 23, 1849, Huntington Library. I have introduced punctuation into the passage for the benefit of the reader.

6. Charles Nahl to his father and stepmother, Sacramento, February 3, 1852, quoted in Moreland L. Stevens, *Charles Christian Nahl, Artist of the Gold Rush, 1818–1878* (Sacramento: E. B. Crocker Art Gallery, 1976), 34.

7. Bayard Taylor, *Eldorado, or, Adventures in the Path of Empire*, 2 vols. (New York: George P. Putnam, 1850), vol. 1, 114.

8. Frank Marryat, *Mountains and Molehills: or, Recollections of a Burnt Journal* (New York: Harper & Brothers, 1855), 42, 45.

9. Read and Gaines, *Gold Rush*, vol. 2, 671.

10. William Rich Hutton, *Glances at California, 1847–1853* (San Marino, Calif.: Huntington Library, 1942), 11. Hutton's drawings and watercolors, together with his diaries and letters, are at the Huntington Library.

11. William McIlvaine, Jr., *Sketches of Scenery and Notes of Personal Adventure, in California and Mexico* (Philadelphia: Smith & Peters, Printers, 1850), 19; New York *Daily Tribune*, June 22, 1849.

12. Carl I. Wheat, ed., *The Shirley Letters from the California Mines, 1851–1852* (New York: Knopf, 1949), 136. In November 1852, seven months after she wrote the letter quoted from, Dame Shirley noted that the thirteen men of the American Fluming Company, which had turned a branch of the Feather River out of its bed, had been rewarded with $41.70 in gold dust for their summer's labor.

13. Enos Christman, *One Man's Gold: The Letters & Journals of a Forty-Niner*, ed. Florence

Morrow Christman (New York: Whittlesey House, 1930), 276. Dragoon Gulch was located near the mining town of Sonora.

14. Schafer, *California Letters of Lucius Fairchild,* 71; Christman, *One Man's Gold,* 179

15. William Swain and David Dewolf are quoted in J. S. Holliday, *The World Rushed In: The California Gold Rush Experience* (New York: Simon & Schuster, 1981), 329, 353; A. P. Nasatir, *A French Journalist in the California Gold Rush: The Letters of Etienne Derbec* (Georgetown, Calif.: Talisman Press, 1964), 121.

16. Carolyn Hale Russ, ed., *The Log of a Forty-Niner* (Boston: B. J. Brimmer, 1923), 180.

9

The Gold Rush and the Beginnings of California Industry

David J. St. Clair

THE CALIFORNIA ECONOMY ON THE EVE OF THE GOLD RUSH

In 1845, California was a sparsely populated, remote, colonial outpost. Not counting the 100,000 unassimilated Indians who continued to live independently, California's population of 17,900 (10,000 assimilated Indians, 7,000 Spanish/Mexican descendants, 700 Americans, and 200 Europeans) was largely clustered along the coast from San Diego to Sonoma.[1] Monterey and Los Angeles were its cultural centers, while San Francisco, then known as Yerba Buena, was only a small hamlet of a few hundred people.

On the eve of the Gold Rush, the missions had been secularized and decaying for more than a decade. Most economic activity was organized around the ranchos, large cattle ranches that produced hides and tallow, the two leading commodities that connected California with the outside world. Along with soap making, the processing of hides and tallow were the only activities that might be described as industrial. The hides, minimally dressed and processed, were sold to foreign merchants. Cattle brought from $4 to $6 per head, reflecting the value of their hides and fat.[2] Ample supply and very limited demand made the meat almost worthless. The export of hides, tallow, and small quantities of wheat, soap, lumber, and gold financed imports. Imported products and local crafts provided Californians with a simple but comfortable life.

California's pre-gold-rush economy was certainly rudimentary. Some historians have gone further, arguing that it was stagnant. In their pioneering economic history, Robert Cleland and Osgood Hardy described California from 1769 to 1848 as "sparsely populated by an unambitious, pastoral people who were seemingly . . . indifferent to all material progress and . . . unmindful of the vast economic opportunities that surrounded them on every hand."[3] Although this stereotypical criticism

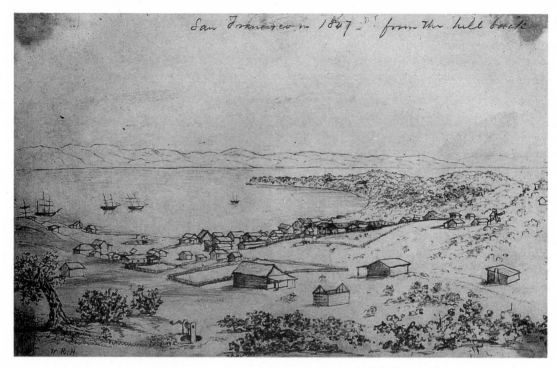

San Francisco in 1847 from the hill back

When the amateur artist William R. Hutton visited San Francisco in September 1847, it was a rough-and-tumble community of adobes, shanties, and frame buildings scattered along Yerba Buena Cove. But following the discovery of gold at Coloma in January, the village was transformed into a vigorous cosmopolitan city. By late 1851 it had a population of some thirty thousand, streets lined with solid brick edifices, and one of the busiest ports in the nation. *Courtesy Huntington Library, San Marino, Calif.*

is unwarranted, there is no doubt that the California economy was small and largely undeveloped.

The Gold Rush unleashed a torrent of change on this pastoral economy. Its first effect was to disrupt the economy. Workers, ranch hands, and shopkeepers rushed off to seek their fortunes in the gold fields. One San Francisco newspaper printed its last edition in 1848 with the following declaration:

> The majority of our subscribers and many of our advertising patrons have closed their doors and places of business and left town. . . . We have also received information that very many of our subscribers in various parts of the country have left their usual places of abode, and gone to the gold region. . . . The whole country from San Francisco to Los Angeles and from the sea to the Sierra Nevada resounds with the sordid cry of "gold! GOLD!! *GOLD!!!*" while the field is left half planted, the house half built, and everything neglected but the manufacture of shovels and pickaxes.[4]

Although we have no statistics, production must have suffered. Fortunately, the disruption was only temporary, as many who rushed off in search of fortune returned after finding only hard work and little gold. However, the lure of gold kept labor at a premium, at least at first, and high wages were a common complaint. John Hittell, a contemporary commentator, argued that high wages delayed industrial development in California.[5]

Those who returned from the gold fields found a very different economy. Overnight, gold transformed California's lethargic business world into a surging boom. People rushed in and gold poured out into the world economy, as California became the center of world production of precious metals. The surge of population brought an unprecedented demand that turned the traditional economy upside down. The scrawny Spanish-stock cattle that earlier had sold for $5 per head now brought $300 to $500 per head to feed hungry miners with gold in their pockets.[6]

By the beginning of 1849, California's population had reached 26,000.[7] By the summer, it jumped to 50,000. San Francisco became the world's fastest growing city, its population exploding from 812 in 1848 to 25,000 in 1850. The official census of 1850 recorded 92,597 people living in the state, while unofficial estimates put the correct figure at 115,000. California's population rose to 380,000 in 1860, 560,000 in 1870, and 865,000 in 1880.[8] During its first century as a state, California's population doubled roughly every twenty-five years.

Mining surged, and California agriculture was soon booming as well. Herds of cattle and sheep driven to California augmented local supplies. Wheat output increased dramatically. By 1860, California was producing five times as much wheat as all other western states and territories combined. California wheat exports poured into world markets. Vineyards were also planted and a wine industry took root within a couple of years of James Marshall's discovery. The impact of gold on California agriculture has generally been appreciated, but what about California industry? Was it similarly influenced, or were money, labor, and energy channeled instead only into gold mining and agriculture?

HISTORIOGRAPHY OF CALIFORNIA INDUSTRY DURING THE GOLD RUSH

Historians have offered divergent views of California industry during the Gold Rush. All acknowledge that important first steps were taken during these years, but many argue that industrial development lagged until the last decade of the nineteenth century, or even later. John Hittell began his 1862 survey of California industry, *The Resources of California*, with a list of reasons why the state's industry could not compete with eastern or European producers.[9] High wages, high interest rates, and a lack of coal, iron, and cotton supplies, he argued, were barriers that producers could not

A team of oxen hauls a wagon loaded with barrels of lime from the Davis & Cowell kilns at Santa Cruz, about 1865. The rapid rise of urban California that began with the Gold Rush created a huge demand for lime, an essential element in the making of mortar, plaster, and cement. Lime production emerged as a leading industry of Santa Cruz at midcentury, and by 1868 the company was shipping a thousand barrels a week, helping to make Henry Cowell one of the richest men in the county. *Courtesy Society of California Pioneers.*

hurdle. In the 1879 edition of the same book, Hittell added the following to his list of obstacles retarding industry: a lack of water power near cities, high transportation costs, expensive water in large towns, expensive land prices near deep-water ports, and insecure land titles.[10] According to Hittell, these obstacles prevented California from exporting any manufactures, kept industry only producing crude industrial products, and limited the state's exports to unfinished or semi-finished resources.[11]

To be sure, Hittell's 1879 edition chronicled more industrial activity in the state by that date, but he still described California products as being "mostly of a crude class."[12] He argued that California producers were able to survive because high transportation costs made outside goods less competitive in the California market.

Hittell concluded that "California agriculture and mining industries had reached advanced development in some branches, while our manufactures are backward."[13] Symptomatic of the state's retardation was its failure to embrace steam power, relying instead on its human muscle, to its "great disadvantage."[14]

Hittell's views became less pessimistic in his later work, but historians have echoed his negative themes down to the present. One author of a survey history of the state, Andrew Rolle, observed that large-scale manufacturing in California appeared "tardily on the scene" due to unstable conditions in California and its distance from large eastern cities.[15] Earl Pomeroy concludes that during the Gold Rush "Western industry lagged or even deteriorated while Western agriculture advanced in technique and prospered."[16] According to Pomeroy, the problem was that "Western manufacturers could not compete with the mass production of the older states except in goods that had to be custom-made or cost too much to ship."[17] In addition, San Francisco businessmen "were content to put their capital into the finished goods that came from the East."[18]

Richard Rice, William Bullough, and Richard Orsi note that in 1860 San Francisco ranked fifteenth among American cities in terms of population, but only fifty-first in terms of manufacturing "because conditions then discouraged heavy industry in the city and state."[19] Scarce coal and iron, prohibitive interest rates, and more lucrative prospects in mining, transportation, and land delayed industrialization until the 1860s and early 1870s. They argue that isolation brought on by the Civil War was a factor in stimulating industrial growth, but concede that the industrial demands of new mining techniques were more important.

Other writers argue that the Civil War had a greater impact on California industry. Cleland and Hardy credit disrupted trade with the East Coast with affording more protection for California's infant industries, including the manufacture of boots, shoes, clothing, chemicals and drugs, furniture, iron and steel, distilled liquor, soap, candles, and tobacco products.[20] Rolle argues that the Civil War not only provided infant industry protection to California firms, it also turned San Francisco into an export center for grain, flour, lumber, wool, mineral ores, quicksilver, and other products.[21] The implication in these accounts is that California industry was delayed until the war, an external event, forced California producers to develop their own resources. However, this stimulus was short-lived, making the industries that benefited from the war exceedingly vulnerable to the inevitable downturn that came with peace.

W. H. Hutchinson writes that while California lacked the coal and iron necessary for industrial expansion, the state "quickly established a basic heavy industry because she had to."[22] Cleland and Hardy repeat Hittell's discussion of the obstacles retarding California industrial growth, but nonetheless cite "a material advance" in California industry between 1850 and 1870, especially during the Civil War.[23] However, they argue that higher profits in mining and agriculture meant that little "serious attention" was accorded California industry until 1900.[24] Likewise, Gerald Nash sees California's industrial stage as beginning in 1900.[25]

More positive views have been expressed by historian John Caughey and journalist Carey McWilliams. Caughey writes that California manufacturing developed "hand in hand" with mining, commerce, and agriculture in northern California.[26] McWilliams takes a different tack, arguing that California enjoyed the advantages of a head start in the competition for industry.[27] He sees California becoming a manufacturing center almost at the same time that it became a state.[28] According to McWilliams, California's early start in industrialization was a distinct departure from the norm, a great exception brought about by the novel conditions created by the Gold Rush and California's unique environment. The Gold Rush, he argues, created "certain underlying dynamics" that became the hallmark of the California economy.[29]

THE PACE OF INDUSTRIAL GROWTH DURING THE GOLD RUSH

Disparaging comments about the pace of California industry are not supported by U.S. census data.[30] Statistics for California first appear in the census of 1850. While this census is not entirely accurate (incomplete and lost data resulted in an undercount), it does offer insight and a starting point. Table 9.1 shows estimates of California manufacturing from the 1850 through 1880 censuses.

The 1850 census ranked California manufacturing sixteenth (by value of output) among the thirty-six states and territories, a remarkable achievement in itself in the first year of statehood. By 1860, California manufacturing output had risen to seventh place, growing by 430.6 percent during the 1850s. This growth was far faster than that of any other state. Table 9.1 also shows the number of manufacturing establishments. Between 1860 and 1870, the number of establishments appears to drop precipitously along with a modest drop in the value of manufacturing output. This would be consistent with a revival of competition with the outside world following the war and the opening of the transcontinental railroad in 1869. However, there is a simpler explanation for the decline. Census data for both 1850 and 1860 include "mining" in the "manufacturing" category. Consequently, the Gold Rush of the early 1850s and the consolidation of mining in larger companies after those years appear in manufacturing statistics, thus distorting the data and begging the question at hand.

A better picture of industrial growth emerges when gold mining is removed from these figures. Table 9.2 shows California manufacturing with gold mining excluded. These figures reduce the size of the "manufacturing" sector reported in the census, but still show California with an industrial sector larger than nine other states and territories. More importantly, between 1850 and 1860, California's industrial sector

Two of the first iron works in California, the Pacific Iron Foundry, *left,* and the Vulcan Foundry, *right,* stand silhouetted against the waters of Yerba Buena Cove in a daguerreotype probably made in the winter of 1852–53 from the corner of First and Howard streets, San Francisco. Although steamship repairs played an important role in the early rise of foundries and machine shops, it was the needs of mining that contributed most to the growth of iron working, which by the conclusion of the Civil War was the leading manufacturing industry in the Golden State. *California Historical Society, FN-08432.*

(excluding gold mining) grew by 510.6 percent, faster than the 396.4 percent growth in gold mining. By 1860, California industry (again excluding gold mining) was ranked eighteenth, and was larger than the manufacturing sectors (with mining still included) of twenty-one other states and territories. In addition, when the distortion of gold mining is removed from manufacturing statistics, there is no decline in the number of establishments or output after 1860.

By 1870, California ranked twenty-fourth in population and sixteenth in manufacturing output (gold mining excluded). Table 9.3 shows 1870 population, manufacturing output, and output per capita for California and six other states with larger populations and larger manufacturing sectors. California manufacturing output per capita exceeded that of Ohio and Illinois, but was still well behind the others.

TABLE 9.1
California Manufacturing

Year	Number of Establishments	Value of Output (in dollars)	Percent Change
1850	1,003	12,862,522	
1860	8,468	68,253,228	430.6
1870	3,984	66,594,556	−2.4
1880	5,885	116,218,973	83.6

SOURCE: *U.S. Census of Manufactures*, 1850, 1860, and 1880. *U.S. Population Census, 1870.*

TABLE 9.2
California Manufacturing, Excluding Gold Mining

Year	Number of Establishments	Value of Output (in dollars)	Percent Change
1850	80	3,854,378	
1860	1,426	23,535,895	510.6
1870	3,984	66,594,556	182.9
1880	5,885	116,218,973	74.5

SOURCE: *U.S. Census of Manufactures*, 1850, 1860, and 1880. *U.S. Population Census, 1870.*

TABLE 9.3
Manufacturing Per Capita in 1870

State	Population	Manufacturing Output (in dollars)	Manufacturing Per Capita (in dollars)
California	560,000	66,594,556	118.92
Illinois	2,540,000	205,620,672	80.95
Massachusetts	1,457,000	553,912,568	380.17
New Jersey	906,000	169,237,732	186.80
New York	4,383,000	785,194,651	179.15
Ohio	2,665,000	269,713,610	101.21
Pennsylvania	3,522,000	711,894,344	202.13

SOURCE: Population statistics are from U.S. Department of Commerce, *Historical Statistics of the United States to 1970* (Washington, D.C.: Government Printing Office, 1975). Manufacturing statistics are from *U.S. Census of Manufactures*, 1880. Per-capita figures are the author's calculations.

Output per capita is not a flawless measure of the manufacturing sector, but it is indicative and does compensate for differences in population.

By 1880, California still ranked twenty-fourth in population and fifteenth in agricultural output, but had moved up to twelfth in manufacturing output.[31] California's per-capita manufacturing output in 1880 was about the same as Illinois's, and still greater than Ohio's. California manufacturing per capita also increased relative to all of the states shown in Table 9.3, except Illinois.

By any measure then, California manufacturing grew rapidly during the Gold Rush. Rapid simultaneous development in mining and agriculture, or more rapid industrial growth in later years, do not alter this. It will be argued below that this rapid growth was accompanied by the development of an industrial core that laid the foundation for the state's future industrial growth. There was no significant delay or lag in developing California industry, and while the obstacles to growth were formidable, the history of California industry is a story of overcoming these obstacles, not succumbing to them.

THE EFFECT OF THE GOLD RUSH ON CALIFORNIA INDUSTRIES

The Gold Rush influenced California industries in three ways. First, the Gold Rush precipitated the population boom that created a soaring demand for a wide range of consumer and producer goods. These products often had little or no direct connection to gold mining. In these cases, there was nothing unique about the gold industry, it was merely the sector that fueled an economic expansion from which other industries benefited. Second, direct gains accrued to industries linked to the gold industry. An expanding gold industry demanded inputs and technologies from supplying industries. Third, and perhaps most important, technologies and industrial infrastructure developed for the gold industry were transferred to other sectors and products. The gold industry was the catalyst for the creation of an industrial infrastructure centered around a foundry–machine shop core.

LINKS TO CONSUMER GOODS INDUSTRIES

The increased demand for food, clothing, shelter, transportation, and construction materials was initially met mostly with imports. For example, glass bottles were in such demand that old bottles from Honolulu, Tahiti, and Mexico were collected and shipped to San Francisco.[32] Imports from the East Coast followed, but breakage and transportation costs doubled their price. Local production of glass began in San Francisco as early as 1862. Similarly, the first stone house built in San Francisco was constructed in 1854 of imported Chinese marble.[33] But within two years, stone from

California quarries was replacing imports. Likewise, California initially imported all of its flour, and the first flour mills in the state got their start remilling imported flour that had spoiled in transit. Flour production expanded rapidly as California's wheat crop grew, and flour imports ceased in 1860. California flour production continued to expand, exporting to world markets.

In contrast, California breweries began immediately after the perishable beer shipped from the East Coast spoiled in transit.[34] By 1881, San Francisco had thirty-eight breweries, the first erected in 1850. Many California brewers specialized in "quick-brewed beer" that was brewed in only three days, no doubt sacrificing taste to speed and quantity.

San Francisco grew first as a bustling trade center before becoming the center of California industry. Table 9.4 shows the date and location of selected California industries established by 1860. San Francisco's domination is apparent, as is its diversity. It is also hard to discern any delay or lag here.

By 1860, California's largest industries, in order of size of output, were flour milling, lumber, sugar refining, machinery (including steam engines), and malt liquors. The largest industries in 1870 were flour milling, lumber, machinery, boot and shoe findings, sugar refining, quartz milling, and cigar making. These were mostly consumer goods industries (except machinery and, to a certain extent, lumber) that thrived in the general prosperity initiated by the Gold Rush.

Flour and lumber mills proliferated. Ninety-one flour mills and 279 lumber mills were in operation by 1860, compared to only 2 and 10, respectively, in 1850. The growth of California flour milling is shown in Table 9.5. Flour mills produced half of the food (by value) produced in the state. In addition, flour and lumber mills were capital intensive, further augmenting the demand for California machinery. California flour mills employed more than 12 percent of the state's steam engines in 1870.

California boot and shoe production is shown in Table 9.6. The sharp increase after 1860 in output-value probably reflects the disruption of imports during the Civil War. The figures in Table 9.6 also suggest that California producers were able to weather the competition from the resumption of imports following the end of the war and the completion of the transcontinental railroad.

California woolen mills provide a good example of how California's post-gold-rush agricultural success has drawn attention away from the state's industrial progress. California's first woolen mill was opened in San Francisco in 1858.[35] By 1881, there were thirteen mills operating in the state, consuming 20 percent of the state's wool and producing woolens valued at $4.85 million. Woolen imports in that year amounted to another $5 million to $6 million. Eighty percent of California wool was exported unworked. According to Hittell, the source for these figures, this high export ratio was "one of the most striking examples of the underdeveloped condition

TABLE 9.4

Selected California Consumer Industries Established by 1860

Industry	Year First Firm Established	Location
Beer	1850	San Francisco
Book Publishing	1850	San Francisco
Book Binding	1860	San Francisco
Bricks	1854	Sacramento
Coffee Grinding	1850	San Francisco
Coffins	1860	San Francisco
Comforters	1860	San Francisco
Cordage	1856	San Francisco
Confectionery	1849	San Francisco
Chocolates	1852	San Francisco
Cordials	1852	San Francisco
Crackers	1849	San Francisco
Distillery	1855	San Francisco
Furniture Shop	1850	San Francisco
Furniture Factory	1857	San Francisco
Gold Beating	1853	San Francisco
Granite Quarry	1853	Mormon Island
Jewelry	1853	San Francisco
Lime Kiln	1853	Santa Cruz
Macaroni	1855	San Francisco
Mustard Grinding	1850	San Francisco
Woolen Mills	1858	San Francisco
Paper	1852	Alviso
Printing	1851	San Francisco
Plumbing	1853	San Francisco
Sailmaking	1853	San Francisco
Sugar Refinery	1855	San Francisco
Upholstery	1853	San Francisco
Vinegar	1854	San Francisco

SOURCE: Compiled by the author from various sources.

of our manufacturing industries."[36] However, if California woolen mills had produced woolens sufficient to replace all of her imports in 1881, it still would have exported 60 percent of its wool. The problem, if that is what it should be called, was not an underdeveloped woolen industry, but rather a large wool output.

The Gold Rush also saw the beginnings of many well known names and labels. Domingo Ghirardelli opened a chocolate factory in San Francisco in 1852. Claus Spreckels began his sugar refinery business in San Francisco in 1863. Levi Strauss

David Hewes's steam paddy, which carried sand for bay fill, passes before the San Francisco Sugar Refinery at Harrison and Eighth streets. Constructed in 1856 by a corporation headed by the Forty-niner George Gordon, this was the first sugar refinery in California and the beginning of an industry that ultimately would emerge as the most economically important in the city. Relying at first on raw sugar from Batavia and Manila, Gordon's refinery was capable of processing sixteen thousand pounds of sugar a day. *California Historical Society, FN-10655.*

originally made trousers for California miners and workers. Folgers Coffee and Schilling Spices both got their start in San Francisco. The Studebaker Brothers, later automobile pioneers, started in a carriage shop in the gold-mining town of Placerville.

LINKS TO PRODUCER GOODS INDUSTRIES

Many industries were connected to the gold industry through supplier-customer links. These could be either forward or backward linkages. Forward linkages are connections with "downstream" industries, that is, industries that utilize the product. In contrast, backward linkages are "upstream" connections to industries that provide raw materials or machinery used in the production of the product in question.

TABLE 9.5
California Flour Mills

Year	Number of Mills	Value of Output (in dollars)	Percent Change
1850	2	754,192	
1860	91	4,620,952	512.7
1870	115	9,036,386	95.6
1880	150	12,701,477	40.6

SOURCE: *U.S. Census of Manufactures,* 1850, 1860, and 1880. *U.S. Population Census, 1870.*

TABLE 9.6
California Boot and Shoe Production

Year	Number of Establishments	Value of Output (in dollars)	Percent Change
1860	70	179,235	
1870	42	2,223,457	1,140.5
1880	546	4,666,814	109.9

SOURCE: *U.S. Census of Manufactures,* 1860, 1880. *U.S. Population Census, 1870.* No data is available for boot and shoe production in 1850.

Forward linkages to gold mining included jewelry making, gold beating (to produce gold leaf), and coin minting. Jewelry and gold beating were undertaken in San Francisco, but neither was particularly significant. In 1850, however, private mints in San Francisco began minting gold coins to alleviate California's currency shortage. These private mints operated until a U.S. mint opened in San Francisco in 1854.[37]

While forward linkages were not extensive, gold's backward linkages were very significant. To appreciate these connections, it is important to see gold mining as an *industry,* rather than as a discovery or find. Perhaps the most common image of the California gold miner is that of a bearded, grizzled prospector bent over a stream, panning for gold. While this may have been typical of many of the early Forty-niners, it does not accurately reflect gold mining after it quickly became more of an industry and less of an adventure.

There were different types of gold mining with different links to other industries. The Forty-niners used simple placering techniques, including panning and the use of rockers, toms, and sluices. Before 1860, placer gold mining accounted for about 99 percent of the gold produced in California.[38] All placering techniques used water, motion, and trapping mechanisms such as ridges and cleats to separate gold from mud and gravel. While larger gold flecks could be picked out of the pan or sluice,

The Pioneer Woolen Mills at Black Point, San Francisco, 1865. Though wool was sheared, carded, spun, and woven at the Franciscan missions at least as early as 1786, it was not until nearly three-quarters of a century later that the manufacture of woolen goods arose as an important industry in California. *Courtesy Society of California Pioneers.*

this mechanical separating left most of the gold behind. To improve yields from placering (and other types of gold mining as well), mercury, or quicksilver as it was commonly called, was added to concentrated ores. The mercury formed an amalgam with gold and silver. The amalgam was collected and the mercury driven off with heat, leaving the precious metals behind. Some of the mercury could be recovered for subsequent use, and the gold and silver were separated with acids. The backward linkages from placer mining thus included links to quicksilver, lumber, and the acid industry. To meet the demand from mints and mines, acid production in San Francisco began in 1854. Lumber was needed for rockers, toms, and sluices. Quicksilver, mined from California mines, was indispensable to gold and silver recovery until the invention of the cyanide process in 1890.

By the mid-1850s, however, simple placer mining sites had been played out. Hydraulic mining and dredging, more advanced forms of placering, were developed to

work less accessible ores. Both hydraulic mining and dredging are very capital intensive, with more extensive and significant links to other enterprises. California industry expanded to meet the demand for leather hoses, pumps, and nozzles. The
dams and flumes required for hydraulic mining also dramatically increased the demand for lumber. Lumber mills responded with special planks, narrower at one end
so they could be readily attached end to end, to construct the long wooden channels
for hydraulic sluices. Leather hoses were made in San Francisco starting in 1857. California oak-tanned leather was stronger than leather used by eastern and European
hose producers.[39] As a consequence, California hoses were superior products,
stronger and less expensive. Eventually, California leather hoses were exported
around the world and were used extensively by fire departments until rubber hoses
replaced them after 1874. Nozzles, first made of wood, were soon crafted out of
metal in California foundries. Dredging was initially tried in 1850 on a river boat
converted to the task of capturing gold from river bottoms near Marysville.[40] However, dredging did not become important until after 1880, when court rulings limited
hydraulic mining. The Risdon Iron and Locomotive Works of San Francisco produced a larger dredge in the 1890s that ignited interest in the technology. Dredging
remained an important mining technique into the 1940s.

Quartz, or hardrock, mining had the greatest impact on California industry. Gold
embedded in quartz was discovered as early as 1849, and was followed by a wave of
speculative excitement. But the excitement ended in a bust, and the quartz mining
that survived was carried out on a small and unprofitable basis for many years. Rodman Paul observed that as late as 1859–60, the cash returns to quartz mining could
be written off as unjustified were it not for the unique technologies invented in this
activity.[41] Later, hardrock gold mining in California, Comstock silver mining, and
the development of a California mining equipment industry owed much to the persistence of these early ventures.

Hardrock mining entailed tunneling to reach the ore, digging it out and bringing
it to the surface, and finally crushing and processing the ore. All stages of this activity
were capital intensive and required specialized machinery. To get at the ore, drills and
explosives were used to dig through rock. San Francisco foundries and machine
shops developed drills that reduced friction, breakage, and fuel consumption.[42] Hand
drills were quickly replaced by steam-driven patent drills. Steam engines were originally taken down into the mines to power the drills, but this drastically reduced their
efficiency. The air compressor permitted steam engines to remain above ground
with hoses supplying the compressed air to the drills. More leather hoses were
needed.

Explosives were also used to get at ore. Imported black powder was originally
used, but transporting it was dangerous, and shipments were disrupted by the Civil
War. Within the state, the California Powder-Works opened near the city of Santa

Cruz in 1861 to produce black powder.[43] The company subsequently opened a second facility near Point Pinole to produce its highly explosive "Hercules" powder. Acids were used in the manufacture of these explosives, leading to the development of yet more satellite industries. California explosives were shipped throughout the West for use in mines and railroad construction and were exported to Canada, Hawaii, and Latin America, especially Mexico.[44] California's explosives industry, however, did not lead to the development of an armaments industry, at least not in the nineteenth century. The manufacture of guns remained an eastern specialty. Blasting techniques developed in the gold mines, on the other hand, were applicable to the mining of other minerals. One of the more interesting applications was found in California's marble quarries, where precision blasting of marble blocks was perfected.

All but the shallowest of hardrock mines required drainage, venting, and hoisting. Timbers and lumber were needed for hoists, supports, and shoring. Hoisting machines and steam engines were produced by California foundries and machine shops; San Francisco wire and cable makers made cable for hoists and ore trams. In addition, most mining machines used leather belts in conveyers and drives; by 1861, four San Francisco firms manufactured leather belts superior to competing eastern and European products.[45]

San Francisco foundries also produced most of the pumps used to pump water out of California and Comstock mines.[46] The Risdon Iron and Locomotive Works manufactured water pipe for use in Virginia City, as well as irrigation pipe for Hawaiian plantations, and made the much-acclaimed pumps for the Chollar-Norcross Mine.[47] Pumps provide an interesting example of how California firms overcame the obstacles working against West Coast manufacturing. California foundries produced mostly mining pumps, which were large and designed and manufactured to order. California foundries relied on their design expertise, their proximity to mining company customers, and superior service to compete against cheaper eastern imports. Although they succeeded in securing the bulk of the mining business, they could not compete with eastern firms in the market for smaller pumps for cisterns, household use, or small business applications.[48] Small eastern pumps were mass-produced, employing cheap child labor, and sold for up to 60 percent less than local, West Coast rivals. California producers enjoyed neither the labor force, the low wages, nor the market size that would have enabled them to compete in this market.

California steam engines were also developed for the mines. The 1870 census records forty-two steam engines in use in California mines, many made by California companies.[49] California ranked ninth in the number of steam engines used in mines. This is all the more impressive in light of California's water-power resources. California also ranked first in the use of waterwheels as a power source in mines, employing 70 of the 134 waterwheels in use in the United States in 1870. While steam

A workman poses with one of the massive steam engines at the mill of the Gould & Curry Mine, Virginia City. On the Comstock Lode, powerful engines manufactured in San Francisco drove a range of hardrock mining machinery, including pumps, compressors, hoists, and stamp mills. *Courtesy Huntington Library, San Marino, Calif.*

engines were developed for the mines, their use spread to other California industries. In 1870, there were 604 steam engines in use in the state's manufacturing establishments. The lumber industry, flour mills, distilleries, and the iron trades often utilized steam power. The assertion that California industry lagged because it failed to embrace steam engines is simply not correct.

Processing quartz ores proved to be a formidable challenge. Ore-bearing rock was first broken into smaller, more manageable pieces. This was followed by grinding. California initially imported grinding machines from Europe for this task, but these, according to John Hittell, proved to be "fancy and usually worthless."[50] They were quickly abandoned in favor of *arrastras,* simple Mexican devices that dragged heavy stones over the ore. A Chilean version substituted a mill stone.

Slow and ineffective, *arrastras* were soon replaced by California stamp mills, which used heavy iron feet, mechanically lifted and dropped, to grind the ore. They were produced by California foundries and machine shops. Rodman Paul calls hydraulic mining and the California stamp mill the crowning technological achievements of the California Gold Rush. The stamp mill was especially important in encouraging the development of local foundries and mining technology.

Because about two-thirds of the gold in quartz ores was not recovered by early processing methods, California miners, working with local foundries and machine shops, rapidly developed other techniques to improve yields. Paul claims that more progress was made in the first twelve years of the California Gold Rush than had occurred over the previous several centuries.[51] Californians invented concentrators, machines that generally used conveyer belts and shaking motion to further concentrate ores before amalgamation. They also developed a second grinding process, often with mercury added. In the late 1850s, metal pans with mechanical stirring devices and steam heat emerged to facilitate amalgamation. These techniques were later incorporated into the vats used in the Washoe process on the Comstock.

All these mining developments stimulated California industry. The effect on the metal working industries appeared immediately in census data. In 1850, half the state's manufacturing establishments not involved in gold processing were blacksmith shops. Since there were no separate census categories for "foundries" or "machine shops," these were included in blacksmithing. In terms of value of output, California blacksmithing ranked third in the nation, behind only New York and Pennsylvania. This is remarkable for a state that was less than two years old. By 1880, the output-value of California foundry and machine shops, now separately enumerated, ranked eleventh among the states, but seventh on a per-capita basis.[52] In blacksmithing, California ranked seventh in output, and second in output per capita.

The size of the iron working trades is obscured by the increasing complexity of the census. This category includes blacksmithing, foundries and machine shops, wire and cable making, iron pipe, pumps, steam engines, saws, shipbuilding, wheelwrighting, and other types of enterprises. These activities formed the core of nineteenth-century industry. After 1850, successive censuses expanded the reporting categories. While this was more accurate and useful for some purposes, the growth of iron working in the aggregate is lost. Table 9.7 recombines these separate categories in the census into an aggregate "iron working trades" industry. The increase in iron working trades, despite the state's poor natural endowment of iron ores and coal, is striking.

TABLE 9.7
California Iron Working Trades

Year	Number of Establishments	Value of Output (in dollars)
1850	42	1,158,200
1860	376	5,853,158
1870	861	8,518,768
1880	994	10,889,437

SOURCE: Calculated from data in *U.S. Census of Manufactures*, 1850, 1860, and 1880. *U.S. Population Census, 1870*. "Iron working trades" includes all iron working census categories.

THE SPREAD OF GOLD INDUSTRY TECHNOLOGIES

Technologies developed for the gold industry were not confined to that sector. As pointed out above, such devices as hoses, steam engines, and pumps all found their way to other sectors of the economy. Nathan Rosenberg has called this process "technological convergence," and maintains that it was vital to creating the machine tool industry on the East Coast in the early nineteenth century.[53] The textile industry, he argues, was the initial catalyst for technological convergence on the East Coast.

Technological convergence can be seen in California, but with gold mining serving as the catalyst. The blacksmith shops, foundries, and machine shops that produced the equipment for the gold industry also created technologies and an industrial base that could later be employed in shipbuilding, in the defense industry, and in other types of manufacturing. By the 1880s, for example, California firms were supplying most of the machinery used on Hawaiian plantations and in sugar cane processing, replacing European imports.[54] California's hydroelectric power also had early connections to the Gold Rush.[55] The first hydroelectric operation in the state was undertaken in northern California in 1879. Soon after, Lester A. Pelton, a millwright and carpenter in the Mother Lode town of Camptonville, created the turbine wheel generator, building on technology developed for gold mining.

The cable industry provides another example of technology dissemination. A. S. Hallidie, president of the California Wire-Works Company, made screens for quartz mills and flour mills, riddles, birdcages, fenders, fireguards, and many other wire products for use in kitchens and industry. In 1868, Hallidie invented a wire ropeway for transporting ores. Soon after, he used the same technology to invent the cable railway, which powers San Francisco's famous cable cars.[56]

California's oldest foundry, the Union Iron Works, also illustrates how gold mining technologies were transferred to other industries. Founded in 1849 by three brothers, Peter, James, and Michael Donahue, the Union Iron Works overcame the iron shortage by buying scrap iron made plentiful by the fires that destroyed San Francisco in the early 1850s. As did a host of other San Francisco foundries, it used the scrap metal and iron imported as ballast to make mining equipment. The Union Iron Works produced a large share (90 percent by one estimate) of the mining equipment used by California and Comstock mines.[57] From mining equipment, the Union Iron Works branched out to supply other iron working industries. It built the first locomotive on the West Coast in 1865. It repaired ships, made ship engines, and assembled ships, including the first steel ship made on the West Coast, the collier *Arago,* in 1885. The company then won one of the first major Navy construction contracts awarded a California firm and built the first steel warship produced on the West Coast, the *Charleston,* in 1888. In addition, Peter Donahue was instrumental in constructing street railroads.

One striking difference between California producers and their eastern counterparts that encouraged technology dissemination was the degree to which California producers did *not* specialize. Eastern foundries and machine shops tended to specialize in the production of a few products. However, with many smaller local markets, California foundries often made more than twenty products, "everything that is in demand, from mining-machinery, locomotives, steamship engines, sugar-mills, and architectural iron-work, down to the various small articles required for every-day use."[58] Diversity was also typical of California's agricultural equipment producers.[59]

The difference between eastern and western foundries was probably due to the wider markets in the East, which facilitated specialization. It was also due to the mining origins of western foundries. Mining equipment was very diverse and often custom-made. San Francisco foundries survived by staying flexible, by experimenting, by innovating, and by producing a wide array of products. Carey McWilliams argued that a willingness to experiment was a long-standing hallmark of California that had taken root in the state's mining past.[60] Equally important, the diversity of California foundries and machine shops probably speeded up the process of technological diffusion because it became more of an in-house process on the West Coast, facilitating easier transfer of technology from product to product.

Finally, the discovery of other minerals was often a by-product of the search for gold during the Gold Rush. Silver, borax, petroleum, coal, chromite, and copper were discovered as gold seekers scoured the countryside. The Comstock Lode, primarily silver, was discovered by California miners looking for gold.

There was, however, one notable exception to this pattern. When California was still part of Mexico, quicksilver was discovered at New Almaden, near San Jose, in 1845. While its discovery and initial development preceded Marshall's discovery, the New Almaden Mine (and the other California quicksilver mines that soon fol-

San Franciscans press forward to watch the launching of the ironclad monitor *Camanche* on November 14, 1864. Assembled at the Union Iron Works with parts manufactured in the East and sent around the Horn, it was the second warship built in California. Slightly more than twenty years later, the Union Iron Works made a successful bid to construct the U.S. Navy's Cruiser No. 2, the *Charleston,* one of the first vessels in the country's "New Navy" and the ship that inaugurated the modern era of shipbuilding in California. *Courtesy Society of California Pioneers.*

lowed) enjoyed robust demand during the Gold Rush. Among mineral industries, quicksilver was second only to gold in output-value until the end of the nineteenth century. More importantly, it is hard to imagine what the Gold Rush and the Comstock silver rush would have been like in the absence of local supplies of quicksilver. In the last half of the nineteenth century, California produced half of the world's supply of mercury, breaking a world quicksilver cartel by flooding world markets with cheap quicksilver.[61]

CONCLUSION

Through backward linkages, a California industrial nexus was created in the Gold Rush. Its features and characteristics were determined by the responses of industrial firms to increasing consumer demand and to the demands emanating from the gold mining industry. In the process, California's industrial capacity was created. An industrial core, centered around foundries, machine tool companies, and the iron working trades, developed. This base became the foundation for future industrial expansion.

While the Gold Rush increased the demand for both consumer and producer goods, care must be taken to keep this factor in perspective. Demand is never sufficient alone to explain development. Boomtowns the world over have generated similar demands, but few managed to create an economic base that survived the exhaustion of the mineral that brought them into being. Virginia City, for example, did not become another San Francisco. Gold presented the opportunity, but the real story is found in the response. Perhaps the greatest legacy of the Gold Rush was not its ability to attract gold miners, but its ability to attract entrepreneurs who seized the opportunities that gold offered.

NOTES

1. Population figures are from Andrew Rolle, *California: A History* (Arlington Heights, Ill.: Harlan Davidson, 1987), 2, 146, 166, 241.

2. Robert Cleland and Osgood Hardy, *The March of Industry* (San Francisco: Powell, 1929), 36.

3. Ibid., 1.

4. *The Californian*, May 29, 1848.

5. John S. Hittell, *The Resources of California* (San Francisco: A. L. Bancroft, 1879), 186.

6. Cleland and Hardy, *March of Industry*, 36.

7. Rolle, *California*, 166.

8. U.S. Department of Commerce, *Historical Statistics of the United States: Colonial Times to 1970* (Washington, D.C.: Government Printing Office, 1975), 25.

9. John S. Hittell, *The Resources of California* (San Francisco: A. Roman, 1862), 304.

10. Hittell, *Resources of California* (1879), 183–84.

11. Ibid.

12. Ibid.

13. Ibid.

14. Ibid., 184.

15. Rolle, *California*, 229.

16. Earl Pomeroy, *The Pacific Slope* (Lincoln: University of Nebraska Press, 1965), 111.

17. Ibid., 112.

18. Ibid., 113.

19. William A. Bullough, Richard J. Orsi, and Richard B. Rice, *The Elusive Eden: A New*

History of California (New York: McGraw-Hill, 1996), 279. The role of energy shortages in deterring the development of California industry has been discussed in James C. Williams, *Energy and the Making of Modern California* (Akron, Ohio: University of Akron Press, 1997).

20. Cleland and Hardy, *March of Industry,* 134.

21. Rolle, *California,* 229.

22. W. H. Hutchinson, *California: Two Centuries of Man, Land, and Growth in the Golden State* (Palo Alto, Calif.: American West Publishing, 1969), 207.

23. Cleland and Hardy, *March of Industry,* 134.

24. Ibid., 133–34.

25. Gerald D. Nash, "Stages of California's Economic Growth, 1870–1970: An Interpretation," in *Essays and Assays: California History Reappraised,* ed. George H. Knoles (Los Angeles: Ward Ritchie Press, 1973), 39–53.

26. John W. Caughey, *California: A Remarkable State's Life History* (Englewood Cliffs, N.J.: Prentice-Hall, 1970), 202.

27. Carey McWilliams, *California: The Great Exception* (New York: A. A. Wyn, 1949), 216.

28. Ibid.

29. Ibid., 214.

30. Census data refers to *U.S. Census of Manufacturers,* taken in 1850, 1860, and 1880. There was no census of manufacturing in 1870. However, manufacturing data is found in the 1870 *U.S. Population Census.*

31. *U.S. Census of Manufacturers* (1880), xii.

32. John S. Hittell, *The Commerce and Industries of the Pacific Coast of North America* (San Francisco: A. L. Bancroft, 1882), 524.

33. California Division of Mines, *Geologic Guidebook of the San Francisco Bay Counties,* Bulletin 154 (San Francisco: Division of Mines, 1951), 235, 238.

34. Hittell, *Commerce and Industries of the Pacific Coast,* 572–75.

35. Ibid., 435. The following discussion is from this source.

36. Ibid., 436.

37. For a discussion of private coinage in California, see Edgar H. Adams, *Private Gold Coinage of California, 1849–55: Its History and Its Issues* (Brooklyn: Edgar H. Adams, 1913).

38. Rodman W. Paul, *Mining Frontiers of the Far West, 1848–1880* (New York: Holt, Rinehart and Winston, 1963), 31–32.

39. Hittell, *Commerce and Industries of the Pacific Coast,* 520–22.

40. This discussion is drawn from Bullough, Orsi, and Rice, *Elusive Eden,* 196. Gold dredging is also discussed in Lewis E. Aubury, *Gold Dredging in California,* California State Mining Bulletin No. 57 (Sacramento: California State Printing, 1910).

41. Paul, *Mining Frontiers of the Far West,* 33.

42. Hittell, *Commerce and Industries of the Pacific Coast,* 657.

43. Ibid., 709.

44. Ibid., 707.

45. Ibid., 521.

46. Ibid., 657.

47. Ibid., 660.

48. Ibid., 658.

49. *U.S. Population Census, 1870,* 760. The figures immediately following on steam engines are from this source (pp. 496–98).

50. Paul, *Mining Frontiers of the Far West,* 31.

51. Ibid., 31–32. The following discussion is from this source as well.

52. *U.S. Census of Manufacturers* (1880), xxi.

53. Nathan Rosenberg, "Technological Change in the Machine Tool Industry, 1840–1910," *The Journal of Economic History* 22 (December 1963): 414–43.

54. Hittell, *Commerce and Industries of the Pacific Coast,* 653.

55. Hutchinson, *California,* 218–19.

56. Hittell, *Commerce and Industries of the Pacific Coast,* 425–26, 668.

57. Ruth Teiser, "The Charleston: An Industrial Milestone," *California Historical Society Quarterly* 25 (March 1946): 39–52. The following discussion of the Union Iron Works is drawn from this source, as well as from Richard H. Dillon, *Iron Men* (San Francisco: Candela Press, 1984).

58. Hittell, *Commerce and Industries of the Pacific Coast,* 659.

59. For a similar observation about California agricultural implement producers, see McWilliams, *California,* 224.

60. Ibid., 221.

61. For a discussion of New Almaden and California quicksilver see David J. St. Clair, "New Almaden and California Quicksilver in the Pacific Rim Economy," *California History* 73 (Winter 1994/95): 278–95; Jimmie Schneider, *Quicksilver: The Complete History of Santa Clara County's New Almaden Mine* (San Jose, Calif.: Zella Schneider, 1992); David J. St. Clair, "California Quicksilver in the Pacific Rim Economy," in *Studies in the Economic History of the Pacific Rim,* ed. Sally M. Miller, A. J. H. Latham, and Dennis O. Flynn (London: Routledge, 1998), 210–33.

10

From Hard Money to Branch Banking

California Banking in the Gold-Rush Economy

Larry Schweikart and Lynne Pierson Doti

If Americans associate any event with the early history of California, it is the Gold Rush. While the impressions of most people are that the Gold Rush "came and went," more or less, with little lasting legacy other than to alert outsiders to the vast wealth to be found in California, the economic development of the state actually took on much of its early form based on the experiences of the Forty-niners. Banking and the financial sector, in particular, evolved in often distinctive ways because of the gold-rush economy. More important, the abundance of gold on the West Coast provided an interesting test case for some of the critical economic arguments of the day, especially for those deriving from the descending—but still powerful—positions of the "hard money" Jacksonians.[1]

By the time banks appeared in California, commercial banking was well established east of the Mississippi, and had made inroads in Missouri.[2] The process by which banks came into existence was common, but not uniform: usually a merchant or freight agent would accept deposits from local entrepreneurs who wanted a safe storage for their money or gold, exchange drafts written from out-of-town companies and pay out gold, and often extend credit to valued customers. The combination of accepting deposits, exchanging drafts, and making loans endowed those merchants with the essential functions of banks. When their business reached such a level that it equaled or surpassed their mercantile or freight activities, they often sought a banking charter from the state legislature, although not all "bankers" had charters. The charter usually empowered the banker to issue paper money, called "banknotes" or simply "notes." Money thus circulated, and competed, against other privately issued money by relying on gold as a standard of measurement, since all notes had to be convertible into gold at some point. More often than not, however, the real determinant of a note's value rested on its reputation—or, more precisely,

A row of solid brick banks lines the west side of Montgomery Street in a charming watercolor executed in the early spring of 1851 by an unidentified French artist. Visible, *left to right,* are the offices of the San Francisco Savings Bank, E. Delessert & Cordier, James King of William, and, across Commercial Street, the bank of B. Davidson, agent for Messrs. Rothschild. The concentration of so many financial institutions had, the previous year, led a newspaper to declare that "this beautiful street may well be called the Wall Street of San Francisco." *California Historical Society.*

that of the issuer—and many banks reflected the apparently paradoxical condition of having low reserves of gold and yet high levels of soundness and solvency. Of course, that paradox was understood if it was kept in mind that *instability* was related to a weak reputation more than to low reserves of gold.[3]

When banking appeared in California, the debate over whether banks should be prohibited from issuing notes at all was decided in favor of the private note. The Panic of 1837 had made several states hostile to banks, with Arkansas and Wisconsin actually prohibiting banks (as Texas later would do). Of course, note-issuing banks still appeared, generally under the inventive title of "Marine and Fire Insurance and Banking Company," or "Railroad and Banking Company." Governments found they could not eliminate the demand for banks—or paper money—and often, "bankless" states, such as Iowa in the 1850s, found that the business they lost to neighboring states caused them to rethink their inflexible positions.[4] California, therefore, by 1849, had plenty of evidence about what worked and what did not work when it came to bank structure. Yet none of the experiences of banks in other states had the key ingredient that California possessed: abundant gold, capable of sustaining a metallic currency.

The discovery of gold on January 24, 1848, at a mill owned by John A. Sutter sparked a stampede to the mines of northern California. Likened to a "hysteria" or to a dam bursting, the Gold Rush brought in thousands of people from everywhere in the world, and with them came a new outlook on life: Mark Twain facetiously reported haircuts going for $1,000, and yet people "happily paid it, knowing that we would make it up tomorrow."[5] Gold poured out of the mines and streams in large enough amounts to run any economy, and indeed, "if a metallic-based economy could survive anywhere, if metallism, as the Jacksonians preached, was a desirable alternative to banks and paper money, then it should have taken root ... in California."[6] According to the Jacksonian principles of banking, there should have been little need for bankers, the much disparaged "middlemen." Instead, the California experience demonstrated the critical role that financial intermediaries play in evolving market systems, even when a suitable "money" was widely available.

Prior to the Mexican-American War in 1846, California lacked banks altogether and had a chronic shortage of paper currency and minted coin. Indians had devised the earliest common currency of the state, meticulously carved round pieces of shell with holes in the center so the "coins" could be strung on long leather thongs to create an early wallet. When the Spaniards arrived and began trade, the strings of coin traded at the rate of a yard to a Spanish dollar. Still, from the founding of the first mission in San Diego in 1769 until Mexican independence in 1821, most trading was by barter. As the missions were closed by the Mexican government after 1833, the economy focused on a few hundred large cattle ranches. These ranchos were basically self-sufficient empires with little need for banks or money. Cowhides, dry, flat, and stiff enough to sail like Frisbees off a cliff, were known as "California dollars."[7] Tallow, hides and furs, classed under the general moniker "fur money," had been a constant in the frontier fur trading areas from the Mississippi to the Rockies, and the Bank of St. Louis, on the main route east from the trapping grounds, accepted pelts and issued money on that security.[8] California cattle hides, also called "California Bank Notes," circulated as a popular form of early money.[9] As an example, Captain William Davis of the USS *Eagle* recorded a transaction in which he sold some goods to Friar Mercado of the Santa Clara Mission in 1844 and received two hundred hides.[10] Despite the obvious fact that a skin-based currency demanded little in the way of safes or vaults, Davis claimed himself as the one to have brought the first safe to California in 1846.[11]

After the state was abruptly wrested from the control of Mexico by the war in 1846, the American population slowly increased. Settlers following the Oregon Trail to the Northwest veered south to find the fabled lush and massive Central Valley between the mountains and the coast. Soldiers passing through Monterey, San Diego, and inland long after remembered the ideal climate and the vast amount of empty land. Some returned, and some influenced others to settle in California. The economy began to develop markets as many of the ranchos were subdivided and the smaller landholders were less self-sufficient, and these markets created a need for money. American dollars brought by settlers became the most common, though still rare, money.

As elsewhere in the West, the local residents expressed more of a concern for the scarcity of currency and coin than for the absence of banks. As two historians of the subject concluded, the "cry 'There is no money in Kansas' might well have described the situation in neighboring plains states as well," and also in California, at least before the discovery of gold.[12] Of course, everything changed when James Marshall, on January 24, 1848, presented a sample of ore from the South Fork of the American River to John Sutter, a Swiss-born adventurer who had hired a group of Mormons to construct a sawmill for him. Quickly, the California economy was changed: by summer, reports of gold had drawn hundreds of people from other parts of California to the region, and then, as news of the discovery spread, thousands of prospectors and miners arrived at San Francisco, from which they would take boats up the Sacramento River, then walk uphill to the gold fields some forty miles from Sacramento. There, they found gold in impressive—indeed, absolutely phenomenal—amounts. Between 1848 and 1860, according to one estimate, gold exports from California topped $650 million at $16 an ounce.[13]

San Francisco reflected the boom in its population, which had stood at barely 150 in 1846, only to swell to 50,000 a decade later. Each new immigrant seemed to add to the news traveling back home that anyone could get rich in California, and regular reports by field agents of express companies, such as William Rochester of American Express in 1851, contributed to the excitement. That year, gold production rose from $41 million to $76 million, leading one resident to comment, "Gold never was known so plenty in San Francisco as this season."[14] Yet despite the abundance of gold, the United States did not open a mint in San Francisco until 1854, meaning that the scarcity of coin persisted amidst an ocean of gold. All customs had to be paid in U.S. coin, which led to hoarding of the few pieces of metallic currency that existed.[15]

Using gold ore or dust for daily business transactions proved difficult because the measurement and valuation of gold in such forms constituted an inexact science, even for the experienced. Gold as it came from the mines was rarely pure. Even nuggets could contain spots of other metals or dirt, and the more common "dust" really consisted of several materials mixed together. Dealers usually weighed the dust

An advertisement from the San Francisco Business Directory of 1856 for Kellogg & Humbert, located at 104 Montgomery Street. In addition to providing assaying services, the firm produced gold bars and operated a private mint. *California Historical Society, FN-30964.*

to ascertain value, and an experienced assayer prided himself on his ability to determine by color exactly where a particular batch of gold had been found.

The difficulty of determining the purity of gold as it came from the mines was only the first problem of using gold as money. Since value depended on weight, every party to a transaction wanted scales. Not only did a miner on a shopping trip have concerns about carrying his leather pouch of gold along, but he had to bear a second pouch containing a miniature set of scales and weights. Differences in calibration between buyers' and sellers' scales placed a premium on negotiation skills. No wonder at least two dozen private mints operated in California.[16] Those mints charged customers to refine their gold and exchange it for coins stamped with the mint's verification of weight and purity. Miners worried about protecting their gold, too, after it was mined and especially when they were in town for their nights out after replenishing their supplies.

A dependence on metallic money presented another problem for miners and merchants in California. At first, there were no local sources of mining equipment. Clothing, blankets, flour, and whiskey all had to come from the East Coast or another distant location. To restock the stores, someone had to travel back with the gold to make the purchases. Many miners also wanted to send payments back east or out of the country to families left behind.

Valuing, transporting, and safely storing gold all contributed to stimulating early banking functions in California. But identifying the "first bank" in California involves determining which of several banking functions or services an individual or business provided—not an easy task, considering that many of the early merchants and entrepreneurs performed most banking functions at some time or another, but seldom all functions at the same time. As late as 1847, of the 169 men who provided their occupations for a newspaper article, none listed themselves as bankers. Robert A. Parker, who later established the Parker House Hotel, was possibly San Francisco's first banker, conducting primitive banking operations from his store on Dupont Street in 1848.[17] Other firms, for example, Mellus, Howard & Co. and B. R. Buckalew in San Francisco and Dickson and Hay in Sacramento soon advertised themselves as "gold dealers," but undoubtedly exchanged drafts and took deposits.[18]

The early gold dealers had provided drafts or exchange for gold, giving the prospectors a liquid and divisible medium for a less liquid and less divisible metal or for notes from other regions that were less well known, and therefore, less reliable. Dealers purchased gold at $8 to $16 an ounce and sold it on the East Coast for $18. This operation allowed merchants and miners to pay local dealers in gold, and get drafts that could be more cheaply and easily transported to pay suppliers or family. Gold dealers then shipped gold in large shipments for sale on the East Coast. Bringing money from outside California was more of a problem, since gold or gold-backed paper was the only locally accepted money. Exchanging local paper for out-of-town notes (called "foreign" notes, even if they originated in another California town) carried a fee—a "discount" based on distance and risk—to redeem the draft or note. An early advertisement for C. V. Gillespie, a San Francisco merchant, read "Wanted: Gold Dust at a high rate of interest for which approved security is offered," and touted loans "negotiated in Gold Dust for both long and short time, interest payable monthly, quarterly, or with the principal at maturity of engagement."[19]

Companies that shipped gold also soon found themselves in the exchange business. Adams & Co., one of the first important express companies in California, became one of the major exchange dealers prior to 1855. Likewise, in Stockton, C. M. Weber, who started the town's first express company, had built a vault and obtained a safe in 1851 for the purpose of accepting packets for storage.[20] Wells Fargo, initially in the express business and eventually also in the stage business, entered banking in California in July 1852, when it first issued certificates of exchange.[21] Familiar with the uncertainties of early transportation, Wells Fargo sent three copies with different carriers between remitters and receivers in the East and West, with the first certificate received recorded as the official transaction and paid, and the others treated as void if and when they arrived. The banking services at Wells Fargo had grown so important by 1852 that an advertisement in the *San Francisco Business Directory* only mentioned the express business in tiny letters, while below it, a huge headline proclaimed "Bankers and Exchange Dealers."[22] Wells Fargo's banking operations grew so fast that by 1855 the company had expanded its services to Sacramento, Stockton, and Portland, and when Wells Fargo opened its office in Los Angeles, its capital reached $1 million.[23]

A final breeding ground for early banks was the general store or merchant. Most merchants allowed reliable customers to "run a tab"—an early form of credit extension—and many already had safes to protect their own daily cash balances. It did not take long for merchants to offer space in their safes for valuables or cash, giving the depositor a receipt, which still other merchants honored or discounted against. One such merchant, Darius Ogden (D. O.) Mills in 1848 left a budding career as a bank clerk in New York to follow his brothers to California. Abandoning the rigorous life of a miner shortly after he arrived, Mills purchased a stock of goods, which he transported to Sacramento and quickly sold. The profit from this operation was so much greater than in the gold fields that Mills returned to New York, found a financial partner, and bought more goods to take back to Sacramento. After a year as a storekeeper, Mills made another trip to New York to present his business partner with $40,000 in profits from a $5,000 initial investment—in fact, Mills had acquired his first cache of goods with just $40 in cash.[24] When Mills traveled back to Sacramento in the winter of 1849–50, he left orders for a variety of goods to be shipped after him, including a large safe, which became the key feature in the new Bank of D. O. Mills.

The Wells, Fargo & Co. office at the town of Iowa Hill, located near the North Fork of the American River in Placer County, August 1855. Prospectors found gold here as early as 1849, but it was not until five years later that miners struck rich diggings and the camp boomed. Charles T. Blake, the local agent for the famed express and banking company founded by Henry Wells and William G. Fargo, stands in the center doorway. *California Historical Society, FN-24037.*

Whether as an express agent, a gold dealer, or a merchant, the route by which one became a banker usually involved several essential steps, not necessarily in any particular order. A would-be banker had to establish himself (there were no female gold-rush bankers of record) in a business of some type, demonstrating to customers that he could be trusted to exchange currency and gold honestly and effectively, and also presenting a personal testimony that he was successful. That image has been taken for granted by historians, but for the potential customers of the day, it represented a crucial element in convincing them to deposit hard-earned gold or currency with a merchant.

Another critical step toward becoming a banker was to purchase a safe—the path followed by Mills—which established the individual as a person to whom others could entrust money with assurances of physical safety and security. Once a businessman had gained a reputation, amassed a measure of personal wealth, and acquired a safe, the final step was to construct a building. The bank building in the Old West, like the safe and the vault, has been largely overlooked. The structure was the physical symbol of safety upon which a banker's business rested. Western bankers had used a number of innovative temporary facilities and strategies to protect money, including hiring full-time guards, placing money in boxes with rattlesnakes, and hiding real gold in waste baskets while substituting gold-painted rocks in the cash drawers.[25] Those, of course, did not satisfy the demands for a building and an iron safe, and therefore an aspiring banker made it a matter of urgency to construct a facility that not only provided physical protection of assets but also suggested to even casual observers that it was an establishment of permanence and strength. The structure itself often contained the most ornate furnishings and finest wood and brass, rivaled in a typical western town by the saloons perhaps, but by few other buildings. The preference for ornate design, rich woods, marble, brass, and other costly materials did not reflect reckless expenditures on meaningless trappings or extravagance. Rather, the building offered physical security, because a bank was inevitably located in the middle of town, "far enough away from the saloon to discourage alcohol-induced midnight pilgrimages by the bar patrons, but close enough that the next morning those same bleary-eyed (and broke) revelers could obtain more cash."[26]

Inside the bank building, an interior wall might be bordered by another business, with a stone or brick vault usually set into the wall or placed in the basement. Even if someone breached the vault, the thief would have to penetrate the safe. Early ball-safe designs utilized a large, hollow iron ball that held cash and valuables, and that rested on a square base, inside which were stored important papers and deeds. The ball was too large and heavy to carry off, and its round surface made it almost impossible to crack using the blasting powder available at that time. Ball safes soon gave way to the larger, rectangular combination safes produced by Hall Safe and Lock in Cincinnati, Ohio. Bankers tended to place the safe inside the vault, which had barred windows and doors. In this manner the artistically embellished iron box was both protected and displayed, presenting the customer a clear view of the bank's chief symbol of safety.

A bank building, complete with its vault and safe, represented an investment in the community of substantial proportions, costing between $8,500 and $250,000. The investment in a building could represent as much as 50 percent of its total capital: William Ralston's Bank of California building constituted 12.5 percent of the bank's initial capital, while at the Lucas Turner & Co. Bank, managed by William Tecumseh Sherman, the three-story 1854 building that housed the bank and other office space accounted for 27 percent of total capital.[27] Placing so much of a bank's precious capital in a building might seem odd to modern, cost-efficient managers until it is understood that the building constituted the most important source of advertising. In an age when many customers were illiterate or literate but unread, the bank had to transmit the message that it was safe and secure in a clear, public display: the imposing bank building.[28]

It was doubly important that a new bank have physical symbols of safety, because, in the absence of regulation, bankers had to assure customers that they protected the customers' funds. Perhaps in the most unnoticed event of western frontier history, these symbols of safety worked almost to perfection. A thorough search of the records of *all* states west of the Missouri/Minnesota border (not counting Texas, which was still considered "southern") reveals the total absence of bank robberies in early years. Though they became a staple in the western movie, virtually no bank robberies—or, at least, successful ones—occurred prior to the 1920s in the West. Authors have found few incidents that even come close to qualifying: a raid on a bank in Nogales, Arizona (a border town subject to bandit incursions from Mexico); a failed attempt by the Butch Cassidy gang on a Colorado bank, in which the would-be thieves used nitroglycerin to threaten hostages; and a 1912 shoot-out in Newport Beach. Otherwise, the outstanding reality of banking in the West was that symbols of safety worked exceptionally well, not only as visual reassurances of security but as deterrents to assaults on the physical capital of the banks.

Another reason the banks had to maintain an imposing physical presence in the town stemmed from the fact that while a single individual usually stood out as the bank's "founder," in reality many early California banks, reflecting the region's highly transient population, were characterized by a high level of ownership instability, with partners frequently entering and leaving the businesses. Moreover, the names of California banking companies changed as often as did the partners. Consider the banking business of Dr. Stephen A. Wright, who in 1848 established the Miner's Bank out of his exchange operations. In September of the following year, he changed the name to Wright & Company, located at Kearney and Washington in San Francisco. Less than a year later, it was reorganized as Miner's Exchange and Savings Bank. A similar business, Decker and Jewett of Marysville, had started as Cunningham and Brumagin (1850), which became Mark Brumagin & Company (1854), then Decker Brumagin & Company (1858), Decker, Jewett & Paxton (1861), and after 1863, Decker, Jewett & Company. The final name, Decker Jewett Bank, lasted until the bank's closing in 1927.[29]

One exception to the typical career path, through which it was typically merchants, freight agents, or gold dealers who evolved into bankers, was Thomas Wells, a newspaper publisher (and no relation to Henry Wells of Wells Fargo) who moved to California from New England. In August 1849, Wells opened his Specie and Exchange Office, which consisted of a simple room, 15 by 18 feet, with a wooden plank counter. Nevertheless, by the end of that year Wells had emerged as the leading banker in the city, writing to his wife that deposits amounted to $132,000 and

Stephen A. Wright's Miners Exchange Bank, on the northwest corner of Montgomery and Jackson streets, was built in 1854 from designs by Peter Portois, one of the most notable European architects to work in California during the nineteenth century. Wright, whose banking company underwent a series of name changes in the early years, poured $147,000 into the construction of the building, a tasteful exposition of current French fashion, which immediately became a San Francisco landmark. Above a first floor of heavily rusticated granite blocks rise three stories of brick, plastered in simulated stone-work and topped by a towering lantern. *Courtesy Bancroft Library.*

that he was opening two or three new accounts every day.[30] By 1850, he had taken in a partner (who added $50,000 in capital) and started construction on a new "fire-proof building," which a year later he discovered not to be fireproof, at great cost to his own health when he stayed in the bank too long during a fire. (In the mistaken assessment that "fireproof" really meant *fireproof*, several bankers, including James King of William, tried to sit out fires inside their supposedly flame-resistant build-ings; King almost died from smoke inhalation.)[31] At any rate, Wells found that the fire at his bank had wiped out his business, for within six months his notes were protested by another company, indicating that they were not sound. Wells could not cover the bills, and placed the bank, or what was left of it, in the hands of trustees who paid off creditors at the rate of thirty-seven cents on the dollar.

Joining Thomas Wells in the banking business in San Francisco by late 1849 were at least three other banks: Naglee & Sinton (later Naglee & Company), Wright, Burgoyne & Co., and B. Davidson; and a year later three more, D. J. Tallant, Page, Bacon & Co., and F. Argenti & Co., entered into competition with the original group. Still other competitors were de facto banks that did not adopt the title "bank."

Whether these establishments were banks in name or in fact, the rapid emergence of banking businesses in California in 1849 was especially noteworthy because much of what they did was technically illegal. The delegates to the 1849 state constitutional convention (which included only one person described as a banker) had prohibited anyone from issuing paper notes or otherwise exercising banking privileges. If banking was prohibited, where did all the banks come from? How did one reconcile the presence of so much gold and so many bankers, with such clear antibanking legislation?

The California Constitutional Convention, convened in early September 1849, met concurrently with a group of private citizens who considered the "official" body illegal. In the official body's draft were several provisions related to banking, including sections 31, 33, and 36 (general incorporation and limited liability acts); section 34 (which expressly prohibited the legislature from passing a charter for a banking association, but still holding open the possibility of private "associations . . . formed under general laws for the deposit of gold and silver"); and section 35 (prohibiting the legislature from "sanctioning in any manner . . . the issuing of bank notes").[32] California had, perhaps inadvertently, accepted the then-popular notion of "free banking" without some of the features that made free banking especially effective. Free banking allowed anyone to open a bank without the express approval of the government, but often required bankers to assume liability for the loss of depositors' money. Scotland's earlier period of free banking, for example, featured double liability for stockholders if deposits were lost.[33] Far from anticipating the widespread appearance of free banking, though, the constitutional convention, wanting to spare the state from what it saw as the evils of paper money, thought that the mountain of gold upon which the state rested would by itself suffice to eliminate banknotes. That did not prevent some, such as a member of the drafting committee on banking and incorporation, from arguing in his finest Jacksonian rhetoric for providing "the strongest constitutional safeguards against the vicissitudes . . . of this monster serpent, paper money."[34] One committee member, J. M. Jones, tried to eliminate the general incorporation laws and to expressly prohibit banks, including any "associations" that accepted gold and issued receipts that might circulate as money. But others quickly countered that merchants demanded a circulating medium, and that failing to permit free enterprise in the form of banks could well jeopardize the ratification of the constitution by the public. As a result, the convention gave the legislature the power to grant charters for banking, but prohibited such banks from issuing paper money—and a second, separate passage reiterated the ban on paper money—and accepted the general incorporation laws with limited liability. Then, as if to confuse completely the convention's intentions, the first legislature established a rate of interest at no more than 10 percent per year on loans, even as it had prohibited any "evidences of debt" (outlawing I.O.U.s). In reality, the constitution and the legislature's stipulations regarding paper money and banks already had been rendered obsolete and irrelevant by the market, which daily saw hundreds of miners exchange gold for drafts—a reality to which the legislatures finally acceded when laws were passed taxing banks on the gold dust brought in or the *exchange sold*, underscoring the significance of money creation as a central element of early banking.

A threat far more dangerous to California's early banks than contradictory laws was the decline in the mines' gold production after 1852. Miners needed more expensive equipment to reach the gold, as the simple pans and picks of a few years earlier no longer sufficed. From 1854 to 1855, banks in San Francisco experienced several panics, particularly when Page, Bacon & Co. failed, triggering a disastrous run. The main office of Page & Bacon in St. Louis had heavy losses on a midwestern railroad loan, but had raised sufficient gold in California to keep the office open, shipping back to St. Louis by steamer. While the gold was en route, word reached San Francisco that the St. Louis branch of Page & Bacon had folded, and the subsequent run shut down the company, as well as other San Francisco banks, including Adams & Co. and Wright's Miner's Exchange Bank. Eventually, even most offices of Wells Fargo were closed. The *Daily Herald* reported that "No day so gloomy has been witnessed in San Francisco since that disasterous fire of the 4th of May, 1851. Every bank was said to have suspended, and rumors of mercantile failures—most of them false, we are glad to say—came thick and heavy in the afternoon."[35] Another panic occurred when prominent San Francisco citizen Henry Meiggs, who had supplied much of the city's lumber and built Meiggs Wharf, unexpectedly left town owing $800,000 secured with forged city warrants.[36]

Meiggs's sudden departure could be traced to the constant hounding he received on his debts by William Tecumseh Sherman, later the famous Civil War general. Sherman had first come to California as a lieutenant during the war with Mexico. His nearly three years' experience was deemed adequate to make him a valuable representative of Lucas Turner & Co. of St. Louis, when that company opened a bank in San Francisco in 1853. Henry Turner opened the branch early in 1853 by renting a suitable space for $600 a month and hiring two employees. Sherman arrived to assume control in late April after a two-month trip marked by a pair of shipwrecks on the same day: "Not a good beginning for a new peaceful career," he wrote.[37] Finding the California economy still booming and business prospects good, Sherman returned home, resigned his U.S. Army commission, collected his family, and journeyed back to California to stay, at least until 1860 as he had agreed. As a manager, Sherman proved as relentless as he would later be to the Confederates. A reading of Dwight Clarke's edited collection of letters from Sherman shows that the future general mercilessly pressured Meiggs for payments in the period prior to the latter's hasty departure.[38]

That weeding out of banks caused by repeated panics merely opened the door for other ambitious and talented men, including William Chapman Ralston, who had abandoned his steamboating career to become a Forty-niner.[39] While crossing the Isthmus of Panama, Ralston met some old steamboating friends, Captain Cornelius Kingston (C. K.) Garrison and Ralph Fretz, who wanted him to handle the Panama branch of a travel and freight business they had in San Francisco. After dealing with malarial climate, unprepared travelers, and even a major shipwreck, Ralston finally settled in San Francisco in 1854 and opened his own steamboat business, earning profits from shipping passengers and goods and amassing enough in January 1856 to open a bank called Garrison, Morgan, Fretz & Ralston. Charles Morgan and Garrison withdrew from the business in 1857. Now renamed Fretz & Ralston, the firm soon merged with dry goods merchants Eugene Kelly and Joseph Donohoe for additional capital.

During that period, Ralston invested in a variety of local industries: foundries, railroads, and dry goods firms. He also expanded to the north, allying himself with the Ladd and Tilton Bank of Portland, which brought a stern warning from Kelly. To Ralston, the reprimand constituted an opportunity to open his own bank, and he immediately rounded up some of the most prominent local citizens, including D. O. Mills. Ralston wanted his new bank to stand out as the most important in the state, and accordingly he named it "The Bank of California" (with "The" always capitalized in the title).[40] Mills became the new president, bringing to the position his reputation, while Ralston took the daily management job of cashier, deciding the investments and loans that the bank would make. When the bank opened on July 1, 1864, its charter specifically listed its business as banking, the first allowed under an 1862 revision of the state's constitution. The Bank of California thus became the first incorporated bank in California, drawing its customers and investment profits primarily from the increasingly successful Comstock silver mines.[41]

Silver mining offered tantalizing opportunities for wealth. The silver veins dove deep into the mountains, and became accessible only by digging expensive shafts, which required extensive capital. Silver miners might easily discover a vein of the blackened metal near the surface, but the pursuit of silver veins required deep mines with reinforced tunnels, ore cars and rails, and pumps and blowers to keep the miners alive, as well as elaborate mills and separators to process the ore. A lively market for mine stocks developed as people realized that capital invested in a mine might not pay off for years or make one rich in a day. Silver mining launched the Pacific Coast Stock Exchange. It also stimulated the production of timber to reinforce deep mines, and railroads to transport timber from the Sierra Nevada to the desert area of Virginia City. Of course, mining constituted a volatile business, with the constant threat of cave-ins, floods, or fires.

It did not take Ralston long to appreciate the close relationship his bank had with the fortunes of the mines: when a miner's pick hit a subterranean water vein and flooded the shafts, mining stocks plummeted and Ralston's correspondent bank in Virginia City failed. That episode served to convince Ralston that he needed his bank to have its own branch in Virginia City, prompting him on the recommendation of a friend to hire William Sharon. When Sharon arrived in Virginia City, he dove into the thorny problem of the long-term profitability of the Comstock Lode, visiting chilly caverns and hot, sulfurous shafts. Floods proved the most frequent, and vexing, problem. Yet all that was required was some way to pump out water. After a particularly disastrous flood swamped one mine, stopping production, Ralston, with typical energy and optimism, installed a 50-horsepower pump—the biggest yet created. But the pump proved so ineffective against the rising lake inside the mines that within eight months the water engulfed the outmatched machine. It was typical, however, of Ralston to order the Vulcan Foundry, which he helped support with his investments, to construct a 120-horsepower pump.

While Ralston struggled with the water problem in the mines, he grew concerned that his bank had made far too many—and too generous—loans. In the process, though, the bank had helped to start woolen mills, a sugar refinery, an insurance company, a railroad equipment manufacturing company, a winery, lumber mills, gas and water companies, and the Sacramento Valley Railroad, as well as invested in other existing projects, such as the Vulcan Foundry. In these early days, banks not only loaned to businesses but also owned substantial portions of a number of enterprises. Of course, with each new investment, Ralston either became an official or de facto member of the board, or the manager of the business. Ultimately, so many businesses owed at least some part of their existence to Ralston's Bank of California that Ralston biographer George Lyman called him the "Atlas of the Pacific," for upon his shoulders "rested the financial structure of the Pacific Coast."[42]

By establishing a branch for his bank in Virginia City, Ralston had presented California with a gift for posterity. Branch banking existed in many parts of the world, including the antebellum American South.[43] Other California bankers had established small branches, but the practice was certainly not universal, nor were the benefits and efficiencies of branching well publicized outside the South. But Ralston realized that San Francisco's economy differed somewhat from Virginia City's, and that the more flexibility his bank had to shift resources back and forth, the more likely it could withstand crises, which were sure to come given the vicissitudes of mining. In Ralston's first big gamble with mining investments, it looked as though even the more resilient branch structure might not save him: he received constant pleas from Sharon for more cash, to the tune of more than $650,000, to keep the

Comstock drills going. Silver existed in abundance, Sharon reassured Ralston, and "Atlas" went beyond what traditional bankers would have seen as their obligations in financing all of the mining ventures. Ralston's gamble paid off in 1865, when the Kentuck mine produced silver. Within a year it yielded $2 million of the metal, making the Bank of California flush with more than $1 million in profits.

Ralston plowed much of the profit back into the bank, building the most elaborate financial headquarters west of the Mississippi, with tall arched windows and nineteen-foot-high ceilings capped by ornamental vases. The bank's interior sported polished dark wood counters, and though it lacked the traditional tellers' cages, the bank advertised its four massive vaults, each formed of a three-inch-thick wall of stone. Enclosed in green glass were inner offices where Ralston and the cashier worked. Contrary to the layout of most banking houses of the day, there was no "ladies banking room." The bolder sort of women who lived in California deposited their funds with the same dark-suited tellers who served the men. To attract Chinese customers, Ralston employed Chinese tellers, whom he exempted from his dress codes by allowing them to wear dark silk robes and their customary long braids.

Beyond the bank, Ralston's influence ran deep. He built the huge, unrivaled Palace Hotel, and, to internalize the costs of construction, he purchased foundries, furniture businesses, and other supporting enterprises. He lent money to the Japanese government to buy railroad engines from California manufacturers. In 1874, he created a new silver coin, called the "trade dollar," to encourage Asian suppliers to hold money earned in trade.

By August 1875, however, Ralston's overextended empire caught up with him. That year, a nationwide financial panic reached California, sparking runs that closed the Bank of California. The day the bank closed, Ralston, perhaps facing the impending bankruptcy of his personal estate, went for his regular swim in San Francisco Bay. He was observed in a brief struggle but died before he could be brought ashore. The "Atlas of the Pacific" had put down the globe for good, but the bank managed to reopen in October of the same year.

Prior to his demise, however, Ralston also demonstrated another characteristic of early California banking, that of domestic capital investment that eventually became capital export. Far from the claims of some contemporaries and historians that eastern interests used the West as a "colony," the California banking experience suggests just the opposite—California's banks, built by men with little imported capital, prospered to the extent that they reinvested their fortunes in the state's economy. The "Irish Four" of John Mackay, James Fair, James Flood, and William O'Brien, who opened the Bank of Nevada in San Francisco in the early 1870s, had started as saloon owners and miners. Although they all became rich from investments in the Comstock Lode, Flood could not hang onto his money, going broke first in the 1850s and having to work as a carpenter to pay his debts. Flood rebuilt his empire, but again

Designed by the Scots Argonaut David Farquharson, the Bank of California was constructed in 1866 and 1867 of granite quarried on Goat Island in San Francisco Bay and proved more solid than the fortunes of its founder, William C. Ralston. For his design of the most powerful banking house in the American West, the architect drew freely on Jacobo Sansovino's Library of St. Mark, creating an elegant Renaissance Revival temple of finance. The interior, equally as distinguished as the façade, was richly finished in black marble and Spanish mahogany. *Courtesy Society of California Pioneers.*

lost it all in a wheat speculation with Mackay that cost the partners as much as $12 million. But the mere fact that a pair of California ex-saloon owners could become major investors in the wheat market provides some evidence as to their wealth.

The diminished fortunes of Mackay and Flood after the 1870s paved the way for the arrival in San Francisco of another early California financial legend, Isaias Hellman, who had come to Los Angeles in 1859 from Bavaria.[44] The dry goods store he started featured a Tilden & McFarland safe, allowing him to diversify into banking activities as early as 1865. His was not the first incorporated bank in Los Angeles, an honor that belonged to James A. Hayward and John G. Downey, who started their bank in 1868. But Hellman quickly developed a reputation as one of the most solid businessmen in the region, and in 1871 he merged his bank with Downey's, bringing in twenty-three other local business and agricultural leaders to form the Farmers & Merchants Bank of Los Angeles. In 1876, Hellman replaced Downey as president after a panic nearly closed the institution. The Farmers & Merchants Bank prospered, and Hellman's business interests extended throughout the state. When in 1891 directors were looking for a new president to take over San Francisco's Nevada National Bank, which the Mackay-Flood losses had weakened, Hellman left Los Angeles to accept the position. He led the bank's return to prominence and its merger with Wells Fargo Bank and Union Trust Company. Like his contemporaries, Hellman invested heavily in California, organizing railroads and becoming a local philanthropist.

In many ways, the ascension of Hellman and the passing of Ralston and the Irish Four marked the end of the frontier period in California's banking history, essentially closing the frenzy begun with the Gold Rush. The early merchant-banker, who relied on safes, vaults, personal reputation, and customer loyalty to maintain business, gave way to a new, professional class of managers. In addition, the regulation of banks—while still largely in the hands of the bankers themselves—came to be viewed as a public policy issue, at least to some degree.

The 1860s and 1870s brought depression and disruption to the California economy. Completion of the transcontinental railroad in 1869 had caused unemployed railroad workers to descend on the cities. Speculation increased land prices dramatically, and droughts in southern California thinned the cattle herds. Ranchers who had borrowed against their land to expand when gold and silver had made the state prosperous found themselves overextended and often lost their land to lenders.[45] Sympathy for the economically distressed, combined with the traditional antibanking sentiment, led legislators to further regulate banks. The resulting state Banking Act of 1878 created a Board of Bank Commissioners and required all banks to pay a license fee, to file reports, and to submit to examinations twice a year. Only Indiana, Iowa, and four New England states preceded California in requiring examinations.[46]

Civil War measures by the Union government had also centralized and nationalized control over American banking far more than ever before. After 1864, notes issued by private, state-chartered banks were taxed nearly out of existence. Money from the newly created national banks circulated, replacing private and state banknotes. While still only connected in the loosest of associations through the federal government and supervised liberally by the Comptroller of the Currency, the national banks nevertheless indicated a new attitude toward bank regulation. With the new national charters, however, came increased examination and supervision by the federal government. A national banker could not merely publish the balance sheets or income statements, but rather had to submit to routine inspections, after which the government examiner would declare the bank "safe and sound" (assuming, of course, that it passed). When California began examining the state-chartered banks in 1878, of the first five banks examined, examiners closed the first and passed the second. The next three closed before the inspectors arrived.[47]

The growing but gradual changes in the supervision of banks by state and federal agencies often are viewed by historians as reforms resulting from public outcry. In reality, increased regulation often *shifted* the public's perceptions of a bank's stability from visual and material symbols, such as the building or the banker's personal wealth, to more "professional" and "expert" endorsements that perhaps in the long run were of far less value. Involvement by the federal government, through the national banking system, also began the relentless transfer of local control over financial institutions to the central government.

Control demanded that as many banks as possible be brought into the national bank system, and federal authorities assumed that the privilege of issuing national banknotes—and the corollary taxing of private or state banknotes—would do the trick. California banks, however, had developed a much different commercial emphasis than had many state banks in other regions, where the issuing of notes constituted a major element of the institution's business. In California, with its abundance of gold, the banks had concentrated on loans and investments, not note-issue, and therefore when the national banking system was established, its most valuable prize for a bank joining the system—the authority to issue tax-free and easily recognized national banknotes—enticed very few California banks to join.

Californians demanded coin in almost all daily transactions, and few trusted the Union government's supplemental Civil War paper currency, known as "greenbacks" (which, unlike national banknotes, were issued directly by the government). When the California Supreme Court upheld a law allowing contracts to specify the type of money acceptable in payment, it essentially defied the U.S. government's contention that greenbacks were "legal tender."[48] Most lenders demanded gold in payment, leaving the U.S. customs collectors as almost the only people in the state willing to accept greenbacks. Congress realized that as long as gold circulated as freely as it did, the national banking system could not make any inroads in California. Accordingly, in 1870, Congress amended the National Bank Act to provide for the creation of national gold banks, with new notes payable in gold coin. Congress required that the banks hold a 25-percent reserve in specie—substantially higher than most antebellum private banks would have held—and limited the total amount of outstanding gold notes to $45 million.[49] Ten gold banks were organized in California, and when all national banknotes became redeemable in specie in 1879, all ten switched to standard national charters.[50]

Even though the "gold" period in California's banking history did not end until the demise of the gold banks, the gold-rush era had closed with the end of the Civil War, if not sooner. California banks passed from the frontier stage, characterized by individual responsibility for bank solvency and safety, to the managerial stage, in which trained professionals directed the activities of the banks under the oversight of state, then later state and federal, authorities. Yet the conditions that had given birth to Ralston, Hellman, the Irish Four, and D. O. Mills still shaped the state's financial institutions. Branch banking was tailor-made for a state as large as California, with its diverse economy.

By the end of the frontier era in California's banking history, several enduring features had been established. First, despite Americans' traditional suspicions of banks, the mere presence of banks from the earliest times led Californians to a certain comfort level with the institutions. Despite concerns by legislators, and in the twentieth century attacks by radical groups or "public interest" spokesmen, most Californians accepted banking as a necessary and useful part of daily economic life. Except for the early constitutional debates, banks generally escaped the harsh criticism or outright ostracism frequented on institutions in Wisconsin, Arkansas, Mississippi, or Iowa, where at various times the practice of banking or the establishment of a bank was prohibited by law or all but eliminated. That acceptance, in turn, meant that Californians—from farmers to millers to shippers to innkeepers—did not hesitate to seek new capital to expand agriculture, commerce, trade, and industry.

Second, the symbols of safety worked as planned, suggesting that consumers were more capable of judging the vitality of their financial institutions than many advocates of regulation have thought. Certainly, many of the early banks eventually failed. But that neither dissuaded consumers from using banks, nor other entrepreneurs from starting new ones. Moreover, of those banks that failed, few collapsed because of the actions of a villain who profited at public expense. In almost all cases, the founder or owner sacrificed everything to keep the institution alive and to meet obligations, even to the point that individual fortunes were exhausted for the sake of the bank.

That point underscores a third characteristic of early California banking, which was the persistent use of coin as currency. While popular for a time, the use of gold dust in daily transactions proved neither practical nor desirable, and coin, and soon paper money, quickly found their way into circulation. Paper money, however, had to be redeemable in gold. Californians hesitated to accept greenbacks, not because they were paper money, but because they were *unbacked* paper money from the government. Evidence from other sections of the country suggests that the "free bank" era of private note-issue was a success, and a substantially revised interpretation of that period, which has been emerging for over a decade, now appears to be the accepted position among economic historians. Far from demonstrating that paper money, and privately created paper money at that, would not work, experience in California showed that consumers will select a variety of exchange mechanisms as these suit their needs, and that the *least* desirable of all money was that issued by the government as "legal tender."

Finally, California's adoption of branch banking, while not prevalent in the early frontier era, proved a critical step in the long-term economic vitality of the state. It was the perfect system for a large, economically diverse state (while, in contrast, branching proved less effective in states with more homogenous economies, such as Nevada or South Carolina in the 1920s).[51] The state, sometimes through deliberate action, occasionally by accident, developed a thriving, diverse, flexible banking structure that by the 1980s saw the temporary ascension of a California bank, Bank of America, as the largest bank in the world. That bank was then only one of many large competitors in the state, suggesting that the attitudes and structures generated by, and during, the Gold Rush proved exceptionally durable and flexible over the subsequent century and a half.

NOTES

1. The most recent and thorough survey of these debates appears in Larry Schweikart, "U.S. Commercial Banking: A Historiographical Survey," *Business History Review* 65 (Autumn 1991): 606–61, as well as his introduction to *The Encyclopedia of American Business History and Biography: Banking and Finance to 1913* (New York: Facts on File and Bruccoli Clark Layman, 1991). Also see Benjamin J. Klebaner, *American Commercial Banking: A History* (Boston: Twayne, 1990), and Larry Schweikart, *Banking in the American South from the Age of Jackson to Reconstruction* (Baton Rouge: Louisiana State University Press, 1987).

2. See Timothy Hubbard and Lewis Davids, *Banking in Midamerica* (Washington, D.C.: Public Affairs Press, 1969), and R. S. Cole, "Early History of Money and Banking in Missouri" (M.A. thesis, University of Missouri, 1906).

3. For example, the experience of the antebellum North Carolina banks, in Schweikart, *Banking in the American South*, passim.

4. Earling A. Erickson, "Money and Banking in a 'Bankless' State: Iowa, 1846–1857," *Business History Review* 43 (Summer 1969): 171–91; Larry Schweikart, "Arkansas Antebellum Banks," *Southern Studies*, 26 (Fall 1987): 188–201; Joseph M. Grant and Lawrence L. Crum, *The Development of State Chartered Banking in Texas* (Austin: University of Texas, Bureau of Business Research, 1978).

5. Robert Glass Cleland, *From Wilderness to Empire: A History of California, 1542–1900* (New York: Knopf, 1944), 240.

6. Lynne Pierson Doti and Larry Schweikart, *California Bankers, 1848–1993* (New York: Guinn, 1994), 9.

7. Richard Henry Dana, *Two Years Before the Mast* (New York: A. L. Burt, 1840), passim.

8. Lewis E. Davids, "'Fur' Money and Banking in the West," *Journal of the West* (April 1984): 7–10.

9. Dana, *Two Years Before the Mast*, 9.

10. Ira R. Cross, *Financing an Empire: History of Banking in California*, 4 vols. (Chicago: S. J. Clarke, 1927), vol. 1, 22.

11. William Heath Davis, *Seventy-five Years in California*, ed. Harold A. Small, 3rd ed. (San Francisco: John Howell Books, 1967).

12. Lynne Pierson Doti and Larry Schweikart, *Banking in the American West: From the Gold Rush to Deregulation* (Norman: University of Oklahoma Press, 1991), 10.

13. Thomas Senior Berry, *Early California: Gold, Prices, Trade* (Virginia: The Bostwick Press, 1984), 78.

14. Robert J. Chandler, "Integrity Amid Tumult: Wells, Fargo & Co.'s Gold Rush Banking," *California History* 70 (Fall 1991): 261. For the growth of San Francisco, in general, see Roger W. Lotchin, *San Francisco, 1846–1856: From Hamlet to City* (1973; reprint, Lincoln: University of Nebraska Press, 1979), as well as J. S. Holliday, *The World Rushed In: The California Gold Rush Experience* (New York: Simon & Schuster, 1981), 316–17.

15. See Cross, *Financing an Empire*, vol. 1, 125–27.

16. The Smithsonian Museum of American History displays the Polk Collection of California's privately minted coins from many of those businesses.

17. Cross, *Financing an Empire*, 44.

18. See Fred R. Marckhoff, "The Development of Currency and Banking in California," *The Coin Collectors' Journal* 15 (May–June 1948), and Benjamin Cooper Wright, *Banking in California, 1849–1910* (San Francisco: H. S. Crocker, 1910), 15.

19. Cross, *Financing an Empire*, vol. 1, 41.

20. Ibid., 90.

21. Wells Fargo History Department, "Historical Highlights," pamphlet published by Wells Fargo Bank, 1982, 5.

22. Ibid.

23. W. Turrentine Jackson, "Wells Fargo: Symbol of the Wild West?" *Western Historical Quarterly* 3 (April 1972): 179–96. Also see his many articles on Wells Fargo, including "A New Look at Wells Fargo, Stagecoaches, and the Pony Express," *California Historical Society Quarterly* 45 (1966): 291–324; "Stages, Mails and Express in Southern California: The Role of Wells, Fargo & Co. in the Pre-Railroad Era," *California Historical Society Quarterly* 56 (1974): 233–72; "Wells Fargo Staging Over the Sierras," *California Historical Society Quarterly* 44 (1970): 99–133; and "Wells Fargo's Pony Expresses," *Journal of the West* 11 (1972): 412–17.

24. Lynne Pierson Doti, "D. O. Mills," in Schweikart, *Encyclopedia of American Business History*, 316–20.

25. These and other unorthodox methods of protecting money and valuables are discussed in Pierson Doti and Schweikart, *Banking in the American West*, 1–37, and Larry Schweikart, *A History of Banking in Arizona* (Tucson: University of Arizona Press, 1982), chaps. 1–2, passim.

26. Pierson Doti and Schweikart, *Banking in the American West*, 39.

27. Neill Compton Wilson, *400 California Street: The Story of the Bank of California, National Association, and Its First 100 Years in the Financial Development of the Pacific Coast* (San Francisco: Bank of California, 1964), 26, 29; Dwight L. Clarke, *William Tecumseh Sherman: Gold Rush Banker* (San Francisco: California Historical Society, 1969), 18. Sherman's building, unlike his business, survives today.

28. A good discussion of bank architecture appears in Christopher Nelson, "Bank Architecture in the West," *Journal of the West* 23 (April 1984): 77–87. See also "Bank Architecture in New York," *Bankers Magazine*, February 1855, for an appreciation of how well in tune with recent developments on the subject California bankers were, and Philip Sawyer, "The

Planning of Bank Buildings," *The Architectural Review* 12 (1905): 24–31, for the rationale behind the floor layout of the banks.

29. These changes are detailed in Cross, *Financing an Empire*, vol. 1, 86–89.

30. Ibid., 52.

31. Ibid., 58–61. Also see Pierson Doti and Schweikart, *Banking in the American West*, 39.

32. J. Ross Browne, "Report on the Debates of the Convention of California on the Formation of the Constitution in September and October, 1849" (Washington, D.C., 1850), 108–36. Also see David Alan Johnson, *Founding the Far West: California, Oregon and Nevada, 1840–1890* (Berkeley: University of California Press, 1992), 122–25.

33. By that time, the evidence on free banking in Scotland was abundant, but the experiments in the United States were still ongoing. See Lawrence H. White, *Free Banking in Britain: Theory, Experience, and Debate, 1800–1845* (New York: Cambridge University Press, 1984); "Scottish Banking and the Legal Restrictions Theory: A Closer Look," *Journal of Money, Credit and Banking* 22 (November 1990): 526–36, and, with George Selgin, "The Evolution of a Free Banking System," *Economic Inquiry* 25 (July 1987): 439–58; as well as Donald R. Wells and L. S. Scruggs, "Historical Insights into the Deregulation of Banking," *CATO Journal* 5 (Winter 1986): 899–910. Several states had used general incorporation laws to establish "free banks" that had *limited* liability but that relied on bond deposit with the secretary of state to ensure that noteholders were reimbursed if an unscrupulous owner left town with the bank's capital. Several articles by Arthur J. Rolnick and Warren Weber show that the culprit in most free bank failures was faulty drafting of the laws that did not specify *market* value of bonds, only *par* value, making it possible for an unscrupulous owner to take advantage of plunges in the prices of bonds the bank had on reserve with the secretary of state. See their "Banking Instability and Regulation in the U.S. Free Banking Era," *Federal Reserve Bank of Minneapolis Quarterly Review* (Summer 1985): 2–9; "Free Banking, Wildcat Banking, and Shinplasters," *Federal Reserve Bank of Minneapolis Quarterly Review* (Fall 1982): 10–19; "New Evidence on the Free Banking Era," *American Economic Review* (Fall 1981): 1–17; "Inherent Instability in Banking; the Free Bank Experience," *CATO Journal* 5 (December 1983): 1080–91; "The Causes of Free Bank Failures," *Journal of Monetary Economics* 14 (November 1984): 267–91; and "Explaining the Demand for Free Bank Notes," *Journal of Monetary Economics* 21 (January 1988): 47–71. Others have challenged elements of their hypothesis, but the structure still remains intact. See Kenneth Ng, "Free Banking Laws and Barriers to Entry in Banking, 1838–1860," *Journal of Economic History* 48 (December 1988): 877–89; Hugh Rockoff, "Lessons from the American Experience with Free Banking," Cambridge, Mass.: National Bureau of Economic Research Working Paper No. 9, Series on Historical Factors in Long-Run Growth, 1989; Andrew Economopolous, "Free Bank Failures in New York and Wisconsin: A Portfolio Analysis," *Explorations in Economic History* 27 (October 1990): 421–41, "The Free Banking Period: A Period of Deregulation?" *New York Economic Review* 17 (1987): 24–31, "Illinois Free Banking Experience," *Journal of Money, Credit and Banking* 20 (May 1988): 249–64, and his "The Impact of Reserve Requirements on Free Bank Failures," *Atlantic Economic Journal* 14 (December 1986): 76–84.

34. Quoted in Cross, *Financing an Empire*, 101.

35. Ibid., 183.

36. Ibid., 177.

37. Clarke, *William Tecumseh Sherman*, 17.

38. Ibid., 69–70.

39. Cecil G. Tilton, *William Chapman Ralston: Courageous Builder* (Boston: Christopher Publishing House, 1935); David Lavender, *Nothing Seemed Impossible: William C. Ralston and Early San Francisco* (Palo Alto, Calif.: American West Publishing Co., 1975); and Lynne Pierson Doti, "William Chapman Ralston," in Schweikart, *Encyclopedia of American Business History,* 398–408.

40. Pierson Doti, "D. O. Mills," 316–20.

41. James Joseph Hunter, *Partners in Progress, 1864–1950: A Brief History of the Bank of California N.A. & of the Region It Has Served for 85 Years* (New York: Newcomen Society in North America, 1950).

42. George D. Lyman, *Ralston's Ring: California Plunders the Comstock Lode* (New York: Scribner's, 1937), 56.

43. For material on the southern branch banking system, and branching in general, see Schweikart, *Banking in the American South*; Charles Calomiris and Larry Schweikart, "The Panic of 1857: Origins, Transmission, and Containment," *Journal of Economic History* 51 (December 1991): 807–34, and their "Was the South Backward? North-South Differences in Antebellum Banking during Normalcy and Crisis," Federal Reserve Bank of Chicago Working Paper, 1988; John Martin Chapman and Ray B. Westerfield, *Branch Banking, Its Historical and Theoretical Position in America and Abroad* (New York: Harper and Row, 1942); Gary C. Gilbert and William Longbrake, "The Effects of Branching by Financial Institutions on Competition Productive Efficiency and Stability: An Examination of the Evidence," *Journal of Bank Research* 4 (Winter 1974): 298–307; Paul M. Horwitz and Bernard Schull, "The Impact of Branch Banking on Bank Performance," *The National Banking Review* 11 (December 1974): 143–89; Shirley Donald Southworth, *Branch Banking in the United States* (New York: McGraw-Hill, 1928); and Eugene N. White, *The Regulation and Reform of the American Banking System, 1900–1929* (Princeton, N.J.: Princeton University Press, 1983).

44. Material on Hellman appears in Robert Cleland and Frank Putnam, *Isaias Hellman and the Farmers' and Merchants' Bank* (San Marino, Calif.: Huntington Library, 1965), and Michael Konig, "Isaias W. Hellman," in Schweikart, *Encyclopedia of American Business History,* 249–60.

45. Walton Bean, *California: An Interpretive History* (New York: McGraw Hill, 1968), 205.

46. Lynne Pierson Doti, *Banking in an Unregulated Environment: California, 1878–1905* (New York: Garland, 1995), 35.

47. Ibid.

48. See Lavender, *Nothing Seemed Impossible,* 170.

49. Wright, *Banking in California,* 51.

50. For a social-choice interpretation of the gold banks, see Robert L. Greenfield and Hugh Rockoff, "Yellowbacks Out West and Greenbacks Back East: Social-Choice Dimensions of Monetary Reform," *Southern Economic Journal* 62 (April 1996): 902–15.

51. For an assessment of the relative ineffectiveness of branching in some other states during the 1920s, see Charles Calomiris, "Is Deposit Insurance Necessary? A Historical Perspective," *Journal of Economic History* 50 (June 1990): 283–295, and his "Deposit Insurance: Lessons from the Record," *Economic Perspectives* (May–June 1989): 10–30. Also see Larry Schweikart, "A New Perspective on George Wingfield and Nevada Banking, 1920–1933," *Nevada Historical Quarterly* 35 (Winter 1992): 162–76.

11

"Property of Every Kind"

Ranching and Farming during the Gold-Rush Era

Lawrence James Jelinek

The Gold Rush brought about profound changes in California agriculture. Prior to 1848 California had been defined by its almost self-sufficient missions, complete with herds, gardens, and orchards nourished by the introduction of irrigation. With the emergence of the Californio ranchos after the 1820s, the hide and tallow trade had fueled the economy, and modest progress had been made in the pueblos, especially Los Angeles, by the expansion of its irrigation system. Following the Mexican-American War, between 1846 and 1848, some growth occurred in farming by Americans and immigrant settlers, particularly in the valleys of northern and central California. With the discovery of gold, new settlers and higher cattle prices gave the rancheros short-term prosperity, but they also contributed to the demise of the open-range cattle grazing era. Once the gold fever had begun to wear off, many newcomers abandoned mining and took up agriculture. By 1872, cattle ranching had changed from primarily open-range grazing to breeding and fattening ranches. Wheat had become a major export crop with major profits. Finally, fruit cultivation had grown in importance throughout the state.[1]

Changes in California's population and demographics reflected the tide of the Gold Rush and dramatically stimulated agricultural markets and production systems. At the beginning of 1849 the state's population, excluding Native Americans, was estimated to be only 26,000, but by the end of that year, the population had risen to approximately 115,000. Males seeking gold were in large measure responsible for California's growth to 225,000 people by 1852. As the gold seekers turned into settlers and established families, the population continued to burgeon to 380,000 in 1860 and 560,000 by 1870.

Rancheros found a new market for their cattle, as beef became a highly sought commodity to feed the growing population of the mining communities. The hide

A California cattle roundup, as portrayed by the British-born historical painter James Walker, who came west in 1875 and executed several paintings, including this one, from drawings made while visiting Rancho Santa Margarita. By the time of Walker's arrival, the great days of the open range and the long drives north had passed, and cattle raising was largely confined to breeding and fattening ranches. *California Historical Society.*

trade declined as beef cattle prices in the mining districts rose from four dollars a head before the Gold Rush to five hundred dollars a head at its high point in 1849. Herds of seven hundred to a thousand animals were driven by vaqueros from southern California up through the San Joaquin Valley or along coastal trails to grazing ranges outside Sacramento, Stockton, and San Francisco. There the herds were sold to buyers for processing.[2]

Mine and town demands soon outstripped the ability of rancheros to supply them with enough good beef. They also found competition from cattlemen in Texas, the Middle West, and Mexico, who began driving herds overland to the Sacramento Valley. By 1855, up to forty thousand head of cattle were driven to California annually. About this time sheep drives were also begun. California's herds included only 17,500 sheep in 1850. New Mexico, Chihuahua, and the Middle West sent herds numbering 135,000 head in 1850 and 200,000 head in 1856, the peak years for such drives.[3]

The rancheros enjoyed substantial profits from the livestock boom, but failed to forestall the bust that was to follow. Instead of restocking their herds by introducing the meatier American stock, rancheros assumed little had changed in the switch from hides to beef. They spent their profits lavishly and went into debt, often at a rate of 5 percent a month, compounded, making them vulnerable to the changes that followed.[4]

In 1856, a severe drought caused heavy losses of California cattle. Many rancheros had already incurred serious debt because of competition with the better breeds of American cattle and sheep, which lowered the price of California-raised cattle. These problems were exacerbated by property taxes levied by a legislature controlled by northerners, especially miners, who held more personal property than real property, and who insisted that the property tax pay for state expenditures. As a result, rancheros began to lose their herds, their lands, and their homes, ending the "golden age of the cattle business."

The Treaty of Guadalupe Hidalgo (1848) accorded Californios American citizenship and obligated the U.S. government to confirm their valid claims to "property of every kind." Miners, however, who decided to switch from mining to agriculture, demanded that the federal government allow them their American birthright to claim homesteads. Land, which had been cheap when the treaty was signed, was suddenly made valuable by the Gold Rush. Congress did nothing to resolve the issue, failing to pass land legislation as it had previously done for Oregon and Washington, which would have enabled settlers to claim free homesteads of from 320 to 640 acres on public land in return for occupying the new territory. Newcomers refused to accept the idea that the government would allow several hundred "defeated Mexicans" to control millions of acres of the choicest land in the state. Hordes of defiant squatters invaded and laid claim to northern rancho lands. Finally, under pressure from these conflicting claims, Congress passed the Land Act of 1851 to determine the validity of all rancho grants.[5]

According to the provisions of the act, each claimant was allowed two years to appear before a three-member land commission to prove title. The commission's judgments could be appealed to the federal district court and then to the U.S. Supreme Court. Once a grant was confirmed, it had to be surveyed and issued a patent by the federal government. In the process of securing a claim, rancheros faced several obstacles. They might lose their claims outright. If their claims were confirmed, the boundaries could be changed, reduced, or increased at the hands of the surveyors. The surveyors were susceptible to squatter intimidations as well as to ranchero bribes. By 1856, when the commission ceased to function, judgment had been made on 813 claims. After the various appeals processes, some of which dragged on for decades, 604 grants were ultimately confirmed and 209 were rejected.

California chroniclers overwhelmingly agree that the Land Act was pro-settler in design and led to immoral and illegal confiscation of the property of Californios. Discrimination was extensive and fundamental. The burden of proof rested on rancheros instead of on the government. Hearings were conducted in English, and no commissioner was able to read documents written in Spanish. American standards for granting ownership took precedence over the Mexican system, which tended to have fewer archival records and less precise descriptions. Because of cumbersome litigation procedures, which required administrative and judicial hearings in San Francisco and Washington, D.C., to confirm and patent each title, most titles were not cleared for fifteen years. Some commissioners were fair-minded despite the biased framework, but lawyers on both sides of the issue were not. Unnecessary harassment resulted when government lawyers refused to let individual cases serve as precedents. On the other hand, ranchero lawyers demanded large fees that often had to be paid in land or cattle. After extensive litigation, rancheros often found that, although they had won their claims, they had to relinquish much of the land as payment to their lawyers.[6]

On the other hand, distinguished historian of land law Paul W. Gates took the view that the squatters were right, and that the federal government would have been wrong to uphold an essentially unproductive feudal order in American California. Gates claimed that the land commission prolonged the ownership turmoil by showing "too much regard for the inchoate rights of land claimants." Gates pointed out that of the 813 grants, 494 had been made in the 1840s. Many of the grantees failed to meet the occupancy and improvement requirements of the American takeover. In anticipation of higher land values upon completion of the American takeover, many of the 68 grants supposedly made in 1845 and the 87 grants made in 1846 had been fraudulently dated. Even so, a majority of claimants who could provide reasonable proof, even if it was deficient, that they possessed a grant and occupied it, had their claims confirmed. Gates also argued that government lawyers did accept early cases as precedent, and that given the value of ranchero holdings, the ranchero lawyers' fees were not excessive. Gates blamed the loss of ranchero land, cattle, and money on drought, extensive inheritance litigation, high living, taxes, and an inability to become competitive by American standards. He also maintained that from one-quarter to one-third of the transfers of grants from Mexican to non-Mexican owners was due to economic vulnerability, not to the Land Act. Gates did acknowledge that the Land Act failed to provide confirmation losers with a homestead tract out of their rejected claims. He also blamed Congress for being unconcerned about establishing public land boundaries promptly and clearly. This foot-dragging caused squatters and rancheros to resort to violence and deceit against each other.[7]

Historians on both sides agree with Gates concerning the dereliction of Congress. It took Congress three years to pass legislation pertaining to rancho grants and five years to establish a public land survey. By refusing to offer settlers free homesteads promptly, Congress plunged California into some of the most violent land disputes in American history. Clouded rancho land titles hindered economic development in rural and urban California for decades.

The weather delivered the final blow to rancheros, who were already suffering from falling cattle prices, taxes, and litigation. Extensive rainfall in the winter of 1861–62 created a runoff lake approximately 250 to 300 miles long and 20 to 60 miles wide in the Central Valley. Nearly 200,000 head of cattle drowned statewide. This was followed in 1862 to 1864 by the "great drought." Hundreds of thousands of cattle died from dehydration, starvation, and suffocation due to dust inhalation. In one decade, 1860 to 1870, California cattle ranges were reduced from three million head to only 630,000. Unable to sell their cattle for profit, rancheros sold their lands, often at ten cents an acre. By the 1870s, many rancheros had become day laborers in the towns.

Wealthy Americans or immigrants took over most of the ranchos.[8] Concentrated land ownership intensified dramatically in American California as speculators and individuals hopeful of becoming large ranchers and farmers bought most of the public lands that came up for sale in the 1850s and 1860s.

Federal legislation passed in 1851 and 1852 allowed California to finance public needs through the sale of 8,702,140 acres of land given to the state by the federal government. To finance public schools, 5,534,293 acres were to be sold; more than two million acres of swampland were designated for sale and reclamation; 500,000 for internal improvements; 46,080 acres for a university; and 6,400 acres for public buildings. The Morrill Act of 1862 set aside an additional 150,000 acres to finance an agricultural college.

California began disposing of its lands before establishing a state agency to administer the selling, surveying, and patenting of them. The agency that was created in 1858 followed no regular practice of informing the federal government of which lands the state had selected for its public domain or when settlers had laid claim to specific parcels within it. The Preemption Act of 1841 and the Homestead Act of 1862 allowed settlers to claim land within the federal public domain, but claimants were often unsure if the land they had selected was state or federal land, land in dispute, or confirmed rancho land. Collusion between officials in the land offices and speculators and would-be landowners was common. Settlers who had waited a long time for their claims to be certified might find that after making improvements, they had to buy the land from a speculator at an inflated price or abandon it when a "paper owner" refused to sell.

During the 1860s, an estimated eight million acres of public land passed into private ownership, according to Paul W. Gates. Much of this land was limited by legislation to grants of 160 acres. Fifty thousand farms of 160 acres should have been created during the decade, had the land laws been enforced. However, only 7,008 new farms were established, 2,848 of which should have come under the Homestead Act. An undetermined number of the remaining farms were the result of northern rancho land sales.[9] This type of misappropriation was experienced in all other states

The family of Vicente Lugo poses about 1892 with several hired hands at the country *casa* Lugo had built nearly half a century earlier on Rancho San Antonio, granted in 1810 to his father, Antonio María Lugo. Like other rancheros, Don Vicente saw his once-vast estates diminished in the 1850s and 1860s through high taxation, expensive litigation, and deadly drought. As a youth Lugo possessed two leagues of land and ran thousands of head of cattle over his domain, but by 1870 he was reduced to several hundred acres surrounding his adobe in present-day Bell Gardens, near Los Angeles. *California Historical Society/Title Insurance and Trust Photo Collection, University of Southern California.*

disposing of public land; however, in most of these states large concentrations were eventually broken up. California was unique in the scale of its misappropriation and in the determination of prominent Californians to maintain the greatest concentration of land ownership in the United States. It became so difficult to purchase land at reasonable prices in some regions that some prospective landowners were forced to accept work in the cities and towns, move to the Northwest, or return to their eastern homes. Settlers who could afford to buy land sometimes bore the heaviest burden of taxation because speculators tended not to improve their lands, and thus often paid relatively lower tax assessments.

The most distinctive member of the new land elite was William S. Chapman. Seeing agricultural potential in the vast tracts of the San Joaquin Valley, Chapman quickly became California's largest landowner after arriving from Minnesota in the early 1860s. He bought public land on his own and also in conjunction with a group of fellow San Francisco businessmen known as the "German Syndicate." By 1871, Chapman owned more than a million acres in the valley that earlier arrivals had scorned as wasteland. Chapman contributed to California's economic growth in many ways. He assisted the valley's farmers in producing large yields of high-quality wheat by experimenting with cultivation techniques. He was instrumental in modernizing the state's cattle industry through the introduction of alfalfa. More importantly, at great personal expense, Chapman, together with other prominent landowners, brought irrigation to large tracts of the valley. They established the Fresno Canal and Irrigation and the San Joaquin and Kings River Canal and Irrigation companies.[10] New crops and new cultivation methods were greatly facilitated by Chapman's willingness to experiment, combined with the availability of irrigation.

Unlike some of his peers, Chapman showed concern over the extensive concentration in land ownership. He sold parcels of land to settlers at substantial but not exorbitant prices, hoping that by helping them get started, their land improvements would increase the value of his remaining holdings. Along these lines he also encouraged colonies to create more concentrated and efficient settlement. A colony of German settlers bought 80,000 acres in Fresno County from Chapman at an average price of $1.80 per acre, only 55 cents an acre more than the federal government was asking for neighboring land. Chapman also donated land, funds, and cultivation information to the membership of the Central Colony of Fresno County in 1875.

Chapman and other large landholders did not escape criticism. The San Francisco *Evening Bulletin* published a series of articles in 1868 blaming speculators like Chapman for preventing settlers from buying good land at reasonable prices and, as a result, slowing California's development. Chapman wrote a letter to the *Bulletin* defending the speculator's role in California:

> Men who bought of me at $2.50 per acre, payable in one year (with privileges of another year's time, if the crop should fail) have this year harvested a crop which will very nearly ten times over pay back their purchase money. . . . Scores of thousands of bushels of wheat have been raised in that region (the San Joaquin Valley) this year, and hundreds of thousands will be during the coming season, over and above what would have been carried through the Golden Gate, had no "speculator" seen the capacity of that region for wheat raising, and by circulation of documents, and by all other available means directed the attention of farmers to the land in question.
>
> I think you err in charging those who have entered a few hundred thousand acres of Government land (for nine years going begging for a purchaser) with ruining the agricultural prospects of the State by holding lands at an enormous rate, and thus repelling immigration.[11]

Chapman did exercise considerable influence on employees in the federal and state land offices. His use of dummy entrymen to file claims for 160-acre home-

A phalanx of steam-powered harvesters moves across a vast landscape in an image symbolic of both the immense size of California farms and the astounding richness of the Golden State's soil. Wheat farming, the first great agricultural industry in California, was highly mechanized from the outset. Steam plows were introduced as early as 1871, and before the end of the following decade, huge machines could turn a quarter section of land in a day. *Courtesy California State Library.*

steads, which they turned over to him for a prearranged fee, would make it easy to conclude that Chapman built his empire at the ultimate expense of settlers and the state. One should keep in mind, however, that this land had been available, but had remained unclaimed, for a decade or more and that due to federal and state mismanagement of land sales, this land could easily have been purchased by a speculator with a much less developed sense of social consciousness. Since a 160-acre homestead was not large enough to grow wheat profitably, Chapman's insistence that settlers buy larger tracts from him worked to their advantage. Finally, as Chapman pointed out, settlers had not wanted the land until he had demonstrated its potential. Chapman's willingness, furthermore, to supply cultivation information to settlers who bought land from him also provided a service neglected by federal and state agencies.

Henry Miller, a German immigrant, and Henry Lux, an Alsatian immigrant, both wholesale butchers in gold-rush San Francisco, soon surpassed Chapman's holdings. Miller bought rancho land in the northern San Joaquin Valley to pasture cattle and to grow feed grains. Then in partnership with Lux, Miller increased his purchases by acquiring large tracts of swampland and dry land in the valley. While Lux oversaw their interests in San Francisco, Miller used both straightforward and devious methods to expand their holdings in the valley. Miller bought swampland from the state for no more than $1.25 an acre and was reimbursed his purchase price by the state by swearing that a like amount of money had been spent reclaiming the land. He also acquired large tracts of more expensive land at the same price by claiming to an understaffed state land office that it was swampland. Miller is reputed to have sworn that he crossed these lands by boat. He neglected to say that the boat was resting on a wagon pulled by horses at the time. Eventually, Miller and Lux owned both banks of the San Joaquin River from west of Modesto to near Madera, as well as a fifty-mile strip along the Kern River. They built an empire of more than a million acres by cheaply buying scrip land warrants issued to veterans and then cashing them in to acquire free federal land, by foreclosing on settlers to whom they lent money, and by controlling vast stretches of additional acreage through the possession of water rights. They owned 700,000 acres in the San Joaquin Valley alone. In addition, they had holdings of two million acres in Nevada and Oregon. Miller and Lux were not concerned with concentrated land ownership as Chapman had been. Miller's philosophy was, "Wise men buy land, fools sell."[12]

Other prominent landowners who began their operations in the 1860s were James Ben Ali Haggin, General Edward F. Beale, James Irvine, and George Hearst. Haggin's San Joaquin Valley holdings later formed the basis of the Kern County Land Company. Beale acquired 172,537 acres by purchasing three ranchos for approximately $25,000. Along with Llewellyn Bixby, Dr. Thomas Flint, and Benjamin Flint, Irvine formed the Irvine Ranch, covering more than a hundred thousand acres, from three rancho purchases. Hearst established San Simeon Ranch, along the coast northwest of San Luis Obispo, from three ranchos that originally were part of Mission San Miguel. Many others owned substantial amounts of land, but their holdings did not measure up to the very largest. In response to settler criticism, large landowners claimed that the size of the ranchos was not a problem, rather that the Californios had been unable to make them productive.

Leadership from ranchers like Chapman, Miller and Lux, and Beale helped transform California's cattle industry, which had been decimated by low cattle prices resulting from overstocking in 1853 and the droughts of 1856 and 1862 to 1864. These large landowners used their wealth to import meatier and heavier breeding stock and introduce modern feeding and breeding techniques. They also fenced ranges to ensure the quality of their herds. Other large-scale ranchers quickly adopted these methods. Most of the 630,000 head of cattle in California in 1870 were the new stock. The change to beef cattle is reflected in hay production, which increased from 2,038 tons to 551,773 tons between 1850 and 1870. During this period, dairy herds

Haying at Buena Vista Farm, one of a series of magnificent mammoth plates made about 1888 or 1889 by Carleton Watkins on the extensive Kern County holdings of James Ben Ali Haggin, a highly successful lawyer and financier who had come west in the Gold Rush. Haggin began buying land in Kern County in 1873, and in less than a decade, he and his associate, William Carr, owned three hundred thousand acres, some forty thousand of which were under irrigation. *Courtesy Huntington Library, San Marino, Calif.*

were also introduced, especially around San Francisco Bay and in Humboldt County. Milk cows numbered only 4,280 in the state in 1850, but that number had increased to 164,093 by 1870. California was producing six million pounds of butter and three million pounds of cheese in 1867.

The sheep industry underwent a similar transformation. Sheep had been almost as numerous as cattle in the mission period, but their numbers rapidly declined during the rancho period. Mutton became important during the Gold Rush, surpassing beef as a miner staple until the herds were decimated by the drought of 1862 to 1864. Prominent stockmen such as James Irvine, W. W. Hollister, and Jotham, Llewellyn, and Marcellus Bixby improved sheep quality, a necessity to the resurgence of the industry. In 1849, there were only 20,000 sheep in California, but this number increased to a million in 1860 and 2.75 million in 1870. The stockmen introduced French and Spanish Merinos, English Cotswolds, Leicesters, Southdowns, and even Australian sheep. Improved stock and a demand for wool in the northern states created by the Civil War produced boom conditions until the 1880s. Due to the poorer quality of the herds in 1860, only two million pounds of wool was marketed, but by 1870, the total had increased to eleven million pounds. Monterey, Los Angeles, San Luis Obispo, and Santa Barbara counties were the centers of the industry. After 1880, the sheep market declined due to the rise of land values, as well as expanding ranches, towns, and farms, which reduced the available pasturage and water supplies, and blocked many of the migration routes.

Crop-cultivation had been brought to a near standstill by gold fever during the early years of the Gold Rush. The exhausting work of placer mining, diminishing supplies of surface gold, and growing numbers of miners led in-state farmers to return to their farms.[13] Many out-of-state rushers who had been farmers returned to the land as well, as feeding the miners became a more stable way of making a living by 1853. Barley had been the principal grain grown by American farmers before the Gold Rush, but due to the needs of miners, wheat became a major grain by 1860, production standing at six million bushels. By 1870, wheat production had increased to 16,750,000 bushels, with 72 percent coming from the Sacramento and northern San Joaquin valleys, the centers of the American farming population. Wheat production on the big ranches, as well as the small farms, caused the supply to quickly outstrip local demand. Although flooding and drought in the early 1860s sharply reduced output, by 1872 railroads had penetrated 150 miles into the San Joaquin Valley, 50 miles into the Sacramento Valley, and 30 miles into the Salinas Valley, which opened prime wheatlands to settlement.

San Francisco middlemen began exporting much of the wheat surplus by sailing ships to Great Britain, Australia, New York, and China during the early 1860s. California's export suffered from uncertain demand and price conditions since each of these markets already had major sources of wheat. Another market for California's crop came from the war-ravaged South, which had put a serious drain on the availability of midwestern and eastern grains. Severe fluctuations in production, combined with the temporary nature of existing export connections, made it unclear if California would fulfill its potential as a major source of wheat. The gold-rush period was important in that the population increase not only reinvigorated cultivation but established it on a substantial scale. As the cattle industry diminished in importance, for the first time in California history, wheat became more important than cattle.

The transition from cattle to cereal production was not healthy in every respect. Wheat is easy to grow, but it depletes the soil. Eager for maximum returns, many large-scale growers ignored good agricultural practices such as soil replenishment and crop rotation. California's grain farms, many of which were established on rented land and hence lacked long-term commitment from growers, were criticized by many rural travelers for their lack of buildings or other signs that owners intended permanent cultivation.

Exploitation of wheat also required wheat growers to put together large gangs of itinerant workers for cutting and threshing. Indeed, because of large landholdings and scant rural population in the state, all types of agriculture relied on itinerant laborers, and because there was a chronic labor shortage in the 1850s and 1860s, Native Americans, Chinese, Mexicans, displaced squatters, and disillusioned miners filled the ranks of these gangs, inadequately at first. Native Americans and Chinese gained acceptance as laborers because they were more readily available, worked hard, and accepted the lowest wages. While Americans and Mexicans tended to bargain and complain individually, Native American and Chinese laborers simplified grower contact with workers by using one of their own as boss and doing what they were told. Minimum decencies given American and Mexican laborers were not accorded to Native American and Chinese laborers.[14] Some of these laborers, which began to include southern and eastern Europeans, became farm entrepreneurs.

Between 1848 and 1872, major strides also were made in fruit growing. Viticulture experienced the most important developments. Through the rancho period, grapes remained important because knowledge was developed about locations and techniques, because there was a market for wine and brandy, and because these commodities were relatively nonperishable. Grape growing became more profitable than any other form of cultivation between 1850 and 1860 because of the heavy consumption of alcohol by miners. This stimulus caused developments in the 1850s that laid the foundation for California's modern wine industry.

Prior to the Gold Rush, grapes had been confined largely to the Los Angeles area, but in order to bring producers closer to the miners and the large urban populations of San Francisco and other rising northern towns, vines were soon planted around San Francisco Bay, in the southern Sacramento Valley, in the northern San Joaquin Valley, and in the Sierra Nevada foothills. The market, however, continued to be dominated by a few prominent Los Angeles-based men such as Pierre and Jean Louis Sansevain, Charles Kohler, John Frohling, and William Wolfskill, who were growers, wine makers, and wine merchants. They were joined by a growing number of smaller-scale growers and unknowledgeable wine makers, who turned out palatable but debased concoctions. In their search for profit, these novices undermined the reputation of California wines for almost fifty years; however, they did determine where most of the state's principal wine growing areas were and were not located.

True viticulture was left to exceptional individuals. Colonel Agoston Haraszthy, a Hungarian nobleman, is generally regarded as the father of California's modern wine industry. Haraszthy came to San Diego from Wisconsin in 1849, searching for relief from asthma and for better economic opportunity. By 1851, Haraszthy had planted the Mission grape and several varieties of Hungarian grapes. He was elected sheriff in 1850 and was elected to the state assembly two years later. During this time

Farm laborers take a rest from the harvest in San Joaquin County to pose for a picture. Beginning with Indians and then Chinese, a succession of ethnic groups, including Japanese, Mexicans, and Okies, predominated in the itinerant work gangs that labored in what Carey McWilliams would term "factories in the field." *California Historical Society, FN-01025.*

he purchased fifty acres near Mission Dolores in San Francisco and a large tract of land near Crystal Springs in what is now San Mateo County. Haraszthy was appointed assayer at the San Francisco branch of the U.S. mint, and he took over the important positions of melter and refiner. When he resigned after being wrongly accused of embezzling gold, Haraszthy subsequently devoted most of his attention to viticulture. He soon realized that coastal fogs adversely affected the sugar content of grapes by depriving them of needed sunlight. In 1857, he bought 560 acres in Sonoma County, an area already proven to have superior grape-growing conditions.

In a year's time, Haraszthy had planted 85,556 vines on his Buena Vista ranch and had 462,000 rooted cuttings in his nursery. In 1860, to improve the quality of California wines, he brought back from Europe 200,000 cuttings and rooted vines representing 1,400 fine varieties. Haraszthy proposed to have the state buy and distrib-

The celebrated viticulturist Agoston Haraszthy stands before his Buena Vista Winery, near the town of Sonoma, 1865. Although modern scholarship has stripped the enterprising Hungarian of his title, the "Father of California Viticulture," Haraszthy is acknowledged for his important role in the development of California winegrowing. He established what was then the largest vineyard in the United States, imported hundreds of varieties of vinifera, and vigorously promoted California wines to a national market in his *Grape Culture, Wines and Wine-Making* (1862) and other writings. *California Historical Society, FN-00301.*

ute the cuttings and vines as well as supervise growing and winemaking operations. Faced with legislative opposition to this expensive plan, he sold many of the cuttings and vines to unskilled vintners. Although progress was noticeably retarded, Haraszthy had been instrumental in introducing improved grape varieties and in moving grapes from a pastoral to a commercial base.[15]

Despite the importance of varietal introductions, the Mission grape dominated the industry until the 1880s. Given the transitional stage of development, vine plantings were nonetheless impressive. There were an estimated one million vines in 1855; only five years later there were eight million and by 1870 there were twenty-eight million vines. At this time some 40,000 acres of bearing and nonbearing vines had been planted, producing two million gallons of wine. Los Angeles County was responsible for one-fourth of this production, with one-sixth coming from Sonoma County. Table grapes also gained in prominence in the 1850s and 1860s to meet the demands of miners and townspeople.

Although orchard fruit underwent expansion during this period as well, its progress was much slower. Deciduous and citrus trees were more expensive to purchase and required a longer maturation period. In a mobile society overly concerned with quick wealth, these factors were a liability. In addition, local consumption was too limited for extensive plantings. While all types of deciduous trees capable of prospering in California had been planted by 1870, apple trees, of which there were twenty varieties, were the most numerous. There were two million apple trees, 750,000 peach trees, and 330,000 pear trees in that year. Modest numbers of almond, walnut, and olive trees were also planted. Sacramento, Sonoma, Yuba, Solano, and Alameda counties had the most deciduous tree plantings, with the San Joaquin Valley accounting for only 7 percent, and the counties from Santa Barbara south containing only 6 percent.

The need for more capital and irrigation combined with less population in the south, and the resistance of southern rancho owners to subdivision, retarded the development of citrus production. Most of the groves, which contained 4,000 orange trees and 600 lemon trees in 1860, belonged to William Wolfskill and were located in Los Angeles County. By 1870, plantings had increased to 45,000 citrus trees in the region, with another 5,000 to 6,000 trees located in the northern counties.

The mounting realization that gold could not permanently underwrite a healthy economy benefited agriculture. The state took action as cultivation gained attention. The State Agricultural Society was chartered in 1854 to establish experimental farms, to hold state fairs and stock shows, and to inspect quality improvements. The State Board of Agriculture, established in 1858, offered bounties on new crops and facilitated the transfer of information from prominent experimenters to other farmers. Before cotton and rice crops had a future in California, bounties were offered on them. The French immigrant Louis Prévost's prediction that silk raising would become the state's most profitable commodity led to the planting of 1.8 million mulberry trees by 1870. Bounties were also offered for sugar cane and tobacco, and after being introduced in El Dorado County by Japanese farmers, tea shrubs.

The importance of the Gold Rush to cultivation, according to historian John W. Caughey, can be seen in the state's fence laws. When cattle reigned supreme, the Trespass Act of 1852 required that a farmer had to build a "lawful fence" in order to collect crop damages from a rancher for livestock depredations. Because of soaring lumber prices, fences, had they been built, would have been worth much more than the land. In 1872 a "no-fence" law was passed, making ranchers responsible for damages caused by their unfenced livestock. Pastoral California had given way to agricultural California.[16]

NOTES

1. Ellen Liebman, *California Farmland: A History of Large Agricultural Landholdings* (Totowa, N.J.: Roman and Allanheld, 1983), 1–28; Lawrence J. Jelinek, *Harvest Empire: A History of California Agriculture,* 2nd ed. (San Francisco: Boyd & Fraser, 1982), 23–38; Richard J. Orsi, comp., *A List of References for the History of Agriculture in California* (Davis, Calif.: Agricultural History Center, 1974); Rodman W. Paul, "The Beginnings of Agriculture in California: Innovation vs. Continuity," *California Historical Quarterly* 52 (1973): 16–27; Ralph J. Roske, *Everyman's Eden: A History of California* (New York: Macmillan, 1968), 391–412; Paul W. Gates, ed., *California Ranchos and Farms, 1846–1862, Including the Letters of John Quincy Adams Warren of 1861* (Madison: State Historical Society of Wisconsin Press, 1967); Osgood Hardy, "Agricultural Changes in California, 1860–1900," in American Historical Association, Pacific Coast Branch, *Proceedings* (1929): 216–30; Robert Glass Cleland and Osgood Hardy, *March of Industry* (Los Angeles: Powell, 1929), 36–130; and E. J. Wickson, *Rural California* (New York: Macmillan, 1923), 60–207.

2. James M. Jensen, "Cattle Drives from the Ranchos to the Gold Fields of California," *Arizona and the West* 2 (1960): 341–52.

3. L. T. Burcham, *California Range Land: An Historico-Ecological Study of the Range Resource of California,* University of California Center for Archaelogical Research at Davis, Publication No. 7 (Davis, 1982), 118–61.

4. Albert Camarillo, *Chicanos in a Changing Society from Mexican Pueblos to American Barrios in Santa Barbara and Southern California, 1848–1930* (Cambridge, Mass.: Harvard University Press, 1979), 33–52, and Leonard Pitt, *The Decline of the Californios: A Social History of the Spanish-Speaking Californians, 1846–1890* (Berkeley: University of California Press, 1966), 83–129.

5. Richard B. Rice, William A. Bullough, and Richard J. Orsi, *The Elusive Eden: A New History of California* (New York: Knopf, 1988), 204–13, and John Caughey with Norris Hundley, Jr., *California: History of a Remarkable State,* 4th ed. (Englewood Cliffs, N.J.: Prentice-Hall, 1982), 135–38.

6. John S. Hittell, *The Resources of California* (San Francisco: A. Roman, 1863), 453–61; Hubert Howe Bancroft, *History of California,* vol. 6: *1848–1859* (San Francisco: The History Company, 1888), 529–81; Josiah Royce, *California, From the Conquest in 1846 to the Second Vigilance Committee in San Francisco* (Boston: Houghton, Mifflin, 1892), 466–501; Robert Glass Cleland, *The Cattle on a Thousand Hills: Southern California, 1850–1870* (San Marino, Calif.: Huntington Library, 1941), 46–71; Pitt, *Decline of the Californios,* 83–119, 282–84; and John W. Caughey, *California: A Remarkable State's Life History,* 3rd ed. (Englewood Cliffs, N. J.: Prentice-Hall, 1970), 242–55.

7. Paul W. Gates, "Adjudication of Spanish-Mexican Land Claims in California," *Huntington Library Quarterly* 21 (1958): 213–36; Gates, "California's Embattled Settlers," *Califor-*

nia Historical Society Quarterly 41 (1962): 99–130; and Gates, "Pre-Henry George Land Warfare in California," *California Historical Society Quarterly* 46 (1967): 121–48.

8. Robert Glass Cleland, *The Irvine Ranch*, 3rd ed. (San Marino, Calif.: Huntington Library, 1978), passim; Theodore Saloutos, "The Immigrant in Pacific Coast Agriculture, 1880–1940," in *Agriculture in the Development of the Far West*, ed. James H. Shideler (Washington: Agricultural History Society, 1975), 182–201; and John W. Caughey, "Don Benito Wilson," *Huntington Library Quarterly* 2 (1939): 285–300.

9. Paul W. Gates, "Public Land Disposal in California," *Agricultural History* 44 (1975): 158–78.

10. Donald J. Pisani, *From the Family Farm to Agribusiness: The Irrigation Crusade in California and the West, 1850–1931* (Berkeley: University of California Press, 1984), 1–77.

11. Excerpts from Chapman's letter to the San Francisco *Evening Bulletin* are reprinted in Gerald D. Nash, "Henry George Reexamined: William S. Chapman's Views on Land Speculation in Nineteenth Century California," *Agricultural History* 33 (1959): 133–37; the letter appears on pp. 135–37. Also see Nash, "Problems and Projects in the History of Nineteenth Century California Land Policy," *Arizona and the West* 2 (1960): 327–40.

12. Edward F. Treadwell, *The Cattle King: A Dramatized Biography* (New York: Macmillan, 1931), 59.

13. Robert L. Kelley, *Gold vs. Grain: The Hydraulic Mining Controversy in California's Sacramento Valley* (Glendale, Calif.: Arthur H. Clark, 1959), 57–84.

14. For a discussion of Chinese farmers, see Sucheng Chan, *This Bittersweet Soil: The Chinese in California Agriculture, 1860–1910* (Berkeley: University of California Press, 1986), 79–105; and Ping Chiu, *Chinese Labor in California, 1850–1880: An Economic Study* (Madison: State Historical Society of Wisconsin, 1963), 67–88.

15. Vincent P. Carosso, *The California Wine Industry, 1830–1895: A Study of the Formative Years* (Berkeley: University of California Press, 1951), 38–48, and Joan M. Donohue, "Agoston Haraszthy: A Study in Creativity," *California Historical Society Quarterly* 48 (1969): 153–63.

16. Caughey, *California*, 201–2.

12

The Golden Skein

California's Gold-Rush Transportation Network

A. C. W. Bethel

To Americans at the beginning of the Gold Rush, California seemed—and was—remote and isolated. In 1849, Rufus Porter, the editor of *Scientific American,* formed a joint-stock company to construct an eight-hundred-foot steam-powered dirigible intended to carry fifty to one hundred passengers "safely and pleasantly" from New York to California in three days.[1] It wouldn't have worked, but his proposal shows the spirit of the times: mid-nineteenth-century Americans were people in a hurry, and they sought to move faster using steam, iron, and electricity.[2]

But before the Gold Rush, transportation in thinly settled, cash-poor, pastoral California was limited. The roads that connected the small settlements near the coast were pack trails, improved locally for two-wheeled oxcarts. A few launches propelled by oars or sails carried passengers and freight on San Francisco Bay and the lower reaches of the Sacramento-San Joaquin river system. What manufactured goods Californians enjoyed were bartered for cattle hides and tallow from foreign-flag ships trading along the coast.[3]

Thus, adequate transport had to be improvised for an influx of gold seekers and merchants who multiplied California's population tenfold. Moreover, because most gold-rush emigrants didn't plan to stay in California, they sought only high-yield, short-term investments, and those who did plan to stay sought advantage for their own city's commerce, often at another city's loss. Fortunately the flood of new gold-rush wealth created economic incentives for fast transportation, and enterprising individuals quickly created an up-to-date transportation system, including an infrastructure of roads, wharves, bridges, ferries, express offices, shipyards, foundries and factories. Innovative shipbuilders soon devised new types of scows, schooners, and steamboats suited to California conditions.

Except for mail subsidies, development was driven by perceived demand. Large

A lithograph published in New York in 1849 by Nathaniel Currier caricatures the desperate attempts of Americans to transport themselves as speedily as possible to the gold fields of California. The steam-powered dirigible, *upper left*, was inspired by the published design of Rufus Porter, editor of *Scientific American*, who early in the year offered Argonauts passage overland, at $200 each, in his "Aerial Transport," which he anticipated placing in operation by April. *California Historical Society.*

companies, often near-monopolies, later consolidated services begun by individuals who happened to own a horse or a boat, but the efficiency gained through economies of scale rarely raised barriers to entry enough to prevent competition, and fares and freight rates declined throughout the Gold Rush.

But at the beginning of the Gold Rush, none of this was in place.

THE PANAMA ROUTE

The fastest way to get to California from the East was to take a steamer to Panama, cross the narrow isthmus to the Pacific, then take another steamer to San Francisco. At first the sixty-mile Panama crossing utilized large dugout canoes, called bungos, to reach the head of navigation on the Chagres River, then followed a mule trail over the divide to Panama City. Shallow-draft steamers soon replaced the bungos; the mule trail was improved; and in 1855 a railroad shortened the total transit time across the isthmus to a few hours.[4]

At Panama City, gold seekers impatiently awaited passage north; until steamer schedules were better coordinated, they sometimes waited for months. Meanwhile they fretted in the unhealthy climate, unimpressed by their picturesque surroundings and intolerant of the local Hispanic culture.[5] The three steamships that the Pacific Mail steamship company had built to satisfy its 1847 mail contract were inadequate for the unanticipated gold-rush traffic. *California*, built to carry 250 passengers at most, inaugurated service by steaming into San Francisco in 1849 with 365 crowded on board. Larger and faster steamers were quickly added: Pacific Mail had fourteen ships by 1851 and twenty-three by 1869.[6]

Panama steamers were wooden-hulled side-wheelers driven by massive single-cylinder steam engines. Low boiler pressures required engines with bores and strokes measured in feet to yield a few hundred horsepower. Because these big engines turned slowly, higher speeds required paddlewheels larger in diameter, up to thirty feet or so, and the big paddlewheel boxes gave the black-hulled ships a look of massive power. All the Panama steamers had masts and occasionally supplemented steam power with sails.[7]

Pacific Mail first- and second-class passengers slept in well-ventilated, carpeted staterooms and had access to elegantly furnished public rooms; amenities sometimes included a barber shop and a bath. Steerage passengers slept on canvas bunks stretched over pole frames and stacked three high. Later, space was made for dining tables, and separate dormitories were provided for men and women. Food on the early voyages was monotonous, but Pacific Mail's management made strenuous efforts to improve it, and the line had earned a generally good reputation by 1852. By contrast, passengers traveling on rival lines protested poor food, insolent service, overcrowding, and lack of clean linens.[8]

The usual running time from Panama to San Francisco was eighteen to twenty-one days at first, later reduced to thirteen or fourteen days. Once the Pacific and Atlantic steamer schedules were coordinated, the whole trip could be made in thirty-five days; faster ships and the Panama railroad eventually shortened this to twenty-one. The frequency of sailings from San Francisco was increased from monthly to twice monthly in 1850, and to every ten days in 1860. At San Francisco the departure of a mail steamer—"steamer day"—was the frantic occasion for businessmen to settle accounts and prepare correspondence for the States.[9]

Pacific Mail's operating costs were high. The steamers' inefficient boilers consumed huge quantities of expensive, imported coal, and because there were no repair facilities on the West Coast, Pacific Mail had to build its own docks, ironworks, and machine shops at Benicia, on the Carquinez Strait. They were closed in 1861, when California's industrial base had grown enough to provide alternative repair services.[10]

Despite high expenses, Pacific Mail generally paid substantial dividends, and these profits attracted competition throughout the gold-rush period. In 1851, Cornelius Vanderbilt began developing a crossing at Nicaragua, which short-hauled

A train of the Panama Railroad pulls into the terminus of the line in December 1854. Completed just a month later, after five years of construction, the road greatly reduced the time and cost of crossing the isthmus. Whereas the Forty-niners paid the better part of $100 for a difficult and dangerous five-day trip by dugout canoe and muleback, later travelers could ride coast to coast in three or four hours for $25, enjoying splendid views of wild tropical jungles from the relative comfort of their cars. *Courtesy Huntington Library, San Marino, Calif.*

Panama by four hundred miles. Reputedly a healthier place than Panama, Nicaragua offered an easier passage by small steamers up the San Juan River and across Lake Nicaragua, then by stagecoach to the Pacific. Between 1853 and 1855, the Nicaragua route drew nearly as many passengers as the Panama crossing. Completion of the Panama railroad and political instability in Nicaragua combined to make the Nicaragua route unattractive after 1856, though it was operated sporadically by Vanderbilt's successors until 1868. Pacific Mail had bought out Vanderbilt in 1859 with a substantial block of company stock that tied his fortunes to theirs.[11] Pacific Mail ships were generally well-managed and safe, despite some spectacular wrecks. Pacific Mail's rivals were less meticulous, however. Survivors ascribed the loss of the Independent Line's *Union* to a drunken crew; and when the Opposition Independent Line's *Yankee Blade* went aground, unsupervised crewmen beat and robbed passengers left on board, the captain having already put himself ashore.[12]

Between 1848 and 1869, about 600,000 passengers used the Panama route, more than 46,000 traveling in 1859, the peak year. By contrast, a total of about 156,000 went via Nicaragua. Because freight rates were high—never less than forty cents per pound—only very high priority freight went westbound via Panama: express way-bills mention clothing, liquor, medicine, books, and firearms. But more than three-quarters of a billion dollars in coined gold was transported across the isthmus eastbound, nearly $48 million in 1864, the peak year. The importance of the Panama route declined with the opening of the first transcontinental railroad in 1869; the Pacific Mail then concentrated on its transpacific steamship routes, which it operated into the 1920s.[13]

GOLD-RUSH MARITIME TRADE

Pastoral California's rudimentary economy could not begin to supply the sudden influx of gold seekers. Until the mid-1850s, even food supplies had to be imported. Provisions came from China, Australia, Chile, and the eastern United States, but they were all three to six months sailing time to California. Hawaii was only three to five weeks away, and had already developed commercial agriculture to provision whaling ships, which had concentrated in the Pacific by the 1840s. In 1850, 469 ships arrived at San Francisco from Hawaii, their trade valued at $380,000. But after 1851, Oregon supplied California's agricultural imports; Oregon was less than half the sailing time away, and its products were cheaper and better. China continued to send foods preferred by Chinese emigrants, Hawaii shifted to tropical products, especially sugar, and the Pacific Northwest later became an important supplier of lumber and coal.[14]

By 1856 San Francisco had become a well-built and settled city of fireproof masonry commercial buildings, extensive piers, planked streets, and handsome residential blocks. For lack of local supply, bricks had been imported from New Zealand and Tasmania and granite from Hong Kong, and prefabricated corrugated iron buildings had come from Britain, Asia, and Australia. The demand for lumber quickly outran the capacity of existing California sawmills, and lumber was imported from the East Coast until 1855—eighty million board feet in 1852.[15]

San Francisco builders valued coastal redwood for its long, straight grain and resistance to fire. Stands of redwood in the Oakland hills and in the Santa Cruz Mountains had been exploited since Hispanic times, but the largest stands of redwoods occupied a four-hundred-mile coastal belt about thirty miles deep stretching from the north shore of San Francisco Bay to the Oregon border. By 1852, sawmills were turning out lumber at Humboldt Bay and along the Mendocino coast. Much of this cut went to San Francisco, but there were foreign exports as well: by 1854, Humboldt Bay was shipping lumber to Australia, and later to China, Hawaii, Chile, and Tahiti.[16]

Navigation along the redwood coast was hazardous. Humboldt Bay offered a protected anchorage, but heavy seas broke over a shallow sandbar at the entrance. Along the eighty-five-mile Mendocino coast, lumber mills were sited on steep bluffs above narrow estuaries, where often the only practical way to deliver lumber to a moored ship was by skidding it down a wooden chute slung from cables. Surging tides, fogs, and submerged rocks made navigation into these "dog-hole" ports dangerous. Steam power, which gave captains better control, would not be fitted to coastal lumber schooners until the 1880s.[17]

To meet the special demands of the traffic, shipyards along the West Coast began delivering handy, flat-bottomed, broad-beamed, single-decked sailing schooners of one hundred tons or so beginning in the 1850s. These craft had oversize hatches for quick loading, and could carry as much lumber above deck as below. Deck loads were chained down to prevent dangerous shifting during the voyage. Broad-beamed hulls made the schooners stable even when empty so that they could return northward safely without cargoes.[18]

Forty-niners emigrating by way of Cape Horn cleared eastern ports of old ships, and the fast clipper designs that had evolved by the early 1840s now dominated a burst of new construction that briefly eclipsed steam and made America's merchant marine a rival to that of Great Britain. The new clippers had narrow hulls and long, concave bows that cut easily through the sea. Above water, their long, black, flush-decked hulls, often accented by a narrow stripe of white or color, had a sleek, racy look. Clippers spread very large sail areas, and their captains were willing to risk sprung masts and snapped yards in gale-force winds in order to gain a fast passage. The clippers' sailing rigs required large crews; poorly paid, the men were hard to manage, and their officers frequently enforced orders physically. Until well into 1851 it was hard to keep a crew from deserting to the mines at San Francisco, and shipping agents recruited men by offering high wages, or by shanghaiing them.[19]

The clippers' impressive performances were aided by the publication of Matthew Maury's charts of ocean winds and currents, which showed that the fastest course under sail was not always the shortest in miles. By following Maury's directions, captains reduced their sailing times to California by forty days or so, whether their ships were clippers or not.[20]

The clippers' hollow lines and vee-shaped bottoms limited their cargo capacity to perhaps half that of a fuller-bodied ship, and their operating expenses were high. In 1850–51, when high-priority freight rates to California were as much as sixty dollars a ton, or one dollar per cubic foot, a single voyage could repay more than the clipper had cost; but freight rates slipped to thirty dollars a ton by 1853, and to $7.50 a ton by 1858, half of the rate that clippers needed to break even. After the Civil War, America's wooden-hulled merchant marine entered a long decline, and British iron-hulled sailing ships dominated California's growing wheat trade with Liverpool.[21]

The *Flying Cloud,* probably the most famous of all clipper ships, prepares for her maiden voyage, from East Boston to San Francisco, in a wood engraving that appeared in *Gleason's Pictorial Drawing Room Companion* in May 1851. Built for speed, clippers carried less freight and fewer passengers than slower vessels, but Forty-niners willingly paid premium prices—as much as $1,000—for passage on one of these glorious vessels. Young Josiah Creesy, who first captained the *Flying Cloud,* drove her around Cape Horn in midwinter and passed through the Golden Gate in a record eighty-nine days, some two or three months faster than broader-beamed ships. *California Historical Society, FN-30960.*

BAY AND RIVER TRAFFIC

San Francisco became gold-rush California's entrepôt because its location just inside the Golden Gate was convenient for arriving ships, and it gave easy access to the Sacramento–San Joaquin river system, which became a supply highway to the mines. River towns—Stockton, Sacramento, Marysville, Colusa, and Red Bluff—grew as centers where goods brought from San Francisco by riverboat could be forwarded by pack train or wagon to the mining towns. Sacramento, the busiest of the river ports, received at least 165,000 tons of freight in 1852, of which perhaps 10 percent was used locally and 15 percent was forwarded upriver, and the rest sent on to the mines,

The side-wheeler *Yosemite* departs for Sacramento from the Broadway wharf of the California Steam Navigation Company, about 1865. Steamboats not only provided a swift and reliable mode of transportation for passengers and freight, but also offered an agreeable way of seeing the California countryside. After an excursion from San Francisco to the state capital in the spring of 1859, the publisher of *Hutchings' California Magazine* declared he "could not recommend a tour which can be made with so much ease, and is so generally calculated to please every variety of tastes, as a trip on the bay and river." *Courtesy Society of California Pioneers.*

three hundred to four hundred tons a day at the height of the season.[22] At first the trip upriver from San Francisco to Sacramento or Stockton usually took about a week. Labyrinthine sloughs could easily disorient navigation, and riverbank foliage sometimes screened off the wind so that the boats had to be rowed or hauled from shore. Clouds of voracious mosquitoes added to the passengers' discomforts.[23]

To expedite bay and river freight, local boatyards developed a distinctive, blunt-ended, flat-bottomed scow schooner in the early 1850s. These surprisingly fast and handy boats carried bulk cargoes, such as hay and potatoes, stacked so high on their decks that the helmsman steered from a raised "pulpit" in order to see ahead.[24] The first steamboats were serving bay and river ports by late 1849; there were about fifty in service a year later. Competition for fast passages soon led to spirited racing, in which steamboat pilots tried to push rival boats ashore or zigzagged to keep them from passing. Passengers wagered on the outcome and sometimes fired pistols at the competition's boat. Deadly boiler explosions resulted from excess steam and deferred maintenance, snags and collisions sank boats, and shifting sandbars in poorly charted rivers stranded them.[25] Racing was ended and tariffs were stabilized by the 1854 merger of several competing steamer lines into the California Steam Navigation Company. Because it was fairly easy to finance a steamboat, the merger never achieved a total monopoly, and there were still occasional rate wars, but increased demand generated enough business for these additional boats, which were often eventually absorbed into the merger.[26]

Fast, elegantly furnished side-wheel steamers provided daily service connecting San Francisco with Sacramento and Stockton in nine or ten hours, though the Sacramento trip was once made in less than six. Smaller stern-wheel steamboats that drew as little as two feet of water served points on the shallow, tortuous stretches of the upper rivers. Because shallow hulls lacked internal stiffness, the smaller, upriver steamers had to be strengthened externally with a cat's cradle of cables attached to a vertical post, called a "hog post," that extended above the superstructure. The little steamers could tow barges by means of a cable attached to a swivel mounted on the hog post, an arrangement that kept the towing cable clear of the stern-wheel and gave the boat's rudders good leverage against the resistance of the barge.[27]

Initially there was only a little downriver freight, mostly in hay and cordwood, but tonnages grew with the development of California's bonanza grain-based agriculture, and downriver freight equaled upriver freight by 1861. Throughout the river system, hundreds of landings, some improvised from brush and planks, became shipping points for otherwise isolated farms, where steamboats would stop for a flag or a lantern signal. Red Bluff was the head of navigation on the Sacramento after snags were cleared above Colusa in 1852. At first, upriver boats regularly reached Marysville on the Feather River, but water diversion and silting impeded navigation after 1855. During the high-water season, from January until July, small, shallow-draft boats steamed south almost to Fresno on the San Joaquin.[28]

PACKING TO THE MINES

In the absence of roads, supplies at first reached the mining camps by pack mules. The mules were managed by experienced Mexican muleteers, or *arrieros*. Their Mexican pack saddles rested the load on a straw-stuffed leather bag, called an *aparejo,* instead of on wooden crossbucks. The *aparejo* was heavier, but it was easier on the animals' backs, and the Army later also adopted it. A mule could pack from 200 to 350 pounds of freight twenty-five to thirty-five miles a day, depending on terrain. Mule loads included flour, beans, whiskey, chairs, tables, plows, pianos, and iron safes.[29]

Because each miner consumed at least a pound of supplies daily, packing to the mines required large numbers of mules: 2,500 mules carried freight from Marysville to Downieville, for example, providing employment for perhaps four hundred men. One thousand pack mules left Marysville in one day, carrying one hundred tons of freight, the equivalent of two steamboat loads. Packing was a seasonal business, but sometimes pack trains operated in the Sierra winter, carrying barley along with the freight because there was no forage for the animals. Sometimes animals and muleteers froze to death. Other mules perished in falls caused by shifting packs or unstable ground, and robbers and hostile Indians sometimes attacked the trains.[30]

WAGON ROADS, BRIDGES, AND FERRIES

Wagon freighting had natural advantages over packing: a mule could draw about two thousand pounds, many times the load that it could pack, and wagons did not have to be unloaded every night. But because wagons could not follow a contour line, wagon roads first had to be graded into the Sierra foothills from the river ports. Some roads were built and maintained by joint-stock toll road companies—there were sixty-four of them in California by 1858—but merchants and civic boosters often subscribed for road improvements without charging tolls, and counties built some roads with public funds. Many gold-rush road improvements were just enough to get the wagons through, with hairpin turns and grades as steep as fourteen degrees, but other construction was substantial. Cuts were blasted with black powder and then cleared with picks and shovels.

Bridges—117 by 1856—crossed ravines, and rock cribbing supported fills. Culverts and diversion ditches sometimes drained roadbeds, though heavy rains still left them so muddy that wagons mired to the hubs. In the winter, scrapers and the tramping of animal hooves cleared some snow, though many mountain roads could be operated only during warmer and drier seasons. These roads were often only a foot or so wider than the wagons that used them. Frequent turnouts allowed wagons to pass, and loaded wagons going uphill had the right of way. Iron tires crashing over uneven, rocky ground announced their coming, as did jangling brass bells, tuned to a chord—usually C, E, G, C—and fastened to flattened hoops above the collars of the lead span.[31]

Swift-flowing rivers dissect the Sierra foothills, so ferries and bridges became nodal points in the road system. The first ferries were skiffs—wagon boxes were floated across—but skiffs were soon replaced by flat-bottomed barges large enough to carry a wagon and team. Some early bridges that replaced ferries were plank roadways floated on pontoons, but wooden truss bridges were introduced in 1850. The trusses were often housed over to protect their structural members from the el-

A pack train makes its way through a snow storm in a wood engraving after a design by Charles Nahl, 1856. Packers and their mules encountered a variety of dangers in carrying supplies to mining camps, but winter trips were especially hazardous. When a tremendous storm caught one train between Grass Valley and Onion Valley, all but three of forty-five mules perished before the snows lifted. *California Historical Society, FN-30968.*

ements, though floods swept away ferries and bridges alike. Wire rope, widely used in mining, was adopted for suspension bridge construction by 1854.[32]

FREIGHT WAGON TECHNOLOGY

California freight wagon boxes were flat-floored and long—sixteen to twenty feet— but only three or four feet wide. Their sides were often overtopped by bulky loads stacked as high as fifteen feet. For oversized loads, such as boilers, the box was removed and the load was secured directly to the running gear. Six-foot-high rear wheels and iron tires up to four inches wide reduced the pulling effort required of the animals. Wagon builders selected different hardwoods for different structural functions, then seasoned the wood for three to five years to prevent shrinkage. Rugged freight wagons could weigh nearly two tons empty, and loads of six to eight tons were common. With a trailer, or "back-action," the load could be roughly equal to one of today's long-haul trucks.

The number of mules used depended on the load and the terrain; sometimes there were twelve to twenty or more mules, all controlled by a single rein, called a jerk line, that ran forward to the bit of the left leader. The mules were trained to act as a coordinated team, and when the wagon rounded a turn, some of the mules would jump over the chain that harnessed them to the wagon tongue and pull tangent to the curve, because a force at an angle to the wagon tongue would only tend to pull the wagon off the road. Teamsters were famous for their foul vocabulary, and they encouraged their teams with whip-crackings and tossed pebbles, but most of them treated their animals humanely for reasons of both prudence and affection. Still, the work was hard, and on steep grades the animals could sometimes pull only forty or fifty feet before needing a rest.[33]

THE TRANS-SIERRA ROADS

Covered-wagon emigrants opened the first roads across the Sierra. At first some of these roads were so steep and rugged that wagons had to be disassembled and packed piecemeal over the rougher stretches. California communities that hoped to gain the emigrants' commerce improved these roads with some bridging and grading. By 1852, half a dozen of them were in passable condition, and the emigrant's choice of route depended on his or her destination. The Carson route, which went from Nevada south of Lake Tahoe to Placerville, attracted the most traffic in spite of its double summit; the Donner Pass route had only a single summit, but it fell out of favor because of repeated, difficult fords in the Truckee River canyon.[34]

California's isolation furnished another motive for trans-Sierra roadbuilding. Popular enthusiasm expressed in organized meetings and petitions resulted in state legislation in 1854 to build a trans-Sierra highway, despite steamship company opposition. Although state courts invalidated this legislation on constitutional grounds—Article VIII required that large expenditures be submitted directly to the voters—Sacramento, Placer, and Yolo counties subscribed $50,000 for an improved Placerville–Lake Tahoe road, to be graded twelve feet wide and cleared of all brush and rocks. It opened in 1858. The discovery of the Comstock silver lode in 1859 made the Placerville road a major freight and stagecoaching highway, supplying a Nevada population of up to 40,000 people. In 1863, 30,000 tons of freight and 56,500 people passed over the road. Traffic was so dense that it was difficult for a wagon to re-enter the traffic stream from a turnout, and delays limited a day's

A huge freight schooner pulled by a six-span team of mules pauses at Webster's Station, in the shadow of Sugar Loaf Mountain on the Placerville Road, about 1865. Built along stretches of the old Johnson's Cutoff, an alternative to the Carson Emigrant Trail, the road opened in 1858, and until the decline of the Comstock Lode in the mid-1860s, it was the great artery of travel over the Sierra Nevada. In addition to the tons of freight that rumbled over the road, thousands of overland travelers passed this way, including Horace Greeley and Mark Twain. *Courtesy Society of California Pioneers.*

progress to eight miles or so. Toll toad companies financed extensive improvements that cost up to $5,000 per mile, and maintenance costs were $2,000 to $3,000 per mile yearly, but freight alone brought in at least $3 million in tolls in 1862.[35]

Then in 1862, the Central Pacific Railroad began construction east from Sacramento, with the goal of laying track along a continuous ridge rising from Auburn to Donner Pass, down the Truckee River canyon, and from there east across Nevada. The Pacific Railroad Acts of 1862 and 1864 authorized loans of federal government bonds to subsidize this construction, but the bonds were slow to arrive and did not remotely cover construction costs. To generate badly needed revenue, the railroad graded the Dutch Flat toll road parallel to the planned rail line, in order to provide a connection to the Comstock from the end of the advancing track. Completed in 1864, it cost the chronically cash-poor railroad $350,000, but teamsters soon preferred it to the Placerville road, and it yielded a million dollars in revenue yearly. The road proved to be the most important trans-Sierra highway until the railroad was completed to Nevada in 1868.[36]

THE EXPRESSES

For lack of resources, there was no government mail service to California's mining camps at first, and the wait at the San Francisco post office could be hours long. By late 1849, enterprising private-sector expressmen filled the gap, charging miners in the mountains a dollar for asking after their mail, and an ounce of gold for each letter that they brought back from San Francisco. Expressmen soon added other services, such as carrying gold dust to San Francisco and bringing back newspapers. Express was packed on mules or, in winter, by the expressmen themselves, using snowshoes or skis; the latter were introduced into California by Norwegian-born expressman John Thompson.[37]

By the 1850s, over sixty express companies served the mining camps. Most of these companies were one-man operations, with a service area defined by steep ravines and ridges. Consolidation began in 1849, when Adams & Company, which had been in the express business in the east since 1840, opened a California branch and contracted with small California express companies to carry parcels east by ship. By 1853, Adams was an important California business house, though one with a reputation for sharp and shady dealing.

Wells Fargo, organized in 1851 by some of the founders of American Express to do business in California, purchased smaller expresses and quickly developed a statewide network of branch offices, operating 56 of them by October 1856, and 147 by 1860. These branch offices accepted banking deposits, bought gold dust, provided secure, fireproof storage, and accepted and distributed express. Wells Fargo carried first-class mail until 1895 federal legislation prohibited it; patrons willingly paid express charges on top of U.S. postage. The business panic of 1855, which ruined Adams & Company in California, distracted Wells Fargo only briefly, a reflection of the firm's sound management and reputation for business integrity.[38]

STAGECOACHING

Stagecoach routes soon radiated from the river ports to the foothill mining towns. Other routes crossed the valley floor to link Stockton, Sacramento, and Marysville,

Marysville with Colusa, and Stockton with Oakland via Livermore Pass. Stages covered the 188-mile route from Sacramento to Shasta in about thirty hours, and competed successfully with upriver steamboats. Visalia, about 150 miles south of Mariposa, became a staging center for the Kern River mines in 1862; these mines could also be reached by stage from Los Angeles over Tejon Pass by 1865. By 1853 a dozen different stagecoaching companies operated from Sacramento—the busiest staging center—employing three to twelve coaches and from 35 to 150 horses. Large-scale operation offered the advantages of lower costs, convenient connections for longer journeys, and better equipment. In 1854, as happened with river steamers, about five-sixths of California staging was consolidated into the California Stage Company, capitalized at a million dollars. Despite consolidation, competition remained vigorous. Some Stockton lines and all the southern California lines remained independent, some lines were later returned to their original owners, and independent operators continually added new routes.[39]

Stagecoaching across the Sierra over the Placerville–Lake Tahoe road began in 1857, and by 1864 Louis McLane's Pioneer Line was running four coaches each way daily. After the completion of the Sacramento Valley Railroad from Sacramento to Folsom in 1856, coordinated steamboat, rail, and stage schedules reduced the San Francisco–Virginia City trip to twenty-four hours. Wells Fargo acquired the Pioneer Line in 1864 and the California Stage Company's Dutch Flat route the next year, though this was not generally known until their grand consolidation of most staging operations west of the Missouri River in 1866.[40]

Continuing complaints of dilatory steamship mail service led Californians to agitate for overland mail delivery. The first such service was the heavily subsidized but underutilized San Diego–San Antonio mail of 1857; the next year, John Butterfield's Overland Mail began running on a twice-weekly, twenty-five-day schedule between San Francisco and the railheads for Memphis and St. Louis. The roundabout route by way of Yuma allowed year-round operation but probably also reflected the postmaster-general's southern sectional orientation. The well-managed line operated regularly, often ahead of schedule, and by 1860 the stages were carrying more mail than the steamers did. Stages ran day and night, and passengers slept on board despite the rough ride. The coaches required eighty hours to cover the route between San Francisco and Los Angeles, via Pacheco Pass, Visalia, and San Fernando Pass, so the average speed was only about five miles an hour.[41]

In 1861 the Overland Mail was briefly rerouted along the coast via Santa Susana Pass, Santa Barbara, Gaviota Pass, and San Luis Obispo. This route later passed through a series of owners who offered indifferent service until a competent superintendent took charge in 1868, a year in which the coast line began providing daily departures using 272 horses and 23 stages. San Diego stagecoaches made connections with the overland and coast lines at Los Angeles, and also offered direct service to San Bernardino via Temecula and, in 1868, to Yuma.[42]

A federally subsidized monthly mail had used the Placerville–Salt Lake route since 1851; in 1861, the Overland Mail was shifted to this route, receiving a million-dollar subsidy to operate a daily mail and a semi-weekly pony express that moved the mail faster, but for very high charges. The Pony Express, begun by the Central Overland and California Pike's Peak Express the previous year without a subsidy, ran only until the completion of the overland telegraph in October 1861, unable, as they then said, to compete with lightning.[43]

STAGECOACH TRAVEL AND TECHNOLOGY

At first, staging was by spring wagons drawn by mustangs or mules, but soon experienced stage operators imported better livestock and Concord coaches. The Concord's curved ash body rested on long leather thoroughbraces that divided the 2,500-pound weight of the coach into two parts, reducing the shock of a rough road and making it easier for the team to start the coach. Nine to twelve passengers rode inside, and up to a dozen more on the flat roof. On difficult roads, stage operators substituted thoroughbraced "mud wagons" that were canvas-roofed, lighter, and lower-slung than the Concords.[44]

Because they served passengers, stagecoach drivers (or reinsmen) generally had more social graces than wagon freighters, had much higher social status, and were usually better educated. Reinsmen were popularly called "jehus," after the furious charioteer of 2 Kings 9: 20. The subtle hand movements by which they tightened or slipped the reins to control each pair of animals separately were scarcely noticeable even to passengers sitting beside them, who sometimes mistakenly attributed the driver's skill to the native intelligence of the team. The horses were hitched loosely, so that jolts to the wheels that jerked the wagon tongue were not transmitted to the animals. Drivers usually made no effort to avoid potholes or rocks, allowing the horses to find their own way so that they would be reliable in darkness or bad weather. Although there was some racing between rival stage lines, the horses were usually driven only at the walk or trot.[45]

Passengers had mixed opinions about stage travel. Journalists sometimes wrote derisive verse about their discomforts and inconveniences, but passengers who found the jarring, shaking ride excruciating nevertheless enjoyed the scenery, found the rapid pace exhilarating, and admired the drivers' skill. Some passengers objected to their fellow passengers' constant spitting and foul language, and complained of clouds of choking dust. To make uphill grades easier on the animals, passengers were expected to get out and walk, and the men were expected to push. Accidents

A Concord coach prepares to get under way from a stop at the Oso House in a photograph taken in 1859 by Carleton Watkins. Despite the graceful lines of the celebrated
coach, staging was invariably an ordeal of rough roads, bad company, long days, and clouds
of dust. *California Historical Society, FN-24569.*

were accepted as unavoidable hazards of travel. Top-heavy coaches overturned and
tumbled down ravines, and rough roads sometimes threw drivers from their boxes,
but despite broken bones, they were often able to regain control of their teams. Passengers were advised to stay aboard a runaway coach; when coaches overturned, injuries were often limited to bruises and scratches. In wet weather, deeply rutted,
muddy roads, washouts, and rain-swollen fords slowed travel or stopped it altogether. When high water swept coaches downstream, passengers had to swim or
drown.[46]

SOUTHERN CALIFORNIA GOLD-RUSH TRANSPORTATION

Isolated from the mining regions by the steep and rugged Transverse Ranges, southern California developed as a freighting and stagecoaching center for Arizona and
Utah.[47] Commercial freighting between Los Angeles and the rude harbor at San Pe-

dro began before the Gold Rush, and by 1853 rival stagecoach operators were racing each other over the rough twenty-mile road. A year later, the transportation partnership of Phineas Banning, an energetic freighter and stage driver, and David Alexander used five hundred mules, thirty or forty horses, forty wagons, and fifteen stages.

In 1857, Banning began dredging the marshy back bay behind Rattlesnake (now Terminal) Island to create a channel six to ten feet deep leading to a protected wharf for shallow-draft coastal vessels and for lighters—barges that Banning used to unload cargo from larger ships that had to anchor in deeper water. In 1858 and 1859, Banning's wharf—he named the place Wilmington, after his Delaware hometown—imported 7,000 tons of merchandise and more than 1.5 million board feet of lumber. Exports were agricultural products, especially grapes and, after the Owens Valley mines began production, silver bullion. In 1869, southern California's first railroad connected Los Angeles with Wilmington.[48]

Beginning in 1847, Mormons had pioneered a freighting corridor from Salt Lake City south and west through Provo, Cedar City, Las Vegas, and Cajon Pass to their satellite settlement at San Bernardino. In 1855, Banning and Alexander and others began hauling freight to Salt Lake City over the all-year road. When winter closed the Sierra passes, freight from northern California was shipped to Los Angeles to be forwarded over the corridor to Utah; some freight was shipped as far as Idaho and Montana. Sometimes a hundred tons of freight were warehoused in Los Angeles awaiting shipment. The road was challenging: Cajon Pass had grades as steep as 30 percent until 1861, and one stretch of fifty-five miles had no source of water; the federal government allocated an inadequate $25,000 for improvements in 1854.[49]

Although the Mormon colony left in 1858, San Bernardino developed as a lumbering and agricultural center and generated freight in its own right. During the Civil War, Los Angeles-based freighters supplied military posts at Yuma and Tucson in Arizona from the quartermaster depot at Wilmington. Gold discoveries on the Arizona bank of the Colorado River in 1862 generated traffic over the Bradshaw road east from San Gorgonio Pass to Ehrenberg and La Paz. Finally, freight traffic to and from the Owens Valley mines grew from the mid-1860s.[50]

From 1857 to 1861, twenty-eight of the Army's camels were based at Fort Tejon, in the Transverse Ranges north of Los Angeles. The camels had been imported in response to dramatic increases in military transportation costs after victory in the Mexican-American War led the United States to annex large tracts of desert. Camels could pack seven hundred pounds easily, though their swaying gait required special packing techniques. The Civil War ended the experiment, however, and the unloved animals were sold. Civilian freighters used camels across the Sierra and in Nevada, but the beasts so frightened horses that public opinion restricted their use. Most were eventually turned loose to fend for themselves.[51]

THE BEGINNINGS OF EAST BAY COMMUTING

Since 1851, a ferry had run from San Francisco across the bay to the foot of Broadway, on the estuary separating Oakland from Alameda, but the shallow sand bar at the estuary mouth limited the size of the boats and made navigation slow and tricky. A shorter, more direct route from San Francisco to Oakland Point opened in 1862, connecting with a commuter train that steamed along Seventh Street to downtown Oakland. Demand soon justified six round trips daily. A similar rail and ferry system was introduced across the estuary at Alameda, and in 1866 this line introduced the double-ended, beam-engined, side-wheel ferryboat that soon came to typify San Francisco commuting. This technology functioned alongside much newer types of propulsion until well into the twentieth century, when automobiles and bridges made the ferry system redundant.[52]

At the beginning of the Gold Rush, the eastern shore of San Francisco Bay had been important only as a route to the mines, but by the early 1860s, helped by a sunnier climate than San Francisco's, Oakland and Alameda were growing as commuter suburbs. These communities attracted people who wanted churches, schools, and shaded, spacious neighborhoods, and who thought that San Francisco catered to vice and corruption. By the end of the decade, a settled metropolitan area was emerging around San Francisco Bay from the confusion of the Gold Rush.

CONCLUSION

During the Gold Rush, Californians extemporized a modern, statewide transportation network of ocean and river navigation, wagon roads, telegraph lines, and the beginnings of a railroad network. The railroads would soon transform California yet again, making shipping and traveling faster, cheaper, and easier, making the trans-Sierra roads irrelevant, and with the development of agriculture and the decline of mining, reorienting the axis of travel away from the foothills to the length of the Central Valley. Some stagecoaching and wagon freighting would continue into the early twentieth century, but only as feeders to the railroads. Then motor vehicles running on a new system of hard-surfaced roads would make them redundant, along with much of the state's railroad mileage. River traffic would continue well into the first half of the twentieth century, sometimes prospering. So would coastal steamers, though the convex contour of California's coastline lengthened their routes compared to the more direct rail lines. The Panama route would not be important again until the opening of the canal in 1914. Thus it is tempting to look at gold-rush transportation as a twenty-year preliminary to the very different transportation pattern that evolved later. In any case, it was a marvel of improvisation and ingenuity.

NOTES

1. The only general history of California transportation is Rockwell Dennis Hunt and William Sheffield Ament, *Oxcart to Airplane* (Los Angeles: Powell, 1929); it is engagingly written but thinly documented. H. Wilbur Hoffman, *Sagas of Old Western Travel and Transport* (San Diego: Howell-North, 1980), is well illustrated, readable, accurate, and enlivened with invented conversations; its scope is broader in time and space than this essay, but gold-rush California is included. Hubert Howe Bancroft, *History of California*, 7 vols. (1886–1890; reprint, Santa Barbara: Wallace Hebberd, 1970), weaves gold-rush transportation through other material in vols. 6 and 7; the only good index is Everett Gordon Hager and Anna Marie Hager, *The Zamorano Index to "History of California" by Hubert Howe Bancroft*, 2 vols. (Los Angeles: University of Southern California, 1985). James D. Hart, *Companion to California*, rev. ed. (Berkeley: University of California Press, 1987), is encyclopedic. Topical maps accompanied by well-researched text are in Warren A. Beck and Inez D. Haase, *Historical Atlas of California* (Norman: University of Oklahoma Press, 1974). R. N. Preston, *Early California Atlas Northern Edition* and *Early California Atlas Southern Edition* (Portland: Binford and Mort, 1974) enable the reader to trace wagon roads and stagecoach routes with a magnifying glass, eyestrain, and some imagination.

2. T. H. Watkins, "The Revoloidal Spindle and the Wondrous Avitor," *American West* 4 (February 1967), and Kenneth Johnson, *Aerial California* (Los Angeles: Dawson's Book Shop, 1961).

3. Jessie Davies Francis, *An Economic and Social History of Mexican California, 1822–1846*, vol. 1: *Chiefly Economic* (New York: Arno Press, 1976), 509–77, 713–41; Alfred Robinson, *Life in California* (1846; reprint, Santa Barbara: Peregrine Smith, 1970), 55–60; John Bidwell, "Life in California before the Gold Discovery," *Century* 61 (December 1890): 171.

4. John Haskell Kemble, *The Panama Route* (Berkeley: University of California Press, 1943; reprint, Columbia: University of South Carolina Press, 1990), chap. 7; James P. Delgado, *To California by Sea: A Maritime History of the Gold Rush* (Columbia: University of South Carolina Press, 1990), chap. 2.

5. Ibid., 166–78.

6. John Haskell Kemble, "A Hundred Years of Pacific Mail," *American Neptune* 10 (April 1950): 130. For a biography of Pacific Mail founder William Aspinwall, see Col. Duncan S. Somerville, *The Aspinwall Empire* (Mystic, Conn.: Mystic Seaport Museum, 1983).

7. Kemble, *Panama Route*, 53–54, 116–21, app. 1.

8. Ibid., 121–24, 156–63.

9. Ibid., 147–53.

10. Ibid., 134–39.

11. Kemble, "A Hundred Years," 126–29; Kemble, *Panama Route*, 86–87, chap. 3; David I. Folkman, Jr., *The Nicaragua Route* (Salt Lake City: University of Utah Press, 1972).

12. Lack of charts increased the hazards of navigation. Spanish coastal charts were unavailable to Americans; U.S. Coast Survey charts began appearing in 1855, and the first edition of the *Coast Pilot* was published in 1858, but the federal government was unwilling to chart foreign coasts on the Panama route. Oscar Lewis, *George Davidson: Pioneer West Coast Scientist* (Berkeley: University of California Press, 1954), 48–51; Kemble, "A Hundred Years," 127, 133–34, 143–44.

13. Kemble, *Panama Route,* 148, 174–75, 197, apps. 2, 3; Kemble, "A Hundred Years," 131 ff.; Folkman, *Nicaragua Route,* app. B; Oscar Osburn Winther, *Express and Stagecoach Days in California* (Stanford: Stanford University Press, 1936), 69–70.

14. In a sense, gold-rush demand returned California to a hunter-gatherer food economy, but on an international scale. Lary M. Dilsaver, "Food Supply for the California Gold Rush," *California Geographer* 23 (1983).

15. Delgado, *To California by Sea,* 43–44; Roger W. Lotchin, *San Francisco, 1846–1856: From Hamlet to City* (New York: Oxford University Press, 1974), 10–11, 49, 57, 73–74, 166–69, 172–73, 178, 181; Harold Kirker, *California's Architectural Frontier* (Santa Barbara: Peregrine Smith, 1973), 38–39, 79.

16. Sherwood D. Burgess, "The Forgotten Redwoods of the East Bay," *California Historical Society Quarterly* 30 (March 1951), and Frank M. Stanger, *Sawmills in the Redwoods: Logging on the San Francisco Peninsula, 1849–1967* (San Mateo, Calif.: San Mateo County Historical Association, 1967). For North Coast lumbering, see Lynwood Carranco, *Redwood Lumber Industry* (San Marino, Calif.: Golden West, 1982); the gold-rush period is covered in chaps. 9, 11. Lynwood Carranco and John T. Labbe, *Logging the Redwoods* (Caldwell, Idaho: Caxton, 1979), covers the same material but in less detail and without documentation. The Pacific Northwest furnished about 60 percent of San Francisco's lumber by 1860; two regional histories of lumbering are Thomas R. Cox, *Mills and Markets: A History of the Pacific Coast Lumber Business to 1900* (Seattle: University of Washington Press, 1974), and Edwin T. Coman, Jr., and Helen M. Gibbs, *Tide, Time and Timber: A Century of Pope and Talbot* (Stanford: Stanford University Press, 1949).

17. The dangers of the Humboldt Bar and historic efforts to tame it are described in Susan Pritchard O'Hara and Gregory Graves, *Saving California's Coast* (Spokane: Arthur H. Clark, 1991). For the hazards of navigating the Mendocino coast, see Karl Kortum and Roger Olmsted, "'... it is a dangerous looking place': Sailing Days on the Redwood Coast," *California Historical Quarterly* 50 (March 1971).

18. Thomas R. Cox, "Single Decks and Flat Bottoms: Building the West Coast's Lumber Fleet, 1850–1929," *Journal of the West* 20 (July 1981): 66–69; Coman and Gibbs, *Time, Tide and Timber,* 179–80; Carranco, *Redwood Lumber Industry,* 105; Kortum and Olmsted, "'... it is a dangerous looking place,'" 43–45; Cox, *Mills and Markets,* 150–55.

19. Carl Cutler, *Greyhounds of the Sea* (Annapolis: U.S. Naval Institute, 1930); app. 7 shows hull lines and sail plans. K. Jack Bauer, *A Maritime History of the United States* (Columbia: University of South Carolina Press, 1988), 89–92; Raymond A. Rydell, *Cape Horn to the Pacific* (Berkeley: University of California Press, 1952), 134–40, chaps. 7, 8. For crews, see Delgado, *To California by Sea,* 97–99; Cutler, *Greyhounds of the Sea,* 186, 222–23; Bauer, *A Maritime History,* 91; Rydell, *Cape Horn,* 148.

20. Frances Leigh Williams, *Matthew Fontaine Maury: Scientist of the Sea* (New Brunswick, N.J.: Rutgers University Press, 1963), chap. 10; Cutler, *Greyhounds of the Sea,* 108, 217–19, 243–44, 259–61.

21. The last clipper was built in 1857, and few survived more than ten years of hard sailing because the leverage of wind against masts and braces damaged their hulls; Rydell, *Cape Horn,* 141, n. 26. The California grain trade began in the 1860s but reached its peak in the 1880s, well after the Gold Rush; Rodman W. Paul, "The Wheat Trade between California and the United Kingdom," *Mississippi Valley Historical Review* 45 (December 1958). Iron

hulls were lighter, roomier, drier, and cheaper to insure, but America built few of them; Bauer, *A Maritime History*, 241–42, 256–58.

22. Early rivals for San Francisco's trade included Benicia and Vallejo; Lotchin, *San Francisco, 1846–1856*, 31–39; for the growth of San Francisco's infrastructure see ibid., 41–44, 76, 236, and Delgado, *To California by Sea*, chap. 3. For patterns of bay and river transportation development, see Mel Scott, *The San Francisco Bay Area: A Metropolis in Perspective*, 2nd ed. (Berkeley: University of California Press, 1985), and Joseph A. McGowan, *History of the Sacramento Valley*, 3 vols. (New York: Lewis, 1961). Also see Thor Severson, *Sacramento, 1839 to 1874: An Illustrated History from Sutter's Fort to Capital City* (n.p.: California Historical Society, 1973). For tonnages, McGowan, *History of the Sacramento Valley*, vol. 1, 63–67, 74, 79–82; Severson, *Sacramento, 1839 to 1874*, 169; Bancroft, *History of California*, vol. 7, 466.

23. Firsthand accounts of early trips upriver are in Elisha Oscar Crosby, *Memoirs: Reminiscences of California and Guatemala, 1849–1864*, ed. Charles Albro Barker (San Marino, Calif.: Huntington Library, 1945), 19–20; Adolphus Windeler, *California Gold Rush Diary of a German Sailor*, ed. W. Turrentine Jackson (Berkeley: Howell-North, 1969), 14, 28–31; Bayard Taylor, *El Dorado, or Adventures in the Path of Empire* (1850; reprint, New York: Knopf, 1949), 163. Before mining debris shoaled the rivers, ships drawing as much as ten feet could sail directly to Sacramento and Stockton, where many were recycled as improvised wharves and buildings; Severson, *Sacramento, 1839 to 1874*, 50–55, 66, 75, 77, 84–87, 90–91; George P. Hammond, *The Weber Era in Stockton History* (Berkeley: Friends of the Bancroft Library, 1982), 94–95, 108.

24. A well-researched photographic essay with a strong text is Roger R. Olmsted, *Square-Toed Packets: Scow Schooners of San Francisco Bay* (Cupertino: California History Center, 1988); an introductory chapter describes the beginnings of navigation on the Sacramento River.

25. Jerry MacMullen, *Paddlewheel Days in California* (Stanford: Stanford University Press, 1944); 19–21, 24–32, 68–71; detailed appendices list boats, river ports, and distances. See also Bancroft, *History of California*, vol. 7, 466.

26. MacMullen, *Paddlewheel Days*, 19–23; McGowan, *History of the Sacramento Valley*, vol. 1, 303.

27. John Haskell Kemble, "The *Senator*," *California Historical Quarterly* 16 (Part 1, 1932), and also his "*Chrysopolis*: The Queen of the Golden River," *American Neptune* 2 (October 1942); MacMullen, *Paddlewheel Days*, 35, 51–52. For a firsthand account of a trip to Stockton, see "The Great Yo-Semite Valley," *Hutchings' California Magazine* 4 (October 1859), reprinted in Roger Olmsted, ed., *Scenes of Wonder and Curiosity* (Berkeley: Howell-North, 1962). A well-researched photographic essay of the upriver boats, including construction details, is Edward Galland Zelinsky and Nancy Leigh Olmsted, "Upriver Boats—When Red Bluff Was the Head of Navigation," *California History* 64 (Spring 1985): 86–117.

28. Zelinsky and Olmsted, "Upriver Boats," 106–8. An evocative, firsthand account of the river landings is in Captain John Leale, *Recollections of a Tule Sailor* (San Francisco: George Fields, 1939), 46–51. Navigation on the upper Sacramento, McGowan, *History of the Sacramento Valley*, vol. 1, 78–81. For navigation on the San Joaquin and the lower Mokelumne, see MacMullen, *Paddlewheel Days*, chap. 11; app., 144–45. The silting problem was attributed to hydraulic mining; Robert Kelley, *Gold vs. Grain: The Hydraulic Mining Controversy in California's Sacramento Valley* (Glendale, Calif.: Arthur H. Clark, 1959) is an exhaustive political

analysis; his *Battling the Inland Sea: American Political Culture, Public Policy, and the Sacramento Valley, 1850–1986* (Berkeley: University of California Press, 1989) places the silting controversy in the broader context of ongoing attempts to control flooding.

29. A firsthand account is "Packing in the Mountains of California," *Hutchings' California Magazine* 1 (December 1856), reprinted in Olmsted, *Scenes of Wonder.* Details of the Army's adaptation of the *aparejo* are thoroughly illustrated in H. W. Daly, *Manual of Pack Transportation* (1916; reprint, Santa Monica, Calif.: Quail Ranch, 1981), chap. 7. See also McGowan, *History of the Sacramento Valley*, vol. 1, 88–89, 99.

30. "Packing in the Mountains," 117.

31. A scholarly but readable work that includes regional history, road, bridge, and ferry development south from Stockton is Irene Paden and Margaret Schlichtman, *The Big Oak Flat Road to Yosemite* (Oakland: Holmes Book Co., 1959). An article focused on the alignments of roads radiating from Stockton and the development of ferry crossings is Thor Breton, "The Old Mariposa Road," *The Far Westerner* 11 (April 1966); the journal is the publication of the Stockton Corral of Westerners. The road network centered on Shasta City is in part 3 of W. H. Colby, *A Century of Transportation in Shasta County, 1821–1920* (n.p.: Association for Northern California Records and Research, 1982). For Marysville and northern Sierra roads, see Ernest Wiltsee, *The Pioneer Miner and the Pack Mule Express* (San Francisco: California Historical Society, 1931). For evolution of roads, McGowan, *History of the Sacramento Valley*, vol. 1, 18, 49, 79, 101, 112. County road appropriations were sometimes minimal (Colby, *Shasta County*, 28–29), but Sonoma, Napa, and Alameda counties levied taxes for road construction and created a network of roads around San Francisco Bay (Scott, *Bay Area*, 40–41). A cut through solid rock at San Fernando Pass in Los Angeles County was financed with a mixture of public and private funds; Vernette Snyder Ripley, "San Fernando Pass and the Traffic that Went over It, Part 2," *The Quarterly of the Historical Society of Southern California* 29 (September–December 1947), and "Part 3," 30 (March 1948). Also see John W. Robinson, "The Taming of San Fernando Pass," *The Branding Iron* 208 (Summer 1997); the journal is published by the Los Angeles Corral of Westerners. The gold-rush wagon road network is charted in Beck and Haase, *Historical Atlas of California*, map 51. Contemporary photographs showing cuts, fills, and hairpin turns are in Irving Wills, "The Jerk Line Team," *The Westerners Brand Book Nine* (n.p.: Los Angeles Corral of Westerners, 1961). For snowplowing, see Lyndall Baker Landauer, *The Mountain Sea* (Honolulu: Flying Cloud, 1996), 70, and Colby, *Shasta County*, 37. For number of bridges, see Bancroft, *History of California*, vol. 7, 143n. For width of roads, see McGowan, *History of the Sacramento Valley*, vol. 1, 48; rules of the road, 48. For tuned bells, see Wills, "Jerk Line Team," 51–52.

32. For a firsthand description of ferry construction and operation, see Samuel Ward, *Sam Ward in the Gold Rush*, ed. Carvel Collins (Stanford: Stanford University Press, 1949), 121–29. Kramer Adams, *Covered Bridges of the West* (Berkeley: Howell-North, 1963), 13–20, and Colby, *Shasta County*, 21–24, 61–62.

33. McGowan, *History of the Sacramento Valley*, vol. 1, 89; Hoffman, *Sagas*, 46–47, 61, and Wills, "Jerk Line Team," 33, 38–46, 55. Wagon running gear is depicted with wonderful clarity in Nick Eggenhofer, *Wagons, Mules and Men: How the Frontier Moved* (New York: Hastings, 1961), 38–42; California freight wagons were not the Conestogas that Eggenhofer illustrates and discusses, but the wheels and running gear were constructed on the same principles.

34. For trans-Sierra emigrant roads, see George R. Stewart, *California Trail: An Epic*

with Many Heroes (New York: McGraw-Hill, 1962); 206–7, 304–6, and map, 300; and Stewart Mitchell, "Crossing the Sierra," *California Highways and Public Works* 29, nos. 9–10 (1949). For a trans-Sierra road that became important in Chico's development see Anita L. Chang, *The Historical Geography of the Humboldt Wagon Road* (Chico: Association for Northern California Records and Research, 1992). An excellent geographical study of trans-Sierra roads is Thomas Frederick Howard, *Sierra Crossing* (Berkeley: University of California Press, 1998).

35. For a thorough account of trans-Sierra road surveys, see Chester Lee White, "Surmounting the Sierra," *Quarterly of the California Historical Society* 7 (March 1928); Mitchell, "Crossing the Sierra," 61, has a detailed and annotated but difficult map showing how the Placerville–Lake Tahoe road evolved. In 1857, federal legislation appropriated money for three wagon roads to the California boundary: one to Honey Lake, another along the 35th parallel to the Mojave River, and a third to Yuma. For Pacific wagon road legislation, see W. Turrentine Jackson, *Wagon Roads West* (New Haven: Yale University Press, 1964; reprint, Lincoln: University of Nebraska Press, 1979), 161–74. Tolls and freight charges, Bancroft, *History of California*, vol. 7, 541. Road construction is treated briefly in Francis P. Farquhar, *History of the Sierra Nevada* (Berkeley: University of California Press, 1965), chap. 11. Farquhar's book is a good regional history; so is Landauer, *Mountain Sea*. See also Edward B. Scott, *The Saga of Lake Tahoe* (Crystal Bay: Sierra Tahoe, 1956), 364–72. The Placerville, Humboldt, and Salt Lake Telegraph Company strung its wires along the Placerville Road to reach Carson City in 1858 and Salt Lake City in 1861; for an overview of northern California telegraph construction, see McGowan, *History of the Sacramento Valley*, vol. 1, 167–70.

36. Mercantilist urban rivalries stimulated road building but hindered railroad construction; see Ward McAfee, *California's Railroad Era, 1850–1911* (San Marino, Calif.: Golden West, 1973), chaps. 3, 4, 5. For the Dutch Flat wagon road, see McAfee, *California's Railroad Era*, 61, and John Hoyt Williams, *A Great and Shining Road* (New York: Times Books, 1988), 59–60, 91, 135.

37. Winther, *Express and Stagecoach Days* is well documented and readable. His *Via Western Express and Stagecoach* (Stanford: Stanford University Press, 1945) is a more popular treatment, without scholarly apparatus. A handsomely illustrated philatelic treatment of the gold-rush expresses is L. Coburn, *Leaves of Gold* (Canton: U.S. Philatelic Classics Society, 1984); Wiltsee, *Pioneer Miner*, has a similar focus. There is a good discussion of the one-man express companies in Winther, *Express and Stagecoach Days*, chap. 1. On snowshoes, see Landauer, *Mountain Sea*, 66–67.

38. Robert J. Chandler, "Integrity Amid Tumult: Wells, Fargo & Co.'s Gold Rush Banking," *California History* 70 (Fall 1991); Winther, *Express and Stagecoach Days*, 42–48, 51–75; for the causes and course of the panic of 1855, chap. 4. See also Edward Hungerford, *Wells Fargo: Advancing the American Frontier* (New York: Random House, 1949) and Noel D. Loomis, *Wells Fargo: An Illustrated History* (New York: Bramhall House, 1968), which is mostly text, despite the title, and well documented. For Wells Fargo first-class mail service, see Wiltsee, *Pioneer Miner*, chap. 9.

39. Winther, *Express and Stagecoach Days*, 91–96, 158–60. Captain William Banning and George Hugh Banning, *Six Horses* (New York: Century, 1930), 47; Harlan Boyd, *Stagecoach Heyday in the San Joaquin Valley* (Bakersfield: Kern County Historical Society, 1983), 16–18, 35–36, 44–46, 48; maps, xii, 17. See also McGowan, *History of the Sacramento Valley*, vol. 1, 87–89, 93, and Bancroft, *History of California*, vol. 7, 151, and n. 46.

40. W. Turrentine Jackson, "A New Look at Wells Fargo, Stagecoaches, and the Pony Ex-

press," *California Historical Society Quarterly* 45 (December 1966), and also his "Wells Fargo Staging over the Sierra," *California Historical Society Quarterly* 49 (June 1970). These articles are in part refutations of Waddell Smith, "Stage Lines and Express Companies in California," *The Far Westerner* 6 (January 1965). Smith argues that Wells Fargo never operated its own stagecoaches in California and did not operate the Pony Express; Jackson is convincing.

41. LeRoy R. Hafen, *The Overland Mail, 1849–1869* (Cleveland: Arthur H. Clark, 1926; reprint, New York: AMS Press, 1969) is a classic account that includes the ocean mail, the Butterfield Overland Mail, the Pony Express, and the complex history of the central route. Ralph Moody, *Stagecoach West* (n.p.: Promontory Press, 1967) is engagingly written and quotes primary sources, but needs to be read with some caution for accuracy. Another classic work is Roscoe P. Conkling and Margaret B. Conkling, *The Butterfield Overland Mail, 1857–1869,* 3 vols. (Glendale, Calif.: Arthur H. Clark, 1947); vol. 3 is the atlas. The Overland's reliability reflects its interlocking directorate with Wells Fargo, which underwrote the initial cost; Jackson, "A New Look at Wells Fargo," 295–303. Omitting the dogleg to Los Angeles would have been shorter and easier, but Angelenos anxious for better service underwrote the extra expense; Ripley, "San Fernando Pass, Part 3," 43–45. A journalist's firsthand account of the first trip west on the Overland Mail is Waterman L. Ormsby, *The Butterfield Overland Mail,* ed. Lyle H. Wright and Josephine Bynum (San Marino, Calif.: Huntington Library, 1942).

42. Charles Outland, *Stagecoaching on El Camino Real: Los Angeles to San Francisco, 1861–1901* (Glendale, Calif.: Arthur H. Clark, 1973) is opinionated, exhaustive, and carefully documented. Outland argues persuasively, against other sources, that there was no staging over the coast route prior to 1861, chap. 1; for development of the route, chaps. 3, 4, 5. See also Walker Tompkins, *Stagecoach Days in Santa Barbara County* (Santa Barbara: McNally & Loftin, West, 1982). For an account of the dangers of contemporary travel along the central coast, see J. Ross Browne, *A Dangerous Journey* (1862; Palo Alto: Arthur Lites, 1950). For San Diego staging see Richard F. Pourade, *The Silver Dons* (San Diego: Union-Tribune, 1963), 172, and also his *The Glory Years* (San Diego: Union Tribune, 1964), 46–49.

43. Hafen, *Overland Mail,* 110–13, 169–87. The Central Overland and California Pike's Peak was overextended even before it undertook the expense of the Pony Express, and was soon auctioned to stagecoaching magnate Ben Holladay (pp. 227–28). Holladay in turn sold all of his stagecoaching operations to Wells Fargo in 1866 (p. 319). For other pony expresses within California, see Jackson, "A New Look at Wells Fargo," 317.

44. Winther, *Express and Stagecoach Days,* 81–86. For Concord coach and mud wagon anatomy, see Eggenhofer, *Wagons, Mules and Men,* 145–76.

45. Banning and Banning, *Six Horses,* 361–73.

46. Firsthand accounts of stage travel are in "A Stage Incident," *Hutchings' California Magazine* 3 (July 1958), reprinted in Olmsted, *Scenes of Wonder,* 236; McGowan, *History of the Sacramento Valley,* vol. 1, 93; Winther, *Express and Stagecoach Days,* 83, 102–5; Banning and Banning, *Six Horses,* 29–30, 31–32 and n.2; and Boyd, *Stagecoach Heyday,* 22, 40.

47. Three good southern California regional histories that discuss transportation are Joseph S. O'Flaherty, *An End and a Beginning: The South Coast and Los Angeles, 1850–1887* (Jericho: Exposition-Lochinvar, 1972), Henry P. Silka, *San Pedro: A Pictorial History* (n.p.: San Pedro Bay Historical Society, 1984), and George William Beattie and Helen Truitt Beattie, *Heritage of the Valley* (Pasadena, Calif.: San Pasqual, 1939). The Beatties' book is a history of the San Bernardino area. For San Diego, see Pourade's *Silver Dons* and *Glory Years.* Harris

Newmark, *Sixty Years in Southern California,* 4th ed. (Los Angeles: Dawson's Book Shop, 1984) is a detailed but not always accurate reminiscence first published in 1916; W. W. Robinson's informed notes are an asset to the fourth edition. Robert Glass Cleland, "Transportation in California before the Railroads, with Especial Reference to Los Angeles," *Annual Publication of the Historical Society of Southern California* 11 (Part 1, 1918); Frank Rolfe, "Early Day Los Angeles: A Great Wagon Train Center," *Historical Society of Southern California Quarterly* 35 (December 1953); and W. Turrentine Jackson, "Stages, Mails and Express in Southern California: The Role of Wells, Fargo & Co. in the Pre-Railroad Period," *Historical Society of Southern California Quarterly* 56 (Fall 1974). Ripley, "San Fernando Pass," and Robinson, "Taming of San Fernando Pass," are also relevant here. Milton R. Hunter, "Via Mormon Corridor," *Pacific Historical Review* 8 (June 1939) puts the corridor into the larger picture of Mormon history; a firsthand account with a good introductory essay is William B. Rice, "Early Freighting on the Salt Lake-San Bernardino Trail," *Pacific Historical Review* 7 (1937).

48. Silka, *San Pedro,* 22–29, 30–31; Rolfe, "Early Day Los Angeles," 306–7. John W. Robinson, *Southern California's First Railroad* (Los Angeles: Dawson's Book Shop, 1978).

49. Hunter, "Via Mormon Corridor," 184, 188–92, 198–99; Rolfe, "Early Day Los Angeles," 310–13; Jackson, *Wagon Roads West,* 140–41; Beattie and Beattie, *Heritage of the Valley,* 335–37, 400.

50. Military supply routes are in Rolfe, "Early Day Los Angeles," 314–15; for the Bradshaw road, see Beattie and Beattie, *Heritage of the Valley,* 398–400; for more detail, see Francis J. Johnston, *The Bradshaw Trail* (Riverside, Calif.: Riverside Parks Department, 1987). Johnston loves his subject, but his speculations need to be treated with caution.

51. As transportation history, the camels are colorful rather than significant. For the Army's camel experiment, see Harlan D. Fowler, *Camels to California* (Stanford: Stanford University Press, 1950); Fowler's sequel, *Three Caravans to Yuma: The Untold Story of Bactrian Camels in the West* (Glendale, Calif.: Arthur H. Clark, 1980) describes the civilian experiment. See also A. A. Gray, "Camels in California," *Quarterly of the California Historical Society* 9 (December 1930), and Deane Robertson and Peggy Robertson, *Camels in the West* (Sacramento: Arcade House, 1979). For contemporary enthusiasm for camels, see "The Bactrian Camel," *Hutchings' California Magazine* 5 (November 1860), reprinted in Olmsted, *Scenes of Wonder,* 335.

52. Scott, *Bay Area,* 46–47, and Robert A. Ford, *Red Trains in the East Bay* (Glendale, Calif.: Interurbans, 1977), chaps. 1, 2.

13

A Veritable Revolution

The Global Economic Significance of the California Gold Rush

Gerald D. Nash

To many Californians the mention of January 24, 1848, conveys no special meaning, nor is that date widely commemorated in the state. Yet it has a special significance in the history of California, for on that day James Marshall, a moody carpenter from Missouri, discovered the first golden nuggets that resulted in the stampede known as the California Gold Rush. In the remoteness of Sutter's Mill, Marshall could scarcely imagine that his find would set off a succession of events that would have a far-ranging importance for California, the United States, and the world. The timing of the event was crucial also because it happened when the nation was just about to feel the growing impact of the Industrial Revolution—a revolution that in the next half-century would transform the United States from an agrarian society into an industrial giant. Within this broad context the Gold Rush helped to trigger momentous economic changes. In the language of economists, it served as a multiplier—an event that accelerated a chain of interrelated consequences, all of which accelerated economic growth. In both state and nation it spurred the creation of thousands of new businesses, banks, and financial institutions. It stimulated rapid agricultural expansion, quickened the volume of trade and commerce, and created demands for new forms of transportation. Since 1848, the Gold Rush has always had a romantic aura, of course. But it should not be forgotten that it was also a major chapter in California's economic development. As one historian has noted, "The American emphasis on the gold and silver rushes as adventures rather than economic industrialization stood in embarrassing contrast to the more realistic accounts of Mexican, South African, and Australian mining."[1]

The Gold Rush spawned a wide range of entrepreneurial activities and led thousands of individuals in California and elsewhere to embark on new business ventures, in manufacturing as well as in service industries. Food, clothing, hardware, mining

California Argonauts—some dressed in the rough clothing of the mines, others wearing boiled, white shirts and ties—stare confidently at us across a century and a half of time. Aware of the historical moment of the great westward movement, the grand adventure of gathering the golden harvest, the Forty-niners preserved their experiences in countless journals and letters home. Though their sagas of long journeys overland and around the Horn, their tales of hard labor and struggle in the mines, are the stuff of legend, of even greater significance are the economic, cultural, and social consequences of the Gold Rush. *California Historical Society, FN-25814.*

supplies, all kinds of luxuries, and steamboats for river traffic—these were only a few of the items in great demand, and ambitious men and women scurried to provide them. When mining machinery came to be in short supply, newcomers in less than a decade created an iron industry in northern California. There they manufactured stamp mills, steam engines, and nozzles for hydraulic operations. Already by 1861 more than a thousand workers in San Francisco toiled in the manufacture of mining equipment. The city boasted thirteen iron foundries and thirty machine shops. Twenty-three other foundries operated in other parts of the state. Mining also required many auxiliary operations in need of explosives, and as early as 1855 newcomers to California had built two powder works, reducing the need for imports from the East.[2]

Gold mining stimulated other industries as well. It created an enormous demand for lumber, not only for housing, but for mine shafts and tunnels. Within a decade Mendocino and Humboldt counties were producing thirty-five million board-feet annually.[3] California also quickly established itself as one of the most important flour-milling states in the Union. In 1848, California had no commercial flour mills to speak of; but by 1860 two hundred flour mills were operating, supplying not only local demand, but exporting large quantities to the entire Rocky Mountain region, and also to China, Japan, Great Britain, and parts of Europe.[4]

The decade after the Gold Rush was an opportune time for wagon and carriage makers. Among the ablest was a young newcomer from the Middle West who made a name for himself very quickly in Placerville. After making his fortune in pioneer California, John Studebaker eventually returned to Indiana. At the turn of the century he became one of the most important automobile manufacturers in the nation—with capital he had amassed during California's pioneer era.[5]

The state's rapid population increase generated a seemingly unlimited demand for clothing, which local enterprisers quickly filled. Within a decade the Mission Woolen Mills became one of the largest in the West. Levi Strauss, one of the most imaginative clothing manufacturers in San Francisco, had great success when he developed blue jeans, a garment particularly well suited for miners and workmen in the 1850s—and generations of other people in succeeding years. Since there was a large number of cattle in California, development of a leather industry in a very short time was eminently feasible. By 1860 the fabrication of boots, harnesses, saddles, and belts for machines was well established.[6]

Retail trade flourished under the conditions stimulated by the Gold Rush. Creation of instant markets with tens of thousands of eager consumers fostered a wide range of wholesale and retail establishments catering to miners. John Bidwell, Alonzo Delano, and Charles M. Weber were some of the merchants who quickly became highly respected citizens and powerful political leaders in the California of the 1850s. Collis P. Huntington, later a railroad tycoon, laid the basis for his fortune in the wholesale trade in Sacramento. He and his partner, Mark Hopkins, began by building the largest wholesale and retail hardware store there and one of the biggest in the entire West. In later years these men branched out to organize the Central Pacific Railroad, which they justly viewed as a key to further expansion of the economy.[7]

Without a doubt, the Gold Rush was the major stimulant of California agriculture in the 1850s. Certainly farming was hardly less significant than gold mining in laying the foundations of California's new economy. Often, when individuals did not succeed in mining they turned to agriculture. Thousands became small farmers, viticulturists, fruit growers, and dairy farmers. Others became sheep and cattle raisers who found lucrative markets not only in California, but up and down the Pacific Coast. The Gold Rush was not merely a local economic event. California's products found their way to

The Huntington & Hopkins Hardware Store on K Street in Sacramento. It was here on a winter's evening in 1861 that the civil engineer Theodore Judah persuaded four shop-keepers who had made their "piles" retailing goods to miners to invest in his dream of a transcontinental railroad. The building of the Central Pacific created enormous fortunes for the Big Four—as Huntington, Hopkins, Stanford, and Crocker came to be called—and played a powerful role in the course of California history. *Courtesy Mariners' Museum, Newport News, Va.*

the Pacific Rim as well. The Gold Rush coincided with the opening of Japan to trade by Commodore Matthew Perry in 1853, and California benefited more from these contacts than any other American state. Commercial relations with China expanded also as a result of aggressive efforts by San Francisco merchants. They found that California farm products enjoyed considerable success in Asia, as did beef and mutton. By 1860, Henry Miller, a German immigrant, had become the largest rancher in the state, with more than three million head of cattle. And the one million sheep reported in that year outnumbered the state's inhabitants.[8]

In just a few years after the first gold discoveries California became one of the most productive grain producers in the nation. Stimulated by the population surge prompted by the Gold Rush, thousands of newcomers became wheat farmers, especially in the San Joaquin and Sacramento valleys, where the soil was well suited for grain culture. The Gold Rush occurred at a most propitious moment for California wheat culture. The ships that brought the gold seekers to the Pacific Coast often sailed back to Atlantic ports without substantial cargo. With the development of wheat farming, these empty vessels were able to take on bulky grain shipments, giving Californians access to East Coast, British, and continental European markets.[9] Moreover, the Gold Rush had a dynamic impact on the state's agriculture because it coincided with revolutionary technological advances in the 1850s. Cyrus McCormick had just developed his reaper, a machine that greatly reduced the need for hand labor and did much to increase productivity. Since California during the Gold Rush had a chronic labor shortage, such a labor-saving device was particularly important in boosting production. Moreover, the vast open stretches of virgin land in the San Joaquin Valley were extremely well suited to the development of mechanized farming. In some ways, McCormick can be considered as one of the fathers of mechanized agriculture in California during the gold-rush era and even in succeeding years. In 1850, relying on crude, labor-intensive methods, California farmers produced just seventeen thousand bushels of wheat; ten years later their total was sixteen million bushels.[10] Technology and commercial conditions combined to make wheat no less profitable than gold.

The population drawn by the Gold Rush created exciting new markets for California farmers. Climate and soil aided them in quickly developing a wide range of crops. In the 1850s Californians grew apples and oranges, peaches and plums, cherries and figs, among a wide range of new varieties. In only a few years California was well on the way to becoming the fruit basket of the nation. At the same time, new farmers were producing impressive quantities of vegetables, from corn to carrots, squash, and potatoes. Since the growing season was much longer than in the East, the output of California's farmers was prodigious, and very profitable.

Along with fruits and vegetables, some of the new immigrants of the gold-rush generation also laid the foundations for a successful wine industry. Miners may have liked their whiskey, but quite a few also developed a taste for wine. Agoston Haraszthy, an enterprising Hungarian immigrant, quickly grasped the potential opportunities and planted dozens of varieties imported from Europe, as well as new strains. Deservedly, he became known as the father of the California wine industry, since he not only grew a variety of grapes, but built markets both in the state and around the world.[11]

The growth of mining, business, and agriculture stimulated the establishment of banks and financial institutions. Such expansion was slow in the 1850s only because the California Constitution of 1849 prohibited the creation of commercial banks. The prohibition received widespread support because members of the constitutional convention clearly remembered the Panic of 1837, which, rightly or wrongly, they at-

Workers harvest wine grapes at Talcoa Vineyards, Napa County, under the supervision of Professor George Husmann, *far right*. Among the most scholarly viticulturists of his day, Husmann built on the knowledge established by Agoston Haraszthy and others, and in 1888 he published the handbook *Grape Culture and Wine Making in California*, which helped to advance the industry. *California Historical Society, FN-21172*.

tributed to the lax issuance of unbacked paper money by banks. Before 1849 California had had no banks, but the Gold Rush created new needs. Miners required places of safekeeping for their gold, and individuals desired banks to transfer money. Furthermore, the increasing number of business establishments involved in trade and commerce looked for banks to execute their transactions. Initially, eastern banks established branches to provide such services, Wells Fargo among the most prominent. By the late 1850s Californians were also providing capital to develop mining throughout the West, including Oregon, Idaho, Arizona, and Colorado, but most importantly for the rich silver mines on the Comstock Lode in Nevada.[12] Californians organized hundreds of stock companies to finance such ventures. The lure of greater profits led one of the most powerful financiers, Sam Brannan, to lobby the California legislature for the removal of the constitutional prohibitions on commercial banking. Finally, in 1862, the lawmakers authorized the establishment of state-chartered savings banks; two years later they allowed commercial banking. As the Civil War further fueled an economic boom, scores of new bankers appeared. One of the most important was William Ralston, who in 1864 organized the Bank of California. Along with William Sharon, his manager in Nevada, Ralston became

Officers of Wells, Fargo & Co. stand before the firm's first office, at 124 Montgomery Street, San Francisco, which in July 1852 opened its doors for business. Although the pioneer banking house has evolved enormously since it instituted an express line of coaches from San Francisco to Sacramento and Marysville, it clings to the imagery of its early days and maintains its corporate headquarters on virtually the site of this daguerreotype. *Courtesy Wells Fargo Bank.*

the dominant presence on the Comstock Lode. The bank financed not only the major mining ventures there, but provided capital for new railroads, steamship lines, water companies, hotels, and a wide range of service industries, even including cemeteries.[13] Few examples better illustrated the multiplier effect of the Gold Rush than the California banks that spawned a large number of new enterprises that built an intricate economic structure in the state.

In that structure, transportation played a dominant role, and the Gold Rush did much to underscore its importance. No other event so dramatized California's geographical isolation. From the beginning, the Argonauts scrambling to reach the gold fields encountered arduous difficulties. Whether they came by ship around the Horn, or sailed to Central America and then made their way across the disease-ridden Isthmus of Panama, or whether they came by land across the prairies in covered wagons, the journey was an ordeal. Those who survived the trek were especially eager to link California more closely to the rest of the nation, as were business people in the East. In the minds of most Californians, and many Americans, transportation held the key to a blossoming of the state's economy.[14]

Between 1848 and 1862 Californians experimented with various ways to end their isolation. They tried wagon trains over the Sierra and coastal steamers along the Pacific Coast, and petitioned Congress to appropriate moneys for a transcontinental highway from Missouri to the West Coast. Seventy-five thousand people signed this petition, fully one-half of the state's population. Yielding to such pressure, Congress in 1856 appropriated $500,000 for a road to stretch from Missouri to Carson City, Nevada. Work was completed in September 1858 and almost immediately John Butterfield secured a federal contract for carrying the mails. He also promised passengers that he would deliver them to western destinations in twenty-five days or less. But neither the stage line, nor the Pony Express, nor the transcontinental telegraph lessened the desire for a railroad in the minds of most Americans.[15]

Support for the building of a transcontinental railroad gathered additional momentum with the outbreak of the Civil War, which underscored California's isolation. In California the project was most ardently promoted by Theodore Judah, a young engineer who had come from Connecticut in 1854 to work on the Sacramento Valley Railroad. Unable to raise the capital needed for the enterprise in San Francisco, he made the rounds of wealthy individuals in Sacramento. In 1860 he approached Collis P. Huntington and his hardware store partner Mark Hopkins, as well as other successful merchants such as Leland Stanford and Charles Crocker. Each agreed to provide about $20,000 for experimental surveys of routes across the Sierra. In June of 1861 the five men incorporated the Central Pacific Railroad. Such a vast undertaking could not be accomplished solely by private enterprise, however, and a few months later Judah and Huntington journeyed to Washington, D.C., to lobby for federal aid. Within a year, the wartime Congress, in part responding to Ju-

A jubilant crowd hurrahs the passage of the Sacramento Valley Railroad's locomotive in a spirited wood engraving titled "First Railroad Ride in California," which appeared in the *Sacramento Pictorial Union* in 1856. Completed in February of that year, the road ran from Sacramento to Folsom, a grand distance of twenty-two miles, and reduced travel between the great river port and the mines by a full day. The era of railroading had dawned in California. *California Historical Society, FN-10954.*

dah and Huntington's political pressure, enacted the Pacific Railroad Act of 1862, which granted lands and loans to the company and the Union Pacific Railroad so that the work could begin. Although the transcontinental railway was not completed until 1869, after 1862 the end of California's geographical isolation was in sight.[16] The Gold Rush had hastened removal of yet another obstacle to California's dramatic economic growth.

The population surge prompted by the gold discoveries also stimulated the building of a canal across the Isthmus of Panama. Between 1848 and 1869 tens of thousands of people headed for California across that once-remote area. The sudden influx brought new economic opportunities for some of the region's inhabitants. It also fostered a considerable increase in prices for many goods, benefiting some and injuring others. This influx of tourists prompted a group of American investors to build the Panama Railroad across the isthmus. Although it was only 47.5 miles long, the difficult terrain slowed construction, and it was not until 1855 that the line became operational.[17] But the influence of the Gold Rush on transportation development did not end with the Panama Railroad. The project fixed the dream of a trans-isthmian canal firmly in the minds of many Americans of that generation. The dream persisted so vigorously that the building of the Panama Canal between 1880 and 1914 was in a very real sense a consequence of the California Gold Rush of 1849.[18]

From the very beginning, the Gold Rush had worldwide ramifications. It affected the economies not only of the United States, but of Central and South America, of Europe, and of the Far East. In the Western Hemisphere, Chile proved a prime example of the influence of events in California on world trade. Before 1848, Chilean farmers had found few market outlets for their products. But the Gold Rush quickly afforded them new opportunities as California emerged as a major market. Chileans shipped their wheat and flour, all kinds of fruits, and large quantities of beef at very profitable prices. Even Mexico, which had just emerged from a humiliating war with its northern neighbor, gained some trading advantages from the gold discoveries. In 1849 more than nine thousand Americans passed through northern Mexico on their way to California, purchasing supplies and stimulating an increase in price levels. At the same time, thousands of Mexicans also rushed north to the California gold mines. But the discrimination they encountered there was increasingly discouraging, and by 1854 the flow of Mexican immigrants lessened.[19]

The influence of the Gold Rush on European economies varied. Among those that were profoundly touched was Norway, whose economy was heavily dependent on shipping and trade and commerce. Norwegian merchants and shipowners looked on the newly emerging economic opportunities on the Pacific Coast with a lively fascination. Already in the 1850s the Norwegians were actively discussing the potentials of a canal across the isthmus. At the same time, Norwegian iron manufacturers were hopefully watching California as a potential big market for rails and railroad equipment, a market they expected to develop quickly. So intense was Norwegian interest in the California Gold Rush that many major newspapers prominently featured letters from Scandinavian miners in their pages.[20]

Elsewhere on the European continent, the Gold Rush was also significant. For thousands of young Frenchmen undergoing the throes of the Revolutions of 1848, California beckoned as a source of new job and investment opportunities. They organized at least eighty-three companies in 1850, not only for gold mining, but also for investments in real estate, farming, and service industries. After 1852, French interest ebbed as Louis Napoleon established political stability in France.[21] In Germany the Gold Rush also attracted considerable interest. Of the one million Germans who came to the United States during the 1850s, at least 30,000 settled in California, many as farmers or in the grocery business. By 1860 at least 14 percent of California's population was German. This heavy emigration caused labor shortages in the German states during the 1850s, although it eased population pressures in succeeding years. The Gold Rush also affected the Sardinian and Italian states, where increased price levels brought about by gold production created new capital available for building of railroads and telegraph lines.[22]

Great Britain, perhaps, was most directly touched by the Gold Rush. Of the 500,000 British immigrants who came to the United States in the 1850s, at least

50,000, many of them skilled Cornish, Welsh, and Irish miners, settled in California. But the economic effects on the mother country were more varied than those experienced elsewhere in Europe. As a manufacturing nation, Great Britain depended on imports of food, and needed specie to pay those nations that could not afford to buy its manufactured products. Before 1848 an increasing shortage of gold had hampered British trade. But the new gold coming from the California mines relieved the specie shortage. As annual production of the metal reached $131 million annually between 1850 and 1855, the amount of gold in the world's money markets increased. That raised prices everywhere. And as the cost of goods also rose in California, the demand for British manufactured goods increased as well. By 1856, British exports to California exceeded $2 million annually. As California gold contributed significantly to the worldwide increase in prices, the British economy profited enormously with booming exports. At the same time this increased demand for British goods benefited many workers, whose wages rose faster than prices.[23]

Nations in the Pacific area were also sensitive to the California gold discoveries. The Gold Rush created a critical labor shortage in Hawaii, where a sizable number of sugar plantation workers migrated to the California gold fields. That also brought a marked increase in the prices of consumer goods, especially foodstuffs. In part this was also due to the great increase of agricultural exports to California, which offered very profitable new markets. Hawaiian trade with the more distant Atlantic seaboard declined, as the increasingly multifaceted contact with the Pacific Coast increased. The exodus of workers from sugar plantations between 1848 and 1853 was so great that employers began to import Chinese immigrants to fill the gap, thereby forever altering the ethno-cultural structure of the islands.[24]

The Gold Rush left ripples in China as well. Between 1848 and 1852, thirty-five thousand Chinese left for California; they constituted at least 10 percent of the population during the 1850s. California gold discoveries coincided with the Taiping Rebellion in China, a violent civil war that led to much plunder and famine, and created thousands of refugees. Eager to emigrate, many peasants from Kwangtung (Guangdong) province heard about California from traders there. Once in the United States, in addition to engaging in mining, they performed a variety of services, including laundry, food production and preparation, and construction. In addition, they were quietly involved in a variety of businesses. These included the importation of ready-made clothing from China, and even prefabricated houses. From the beginning of statehood, Californians initiated commercial contacts with their Chinese neighbors, even if they did not treat them as equals during the nineteenth century.[25]

The Gold Rush and the resulting increase of gold in circulation contributed to higher price levels throughout the world. In the decade before 1848, prices had declined in developed nations. The tight money policies of the Bank of England and also the Bank of France had contributed to this decline and led to a shortage of specie. California's gold production changed that situation and precipitated the rise in wholesale and commodity prices. The effects in the United States were also notable. No longer did the nation have to depend mainly on capital brought by immigrants, or produced by imports. Instead, the coinage of gold increased the amount of money in circulation and produced a favorable trade balance for the United States.[26]

Indeed, throughout the second half of the nineteenth century, rising and falling world prices were closely related to gold production in California, and also in South Africa and Australia, where the California experience gave an impetus to the search for new mines. Between 1848 and 1870 increasing gold production raised price levels, but as the output slackened thereafter, the trend was reversed. Prices rose again from 1890 to 1896, boosted by new gold discoveries in Alaska and South Africa. Great Britain profited most from the increase of gold stocks because both the United States and South Africa exported their bullion to buy British goods. As E. Victor Morgan, a prominent British economist, noted in the twentieth century, "The most important single factor in the monetary history of the nineteenth century is the great increase in gold output, following the discovery of the mines of California and Australia."[27]

The Gold Rush had an important effect on the investment policies of European nations, particularly Great Britain. In the first decade after the discovery of gold, British stock companies invested at least $10 million in mining companies in California—most of which were not very successful. That experience led to a lull until 1870, when British investors took another fling in California mines. Between 1870 and 1873, twenty-seven companies poured at least £4 million into mining operations in the state, and more than twice as much in the Comstock Lode in Nevada. High hopes were disappointed, but the experience did much to familiarize British capitalists with California. Hope springs eternal, and between 1873 and the end of the century, British investors broadened their interests. Some, like the California Redwood Company, sent their monies to purchase forests in northern California. Others, like the California Orange and Vineyard Company, entered the southern part of the state and contributed to the economic boom of the late 1880s there. Others bought land and established ranches, as in Duarte. The Glasgow California Land Company reclaimed swamp lands in the San Joaquin Delta. Many of these ventures failed; one scholar estimated losses between 1880 and 1893 to be as high as £150,000. But the infusion of so much foreign capital did much to stimulate California's economy. It facilitated rapid expansion and certainly accelerated the building of railroads.[28] And of course the large volume of gold exports from California contributed mightily to create a favorable trade balance for the United States. Between 1850 and 1900 California's gold production constituted fully 59 percent of total U.S. gold production, totaling about $1.4 billion (or at least $25 billion in 1990 dollars).[29]

The solid stone and brick edifices lining Montgomery Street in the mid-1850s testify to
the transforming powers of gold. Where but a half-dozen or so years earlier a scattering
village of adobes and modest frame buildings had fronted Yerba Buena Cove, now stood
a substantial cosmopolitan city of hotels, shops, theaters, and banking houses. The cost of
John Parrott's elegant Granite Block, foreground, built in 1852 of stone quarried in China,
possibly exceeded the entire value of the frontier settlement that had earlier been galva-
nized by the cry "Gold! Gold! Gold on the American River!" *Courtesy Bancroft Library.*

In many ways, the California Gold Rush precipitated a veritable economic revolution in the state, the nation, and the world. Production of precious metals affected
price levels, labor, wages, capital investment, the expansion of business, finance,
agriculture, service industries, and transportation. True, the California experience
was not entirely unique. Precious metals had influenced the course of civilizations for
thousands of years before 1848. When Emile Le Vasseur, the great French economist, in 1858 traced the historical relationship between the value of gold and the value
of commodities, he identified fourteen major revolutions in world history, of which
the California Gold Rush was the last in his lifetime.[30] Many of his views were
shared by his contemporary, Karl Marx, who just one year later declared that his observations on capitalism were made in direct response to the gold discoveries in
California. As Marx wrote in 1859, "The enormous material on the history of polit-

ical economy which is accumulated in the British Museum; the favourable view which London offers for the observation of bourgeois society; finally, the new stage of development upon which the latter seems to have entered with the discovery of gold in California and Australia led me to the decision to resume my studies from the very beginning and work up critically the new material." Those studies were soon to culminate in *Das Kapital,* a revolutionary book stimulated by the gold discoveries of the 1850s.[31]

The passage of time did not dim assessments of contemporaries as to the revolutionary economic impact of the California Gold Rush. The eminent British economist John Maynard Keynes wrote in 1930 that he viewed the rise and fall of civilizations in relation to precious metals. He surmised, for example, that Sumerian civilization could be explained by the gold of Arabia, the greatness of Athens by the gold of Laurium, and the stagnation of western Europe during the Middle Ages by the scarcity of precious metals. Historians agreed. Fernand Braudel, the French student of world civilizations, exclaimed that "the chapters of world history . . . follow the rhythms imposed by the legendary metals."[32]

In the final analysis, it might be said that the economic significance of the Gold Rush can also be understood in a psychological and philosophical context. As the French philosopher Michel Foucault once wrote, "the signs of exchange, because they satisfy desire, are sustained by the dark, dangerous and accursed glitter of metal. An unequivocal glitter, for it reproduces in the depths of the earth that other glitter that sings at the far end of the night; it resides there like an inverted promise of happiness, and because metal resembles the stars, the knowledge of all these perilous treasures is at the same time knowledge of the world."[33] Thus, the economic impact of the Gold Rush is rooted as much in emotions as in rational behavior. It touched a deep-seated nerve in the human psyche. Consequently, it had a profound influence not only on contemporaries, but on later generations, and is bound to exercise a continuing fascination in the future.

NOTES

1. Howard R. Lamar, "Coming into the Mainstream at Last: Comparative Approaches to the American West," *Journal of the West* 35 (October 1996): 4. The literature on the California Gold Rush is extensive. Two excellent recent works stressing social aspects include Malcolm J. Rohrbough, *Days of Gold: The California Gold Rush and the American Nation* (Berkeley: University of California Press, 1997), and David Goodman, *Gold Seeking: Victoria and California in the 1850s* (St. Leonards, New South Wales, 1994). An older factual account is Rodman W. Paul, *California Gold: The Beginning of Mining in the Far West* (Cambridge, Mass.: Harvard University Press, 1947).

2. Inexplicably, a definitive history of the California economy or business remains to be written. More than one hundred years ago Hubert Howe Bancroft compiled much useful de-

tail. Material in this paragraph is taken from Hubert Howe Bancroft, *History of California,* vol. 7 (San Francisco: The History Company, 1890), 94–97. Older useful compendia are John S. Hittell, *The Resources of California* (San Francisco: A. Roman, 1863), and Robert G. Cleland, *The Cattle on a Thousand Hills* (San Marino: Huntington Library, 1941), 157–83.

3. Bancroft, *California,* vol. 7, 76–78; H. Brett Melendy, "One Hundred Years of the Redwood Lumber Industry," (Ph.D. diss., Stanford University, 1952), chap. 1.

4. Bancroft, *California,* vol. 7, 84.

5. Ibid., 79–80, 315; see also Edwin Corle, *John Studebaker, An American Dream* (New York: E. P. Dutton, 1948).

6. Among original sources see San Francisco *Chronicle,* February 11, 1872, "Our Solid Merchants: The Immense Establishment of Levi Strauss and Company," and San Francisco *Bulletin,* October 12, 1895, which reports on an interview with Strauss. See also Art Roth, "The Levi's Story," *American Heritage* (Fall 1952): 49–51 and Alvin Josephy, "Those Pants that Levi Gave Us," *American West* (July–August, 1985): 30–37; the firm was actually founded by Levi's brother-in-law, Norton B. Stern, who came to San Francisco in 1851, two years before the arrival of Strauss. See William M. Kramer and Norton B. Stern, "Levi Strauss: The Man Behind the Myth," *Western States Jewish History* 19 (April 1987): 257–63. On cattle, see James M. Jensen, "Cattle Drives from the Ranchos to the Gold Fields of California," *Arizona and the West* 2 (Winter 1960): 341–52, and Cleland, *Cattle.*

7. Rockwell D. Hunt, *John Bidwell: Prince of California Pioneers* (Caldwell, Idaho: Caxton Printers, 1942), Norman E. Tutorow, *Leland Stanford, Man of Many Careers* (Menlo Park, Calif.: Pacific Coast Publishers, 1971), and David Lavender, *California: Land of New Beginnings* (New York: Harper & Row, 1972), 159–74, 227–34.

8. E. J. Wickson, *Rural California* (New York: Macmillan, 1923), 208–84; Paul W. Gates, ed., *California Ranchos and Farms, 1848–1862, Including the Letters of John Quincy Warren* (Madison: State Historical Society of Wisconsin, 1967, 1–80) which has an excellent introduction that summarizes California's agricultural history; Gerald D. Nash, *State Government and Economic Development: A History of Administrative Policies in California, 1850–1933* (Berkeley: Institute of Government Studies, University of California, 1964), 63–80, and for Henry Miller, see Edward F. Treadwell, *The Cattle King* (Fresno: Valley Publishers, 1966).

9. Rodman W. Paul, "The Wheat Trade Between California and the United Kingdom," *Mississippi Valley Historical Review* 45 (1958): 391–412.

10. On McCormick see William T. Hutchinson, *Cyrus Hall McCormick,* 2 vols. (New York: Da Capo Press, 1930–1935); also see a good general survey by Lawrence Jelinek, *Harvest Empire: A History of California Agriculture* (San Francisco: Boyd & Fraser, 1979).

11. E. J. Wickson, *The California Fruits,* 8th ed. (San Francisco: Pacific Rural Press, 1919); Vincent P. Carosso, *The California Wine Industry* (Berkeley: University of California Press, 1952).

12. Nash, *State Government,* 83–89; Ira B. Cross, *Financing an Empire: A History of Banking in California,* 4 vols. (Chicago: S. J. Clarke, 1927), vol. 1, 41–94; Fritz Redlich, *History of American Business Leaders,* 2 vols. (New York: Johnson Reprint, 1947), vol. 2, part 1, 43–66; "Banks and Banking in the Fifties: Early Legislative Prohibitions," *Mercantile Trust Review of the Pacific* 13 (1924): 118–28.

13. Robert J. Chandler, "Integrity Amid Tumult: Wells, Fargo & Co.'s Gold Rush Banking," *California History* 70 (Fall 1991): 259–77; David Lavender, *Nothing Seemed Impossible: William C. Ralston and Early San Francisco* (Palo Alto: American West, 1975); Dwight L.

Clarke, *William Tecumseh Sherman: Gold Rush Banker* (San Francisco: California Historical Society, 1969); and Nash, *State Government,* 81–89. A recent study of California bankers and the Comstock Lode is Maureen Ann Jung, "The Comstocks and the California Mining Economy, 1848–1900. The Stock Market and the Modern Corporation" (Ph.D. diss., University of California, Santa Barbara, 1988), 31–60, 104–36.

14. Thousands of diaries have been published. Typical is George P. Hammond and Edward Howes, eds., *Overland to California on the Southwestern Trail 1849, Diary of Robert Eccleston* (Berkeley: University of California Press, 1950). Well-written summaries of such journeys are in George R. Stewart, *The California Trail: An Epic with Many Heroes* (New York: McGraw-Hill, 1952), and J. S. Holliday, *The World Rushed In: The California Gold Rush Experience* (New York: Simon & Schuster, 1981).

15. Roscoe P. Conkling and Mary P. Conkling, *The Butterfield Overland Mail, 1857–1869,* 3 vols. (Glendale, Calif.: A. H. Clark, 1947); W. Turrentine Jackson, *Wagon Roads West* (Berkeley: University of California Press, 1952); and Raymond W. Settle and Mary Settle, *Saddle and Spurs: The Pony Express Saga* (Harrisburg: Stackpole, 1955).

16. Wesley S. Griswold, *A Work of Giants: Building the First Transcontinental Railroad* (New York: McGraw-Hill, 1963); Oscar Lewis, *The Big Four: The Story of Huntington, Stanford, Hopkins, and Crocker, and of the Building of the Central Pacific* (New York: A. A. Knopf, 1938); on Judah see Carl I. Wheat, "A Sketch of the Life of Theodore Judah," *California Historical Society Quarterly* 4 (September 1925): 219–71.

17. John H. Kemble, *The Panama Route, 1848–1869* (Berkeley: University of California Press, 1943), 1–115, 200–209; Oscar Lewis, *Sea Routes to the Gold Fields* (New York: A. A. Knopf, 1949), 261–82.

18. John H. Kemble, *The Panama Canal: The Evolution of the Isthmian Crossing* (San Francisco: Book Club of California, 1965); David McCullough, *The Path Between the Seas: The Creation of the Panama Canal, 1870–1914* (New York: Simon & Schuster, 1978).

19. Ralph J. Roske, "The World Impact of the California Gold Rush, 1849–1857," *Arizona and the West* 5 (1963): 199–200; Doris Wright, "The Making of Cosmopolitan California," *California Historical Society Quarterly* 19 (1940): 326, and ibid., 20 (1941): 66–74; Ralph Bieber, "California Gold Mania," *Mississippi Valley Historical Review* 35 (June 1948): 13, and Ralph Bieber, ed., *Southern Trails to California in 1849* (Glendale: Arthur H. Clark, 1937), 62; James M. Guinn, "The Sonoran Migration," *Historical Society of California Publications* 8 (1907): 33; Richard H. Morefield, "Mexicans in the California Mines, 1848–1853," *California Historical Society Quarterly* 35 (March 1956): 42–43.

20. Wright, "Making of Cosmopolitan California," 20: 67–68.

21. Gilbert Chinard, "The French in California," *California Historical Society Quarterly* 22 (1943): 295; Henry Blumenthal, "The California Societies in France, 1849–1855," *Pacific Historical Review* 25 (August 1956): 253–58; Abraham P. Nasatir, *The French in the California Gold Rush* (New York: American Society of the French Legion of Honor, 1934).

22. Roske, "World Impact," 223–25; Marcus L. Hansen, "The Revolutions of 1848 and German Emigration," *Journal of Economic and Business History* 2 (August 1930): 630–33; Wright, "Making of Cosmopolitan California," 20: 68–69; Andrew F. Rolle, "Italy in California," *Pacific Spectator* 9 (Autumn 1955): 409–11; Francesco M. Nicosia, Dorothy Miller, and Edwin McInnis, *Italian Pioneers of California* (San Francisco: Italian-American Chamber of Commerce of the Pacific Coast, 1960), 12–17.

23. Leland Jenks, *The Migration of British Capital to 1875* (London: A. A. Knopf, 1973),

160–63, 383–84; John H. Clapham, *An Economic History of Modern Britain: Free Trade and Steel, 1850–1886,* 3 vols. (Cambridge: The University Press, 1952), vol. 2, 336–37; Dean Albertson, "The Discovery of Gold in California as Viewed by New York and London," *Pacific Spectator* 3 (Winter 1949): 27–30.

24. Ralph Kuykendall, *The Hawaiian Kingdom, 1778–1854* (Honolulu: University of Hawaii Press, 1938), 319–25, 328, and also his *The Hawaiian Kingdom, 1854–1874: Twenty Critical Years* (Honolulu: University of Hawaii Press, 1953), 16; Theodore Morgan, *Hawaii: A Century of Economic Change* (Cambridge: Harvard University Press, 1948), 155–57; Roske, "World Impact," 189–94.

25. Stephen Williams, *The Chinese in the California Mines, 1848–1860* (Stanford: Stanford University Press, 1930); Ellen R. Wood, "Californians and Chinese: The First Decade" (M.A. thesis, University of California, Berkeley, 1961). For context see the old classic by Mary R. Coolidge, *Chinese Immigration* (New York: H. Holt, 1909), and Ping Chiu, *Chinese Labor in California, 1850–1880* (Madison: State Historical Society of Wisconsin, 1963). Liping Zhu is preparing a study of the Chinese in Idaho.

26. James T. Phinney, "Gold Production and the Price Level," *Quarterly Journal of Economics* 47 (1933): 666–69, 678–79; Wesley C. Mitchell, *Gold, Prices, and Wages* (Berkeley: University of California Press, 1908); Walter B. Smith and Arthur H. Cole, *Fluctuations in American Business* (Cambridge: Harvard University Press, 1935), 89–90; Pierre Vilar, *A History of Gold and Money, 1450–1920* (London: Humanities Press, 1976), 38, 321.

27. Victor Morgan, *The Theory and Practice of Central Banking* (New York: A. M. Kelley, 1965), 154; Milton Friedman and Anna J. Schwartz, *Monetary History of the United States* (New York: Princeton University Press, 1963), 27, 58; Wesley C. Mitchell, *A History of the Greenbacks* (Chicago: University of Chicago Press, 1903), 142–44; Thomas S. Berry, *Western Prices Before 1861* (Cambridge: Harvard University Press, 1943), and also his "Gold—But How Much?" *California Historical Society Quarterly* 55 (1976): 247–55; Paul, *California Gold,* 345–48. *Historical Statistics of the United States* (Washington, D.C.: Government Printing Office, 1960), 346.

28. W. Turrentine Jackson, *The Enterprising Scot* (Edinburgh: Edinburgh University Press, 1968), 211–16, 222–33; W. W. Rostow, *The British Economy in the Nineteenth Century, 1750–1914* (Oxford: Clarendon Press, 1949), 22–23; Jenks, *Migration of British Capital,* 160–63.

29. Berry, "Gold—But How Much?" 247–55.

30. Noted in Vilar, *A History of Gold and Money,* 322; see also Roy Jastram, *The Golden Constant: The English and American Experience* (New York: Wiley, 1977), 212–15, 224.

31. Karl Marx, *Contribution to the Critique of Political Economy,* trans. N. I. Stone (New York: International Library Publishing, 1904), preface, 14.

32. John Maynard Keynes, *A Treatise on Money,* 2 vols. (London: Macmillan, 1930), 150; Fernand Braudel, "Monnaies et civilizations de l'or du Soudan à l'argent d'Amerique," *Annales* (1946): 22; Vilar, *A History of Gold and Money,* 12–13.

33. Michel Foucault, *The Order of Things* (London: Tavistock Publications, 1970), 173; see also Kevin Starr, *Americans and the California Dream* (New York: Oxford University Press, 1970), and Geoffrey Blainey, *The Rush That Never Ended* (Melbourne: Melbourne University Press, 1963).

Contributors

A. C. W. BETHEL's father showed him the excitement of history books and steam locomotives. The layered, kaleidoscopic changes he watched in Los Angeles laid the groundwork for his later focus on California history. He is now professor of philosophy at California Polytechnic State University, San Luis Obispo.

DANIEL CORNFORD is professor of history at San Jose State University. He is the author of *Workers and Dissent in the Redwood Empire* (1987), editor of *Working People of California* (1995), and coeditor (with Sally M. Miller) of *American Labor in the Era of World War II* (1995).

RAYMOND F. DASMANN, emeritus professor of ecology for the Environmental Studies Board at the University of California, Santa Cruz, is the author of thirteen books, including *The Destruction of California* (1965) and *California's Changing Environment* (1981). He has researched wildlife and ecologically sustainable economic development (ecodevelopment) since 1948.

LYNNE PIERSON DOTI, a professor of economics and business at Chapman University since 1971, is the author of *Banking in an Unregulated Environment: California, 1878–1905* (1995) and coauthor of *California Bankers, 1848–1994* (1994) and *Banking in the American West* (1991). She has also written approximately twenty-five articles on banking, using history as a laboratory to test theories of branch-banking, bank structure, and financial regulation. Her doctorate in economics is from the University of California, Riverside.

LAWRENCE JAMES JELINEK is a professor of history at Loyola Marymount University, Los Angeles. He earned his doctorate in history from the University of California at Los Angeles in 1976. He is the author of *Harvest Empire: A History of California Agriculture* (1982).

MAUREEN A. JUNG received her M.A. and Ph.D. degrees in sociology from the University of California, Santa Barbara. In 1989 she received the Theodore Calvin Pease Award from the Society of American Archivists for her article "Documenting Nineteenth-Century Quartz Mining in Northern California." For the past five years, she has owned WordSpring Writing Consultants, located in Sacramento. In addition to writing on mining and regional land use issues, she is a contributing writer to *Living Blues*, published by the University of Mississippi Center for the Study of Southern Culture.

ANTHONY KIRK completed his doctorate in history, with a specialization in American cultural history and art history, from the University of California, Santa Barbara. He is a historical consultant in Santa Cruz, California. He is the author of *Founded by the Bay: The History of the Macaulay Foundry, 1896–1996* (1996) and has recently completed a book-length manuscript entitled "Visions of a Golden Land: California Art and Artists from the Age of Exploration to the Great Earthquake and Fire of 1906."

RONALD H. LIMBAUGH, an Idaho native, received his B.A. degree from the College of Idaho, and earned his M.A. and Ph.D. in history at the University of Idaho. At the University of the Pacific he holds concurrent positions as director of the John Muir Center for Regional Studies, executive director of the Conference of California Historical Societies, and Rockwell Hunt Professor of California History. He has published three books and many articles and book reviews on aspects of western American history. His most recent book is *John Muir's "Stickeen" and the Lessons of Nature* (University of Alaska Press, 1996).

GERALD D. NASH, distinguished professor of history at the University of New Mexico, is the author of many books dealing with the economic history of California and the twentieth-century West. He has served as George Bancroft Professor of American History at the University of Göttingen in Germany. With Richard W. Etulain, he edited *Researching Western History* (1997) and is currently writing an economic history of the twentieth-century West.

RICHARD J. ORSI is professor of history at California State University, Hayward. A graduate of Occidental College in Los Angeles, he received his doctorate from the University of Wisconsin, Madison. He is the coauthor (with Richard B. Rice and William A. Bullough) of *The Elusive Eden: A New History of California*, 2nd ed. (McGraw-Hill, 1996), and coeditor (with Alfred A. Runte and Marlene Smith-Baranzini) of *Yosemite and Sequoia: A Century of California National Parks* (University of California Press, 1993). He is nearing completion of another book, "A Railroad and the Development of the American West: The Southern Pacific Company, 1860–1930." Since 1988, he has been editor of *California History*, the quarterly of the California Historical Society.

DONALD J. PISANI is Merrick Professor of History at the University of Oklahoma. He has published extensively on the history of natural resources in the American West. His most recent book is *Water, Land & Law in the West: The Limits of Public Policy, 1850–1920* (University Press of Kansas, 1996).

JAMES J. RAWLS, a graduate of Stanford University, received his doctorate in history from the University of California, Berkeley. He is the author, coauthor, or editor of more than twenty books on California and U.S. history, including *California: An Interpretive History* (7th ed., 1998), *Chief Red Fox is Dead: A History of Native Americans since 1945* (1996), *New Directions in California History* (1988), *Land of Liberty: A United States History* (1985), and *Indians of California: The Changing Image* (1984). He has served as reviews editor for *California History* since 1983 and is an instructor of history at Diablo Valley College.

LARRY SCHWEIKART is coauthor, with Lynne Pierson Doti, of *Banking in the American West* (1991) and *California Bankers, 1848–1994* (1994). He is currently completing a textbook on American business history titled "Entrepreneurial Adventure."

DUANE A. SMITH received the Ph.D. degree from the University of Colorado and has been professor of history and southwest studies at Fort Lewis College since 1964. His research and writing areas include mining, Colorado, baseball, Civil War, and urban history.

MARLENE SMITH-BARANZINI, the associate editor of *California History* since 1990, is the editor of *The Shirley Letters from the California Mines, 1851–1852* (Heyday Books, 1998). She is coauthor (with Howard Egger-Bovet) of the USKids History Series, which includes *Book of the American Indians* (1994), *Book of the American Colonies* (1995), *Book of the American Revolution* (1994), *Book of the New American Nation* (1996), and *Book of the Civil War* (1998), published by Little, Brown.

DAVID J. ST. CLAIR is professor of economics at California State University, Hayward. His areas of specialization and interest include economic history, urban transportation history, comparative economic systems, and California economic history. He has published in *The Journal of Economic History* and is the author of *The Motorization of American Cities* (Praeger Press, 1986). He received his Ph.D. in economics from the University of Utah and was the 1979 recipient of the Allen Nevins Prize for the year's best doctoral dissertation in U.S. economic history.

Index

accidents, at the mines, 91
"An Act Concerning Corporations" (1850),
    62
Adams, James Capen "Grizzly," 107–8
Adams & Co., 215, 221, 263
African Americans, in the Gold Rush, 5, 84
*After the Gold Rush: Society in Grass Valley
    and Nevada City, 1849–1870* (1982), 13
Agricola, 39, 151
agriculture: 138, 143, 189, 193; changed due
    to the Gold Rush, 233, 276; dominates
    the 18th century, 54; affected by hy-
    draulic mining, 132–33, 169; and water
    rights, 139, 143–44
Agua Fria, 180
air compressor, 199
Alameda, 268
Alameda County, 247
Alaska, 110, 149, 166, 287
alcaldes, 127
Aldrich, Mark, 91
Aleutian Islands, 110
Aleuts, hunting by, 106
Alexander, David, 267
Almaguer, Tomás, 14
Alta California (newspaper), 8, 59, 68, 152
Amador County, 64, 98
Amador County Laborers' Association, 98
Amador War, 98

American Bar, 156
American Express, 212, 263
American Revolution, 126
American River, 28, 30, 105, 179
Americans, hunting by in Rancho era, 106
Anaconda mine, 165
anthropology, wedded to Social
    Darwinism, 125
aparejo, 258
Arago (ship), 204
Arizona: 155, 166, 266, 281; and the "Col-
    orado Doctrine," 139; gold mining in, 152
Arkansas, 56, 127, 210, 228
Arkansas River, 149
Armour, Philip Danforth, 7
arrastra, 39, 202
Ashburner, William, 157
Asia: 254, 285; as source of miners, 5
Asians, banned from mines, 9
Auburn, 9, 85, 262
Austin mining district, 162
Australia: x, 155, 243, 254, 287; Californians
    in, 150, 152; discovery of gold in, 26;
Australians, in the Gold Rush, 5, 86

B. Davidson, bank of, 210, 220
Bacon, H. M., 92
Baja California, 110, 113
Baker, George Holbrook, 174, 176

Bakersfield, 113, 138, 139
ball safes, 217
Bancroft, Hubert Howe, 1, 44
"Bank Crowd," 71, 73
Bank of America, 229
Bank of California (San Francisco), 71, 73,
    160, 217, 222, 223, 224, 225, 281
Bank of D. O. Mills, 215
Bank of England, 286
Bank of France, 287
Bank of Nevada (San Francisco), 224
Bank of St. Louis, 211
bank corporations, prohibited by state law,
    62
banking: during the Gold Rush, 209–29,
    280; panics, 221; robberies of in West,
    218
Banking Act of 1878, 226
banking associations, 65
banknotes, 209, 220, 227
Banks, John, 58, 59
banks: 54; Americans' suspicion of, 228;
    description of typical building, 217;
    process of creation, 209–10, 214
Banning, Phineas, 267
barley farming, 243
Barnhart, Jacqueline Baker, 14
Bartholomew, William N., 167
Bausman, William, 79
Beale, Edward F., 241
Bean, Edwin F., 63
Bear River, 119, 132
beaver: 109; in California, 111
Beecher, Lyman, 27
Bell Gardens, 238
Belmont, 162
Benecia, 252
Bethel, A. C. W., 18, 20
Bidwell, John, 86, 111, 114, 278
Big Bonanza, 160
The Big Bonanza, 154
Big Four, 279
Bigler, Henry William, 1, 11
Birchville, 132
Bixby, Llewellyn, Jotham and Marcellus,
    241

black bears, 107
Black Hills (South Dakota), 159, 165
Black Point, San Francisco, 198
blacksmithing, 202, 203
Blackstone, William, 125
Blake, Eli Whitney, 41
Board of Bank Commissioners, 226
bobcats, 117
Bolivia, 69
"Bonanza firm," 72
"bonanza kings," 159
boots and shoes, production of, 194, 197
borax, 157, 204
Borthwick, J. D., 58
Boss, M. P., 45
Boston, 26, 67
Boston Flat, 92
Bradshaw Road, 267
Brannan, Sam, 281
Braudel, Fernand, 289
Brewer, William, 114, 118, 120
breweries, 194
bridges, 259
British Columbia, x, 91, 152, 155
Browere, Alburtus Del Orient, 181–82
Browne, J. Ross, 28, 44, 166, 169
Bruff, J. Goldsborough, 6, 177, 179
Buckalew, B. R., 214
Buckeye Rovers (Ohio), 58
Buena Vista Ranch, 245–46
Buena Vista Slough, 139
Bullough, William, 189
Butte, Montana, 159, 165, 169
Butte County, 64
Butterfield, John, 264, 283

cable cars, 203
Cajon Pass, 267
Calaveras County, 5, 64, 181
California (steamship), 252
California: influence of on future mining,
    149–70; state constitution of, 62
California as It Is & as It May Be, Or
    a Guide to the Gold Region, 62
California Assembly Committee on
    Corporations, 73

California Constitutional Convention, 220
"California Doctrine," 139
"California dollars" (hides), 211
California dredge, 166, 167
California Emigration Society, Boston, 57
California . . . for Travellers and Settlers (1873), 117
California Gold: The Beginning of Mining in the Far West (1947), 13, 80
The California Gold Rush: A Descriptive Bibliography (1997), 11
California mining company, 72
California News (painting), 176
California Orange and Vineyard Company, 287
California Powder-Works, 199
California Redwood Company, 287
California Stage Company, 265
California stamp mills, 39, 155, 202
California Star (newspaper), 3
California State Bureau of Mines, 44
California State Mining and Smelting Company, 63
California Steam Navigation Company, 257–58
California Supreme Court, 130, 137, 139, 143
California Trail, 177
California Wire-Works Company, 203
Californian (newspaper), 3
California's Golden Jubilee (1898), 11
Californios, 86, 241
Camanche (ironclad monitor), 205
Camptonville, 203
Canada, 28, 200
Cape Horn, 5, 56, 83, 177, 255
capital investment: in California mines, 53, 61; in Nevada, 162
Carolina, 39
Carquinez Strait, 252
Carr, William, 242
Carson, James H., 3Carson Emigrant Trail, 262
Carson River, 152, 160
Carson River mills, 160
Carson River route, 179, 261

Carson Sink, 176
Cashman, Ellen, 166
Cassidy, Butch, 218
Catskill, New York, 181
cattle, 109, 113, 114–15, 185, 233, 241
cattlemen, 125
Caughey, John Walton, 13, 247
Cedar City, Utah, 267
Central America, 5, 155, 178, 285
Central City, Colorado, 163
Central Colony of Fresno County, 239
Central Overland and California Pike's Peak Express, 265
Central Pacific Railroad, 160, 262, 278, 283
Central Valley, 35, 111, 113, 114, 118, 132, 139, 212, 237
Chagres, 178
Chagres River, 251
Chan, Sucheng, 15, 85
Chana, Claude, 85
Channel Islands, 109, 110
Chapman, William S., 238–41
Charleston (ship), 204, 205
Charlotte (brig), 177
Cherokees, discover Colorado gold, 163
Chicago, 42
Chihuahua, 234
Chile: 5, 254, 285; miners from, 82, 84, 86
Chilean mill, 39
China, ix, 110, 243, 254, 278, 279, 286
Chinese: in the Gold Rush, 5, 9, 29, 30, 85, 151, 286; indentured service by, 84; as laborers, 244, 245; prejudice against, 86, 97
Chinese chain pump, 31
Chollar-Norcross Mine, 200
Christman, Enos, 181
chromite, 204
Chrysolite mine, 165
Chumash Indians, 109, 110
Civil War, 130, 142, 144, 153, 189, 199, 221, 255, 283
"claims' associations." *See* squatter clubs
Clappe, Louise Amelia Knapp Smith. *See* Shirley, Dame
Clarke, Dwight, 221

Cleland, Robert, 185, 189
Clemens, Samuel, 155, 211
climate, 120
clipper ships, 255–56
coal, 189, 202, 204
Coeur d'Alene mines, 166
Cole, Cornelius, 44
Collins, John, 66, 67
Coloma, 30, 179, 180, 186
colonial charters, and mineral policy, 126
Colorado: x, 152, 155, 164, 166, 281; Californians in, 163
"Colorado Doctrine," 139
Colorado River, 267
Colorado Supreme Court, 164
Columbia Hill, 132
Colusa, 256, 258, 264
Commentaries, 125
Comptroller of the Currency, 226
Comstock Lode: x, 80, 91, 95, 96, 131, 153–54, 199, 201, 204, 222, 223, 281–82; discovery of, 53, 68, 142, 204, 261, 287; dominated by Californians, 152, 154, 156; effect on the environment, 115; failure of, 160; rise of corporate mining on, 68–73
Concord coaches, 265, 266
condors, 121
Conlin, Joseph, 90
Conness, John, 131
Conquests and Historical Identities in California, 1769–1936 (1995), 14
Consolidated Virginia mining company, 72, 160
consumer industries, in the Gold Rush, 195
Converse Basin, 115
"coolie" system, 85
copper mines: 25, 37, 204; in the Lake Superior District, 127
Cornford, Daniel, 15, 16
Cornish miners, 32, 37, 38, 39, 82, 95, 96–97, 151, 286
Cornwall, 25, 38, 39
corporations: formation of, 64; laws affecting, 63, 134–35; mining, 52, 54; promotions of, 63

corporate economy, in mining areas, 68–73
corporate securities, in mining companies, 62
Council Bluffs, Missouri, 177
Cousin Jacks, 38
Cowell, Henry, 188
Coyote and Deer Creek Water Company, 137
cradle. *See* rocker
Creesy, Josiah, 255
Crocker, Charles, 279, 283
Cross, Ira, 69
Crown Point and Savage mines, 71
Crystal Springs, 245
Cunningham and Brumagin, 218
Curle, J. H., 157
currency, 227, 228
Currier, Nathaniel, 251

D. J. Tallant, 220
Daily Alta California. See Alta California
Daily Herald (newspaper), 221
Dakotas: x; and the "California Doctrine," 139
Daly, George, 165
dams, to contain hydraulic debris, 144
Dana, Richard Henry, 111
Daniels, Douglas Henry, 15
Das Kapital, 289
Dasmann, Raymond F., 17
Davis, William Heath, 111, 211
Davis & Cowell lime kilns, 188
Dayton, Nevada, 46
Deadwood, 165
Decker and Jewett (Marysville), 218
Decker Brumagin & Company, 218
Decker Jewett Bank, 218
Decker, Jewett & Company, 218
Decker, Jewett & Paxton, 218
deer, 107, 117
Deer Creek, 81, 177
Deetken, G. F., 45
Deidesheimer, Philip, 154
Delano, Alonzo, 129, 278
Delavan, James, 66
Denver, Colorado, 163, 169

De Quille, Dan, 154
Derbec, Etienne, 182
Desert Land Act (1877), 138
Dewolf, David, 182
Dickson and Hay, 214
dirigible, 250
doctors, 87
Donahue, James, 42, 204
Donahue, Peter and Michael, 204
Donner Party, 179
Donner Pass, 261–62
Donohoe, Joseph, 222
Doti, Lynne Pierson, 18
Downey, John G., 226
Downieville, 116, 259
Dragoon Gulch, California, 181
dredging, 149, 151, 168, 198–99
Dresel, Emil, 116
Drew, Thomas, 9
drift mining, 32
drought, 115, 235, 237
dry washing (winnowing), 29
Duarte, 287
Duhaut-Cilly, 115
Dupont Street, 214
Dutch Flat toll road, 263, 264
dwellings, 91
dynamite, 37

Eagle, USS, 211
economics: 285; development of California,
    209; in the diggings, 52–74; of gold
    discovery, x, 9;
E. Delessert & Cordier, 210
Ehrenberg, 267
El Dorado County, 64, 247
elk, 107, 112, 121
Elliott, Russell, 162
Engineering and Mining Journal, 156
engineering, 28
England: 158; miners from, 37
English common law, 127
English miners, 151
Enlightenment, 123–25
environment, and the Gold Rush, 105–21,
    169

Eureka, California, 115
Eureka, Nevada, 165
Eureka mining district, 162
Europe: 59, 285, 287; source of investment
    capital, 53; technology in, 28
Europeans, in the Gold Rush, 5
Everett, Edward, 27
explosives, 199, 277
expressmen, 263

Fair, James G., 72, 159, 224
*The Fair but Frail: Prostitution in San
    Francisco, 1849–1900* (1986), 14
Fairchild, Lucius, 176, 181
Falcon (ship), 178
Faragher, John Mack, 13
Farallon Islands, 110
Farallone Egg Company, 112
F. Argenti & Co., 220
Fargo, William G., 216
Farmers & Merchants Bank (Los Ange-
    les), 226
farming, during the gold-rush era, 233–48
Farquharson, David, 225
Feather River, 7, 119, 131, 132, 168, 258
Ferriage of the Platte (drawing), 177
ferries, 259–60, 268
Field, Stephen J., 128–30
Fillmore, Millard, 130
fire, suppression of, 115
Flint, Benjamin, 241
Flint, Dr. Thomas, 241
Flood, James C., 72, 159, 224, 225
flooding, 118–19
flour mills, 194, 197, 278
Flying Cloud (clipper ship), 256
Folgers Coffee, 196
"follow the vein," 134
Font, Pedro, 111
Foote, Arthur and Mary Hallock, 157
foreign miners, 9
forests, in California, 115–16
Fort Ross, 110, 115
Fort Tejon, 267
Fort Vancouver, 111
Fosters Bar, 182

Foucault, Michel, 289
foundries, 199, 200, 202, 203, 204, 277
foxes, 117
Fraser River, gold rush on, 91, 152
free mining, 128–31, 140, 144, 145
Freiburg, Germany, 28
Frémont, John C., 63, 114
French Corral, 132, 133
French miners: 151, 285; prejudice against, 86
Fresno, 138, 258
Fresno Canal and Irrigation Company, 239
Fresno County, 239
Fretz, Ralph, 222
Fretz & Ralston, 222
Frohling, John, 244
fruit cultivation, 233, 244, 247
Fry, Walter, 107
furs, used for clothing, 109

Garcia, Mario T., 15
Garrison, Cornelius Kingston (C. K.), 222
Garrison, Morgan, Fretz & Ralston bank, 222
Gates, Paul W., 236, 237
Gaviota Pass, 264
genocide, 8
Georgetown, California, 154
Georgia: 39; gold rush in, 82
"German Syndicate," 239
Germans, 25, 151
Germany: miners from, 37, 285; mining technology in, 39
Ghirardelli, Domingo, 7, 195
Gill, W. E., 38
Gillespie, C. V., 215
Gilpin County, Colorado, 163–64
Glasgow California Land Company, 287
Goat Island, 225
gold: in the Americas, 3; in Australia, 26; discovery in California, ix, x, 1, 3, 211; discovery in Nevada, 53; in Georgia, Carolinas, Michigan, 25; minting of, 197, 213–14; purity of, 214
Gold Canyon, 152
Gold Hill, 38

Gold Hill mine, 94
Gold Is the Cornerstone (1948), 13
Golden Dreams and Leaden Realities (1853), 10
Golden Dreams and Waking Realities (1851), 10
Goldfield, Nevada, 162
Goodman, David, 82, 83
Goodwin, C. C., 154
Gordon, George, 196
Gould & Curry mine, 69, 72, 153, 161, 201
Granite Block (San Francisco), 159, 288
Grape Culture, Wines and Wine-Making (1862), 246
Grass Valley, 9, 37, 40, 80, 89, 90, 91, 92, 93, 94, 95, 96, 97, 115, 151, 152, 155, 158, 260
Grass Valley Gold Mining Company, 66, 67
"Grass Valley System," 38, 45
grasses and grassland, in California, 106, 113–15
Gray, Charles Glass, 6
grazing, 115
Great Basin, 113
Great Britain: ix, 243, 278, 285–87; miners from, 93, 151
Great Salt Lake, 111
Greeley, Horace, 66, 176
Green, Thomas Jefferson, 9
Greenhorn Cutoff, 179
Gregory, John, 163
Gregory District (Colorado), 163–64
Grinnell, Joseph, 111
grizzly bears, 105, 107, 109, 121
"ground sluicing," 32, 33
Guadalupe fur seal, 110
Guadalupe Island, 110
guns, manufacturing of, 200

Haas, Lisbeth, 14
Habakkuk, H. J., 27
habitat, wildlife, 107
Haggin, James Ben Ali, 139, 241, 242
Hague, James D., 157
Haight, Henry, 98
Hale, Richard Lunt, 182

Hale & Norcross mining company, 72
Hall Safe and Lock (Cincinnati, Ohio), 217
Hallidie, Andrew Smith, 156, 203
Haraszthy, Agoston, 244–46, 280
hardrock mining. *See* quartz mining
Hardy, Osgood, 185, 189
Harte, Bret, 11, 12
Havana, 178
Hawaii, 200, 203, 254, 286
Hawaiians, in the Gold Rush, 5
Haying on the Buena Vista Farm (photo), 242
Hayward, Alvinza, 46, 71, 160
Hayward, James A., 226
Hearst, George, 68, 69, 158, 159, 165, 241
Heckman, Marlin L., 10
Hellman, Isaias, 225, 226, 228
Hell's Delight, 7
Helper, Hinton Rowan, 10
"Hercules" powder, 200
Hester, Sallie, 5
Hewes, David, 196
hide and tallow trade, 185, 211, 233
Highly, William, 31
Highway 49, 116, 120
Hittell, John S., 31, 32, 71, 142–43, 187–89, 202
Hittell, Theodore, 58
Hobbes, Thomas, 141
Holliday, J. S., 5, 11
Hollister, W. W., 242
Homestake mine, 165
Homestead Act: 121; of 1862, 237
honey bucket, invention of, 157–58
Hong Kong, 254
Honolulu, 193
Hopkins, Mark, 278, 283
Hovey, John, 177
Huancavélica, 3
Huaute, Semu, 109
Hudson's Bay Company, 111
Hugill, Peter J., 25
Humboldt Bay, 116, 255
Humboldt County, 109, 242, 254, 278
Humbug Flat, 180
Humphreys, 30

Hunt, Rockwell, 114
Huntington, Collis P., 278, 283–84
Huntington & Hopkins Hardware Store, 279
Huntington Mill, 39
Hurtado, Albert L., 14, 87
Husmann, George, 281
Hutchings' California Magazine, 40
Hutchinson, W. H., 189
Hutton, William R., 179, 186
hydraulic mining: ix, 94, 95, 106, 152, 167, 198–99, 202; companies and/or corporations, 130, 136; development of, 59–61, 151; environmental impact of, 116–120; labor in, 80, 84, 99; laws and, 131–34, 136–40, 143; technology of, 32–36
hydroelectric power, 203

Idaho Springs, Colorado, 163
Idaho: x, 155, 162, 166, 267, 281; and the "Colorado Doctrine," 139
The Idle and Industrious Miner, 79
Illinois, 25, 56, 126, 191, 193
incorporation laws, 54–55
indentured labor, 87
Independence, Missouri, 177
Independent Line, 253
"Indian Jim," 1
Indian Survival on the California Frontier (1988), 14
Indiana, 126, 226
Indians. *See* Native Americans
Industrial Revolution, 276
industry, and the Gold Rush, 185–206, 276
insurance, 223
insurance companies, 54
interest rates, during the Gold Rush, 62
Iowa, 211, 226, 228
Iowa Hill, 216
Ireland, ix
Irish, in the mines, 96, 286
Irish Four, 228
Irish potato famine, 25
iron, 189, 191, 202, 203
irrigation systems, in Los Angeles, 233
Irvine, James, 241, 242

Irvine Ranch, 241
"It's Your Misfortune and None of My Own"
    (1991), 14
Italian miners, 151
Italy, 285

Jackson, George, 163
Jackson, W. Turrentine, 162, 165
jaguars, 107, 121
James King of William, offices of bank, 210
Janin, Louis and Henry, 157
Japan, 278, 279
Japanese, 245, 247
Jelinek, Lawrence James, 18
Jenkins, Gordon, 11
John A. Collins & Company, 66
Johnson, Charles S., 125
Johnson, George H., 124
Johnson, Susan, 84
Johnson's Ranch, 179
joint-stock companies, 55, 58, 83, 84, 94
Jones, J. M., 220
Jones, J. Wesley, 167
Jones, John P., 71, 160
Judah, Theodore, 279, 283–84
Julian, George, 130–31
Jung, Maureen A., 15

Kanaka Bar, 5
Kanaka Creek, 5
Kansas, and the "California Doctrine," 139
Kasson, John F., 27
Kaweah River, 107
Kelley, Robert, 35
Kellogg & Humbert, 213
Kelly, Eugene, 222
Kentuck mining company, 72, 224
Kern County Land and Water Company,
    139, 241
Kern River: 139, 264; "humbug," 152
Keynes, John Maynard, 289
King, James, of William, 19, 219
Kinman, Calvin, 109
Kirk, Anthony, 18
Klondike, 168
Knight water wheel, 31

Kohler, Charles, 244
Korea, 168
Kuchel, Charles, 116
Kunath, Oscar, 12
Kurutz, Gary F., 11
Kwangtung (Guangdong) Province, 286

La Paz (Mexico), 267
La Pérouse, Comte de (Jean-François de
    Galaup), 110
labor, in the mines, 78–99
Ladd and Tilton Bank (Portland), 222
Laird's Hill, 28
laissez-faire, 82
Lake City, 132
Lake Nicaragua, 253
Lake Tahoe, 115, 261
Lakes, Arthur, Jr., 167
Land Act of 1851, 235
land law, 123, 235–36
Land of Gold: Reality Versus Fiction (1855),
    10
land policy, 126, 138
Lapp, Rudolph, 84
Las Sergas de Esplandián (novel), 3
Las Vegas, 267
Lassen's Cutoff, 179
Latin America, 200
*Law for the Elephant: Property and Social
    Behavior on the Overland Trail* (1997), 14
laws. *See* land law, mineral law, resource
    law, water law
lawsuits: and the Comstock mines, 135; in
    the Gold Rush, 67
lawyers, 87, 128
Le Vasseur, Emile, 288
lead mines: 25, 37; in Indiana Territory, 126;
    in the Lake Superior District, 127
Leadville, Colorado, 149, 162, 165
Lee, Abe, 149
Legacy of Conquest (1987), 14
Lemon Cove, 107
Lewis, David Rich, 14
Lewis, Oscar, 7
Leyner percussion drills, 38
Limbaugh, Ronald H., 15, 17

lime production, 188
Limerick, Patricia Nelson, 14
Lincoln, California, 53
Lingenfelter, Richard, 98
Livermore Pass, 264
livestock, grazing by, 105
Locke, John, 123–25
lode mining. *See* quartz mining
logging, 115–16
London, England, 67
London School of Mines, 28
London stock exchange, 63
long tom, 26, 29, 59, 181, 197
Loo Choo (ship), 176
Lord, Eliot, 68
Los Angeles, 138, 185, 215, 225, 244, 264, 265, 266, 267
Los Angeles basin, 113
Los Angeles County, 144, 243, 247
Louis Napoleon, 285
"The Lousy Miner" (song), 7
Lovejoy, Reuben, 174
Lucas Turner & Co. Bank, 217, 221
"The Luck of Roaring Camp," 11
Lugo, Antonio María, 238
Lugo, Vicente, 238
lumber mills, 194, 199, 223
Lux, Charles, 139
Lux, Henry, 240–41
Lyman, George, 223
Lynn, Massachusetts, 177

machinery. *See* technology
Mackay, John W., 72, 159, 224, 225
Madera, 241
Malakoff Diggings, 106, 117
Manhattan Quartz Mining Company, 67
Manifest Destiny, 27, 78, 83, 86
Manila galleons, 110
Mann, Ralph, 13, 16, 80, 83, 90, 91, 92, 93, 94, 95, 115
manufacturing: 189, 190; table re, 192
manzanita, 116
Mare Island, 111
Mariposa, 36, 65, 142, 264
Mariposa County, 5, 63, 64

Mariposa Mining Company, 63
Mariposita, 36
Maritime trade, 254–55
Mark Brumagin & Company, 218
Marryat, Frank, 178
Marshall, James Wilson, discovers gold, ix, x, 1, 2, 3, 180, 187, 212, 276
Marx, Karl, influenced by the Gold Rush, 288–89
Marysville, 69, 91, 118, 119, 144, 168, 218, 255, 258, 259, 263–64, 282
Mason, Col. Richard B., 5, 127
Matteson, Edward E., 32
Mattole country, 109
Maury, Matthew, 255
May, Philip R., 32
Mazatlán, 174
McCormick, Cyrus, 280
McCullough, Dale, 111
McGrath, Roger D., 14
McIlvaine, William, Jr., 180
McLane, Louis, 264
McMurtrie, Wm. B., 176
McWilliams, Carey, 78, 139, 190, 204, 245
Meiggs, Henry, 221, 222
Meiggs Wharf, 221
Mellus, Howard & Co., 214
Memphis, Tennessee, 264
Mendocino Coast, 255
Mendocino County, 278
Mercado, Friar, 211
merchants, 80, 87
mercury ("quicksilver"), 29, 157, 198
Mexican Land Grants, 138, 143
Mexican-American War, 86, 211, 233
Mexicans: 244, 245; banned from mines, 9; laborers in gold fields, 84, 151
Mexico: ix, 69, 155, 193, 200, 234, 285; miners from, 5, 37, 82, 86; mining technology in, 28, 39
Michigan Bluff, 35
Michigan, 82, 126, 127
Middle West, 234
Miller, Henry, 113, 139, 240–41, 279
Miller and Lux ranch, 113, 240–41

Mills, Darius Ogden (D. O.), 215, 216, 222, 228
mineral law, 123
mineral policy, 126
miners: in California, ix; diet of, 90–91; dress of, 87, 277; economic return of, 7, 78; mobility of, 91–92. *See also* strikes, unions, wage laborers
Miners: A Moment at Rest (painting), 182
Miner's Bank, 218
Miner's Exchange and Savings Bank, 218, 219, 221
Miners' Foundry and Machine Works, 42
Miners in the Sierras (painting), 180
The Miner's Return (painting), 182
Mining Act of 1872, 120
Mining and Scientific Press (San Francisco), 71
Mining Camps: A Study in American Frontier Government (1885), 11
Mining Stock Exchanges 1860–1930 (1973), 52
mining claims, 58, 129
mining codes, 9, 58, 68, 127–28, 130, 151
mining companies: in the gold fields, 56–62; organizing of, 55–56;
mining corporations, 52
mining districts, 56–58, 163
mining laws, in Mexico, 127. *See also* resource law
mining unions, 81
Minnesota, 238
Mission Dolores, 245
Mission San Miguel, 241
Mission Woolen Mills, 278
missions, 185, 211
Mississippi, 228
Missouri, 25, 56, 209
Missouri River, 140
Miwok Indians, 84
Modesto, 138, 241
Mojave Desert, 113
Mokelumne Hill, 31
Mokelumne River, 29
Monaghan, Jay, 150
money: metallic, 214, 228; paper, 221, 228

monitors, 33
Montalvo, García Ordóñez de, 3
Montana: 125, 166, 167, 267; and the "California Doctrine," 139; hydraulic mining in, 144
Monterey, California, 3, 8, 113, 185, 212
Monterey Bay, 109
Monterey County, 243
Montgomery Street (San Francisco), 159, 210, 288
Moore's Flat, 132
Morgan, Charles, 222
Mormon Island, 179
Mormons, 212, 267
Mormon's Bar, 30
Morrill Act (1862), 45, 237
"Mother Lode," 36
Mount, William Sidney, 176
Mount Davidson, 72
Mount Ophir Mill, 65
mountain lions, 107, 117
Mountains and Molehills, 179
Muir, John, 114
mules, 258
Murphy's, 118
Murphys Camp, 182
myth, power of, 78–79, 81

Naglee & Sinton, 220
Nahl, Charles, 26, 60, 108, 129, 178, 180, 260
Nancy Bishop (schooner), 174
Napa Valley, 111, 281
Narjot, Ernest, 182
Nash, Gerald D., 20, 190
National Bank Act, 227
Native Americans: 185, 233; clashes with white miners, 8; devise currency, 211; and environment, 107, 114; as laborers, 244, 245; land taken from, 123, 125; as miners, 5, 85, 86–87
nativism, 80
Nebraska, and the "California Doctrine," 139
Nevada, 68, 96, 115, 132, 142, 152, 155, 160, 162, 241, 261, 263, 281, 287

Nevada City, 80, 81, 89, 90, 91, 92, 93, 94, 115, 132, 137, 141, 151, 152, 155, 158
Nevada County, 32, 36, 40, 60, 63, 64, 66, 68, 95, 106, 129, 132, 134, 152, 180
Nevada National Bank, 226
New Almaden quicksilver mine, 157, 204
New England Pioneers (mining company), 174
New Jersey, 6
New Mexico: x, 234; and the "Colorado Doctrine," 139
New Orleans, 174
New South Wales, 150
New York, 26, 202
New York City, 66, 67, 215, 243
New York *Daily Tribune,* 176
New York *Herald,* 55, 176
New York *Tribune,* 66
New Zealand, 167, 254
Newburyport, Massachusetts, 177, 182
Newell, Dianne, 24, 32
Newport Beach, California, 218
Nicaragua, 252, 253
Nidever, George, 110
Nigeria, 168
Nogales, Arizona, 218
Nordhoff, Charles, 117
Norris, Frank, 143
North Bloomfield, 132
North Bloomfield Gravel Mining Company, 106, 169
North Carolina: 155; gold rush in, 82; miners from, 151
North Columbia, 120
North Fork of the American River, 174, 216
North San Juan, 120, 132
Northern Mines, 89
Norway, 285
Notes on California and the Placers: How to Get There and What to Do Afterwards (1850), 66

O'Brien, William S., 72, 159, 224
O'Sullivan, Timothy, 153
Oakland, 169, 254, 264, 268
The Octopus (1901), 143

Ogden, Peter Skene, 111
Ohio (steamer), 178
Ohio, 191, 193
Okies, 245
Oklahoma, and the "California Doctrine," 139
Onion Valley, 260
Ontario, Canada, 28, 32
Ophir Mine, 159
Ophir Mining Company, 68, 69
Opposition Independent Line, 253
Oregon: 106, 155, 235, 241, 254, 281; and the "California Doctrine," 139; gold mining in, 152; miners from, 87
Oregon Trail, 211
Original California Songster (1855), 7
Orsi, Richard, 189
Osgood, Ernest, 125
Osgood, Samuel S., 180
Oso House, 266
Ostrogorsky, Michael, 31
Overland Mail, 264, 265
Overland Monthly, 143
Overland on the California Trail, 1846–1859: A Bibliography of Manuscript and Printed Travel Narratives (1984), 10–11
overland routes to California, 5, 83
Owens Valley, 267

Pacheco Pass, 264
Pachuca, 3
Pacific Coast Stock Exchange, 222
Pacific Gas and Electric, 137
Pacific Iron Foundry, 191
Pacific Islands, as source of miners, 5
Pacific Mail Steamship Company, 178, 252, 253–54
Pacific Mill and Mining Company, 73
Pacific Railroad Acts (1862, 1864), 262, 284
Page, Bacon & Co., 220, 221
Palace Hotel (San Francisco), 224
Palmer, Cook & Company, 63
Panama, 178, 253–54
Panama Canal, 284
Panama City, 178, 251
Panama Railroad, 252, 253, 284

Panama route, 251, 254
Panama steamers, 252
Panamanian isthmus, 5, 56, 83
Panic of 1837, 126
panning for gold, 26
Paris stock exchange, 63
Parker, Robert A., 214
Parker House Hotel, 214
Parrott, John, 159, 288
partnerships, 55, 58
Pattie, James O., 111
Paul, Almarin, 158
Paul, Rodman, 1, 13, 15–16, 36, 39, 44, 46,
    80, 87, 89, 90, 93, 98, 99, 163, 164, 199,
    202
Payson, George, 10
Pelton, Lester A., 203
Pelton water wheel, 31
Pennsylvania, 202
Peoples of Color in the American West (1994),
    14–15
Perseverance Mining Company of
    Philadelphia, 55
*Personal Adventures in Upper and Lower
    California, in 1848–9* (1850), 8
Peru: 5, 69; miners from, 82, 84, 86
petroleum, 204
Philadelphia, 26
Philippine Islands, 168
Phoenix (dredge boat), 167
Pike's Peak gold rush, 153, 162
Pioche, 162
Pioneer Line, 264
Pioneer Woolen Mills, 198
Pisani, Donald J., 17
Pitt, Leonard, 5, 84, 86
Placer County, 35, 64, 136, 216, 261
Placer Herald, 136
placer mining: 87, 89, 141, 158, 197; disap-
    pearance of, 151. *See also* river mining
Placerita Creek, 3
Placerville, 179, 196, 261, 278
Placerville–Lake Tahoe road, 261–63, 264
Placerville–Salt Lake route, 265
plate tectonics, 2
Platte River, 6, 177

Plumas County, 16
Point Pinole, 200
Polk, James K., 126, 130, 174, 177, 180
Pomeroy, Earl, 189
ponderosa pine forest, 116
Pony Express, 265, 283
population: of California in 1845, 185;
    of California in 1848, ix, 187, 233, 284;
    mobility of during the Gold Rush,
    91–92
Porter, Rufus, 250–51
Portland, Oregon, 182, 215
Portois, Peter, 219
Portsmouth Square, 178
Portugal, 168
Potosí, 3
Poverty Hill, 7, 180
Preemption Act of 1841, 125, 237
Prévost, Louis, 247
pronghorn, 107, 113, 121
property law. *See* resource law
prostitutes, 989
Provo, Utah, 267
public domain, 129, 131, 140
public lands, 125
Public Lands Commission, 140
public schools, 237

quarries, 194
quartz deposits, 63, 201
quartz, 66
quartz mining: ix, 66, 94–95, 98, 133, 151,
    152, 163, 164; development of, 59–61;
    labor in, 80, 84, 97, 99; laws and, 134,
    141; technology of, 36–43, 199–202
"quicksilver." *See* mercury

*Racial Fault Lines: The Historical Origins
    of White Supremacy in California* (1994),
    14
racism, 80, 86
raccoons, 117
railroads: 54; drive economic expansion, 52,
    190; transcontinental built, 226, 283
Ralston, William C., 71, 73, 159–60, 217,
    222, 223, 224, 225, 228, 281

ranching, during the gold-rush era, 233
ranchos, 185, 233–37
Randolph, Edmund, 83
Raymond, Rossiter, 28, 32, 36, 44, 155, 156, 157, 164, 166
Red Bluff, 118, 256, 258
redwoods, 115, 254
Reese River (Austin), 162
Reid, John Philip, 14
Relief Hill, 132
Reno, Nevada, 160
resource law: federal, 164; in the Gold Rush, 123–45, 163
The Resources of California (1862), 187
Revolutionary War, 54
Rice, Richard, 189
Rickard, T. A., 157
"right of discovery," 128
riparian rights. *See* water law
Risdon Iron and Locomotive Works, 199, 200
river mining, 59–61
river transportation, 256–58
Robbins, Roy, 126, 140
Roberts, George D., 165
Robinson mine, 165
Rochester, William, 212
rocker (cradle), 29, 30, 59, 94, 181, 197
Rocky Mountains, 111, 149
Rocky-Bar Mining Company, 66
Rohe, Randall, 32
Rohrbough, Malcolm J., 9, 80, 87
Rolle, Andrew, 189
Romans, 25
Rosenberg, Nathan, 203
Roses Bar, 118
Rossland (Canada) mines, 166
Rothschild, Messrs., 210
Rough and Ready, 60, 180
Roughing It, 155
Rowe, John, 38
Royce, Josiah, 9, 12, 58, 141
Russell, William, 163
Russians: hunting by, 106, 110; logging by, 115
Ryan, William Redmond, 8

Sabina (ship), 176
Sacramento, 67, 69, 91, 105, 119, 144, 174, 215, 234, 256, 257, 258, 263, 264, 278, 282
Sacramento County, 64, 247, 261
Sacramento *Daily Union,* 67
Sacramento River, 111, 117, 132, 212, 250, 256, 280
Sacramento Valley, 118, 132, 143, 144, 234, 243, 244
Sacramento Valley Railroad, 223, 264, 284
St. Clair, David J., 18
St. Louis, 221, 264
Salinas Valley, 243
Salt Lake City, 169, 267
San Antonio, Rancho, 238
San Bernardino, 265, 267
San Bernardino County, 144
San Diego, 113, 185, 211, 212, 244
San Diego County, 144
San Diego-San Antonio mail, 264
San Fernando Pass, 264
San Francisco: 5, 42, 66, 67, 68, 91, 92, 144, 152, 156, 174, 178, 182, 185, 212, 234, 236, 241, 244, 251, 254, 255, 256, 268, 282; banking in, 210, 212–15, 218–22; business directory for, 213; manufacturing in, 34, 41, 196–97, 200, 204, 277, 278; news of gold discovery reaches, 3; source of resources for other regions, 158, 160, 189, 243; world's fastest growing city, 187
San Francisco Bay, 109, 110, 115, 132, 242, 250, 254
San Francisco Business Directory, 215
San Francisco County, 64
San Francisco *Evening Bulletin,* 239
San Francisco Mining Stock and Exchange Board: formation of (1862), 69; sales of securities at, 70
San Francisco *Morning Post,* 63
San Francisco Post Office, 263
San Francisco Savings Bank, 210
San Francisco Sugar Refinery, 196
San Gorgonio Pass, 267
San Joaquin and Kings River Canal and Irrigation Company, 239
San Joaquin County, 6, 245

San Joaquin Delta, 287

San Joaquin River, 111, 241, 250, 256, 258, 280

San Joaquin Valley, 113, 114, 118, 138, 234, 238, 239, 240, 243, 244, 247

San Jose, 204

San Juan mining district (Colorado), 157, 162

San Juan Ridge, 116

San Juan River, 253

San Lorenzo, Panama, 178

San Luis de Gonzaga Ranch, 114

San Luis Obispo, 241, 264

San Luis Obispo County, 144, 243

San Mateo County, 245

San Pablo Bay, 132

San Pedro, 266–67

San Simeon Ranch, 241

Sandmeyer, Elmer, 85

Sandon mining district (Canada), 166

Sansevain, Jean Louis and Pierre, 244

Santa Barbara, 264

Santa Barbara County, 109, 144, 243, 247

Santa Clara County, 63

Santa Clara Mission, 211

Santa Clara Valley, 111

Santa Cruz, 188, 199–200

Santa Cruz County, 109

Santa Cruz Mountains, 115, 254

Santa Fe, 111

Santa Margarita, Rancho, 234

Santa Susana Pass, 264

Sarras, Ferminia, 166

Savage Silver Mining Works, 153

sawmill, first in Hispanic California, 115

Sawyer, Lorenzo, 132–33, 134, 169

Schieffelen, Ed, 166

Schilling Spices, 196

schooners, 255

Schweikart, Larry, 18

Scientific American, 250

Scotch broom, 117

sea otters, 106, 109–10

sea routes to California, 5

Sears, Marian V., 52

"Seeing the Elephant" (lithograph), 176

Sequoia National Park, 109

Sequoia-Kings Canyon National Park, 115

Service, Robert, 168

Shady Creek, 117

shaft mining. *See* quartz mining

Sharon, William, 71, 73, 160, 223, 224, 281

Shasta, 264

Shasta County, 64

Shaw, William, 10

sheep, 113, 114–15, 242–43

Sherman, William Tecumseh, 217, 221

Shew, William, 53

Shinn, Charles Howard, 11, 58, 141, 151, 169

shipbuilding, 203

Shirley Letters, The, 7

Shirley, Dame, ix, 7, 79, 87, 181

Sierra County, 5, 64, 129, 132, 141

Sierra Nevada, roads through, 261–63, 264

Silliman, Benjamin, 132

silver, discovery in Nevada, 53, 204, 222

Silverton mining district (Canada), 166

Skunk Gulch, 7

skunks, 117

slavery, 84, 87

slickens, 118, 133

"sliming" ore, 43

sluice box, 28, 59, 94, 181, 197

Smartsville, 118

smelter, 169

Smith, Adam, 125

Smith, Duane A., 17, 144

Smith, H. Grant, 154, 160

Smith, Hamilton, 157

Smith, Jedediah, 111

soap making, 185

Social Darwinism, wedded to anthropology, 125

Society of California Pioneers, 83

Solano County, 247

Sonoma, 113, 185, 245–47

Sonora, Mexico, 84, 89

South Africa, 287

South America, 28, 155, 285

South Fork of the American River, 1, 2, 212

southern California, transportation and, 266–68

Southern Maidu, 9
Southern Mines, 29, 36, 38, 89, 131, 180
Southern Pacific Railroad, 138
Soviet Union, 168
Spain, 25
Spanish explorers, 2
Spanish miners, 151
Specie and Exchange Office, 218
speculators and speculation, 165
Spence, Clark, 55, 135, 149, 165, 167
Spreckels, Claus, 195
squatter clubs, 125
stagecoaching, 263–66, 283
stamp milling, 32
stamp mills, 66
Stanford, Leland, 279, 283
Stanislaus River, 8
State Agricultural Society, 247
State Board of Agriculture, 247
state laws, effect on incorporation, 54
steam engines, 199, 200–1
steamboats, 258, 265, 283
Stegner, Wallace, 139
Stewart, William Morris, 131, 164
Stockton, 69, 91, 215, 234, 256, 257, 258, 263,
    264
Stone, John A., 7
Storms, William H., 46
Stowe, Harriet Beecher, 27
Strauss, Levi, 7, 195, 278
strikes, by miners, 96–99
Studebaker, John, 7, 196, 278
A Study of American Character (1886),
    12
Sugar Loaf Mountain, 262
sugar cane, 203
sugar refinery, 223
Suisun Bay, 132
Sutro, Adolph, 160
Sutter, John, 86, 211, 212
Sutter's Fort, 105, 179
Sutter's Mill, 1, 2, 179, 276
Swain, William, 90, 182
Sweetland, 132
Swickhimer, Laura, 166
"Sydney Town," in San Francisco, 5

Tahiti, 193, 254
Taiping Rebellion, 286
Talcoa Vineyards, 281
Tasmania, 254
Taylor, Bayard, 178
Taylorville, 16
technology: in Colorado, 164; in the
    Gold Rush, 24–47, 62, 151, 156, 276–77;
    manufacturing, 155
Tehachapi Mountains, 107, 138
Tejon Pass, 264
telegraph, 283
Temecula, 265
Ten Mile District (Colorado), 165
Tennessee, 39
"Tennessee's Partner," 11
Terminal Island (Rattlesnake Island), 267
Texas: 218, 234; and the "California
    Doctrine," 139
textile industry, 203
Tharp, Hale, 107
*They Saw the Elephant: Women in the
    California Gold Rush* (1990), 14
Thompson, John, 263
Thoreau, Henry David, 83
Tibbetts, A. C., 113
Tilden & McFarland, 225
Timbuctoo, 118
tin mining, 25
Todd, John A., 134
toll roads, 262
tom. *See* long tom
Tombstone, Arizona, 166
Tonopah, Nevada, 162
trams, 156–57
transportation, in the Gold Rush, 250–68,
    283
Trask, John B., 44
Treasure Hill, 162
Treaty of Guadalupe Hidalgo, 3, 235
Trespass Act of 1852, 247
Trinity County, 5
Truckee River, 176, 261, 262
Truckee Trail, 179
Truro, Cornwall, 38
Tucson, 267

Tulare County, 144
tule elk, 111
Tuolumne County, 5, 64, 141
Tuolumne Miners' Union, 98
Turner, Frederick Jackson, 125
Turner, Henry, 221
Tuscarora, 162
Twain, Mark. *See* Clemens, Samuel
Two Treatises on Government (1690), 123
Two Years Before the Mast, 111
Tyler Foote Crossing Road, 116, 117, 120

Union (steamship), 253
Union Iron Works, 156, 203, 204, 205
Union Mill and Mining Company, 71
Union Trust Company, 226
unions, 96–99
U.S. Commissioner of Mining Statistics, 44
U.S. Geological Survey, 44
U.S. Supreme Court, 130
University of California, Berkeley, 45
Upham, Samuel, 58
Utah Territory: 68, 165, 266, 267; and the "Colorado Doctrine," 139

Vallejo, California, 111
Van Dyke, T. S., 112–13
Vance, Robert, 2
Vanderbilt, Cornelius, 252, 253
Vera Cruz, 174
vineyards, 187
Virginia and Truckee Railroad, 160
Virginia City, Nevada, 45, 154, 155, 160, 161, 200, 206, 223
Visalia, 264
Vulcan Foundry, 191, 223
Vulture Mine, 166

wage laborers, 59, 80, 86, 93–95
wagon freighting, 259–61
Walker, James, 234
Walker's Pass, 114
Walsh, James, 68
Walton, Henry, 181
Washington, D.C., 177, 236

Washington City Company, 6, 177, 179
Washington State: 155, 235; and the "California Doctrine," 139; gold mining in, 152
Washoe, 176
Washoe pan amalgamation process, 28, 158, 202
water law: development of, 151, 164; and mining, 135–40
water rights, 139
water wheels, 31
Watkins, Carleton E., 65, 106, 242, 266
Webb, Walter Prescott, 139
Weber, Charles M., 215, 278
Webster's Station, 262
Wells, Henry, 216
Wells, Thomas, 218, 219–20
Wells, Fargo & Co., 215, 221, 226, 263, 264, 281, 282
Welsh miners, 151, 286
Wenderoth, August, 60, 180
West Virginia, 91
whaling, 110
wheat farming, 132, 187, 240, 243–44, 280
White, Richard, 14
Whitney, Josiah D., 44
Whyte, Toby, 107
Wickenburg, Henry, 166
Wierzbicki, Felix P., 62
wildlife, 107, 117, 121
William D. Peck, Rough and Ready, California (watercolor), 181
Williams, Lucia, 6
Wilmington, California, 267
Wilson, Terry P., 15
Winchester, Jonas, 66
wine making, 223, 245–47, 280, 281
wire rope, 156, 200, 203
Wisconsin: 25, 56, 126, 127, 244; miners from, 151; prohibits banks, 210, 228
Wolfskill, William, 244, 247
wolves, 107, 121
women, in the Gold Rush, 89–90
Women and Men on the Overland Trail (1979), 13
Woodruff, Edwards, 168

Woodruff v. *North Bloomfield Gravel Mining Co.*, 134, 143, 168
Woods Dry Diggings. *See* Auburn
Woodworth, Joseph, 68
woolen mills, 194–95, 223
The World Rushed In: The California Gold Rush Experience (1981), 11
Wright, Dr. Stephen A., 218, 219
Wright, William, 154
Wright, Burgoyne & Co., 220
Wright & Company, 218
Wyman, Mark, 98
Wyoming: 125; and the "Colorado Doctrine," 139

xenophobia, 86

Yankee Blade (steamship), 253
Yankee Jim's, 136
Yeakel, Solomon, 87
Yerba Buena Cove, 185, 186, 191, 288
Yolo County, 261
Yosemite (side-wheeler), 257
Yosemite Valley, 116, 188
Young, Otis, 39, 135
Yuba County, 64, 129, 247
Yuba River, 94, 116, 118, 119, 132, 133, 167, 169, 182
Yukon, 149
Yuma, 264, 265, 267

Zacatecas, 3
zinc, 25

DESIGNER:	Terry Bain
COMPOSITOR:	Integrated Composition Systems, Inc.
TEXT:	11/14 Adobe Caslon
DISPLAY:	Adobe Caslon Regular, Italic and Small Caps
TEXT AND COLOR INSERT PRINTER:	Malloy Lithographing, Inc.
COVER PRINTER:	Southeastern Printing, Inc.
BINDER:	Malloy Lithographing, Inc.